MEGHAN AND HARRY

The Real Story

Lady Colin Campbell

Dynasty Press

Dynasty Press Limited
36 Ravensdon Street
London SE11 4AR
www.dynastypress.co.uk

First published in this version by Dynasty Press Ltd.

ISBN: 978-1-9161317-1-2

Typeset by Biddles Books Ltd., Castle House, East Winch Road, Blackborough End, King's Lynn, Norfolk PE32 1SF

Cover Design by Rupert Dixon

Printed and bound in the United Kingdom

CONTENTS

CHAPTER 1

On May 19th 2018, when Meghan Markle stepped out of the antique Rolls Royce conveying her and her mother Doria Ragland from the former Astor stately home Cliveden to St. George's Chapel, Windsor, where she was due to be married at 12 noon, she was a veritable vision of loveliness. At that moment, one of the biggest names of the age was born.

As the actress ascended the steps of St. George's Chapel, its interior and exterior gorgeously decorated in the most lavish and tasteful spring flowers, she was a picture of demure and fetching modesty, stylish elegance, transparent joyousness, and radiant beauty. The simplicity of her white silk wedding dress, designed by Clare Waight Keller of Givenchy, with its bateau neckline, three-quarter length sleeves, and stark, unadorned but stunningly simple bodice and skirt, coupled with the extravagant veil, five metres long and three metres wide, heavily embroidered with two of her favourite flowers (wintersweet and California poppy, as well as the fifty three native flowers of the various Commonwealth countries, and symbolic crops of wheat, and a piece of the blue dress that the bride had worn on her first date with the groom), gave out a powerful message.

All bridal gowns make statements. Diana, Princess of Wales, according to her friend Carolyn Pride, used hers to announce to the world, 'Here I am. Take notice. I'm not a bit shy and intend everyone to know who I am.' Catherine Middleton's stated, 'I am stylish, athletic, and traditional. I aim to please, and I relish my femininity. I possess exquisite but conservative taste, with just a hint of daring beneath the surface.' Meghan's not only conveyed that she loved clothes, was a feminine woman despite her avowed feminism, and something of an impact specialist where presentation is concerned, but also that she was a thoughtful, considered, deliberate and aware individual who would use traditions as and when they suited her, but was prepared to jettison them when they did not. She struck the absolutely right note for someone who was making her debut into the world's leading royal family, letting the public know that her virtues were sterling and her performance would be polished.

Beneath the message, however, there was controversy. The Queen was said to be surprised that her soon-to-be granddaughter-in-law, already married and divorced once, had chosen virginal white in defiance of all accepted custom in royal and aristocratic circles, where a nod in the direction of reality dictated that no colour lighter than cream should be worn. But Meghan was starting out as she intended to continue. Royal and aristocratic traditions were of scant importance to someone whose self-belief was so rock solid that her father-in-law-to-be, who liked her, had already affectionately nicknamed her Tungsten.

The colour of her dress was not the only surprise Meghan delivered on her wedding day. Traditionally, after the couple signs the register and rejoins the congregation, the bride curtsies to the Queen and the groom bows. It has always been done and it was expected by all that it would be done on the 19th May 2018. Princess Anne did it at her two weddings. Diana did it at hers. So too did Princess Alexandra, the Countess of Wessex, the Duchesses of York, Kent and Cambridge. However, as Meghan rejoined the congregation and set about walking down the aisle with a beaming Prince Harry by her side, she omitted to curtsy when she passed the Queen. This caused consternation throughout the assembled company at St. George's Chapel, one of whom told me, 'No one could believe it. She walked out, sailed down the aisle, with not so much as the merest bob in the direction of Her Majesty.' The Queen is not on record as having made a comment or a complaint, but 'she will have noticed. Everyone did.'

Like many of the people present, I put Meghan's omission down to nervousness and forgetfulness. It really is easy for people who are not used to royal ways to forget each and every dance step in the choreography of royal life, but not everyone took so benevolent a view, especially as the run-up to the wedding had been fraught with scenes, tantrums and demands, most of which were carefully concealed from the public, although by the time of the wedding they were well known in Court circles.

Meghan is wonderfully self-possessed. She has supreme self-belief. She knows what she wants and she sets about achieving it by brooking no opposition. She is astonishingly direct in a way only Americans of a certain background who have made successes of their lives can be. She does not shy away from making demands but expects those who are there to assist her to bring her desires to fruition. Harry adores her forthrightness and strength of character. He admires the fact that she allows no one to prevail when she sets her mind to a task. In Court circles, however, where people dance around issues and no one makes a demand much less asks a direct question or even makes a straightforward suggestion, Meghan was unwittingly making waves. This was laying the ground for the misunderstandings and bad feelings that would soon characterise relations between the couple and many of the people close to them.

With the wisdom of hindsight, it is obvious that Harry should have nipped things in the bud before they degenerated further by pointing out to Meghan that she needed to adopt a more British approach. He should have explained that what works in the film industry in Hollywood goes down like a lead balloon in Britain. People would not admire her for her ballsiness but begin to resent her for what he and she might admire as forthrightness but they would deplore as being difficult, demanding and brash.

Harry, however, handled this dichotomy in the worst possible way. Up to then, he had enjoyed a reputation for affability even if he was also known to be hot-headed and so emotional that he often took things personally when a degree of impersonality would have been the more justified reaction. This more emotional side of his character now came to the forefront in the most unfortunate fashion. He started throwing his weight around, playing the Alpha male protecting his little woman as he backed Meghan up even when he must have known that the more positive response would have been to have a quiet word with her instead of endlessly repeating the mantra, 'What Meghan wants, Meghan gets.' In doing so, he not only allowed her to continue getting people's backs up quite unnecessarily and more than likely unwittingly too, but also antagonised those who had previously had a high opinion of him. In reality, he was adding fuel to the fire when he could easily have doused the flames with one part knowledge and a second part wisdom.

A case in point was the fuss Harry and Meghan made over the emerald and diamond kokoshnik Princess Eugenie had chosen for her wedding. Harry will have known the score. The date of his cousin's marriage had

had to be pushed back to allow him to be married first because he took precedence over her. It would be unfair to deprive Eugenie of the tiara she had chosen. This had once belonged to Grand Duchess Xenia of Russia, Tsar Nicholas II's elder sister. It had been sold to the Royal Family when the grand duchess was given refuge in England following the Russian Revolution and the execution of her brother and many other members of her family at the hands of the Bolsheviks. The Queen had promised Eugenie the use of it. There the matter should have rested, and would have, had Meghan not decided that she wanted to wear Grand Duchess Xenia's kokoshnik at her wedding, and Harry, so eager to fulfill her every wish, neglected to point out that she couldn't be lent something that his cousin had already been promised.

There were, of course, other tiaras from which to choose. Most of the really spectacular tiaras in the British Royal Family's collection actually come from the Russian Imperial Family and were bought by Queen Mary, the present Queen's grandmother and a great collector of art, jewels, and furniture. These include the famous Grand Duchess Vladimir Tiara with the detachable drop emeralds and pearls, which is only ever worn by a present or future queen. As the future wife of a second son of an Heir Presumptive, Meghan never had a choice of the truly spectacular jewels, to include the Vladimir or Greville tiaras, which are worn by Camilla, Duchess of Cornwall. Jewels are allocated according to precedence, and what a senior royal wears, a junior royal cannot.

Although Meghan did have a choice, no incoming bride can just scoop up whatever jewels she wants and wear them as if by right. She has no right to anything. All she can do is accept a loan, and a loan, moreover, that means that the lower down the order of precedence she is, the more limited her choice. Meghan, however, is a clothes horse, and knows what suits her and works best as she presents the image she wants to purvey. She is not the daughter of an award-winning lighting engineer for nothing. From early childhood she was privy to the secrets of good lighting and photography. She is bright and capable and learnt her lessons well. Her many years in front of the camera have also honed her skill in choosing what works well for her. One of her favourite words before she married into the British Royal Family was 'classy'. She also understands glamour as few other women do. Being more intelligent than most, this gives her greater insight into scenarios, and allows her to have a more historic dimension than someone of her background would typically have. There is little doubt that Grand Duchess Xenia's kokoshnik appealed not only because it is more spectacular, but also because its history is more romantic and exotic. Who, with Meghan's sensibilities, would fail to want the more spectacular and historic tiara over Queen Mary's bandeau, made in 1932 to accommodate a brooch which is still detachable?

If Meghan's choice could not be faulted as regards taste, it was on promissory grounds, and the Queen could not very well be expected to ignore her promise to Eugenie, nor would it be appropriate for successive brides to wear the same tiara. The Queen, after all, could not collude with her granddaughter's thunder being stolen by a granddaughter-in-law. So she was put in the onerous position of having to make it clear by way of her trusted dresser, dress designer and good friend Angela Kelly to Meghan and Harry that they would have to accept what was on offer and not demand what was not.

The matter might have rested there, with no one any the wiser, had Harry and Meghan not made an almighty fuss, not only about the tiara, but also about such things as the scent of St. George's Chapel and the ingredients of certain dishes being prepared for the wedding. Meghan, in the questing, forthright way which had hitherto worked so well for her, caused great offence to a member of staff when she implied that that individual was a liar because Meghan claimed to be able to taste the existence of an ingredient which she had banned from a dish. The purported culprit, deeply offended, denied its existence, and Meghan was duly informed that royals don't speak to their staff like that, causing offence all around, for now the bride-to-be had injured feelings as well. There was also the kerfuffle surrounding how St. George's Chapel smelt. Meghan floated the idea of having it sprayed with a perfume of her choice: a suggestion that went down like a lead balloon. As one courtier told me, 'We were really astonished to find that this minor TV actress from California was so demanding that she was giving us the message that we should up our game and satisfy her much higher standards.' While the courtier thought that 'the arrogance and impertinence were breathtaking, exceeded only by the disrespect,' Meghan would have had an entirely opposite view. From her perspective, it was her wedding. She could make any demands she wanted. As Harry kept on saying, what she wanted, she must be given. He knew that, after years of struggle, she had finally achieved the way of life she had always aspired to, and he wanted to have all her desires fulfilled. As far as he and she were concerned, who were these people obstructing her? They were merely employees, irrespective of their pretensions. They were there to serve, and now that she was going to be a member of the Royal Family, they should be doing all in their power to make her happy.

Meghan will neither have foreseen the offence she was causing, nor have realised that she was trampling on sensitivities, though in reality she and Harry were belittling staff and making them feel devalued. As far as she and Harry were concerned, she was their victim; they were not hers. How could they be, when they were there to serve her, and they had failed to do so?

What Harry ought to have known, and Meghan could not have, was that most people at Court work for ridiculously low sums. The rewards of service to the monarchy are all non-financial and what is important to them isn't measured in practical coinage but in terms of the regard their employers and fellow employees have for one another. This was, in actuality, the clash between the straightforward transactionalism of the California way of life and the far more subtle and obtuse royal way, but it also shows why each side regarded itself as entitled to its feelings. The values and traditions of the Old World were now colliding with the requirements and expectations of the New, and though no one knew it at the time, this clash of two different and sometimes incompatible cultures would only worsen, creating problems but also opportunities for all sorts of interest groups, not the least of which were the press, various political entities, and even the couple themselves.

Before the marriage, therefore, the rumblings about Meghan and Harry's behaviour and how they were rubbing people up the wrong way, had begun. The public, of course, remained unaware of any of this. The hope in royal circles was that Meghan was suffering from pre-wedding nerves, that Harry was playing macho man to impress his wife-to-be, but that things would settle down once they were married. That Meghan would dampen down her Californian ways and that Harry, who was rapidly alienating admirers and gaining a well-earned reputation for throwing his weight around in a wholly unacceptable manner, would revert to the right-on, lovable bloke he had been up to then. No one foresaw that Meghan and Harry were on a roll, that they would spark each other to ever greater heights, that they would not buckle to any opposition, that they regarded those who stood in their way as needlessly obstructive, and that, if they didn't get their way, they'd decamp. Certainly no one in royal circles could ever have envisaged a scenario where, within eighteen months, female MPs, the Archbishop of Canterbury and the author Hilary Mantel would be adding their voices to those who claimed that Meghan's failure to adjust to royal life was down to racism, while she and Harry went about moving from the restraints of royalty to the freedom of global celebrity entrepreneurism.

Throughout Britain, in particular in royal, aristocratic, media, political, populist and ethnic circles, people wanted the marriage to be a success. Although in royal and aristocratic circles there had been initial reservations about the suitability of the union when the couple first got together, owing to the celerity with which Harry and Meghan had committed themselves, and the fear that each of them might have been blinded by their desires and might not be well suited for the long haul - the last thing anyone wanted was yet another divorce - once it became apparent that Harry was determined to marry her, the whole Royal Family, and the Court, fell into line. Meghan's virtues were focused upon, not only in terms of her undoubted intelligence and determination, but also her sweetness of manner, her charm, vivacity, sense of humour and last, but by no means least, her heritage. The fact that she was a good looking, stylish, glamorous, photogenic, mature woman with an interest in philanthropy was one thing, but what sealed things in her favour was her ancestry. Not only was she an American, and a well-educated one with a patina of sophistication, but she was also a woman of colour. The Queen, who is well known to be a wit, said to a friend, 'Mr Corbyn will find it much more difficult to get rid of us now that Meghan's in the family.' This conveyed a welcome degree of truth as well as humour, for Meghan's bi-racial identity made the monarchy both reflective and representative of multicultural, multiracial Britain in a way that a white, 37 year old, California-born actress who had been a cast member of a popular television series could never have been.

The British press and general public, as well as the political establishment, also embraced Meghan's mixed-race heritage. There had been other mixed-race unions in other royal houses and the general feeling was that it was high time the British Royal Family caught up with their Continental cousins. The Queen of Denmark's second son had married a Eurasian woman. The Ruling Prince of Lichtenstein's second son had married a Panamanian-born American of colour. Prince Rainier of Monaco's nephew had married a West Indian of colour. Two of the Archduke Geza of Austria's sons had married three Sub-Saharan Africans. The Queen had given her blessing to two of her first cousins once removed, when the Hon James Lascelles married the Nigerian aristocrat Joy Elias-Rilwan in 1999 and Lady Davina Windsor married Gary Christie Lewis, a Maori carpenter/house renovator in 2004. But both these cousins were members of the extended as opposed to the actual Royal Family. Meghan Markle's inclusion in the British Royal Family itself would send out a positive message which would not only play well in Britain, but also in the Commonwealth.

Of course, not everyone everywhere shared this viewpoint. There have always been, and presumably always will be, people who are racist. They will not have been happy with Meghan's inclusion in the Royal Family. But they were sufficiently few and far between to be of no consequence. Moreover, it is a crime in Britain to discriminate against someone on the grounds of race. Hate crimes are rigidly enforced by the authorities, so the racists will have found themselves baying into the abyss, ignored by all but a few like-minded bigots. In fact, they were both voiceless and powerless and would never become a factor, though their existence would confuse the American press into thinking that Meghan was a victim of racism in Britain when nothing could have been further from the truth.

It is fair to say that, the racist minority aside, practically everyone welcomed the marriage, mostly on racial grounds, and no one at Court wanted the behind-the-scenes difficulties to leak out, lest they colour the public's opinion and acceptance of Meghan. Her father's non-attendance was a blip which was managed as well as it could have been, and the day itself went off without a hitch. According to Nielsen Social, 29 million Americans and 18 million Britons watched the wedding, while the BBC estimated that 1.9 billion people tuned in worldwide.

That night, the bride ratified her style credentials by wearing a classical white silk crepe halter neckline evening dress by Stella McCartney to the black tie reception at Frogmore House. Situated on the Crown Estate, Windsor, in Windsor Great Park, it is a five minute drive from the castle. Harry drove Meghan there in an ice-blue E-Type Jaguar which coordinated perfectly with the large emerald cut aquamarine ring belonging to his mother Diana: this Meghan wore on her right hand. It was, according to people who attended it, a great party, with a wonderful atmosphere, and the couple seemed very much in love. 'Not since the early days of Prince and Princess Michael's marriage have I seen a royal couple so in love,' a friend said. 'They couldn't keep their hands off each other. It really was very touching.'

One would have hoped, after such a brilliant start, that the couple would continue to be as feted and admired as they were on their wedding day. Everyone I knew was rooting for them. They even made the mature and, some would say, 'woke' choice of not going on honeymoon immediately. Meghan and Harry both let it be known that they were deeply committed to their work, which would revolve around charitable and humanitarian activities. Being in their mid to late thirties, and, having been living together prior to the marriage, they hardly had need of a honeymoon the way a young couple starting out life together would.

Yet, four days after the wedding, I was having dinner at the house of an influential aristocrat with impeccable palace connections when I heard a report that filled me with foreboding. The day before, Meghan had joined Harry and Prince Charles and Camilla at a garden party at Buckingham Palace to celebrate the Prince of Wales's patronages in recognition of his 70th birthday. What had taken place then, which I will cover later on in this work, was so shocking as to lead all of us to conclude that Meghan was utterly unsuited to the role of royal duchess, and that it would be a miracle if the marriage worked out. None of us envisaged that she and Harry would be resourceful enough to find a way of moving beyond their royal status and that they would remain a couple while forging a non-royal way of life in the United States of America. But if what had happened was true - and it was - there was little doubt that she was no more suited to royal life than Angelina Jolie would be to competitive boxing.

It was hardly surprising that they would lurch from one controversy to another, in the light of Meghan's unsuitability to royal life, and Harry's blanket support for her. His failure to ever enlighten her as to where she was going wrong only ensured that she went from unintentional blunder to unintentional blunder. For every foot that they put right, they put four feet wrong. To those of us who wanted Meghan to remain in Britain as a fully-fledged member of the Royal Family, sprinkling her gold dust as she went about her royal duties and furthered the cause of racial unity throughout the country and the Commonwealth, this was a tragic outcome which could so easily have been averted had Harry enlightened his wife rather than supporting her in a path that would ultimately cause both of them misery and result in their departure. All he needed to do was handle things slightly differently. He could easily have been more instructive, making her aware that she was creating antagonism when it was obvious that she wanted approbation. Then the outcome could have been so different.

As it was, Meghan's conduct was inadvertently creating so much friction and attracting such criticism that it was soon leading the couple and their supporters to question whether the basis was racist. This was not a happy state of affairs for the couple or for any monarchist, though it would prove to be a welcome bludgeon for republicans, anti-monarchists and left-wingers who want to change the social order.

Despite this negative outcome, the problems arising out of Meghan's failure to adjust to the British way did make for a more interesting narrative than would otherwise have been the case, had she slotted into her royal role the way we all hoped. Had any author written a work of fiction with a plot along the lines of the Meghan and Harry story, it would have been dismissed as too fantastical to be believed. Yet, when one looks at their histories, the couple's trajectory has a sense of appropriateness which suggests that they could well pull several rabbits out of their hats and end up just where they want to be: at the apex of celebrity as the most feted, revered royal couple in the United States. For both their sakes, but even more than that, for the sake of the hundreds of millions of people of colour all over the world whose hopes and expectations are vested in their success, I hope they do.

CHAPTER 2

For a couple whose backgrounds are so radically different in worldly terms, Meghan and Harry were born to parents whose unions shared surprising similarities. Both the Prince and Princess of Wales and Mr and Mrs Thomas Markle were mismatched. Once their marriages failed, both sets of parents would try their best to spare their children from suffering from the fallout, in the process exacerbating its effects in unexpected ways. Had Harry and Meghan been born to couples who were more compatible, more evenly matched, and more aware of the need to provide stronger boundaries and less indulgence, it is unlikely that either the Duke or the Duchess of Sussex would ever have had as much in common as they do. For all their differences, they also share such profound similarities that this unique combination has proven to be a potent force binding them together in ways that make them a uniquely strong couple.

Rachel Meghan Markle was born three years before Harry on the 4th August 1981. Her father Thomas Wayne Markle Sr was, according to her, a successful, 37 year old 'lighting director for a soap opera' who had received a Chicago/Midwest Emmy for the television show *Made in Chicago* in 1975, and would later on be a co-recipient of two Daytime Emmy awards for the popular soap opera *General Hospital* in 1985 and 2001. He was nominated on several other occasions as well, and also worked on the long-running series *Married... with Children*, while 'my mom was a temp at the studio when they met'.

Doria Loyce Ragland was four weeks shy of her 25th birthday at the time of her daughter's birth, and had been married for a year and nine months. Meghan likes 'to think he was drawn to her sweet eyes and her Afro, plus their shared love of antiques. Whatever it was, they married and had me. They moved into a house in The Valley in LA, to a neighborhood that was leafy and affordable.' Tom Sr was earning some $200,000 per annum, so, while not wealthy, the family was certainly comfortable.

It might be difficult for people of a certain age to imagine how it was for inter-racial couples four decades ago. The reality is, it took courage for both the Caucasian Tom and the Afro-American Doria Markle to embark upon their union. Admittedly, Hollywood, where they worked, was a lot less colour prejudiced than the hinterlands of Newport, Pennsylvania and Cleveland, Ohio, where Markle and Ragland families came from. But even in California, mixed race couples were still more of an exception than the norm, and Meghan states that some of her early memories were coloured by the embarrassment of people mistaking her mother for her nanny. As they lived in a white neighbourhood, and appear to have been the only mixed race family nearby, the confusion of the other residents as to what role Doria played in the fair-skinned Meghan's life might well have been a matter of ignorance and unthinking expectation rather than prejudice. But, to a proud and strong woman like Doria, it was humiliating nevertheless to be mistaken for her daughter's nanny. There is every indication that this was one of the catalysts which made the marriage as short lived as it was.

Although Meghan was Doria's first, and would prove to be her only, child, her father already had a son and daughter from his first marriage. In 1964, at the age of twenty, Tom had married Roslyn Loveless, a nineteen year old secretary he had met at an on-campus party at the University of Chicago. In November of that year, their daughter Yvonne, now Samantha Marie, was born, followed two years later by Thomas Wayne Markle Jr.

After graduating from college, Tom Sr worked as a lighting director at WTTWTV-Channel 11, the primary Public Broadcasting Service in Chicago, Illinois, winning his first Emmy in 1975. At first, the marriage was happy, but within a few years, Roslyn was feeling neglected. According to her, Tom spent all hours of the day and night working. His aim was to win an Emmy, and while he was bringing in good money, he not only neglected her, but caroused with other women. By the early 70s, the marriage was over and the couple separated.

Tom lived in Chicago and had the children for weekends, but after he was nominated for his first Emmy, he moved to California, settling in Santa Monica. Samantha, who did not get on with her mother or her brother, joined him first. Then a traumatised Tom Jr arrived following an incident when Roslyn's boyfriend apprehended burglars and was shot in front of mother and son. Tom Jr promptly fled to the safety of California, where the one fly in the ointment, from his point of view, was the presence of his sister, for whom he had an innate antipathy.

With both children now living with him, Tom moved to a spacious, five bedroomed house on Providencia Street adjacent to the Woodland Hills Country Club in the San Fernando Valley. Its location made the Markle residence one of the more desirable properties in the area. Even now it is predominantly a white neighbourhood, with some 80% of the population being Caucasian, and less than 3.5% Afro-American, but in the 1980s, there were even fewer people of colour living there. It was a prosperous area, and has remained so, with fashionable Calabasas to its east.

According to the Markles, in the early days of Tom and Doria's relationship, they were extremely happy. She brought a welcome sense of family to the household, unifying them in a way that had not existed before. She herself came from a loving family, and even included the Markles in the Ragland family Thanksgiving celebrations. Tom Jr was surprised at how 'warm and inclusive' her parents and her half-brother Joseph and half-sister Saundra were, and commented that they were 'the kind of family I had always wanted.' Even after Doria's parents divorced and her father married a kindergarten teacher named Ava Burrow, and produced a son named Joffrey Ragland, then divorced, Doria remained close to all of them.

The Raglands were a modest but by no means well-off family. Doria's father Alvin owned an antique shop named *'Twas New*, while her mother was a nurse. They were what would be categorised as *petit bourgeois* in Europe and middle class in America. Doria herself was something of a hippie, which made her warmth and kindness even more appealing to the children than she would have been, had she presented in a more conventional manner. Shortly after moving into the Providencia Street house, she decided that what the family needed was something they could all love. She therefore took Tom Jr to an animal shelter, where they chose a beagle/golden retriever mix which he named Bo and which became a much-loved pet.

Like many twenty five year olds, Doria was not sure exactly what she wanted to do with her life. She had tried her hand at being a make-up artist before Meghan's birth, but, with a baby and two stepchildren to cater to, as well as running a house which would later be described as 'cavernous', and a husband who worked eighty and ninety hour weeks, she found being a housewife less than appealing. She therefore took up yoga, with a view to teaching it, and only too soon was farming out babysitting duties to her mother Jeanette and stepson Tom Jr. Her seventeen year old stepdaughter had no interest in babysitting, preferring instead to be out partying with her friends. There have been reports that Samantha used to refer to Doria as 'The Maid', but these appear to be apocryphal, as both families remember everyone getting on well, even if, in typical teenage fashion, Samantha was focused more on having a good time with her friends than on being an integral part of the family.

Theirs was nevertheless an extremely relaxed household, with pretty much anything going. The children were allowed to come and go as they pleased, to have their friends around, even to smoke pot if they were so inclined.

According to both Toms, Tom Sr was completely besotted with Meghan from the moment of her birth. His every spare moment was spent with her. He was even more in love with her than he was with Doria and he also gave her more of his time and attention than he had ever given his two elder children. This seems to have caused some resentment with Samantha, who was jealous of the little princess when she saw the degree of attention she was getting from her father, but to say that it was a problem would be to exaggerate what was, after all, a perfectly ordinary situation, albeit one laden with possibilities for contemporaneous resentments to find inconvenient expression in the future.

There is also the suggestion that Doria felt sidelined by Tom Sr as he worshipped at the altar of his Flower, as both parents started calling the baby. Reading between the lines of what the family now says, it is likely that Doria's reaction to Tom Sr's fixation on Meghan was akin to Samantha's. Not that Doria did not love her daughter. But she appears to have wanted Tom Sr to be more emotionally engaged with her than he thereafter was. Only too soon, the couple was squabbling. Doria resented being left alone for most of the time with the baby and her step-children, while Tom worked and worked and worked, then when he came home, he made a big deal of the baby, and took his wife for granted.

Up to then, theirs had been an extremely relaxed household, but as tensions developed between the workaholic Tom Sr and the neglected Doria, she too emulated the habits of her stepdaughter and started to come and go as she pleased, often parking the baby with her mother or with Tom Jr.

According to Meghan, when she was two, her parents separated. Her mother went back to her grandmother Jeanette's house, where they lived during the week, while she returned to her father to spend weekends with him. She remembered harmony reigning supreme, with never a squabble or harsh word between the two of them. This was quite possible, though the family remembered superficial civility rather than real warmth between the couple. Meghan seems to have candy-coated a more acrid scenario, and moreover was doing so for good reason. The whispers are that Doria not only realised that she didn't want to be alone with a husband who was never around and took her for granted when he was, but that she actually didn't want to be with a husband at all. Thereafter, she would pursue a life of such extreme privacy that the question has been asked what, if anything, she had to hide. In choosing to lead her life in such a secretive way, she would thereafter be both resolute and independent. The fact that she did so with the quiet dignity for which she has become known, and ensured that civility reigned between her ex-husband and herself, at least until Meghan and Tom fell out (since when he has found her to be unresponsive), is testament to her strength of character and her ability to achieve what she wants in her own quiet and determined way.

Both sides of Meghan's family have confirmed that while she was growing up 'nothing was too good for her.' Her father spoiled her from the time she was a baby. Although her mother lay down boundaries, she also spoiled her, as did the extended families. At the age of two, around the time of her parents' separation, she was enrolled in the Hollywood Little Red School House. This was an exceptional school started by an exceptional woman whose objective was to create exceptional adults.

Ruth Pease, born Stover, was the only child of deaf parents. As a result, she was teased from early childhood and grew up valuing kindness and diversity as well as education and character. During the Second World War, she ran a nursery school for six children at her house. One charge was a half Chinese boy whose parents had had difficulty finding a place for him elsewhere. At the time, the US was at war with Japan, and the child, who was often mistaken for Japanese, attracted such prejudice that no one else would take him in. Ruth's landlord then objected to her running a nursery school from his property, necessitating a move to a house nearby on a quiet, tree-lined street named Highland Avenue. Her husband Robert painted the building red, they expanded to some twenty children, and, to distinguish it from a daycare centre, Pease in 1951 helped to form the Pre-School Association of California. According to her daughter Debbie Wehbe, 'People started referring to it as "the little red schoolhouse."' So they changed the school's name and added the storybook bell tower which became a stand-out feature. Diversity was one of Mrs Pease's aims, and, over the years, the school acquired such a good reputation that its alumnae included the children of the 1950s sex symbol Jayne Mansfield, Johnny Depp, and Flea - bassist for the Red Hot Chili Peppers - as well as diplomats and people from more average backgrounds.

By 1968, new building codes required the tearing down of the old building and the construction of a new one. Meghan therefore arrived in 1983 to a much enlarged and expanding institution, whose reputation for excellence and diversity was second to none locally. By no means cheap (from twenty to twenty five thousand dollars at today's prices), it was by that time one of the main 'go to' centres of learning for the children of the Hollywood elite. Meghan would spend nine years there, flourishing under the ministrations of a progressive but structured regimen based upon the four stages of Cognitive Development formulated by the Swiss psychologist Jean Piaget.

The location of the Hollywood Little Red School House could not have been more convenient for Tom and Doria. He worked at the ABC Studios in nearby Los Feliz while her workplace, where she was training to be a social worker, was a few minutes away and easily accessible to her new home just south of Hollywood. After school, Doria, always physical, would take Meghan for bike rides, runs, or yoga, and they would end the day with mother and daughter making dinner. Meghan now attributes her love of cooking to this early regimen, so clearly it was a happy activity.

In 1992, at the age of eleven, Meghan transferred to Immaculate Heart High School. This again was a school where Hollywood's elite and aspirational sent their children. Founded in 1906 and located on a beautiful hillside property in Los Feliz, LA, it was and remains a Catholic preparatory school for girls from grades 6 - 12. 'We celebrate more than a century of nurturing the spiritual, intellectual, social and moral development of students as they distinguish themselves as women of great heart and right conscience,' the school maintains, and once more, it was a bastion of elitism intermingling with some children of more ordinary background. Alumnae include Tyra Banks, Lucy Arnaz, Mary Tyler Moore, and Diane Disney, as well as several girls who have gone on to make their names in the entertainment industry.

From now until she went to university, Meghan would live mostly with her father. They had moved from the Providencia Street house to a smaller and more modest place near the school and his workplace. She remembered spending afternoons after school, dressed in her distinctive Catholic school uniform, at the studio where her father was working. She learnt all about lights and camera angles and the myriad of other techniques that make up the magic that is Hollywood. She recounted how 'every day after school for 10 years, I was on the set of *Married... with Children*, which is a really funny and perverse place for a little girl in a Catholic school uniform to grow up. There were a lot of times my dad would say, "Meg, why don't you go and help with the craft services room over there? This is just a little off-color for your 11-year-old eyes."'

Ironically, it was race, not sex, that was developing into an issue for Meghan, though it is obvious from all she and everyone who knew her says, that it was a problem she was careful to keep to herself. At least, at the time. There was, for instance, the time she was compelled to fill out a mandatory census questionnaire in her English class. Asked to choose between boxes for white, black, Hispanic or Asian, she was befuddled so asked her teacher which one she should choose. The teacher recommended Caucasian, 'Because that's how you look, Meghan,' she remembered. But she refused to do so. 'Not as an act of defiance, but rather a symptom of my confusion. I couldn't bring myself to do that, to picture the pit-in-her-belly sadness my mother would feel if she were to find out. So, I didn't tick the box. I left my identity blank - a question mark, an absolute incomplete - much like how I felt.'

These are not the words of a child who is comfortable with her identity, but of one who is thoughtful, perplexed with uncertainty and troubled by it. Later on, Meghan spoke to her father, who told her that next time she should simply create her own box and tick that. This suggests that Meghan was trying to reconcile the conflicts arising out of being a child of colour who could be viewed by her peers as white and didn't really know where she fitted in. Many other mixed-race Americans, being asked the same question, would have unquestioningly answered black. The fact that she did not shows that, even at that age, she had a more nuanced view of the subject than many others did. While she was not prepared to deny her African antecedents, nor was she prepared to resile away from her Caucasian. Because she did not look obviously mixed-race, and the only parent who seems to have had any profile at the school at that time was her father, many of her classmates simply assumed she was white. On one occasion, a cabal of girls even asked her to join a White Girls Only Club, her response being a non-explanatory, 'Are you kidding me?'

By her own account, 'my mixed race heritage may have created a grey area surrounding my self-identification, keeping me with a foot on both sides of the fence.' Later on, she would work through the conflict 'to embrace that. To say who I am, to share where I'm from, to voice my pride in being a strong, confident mixed-race woman.' But before she could do so, she had to work her way through the grey to come to the light.

This early conflict would ultimately not only strengthen her but also deepen her. It gave her empathy for those who also did not fit in easily into one of life's many boxes. According to her school friend Elizabeth McCoy, 'If someone was being treated unfairly, she stuck up for them. She was a genuinely decent human being who looked out for people who needed help. She gave a damn about people other than herself.'

Her former homeroom advisor, Christine Knudsen, thought, 'She'd take conversations to a deeper level. She had a lot of depth, probably because of her own experiences and hard knocks growing up,' referring to her parents' divorce, though equally the issues surrounding her racial identity must also have influenced Meghan's thinking.

Tellingly, Knudsen did not remember race being an issue at all at the school. It was 'not a big deal simply because our school is so diverse. There's no looking down on someone because she comes from something different than you do.' A recent breakdown of the diversity of the students shows that 35% were white, 20% Latina, 17% multiracial, 17% Asian or Pacific Islander, 5% black and 6% preferred not to state. The year Meghan graduated, the demographics were similar, the main difference being that there were slightly more black students. These figures mean that Meghan was by no means the only bi-racial student, and indeed, non-Caucasians being a two-thirds majority, she was in the majority rather than the minority, save as her appearance went.

The pattern that emerges is that the pressure Meghan was under regarding her race was to a large extent internal rather than external. She was being affected by the conflicts many other people of colour who inadvertently 'pass' for white have suffered throughout the ages. The singer Marsha Hunt once described her blue-eyed, blonde-haired grandmother of colour, by this time driven insane, staring at herself in the mirror befuddled as to how she could have been categorised as black when she looked white.

Meghan was a clever child and would grow into an intelligent woman. She had witnessed from early childhood how 'my mom, caramel in complexion with her light-skinned baby in tow, (was) being asked where my mother was since they assumed she was the nanny.' One would have to be lacking in empathy to fail to see how such experiences would have coloured the feelings of both mother and daughter. They would have had to be inhuman not to be embarrassed, annoyed, humiliated, aware of the cultural disparity between blacks and whites, and subject to a host of conflicting feelings, few of which would have been comfortable to experience. No child likes being different. No child wants to stand out from the crowd. No child wants to know that people think its mother is its servant. It is therefore understandable that no one has any memory of Meghan ever volunteering information on the subject of her race. Without actively concealing it, she was by omission avoiding the subject.

Because Immaculate Heart was a Catholic school, and Catholicism preaches that there are both sins of commission and omission, Meghan will have been aware that to omit to assert her identity was tantamount to a sin of omission. This awareness can have done nothing to reduce the pressure that she felt as she was mistaken for white, for while she never actively denied her heritage, and was indeed fond of her mother and her mother's family, she also did not assert it actively. Such a dilemma would have been difficult for any child to endure. It must have driven her back into herself, and by her own account, she was a part of no special group and would volunteer for activities to avoid having to eat lunch alone. She was well liked by all and was friendly with many, but she had no actual circle of friends, felt isolated for all her superficial popularity, and was therefore already functioning as a solitary and independent unit. As she put it, 'My high school had cliques: the black girls and white girls, the Filipino and the Latina girls. Being bi-racial, I felt somewhere in between. So every day during lunch, I busied myself with meetings - French club, student body, whatever one could possibly do between noon and 1pm - I was there. Not so that I was more involved, but so that I wouldn't have to eat alone.'

Although Meghan had a best friend, Nikki Priddy, with whom she had been schooled since the age of two, and they would obviously have lunch together some of the time, her statements indicate that she felt that her racial identity was a problem with which she was finding it difficult to deal. However, rather than feeling sorry for herself, or becoming embittered by her circumstances, she was already positive and self-confident enough to find resourceful solutions which kept her occupied and gained her the approbation of her teachers. The message one receives is that this early solution to the problem of isolation helped her develop a self-reliance and independence that not only provided her with positive feedback, but also hid her isolation behind a facade of affability.

These were traits that would serve Meghan well in adulthood. Outstanding success in adulthood might initially be a question of luck, but maintaining it and capitalising upon it to the extent that she has, are a matter of grit, endurance, determination, and discipline. These are all qualities that are enhanced when adults have surmounted early hardship or deprivation, and Meghan's revelations of her early struggles reveal that she did indeed suffer from a sense of alienation as a result of her bi-racialism. Circumstance forced her into being something of a lone wolf, and lone wolves make the best hunters.

Although Meghan's identity struggles were not obvious to anyone when she was growing up, already her determination was. According to Maria Pollia, who taught her Theology in her junior year, she was 'a focused young woman who challenged herself to reflect on the toughest texts.' She did not shy away from challenges, but embraced them, and sometimes even sought them out. A case in point was Meghan's willingness to volunteer after her teacher had mentioned in class that she worked with homeless people. When she informed Pollia that she too had worked with them, and wanted to do so again, she sent her to the skid row kitchen where she herself worked.

'My parents came from little, so they made a choice to give a lot: buying turkeys for homeless shelters at Thanksgiving, delivering meals to people in hospices, giving spare change to those asking for it,' Meghan would later explain. Though her introduction to charity work, like Diana Princess of Wales's, initially came from observing her parents endowing those less fortunate than themselves, it was really through their schools that both women converted an initial introduction into an established practice.

Meghan now spent a year and a half working on skid row, and Pollia said, 'The people that I knew at the kitchen would tell me what a natural she was. Skid row is a very scary place. Once she got over that and she was talking to people, she knew everybody's names.'

For all the care she showed to strangers, Meghan had trouble behaving similarly towards her father. Nikki Priddy remembered that 'as Meg got older she had to parent Tom a little more and she couldn't do that.' Despite the diplomatic tightrope she walked as she carried messages back and forth between her civil parents, Meghan had always been the one both parents had taken care of, and she did not take well to having those roles reversed. Her refusal to do for her father what she was doing for strangers gives an invaluable insight into her character, and shows that even at an early age she knew where she wanted to establish boundaries. Soup kitchens are very much one thing or another. There are no shades of grey. You are either poor and needy or you are helping the poor and needy. The lines of demarcation could not be clearer. Within those parameters, the lonely, sensitive, giving, loving, and emotionally needy have scope to achieve all the human connectedness they yearn for as they are bountiful to strangers. Because the contact between giver and recipient is essentially impersonal in terms of identity while being intensely personal within the moment, the atmosphere is often far more highly charged than it would be in more ordinary circumstances. This is gratifying for both the giver and recipient, and explains why so many people who feel alienated work with the less fortunate. There is little doubt that this dynamic was at play with Meghan. Thereafter, a girl whose identity had caused her both pain and confusion, would seek out those who might seem underprivileged but were, to her, sources of warmth, meaning and human connectedness. And they came without the risks and pitfalls involved with companionship with her peers. Giving to strangers was one thing. Giving to loved ones who she felt should be giving to her was something else.

Pollia remembered how Meghan took to working on skid row with such alacrity that she would update her on the specifics of what Betty was up to and whether Ralph still had his dog or Fred his fish. She had discovered a great way to rise above the barriers of isolation in which the grey areas of her racial identity had bogged her down. Meanwhile, Meghan was learning one of life's most profound lessons: goodness really can be its own reward, and its benefits were both practical and emotional. But, to achieve them, you had to be proactive.

And proactive Meghan certainly was. By this time, she was well on the road to becoming the activist she would later grow into being. Although she now credits Pollia with having provided her with encouragement and inspiration, the most cursory of examinations reveals that her father in fact played at least as fundamental a role. As she herself used to admit, Tom Sr instilled the belief in her that she could achieve anything she wanted, as long as she strove for it. Intensely hard-working, courageous in standing up for what he believed in, and forthright, he encouraged her to have a voice, and to use it. Disparate members of her family attribute the remarkable degree of self-confidence Meghan possesses, and possessed from her youth, to the encouragement her father gave her to cultivate her judgement, trust it, and act upon it. There is, for instance, the matter of the Ivory dishwashing liquid advertisement which has assumed almost mythical status since Meghan became a successful actress, then an even more famous duchess.

Like all myths, cause and effect are problematic, and the numbers don't quite add up, but the basics are indisputable. In 1995, Meghan saw a commercial for Ivory Clear Dishwashing Liquid with the tagline: "Women all over America are fighting greasy pots and pans." According to an account she gave at a United Nations conference in the years when she was still a relatively unknown actress, 'Two boys from my class said, "Yeah. That's where women belong — in the kitchen." I remember feeling shocked and angry and also just feeling so hurt. It just wasn't right, and something needed to be done.' Thomas Markle Sr encouraged her to write letters of complaint, which, by her own account, she did, mailing them to the First Lady Hillary Clinton, the high-profile women's rights advocate Gloria Allred, and Proctor and Gamble the manufacturers of Ivory Clear Dishwashing Liquid. While the First Lady and the controversial lawyer responded, Proctor and Gamble did not. According to Meghan, a month later they replaced the ad with one that said that "People all over America are fighting greasy pots and pans." This led her to believe that her complaint had been responsible for the change. As she put it to the UN, 'It was at that moment that I realized the magnitude of my actions. At the age of 11, I had created my small level of impact by standing up for equality.'

Empowering though that message was, there are four difficulties with the scenario, all of which were picked up once Meghan and Harry started going out seriously and the palace did the background checks it does on all people who become closely involved with the royals. Firstly, Meghan was not eleven in 1995, but fourteen. Secondly, Hillary Clinton was not First Lady in 1992, when Meghan was eleven, but became First Lady in 1993, when Meghan was twelve. Thirdly, there is no evidence that her sole letter altered the course of history. Proctor and Gamble indubitably changed its tagline, but it was optimistic of Meghan to suppose that it did so as a result of one letter written by the eleven or even fourteen year old Meghan Markle. Lastly, no advertising agency could replace an advertisement in a month. Advertisements take months to prepare. They are parts of advertising campaigns in which spontaneity and responsiveness of the sort to which Meghan was laying claim simply do not exist. Had she suggested that hers might have been one of the many letters that led to change; had she not provided such a tight timeline, which proved that her letter could have had no impact whatsoever, she would have been on firmer ground. But by presenting the facts as she did, she undermined the legitimacy of her claims. In the process, she opened herself up to suspicions that would lead a courtier, who values integrity, to conclude that she was a 'typical Hollywood type.....always pushing herself forward in the most obvious manner, when a more modest and realistic approach would have indicated integrity. As it is, when one watches the tape of that speech, one winces at her rank egotism, not to mention the naiveté displayed by so many Hollywood types, who think, because they have said that black is white and pink is green, everyone accepts this fiction as fact.'

In fairness to Meghan, she is a creature of Hollywood. The values there are different from those of palaces. Fantasy and self-promotion are not frowned upon, nor is exaggeration, all of which are viewed as valid tools for 'getting your message across.' A fourteen year old who writes a letter which garners praise from her school, as hers did, and which earns the standard responses that the Hillary Clintons and Gloria Allreds customarily send out to anyone who contacts them, nevertheless has just cause to be proud of her accomplishment, even if she unknowingly mistakes the polite response that public figures send out as being something more personal, and further believes that, because the company then altered its tagline, it did so as a result of her letter.

Be that as it may, this was one of those turning points that each individual has in his or her life. Like any other, it also had long-reaching effects. Just as how it empowered Meghan to conclude that her actions had had more of an effect than they could possibly have had, thereby encouraging her to adopt the role of activist, it also induced people who would otherwise have viewed her neutrally, to suspect her of inflating herself beyond her natural entitlement. This is where the exacting standards of the Old World collide with the embellishments of the New. Self-promotion and exaggeration have traditionally been viewed with suspicion in the royal and aristocratic worlds, where one's word has always been one's bond. There is an elaborate code of behaviour preventing people from too-overtly pushing themselves forward or laying claim to what isn't theirs by right. Indeed, British history is full of people who have gone to the executioner's block or otherwise ruined themselves rather than dishonour themselves by over-egging the pudding or in any other way compromising their integrity. A case in point was Terence Rattigan's 1946 hit play *The Winslow Boy, which* was based upon an infamous case when my late friend Mary Archer-Shee's cousin Martin nearly bankrupted himself to defend his son George against the unfair accusation of having stolen a five shilling postal order, which he denied having taken. While things have loosened up enough for traditionalists to know that it is no longer necessary to endanger one's prosperity to defend oneself against a petty accusation, and to accept that 'hype' forms a more acceptable part of modern life than it used to, people still adhere strictly to the dictum, 'Lay claim only to what is your due.'

This early error on Meghan's part would come back to haunt her once she made the transition from modest Hollywood stardom to the superstardom with which being a member of the British Royal Family invested her, because it was living proof that she was prone to exaggeration. This would doubtless make no dent in the way she was viewed in North America, where Hollywood and its ways have greater acceptance than they do in Britain, but on this side of the Atlantic it did alert people to the fact that the new Duchess of Sussex had both a propensity for exaggeration and a flair for dramatics in a way that the British find suspect.

According to Ninaki Priddy, Meghan's best friend from childhood, attention, approbation and applause have always been driving forces for her. 'Meg always wanted to be a star,' she said. Despite this, she was normal and likeable, even though she did exhibit some of the grit that would later on lead to her outstanding success. The two women knew each other from the age of two, when they started at the Hollywood Little Red House together. At the age of eleven, they transferred to Immaculate

Heart. 'It was always Nikki and Meg. We were so close-knit we came as a two. We were both honorary daughters in each other's homes. We were like family,' she said. Hers is the most trustworthy account of Meghan's early years. It is balanced, truthful, shorn of all side, with no malice or self-aggrandisement to undermine it. She was there, and nothing she says fails to ring true.

According to Nikki, 'Her mum, Doria, was very cool. She was this free spirit who'd dance around the house and have girlie evenings with us. She used to tell Meg to loosen up. She'd say, "You've got to have fun. Keep working at it."' Even at that early age, Meghan was displaying signs of the intensity which would take her so far but which would also interfere with her enjoyment of life unless she kept it in check.

Despite her fun-loving side, Doria had firm boundaries and trained Meghan to be well ordered domestically. 'Tom allowed her more space. He allowed us to get away with things. He provided a less strict household.' But Meghan was the star to both her parents. 'In a way, she was nurtured on a stage. She knew no other life. Tom was a great coach in that respect. He'd take photos of her on stage right from a young age.' The result was that 'Meg always wanted to be famous. She just loved to be the centre of attention. We used to imagine her receiving an Oscar. She used to practise announcing herself.'

Even at that tender age, Meghan displayed character traits that were exceptional. 'I admired the skilful way she handled her parents. She'd have to relay messages. It was literally stuff like, 'Tell your mother' or 'Tell your father.' Controlling her emotions is something she learnt back then. For as long as I knew Meghan, her parents weren't together. It could be hard for her. Sometimes she felt she had to pick sides. She was always trying to make sure each of them was happy.' The result was that she has always been 'very poised, a natural mediator. She was tough, too. If you rubbed her up the wrong way, she'd make it known with the silent treatment.' Whenever there was a problem, Nikki found, 'I'd always be the first to apologise. I just wanted to be besties again. She was stubborn. She digs her heels in the ground.'

So close were the girls that Meghan often slept over at the Priddys' house in North Hollywood. Meghan often swam in their pool. When the girls were fifteen, Dalton and Maria Priddy invited Meghan to join the family, which included Nikki's younger sister Michelle, on a tour of Europe. Nikki was so smitten by Paris that she ended up spending the following summer at the Sorbonne, but Meghan was more turned on by London. They stayed at a hotel near Kensington Palace and of course went to Buckingham Palace, where the duo was photographed sitting on the railings opposite Queen Victoria's statue with the palace in the background.

Nikki confirmed that 'the Royal Family was something she found fascinating. She had one of Princess Diana's books on her bookshelf.' She watched Diana's funeral, was moved to tears as were her friends, and, so obsessed did she become that she and another friend, Suzy Ardakani, got ahold of old videos of Diana's 1981 wedding to Prince Charles and decided to emulate her humanitarian example by collecting clothes and toys to be distributed amongst less privileged children. The lesson she was learning was that the most stylish and glamorous women show how special they are not only in their personal presentation, but through humanitarianism. She had found her role model and 'used to love The Princess Diaries - films about a commoner who becomes part of a Royal Family. She was very taken with that idea. She wants to be Princess Diana 2.0," Nikki Priddy said.

Of course, Meghan had no idea what the future held for her, nor that she would one day have an office in Buckingham Palace, or that she would chafe against palace restrictions in much the same way the mother-in-law she would never meet had resisted hers. At the time, though, Meghan's ambitions were more perfunctory. Her most immediate one was to go to Northwestern University. And to escape from her father, who now needed more reciprocity than she was willing to provide.

In 1990, Tom had won $750,000 in the California State Lottery. Although much of it was dissipated in an ill-advised investment in a jewelry business with a friend from Chicago, it nevertheless provided him with the means to work less and indulge his children even more than he had previously done. All members of the Markle family confirm that Tom was always exceedingly generous. Tom Jr was given the funds to start up a flower shop and Samantha was bought a second car to replace the first gift she had written off, while Meghan's school fees, always expensive, were covered more easily out of the proceeds of the win.

During her years at Immaculate Heart, Meghan threw herself into dramatics more than into anything else. Her ambition, as Nikki has stated, was to be a star. This was an ambition her father shared and fostered. Known at the school as an Emmy award-winning lighting director who was nominated virtually every year, the dramatics department was only too pleased when Meghan delivered him up as the technical director of every production in which she was involved. One cannot help thinking that even at that early age Meghan was learning the benefits of one hand washing the other, of how much of an additional advantage it was when you had something else aside from mere talent to help you along in achieving your ambitions. And of how those ambitions could be further enhanced by the skill of knowledgeable people such as her father.

While Thomas Markle Sr's technical abilities undoubtedly improved the quality of each production Meghan was in, he also used each opportunity to further enhance his daughter's knowledge of what would, and would not, work on stage. He taught her all about finding the light, or the importance of light and shade, of where to stand on stage, even what angle to deploy for maximum effect. He would also take an endless stream of photographs of her, so that she could see for herself what he meant when he told her to do this and not do that. This technical knowledge was invaluable, for he was teaching her at the cradle what most actors only learnt when they were approaching the grave after a lifetime of trial and error.

The former child actress Gigi Perreau taught acting at her alma mater as well as helped with the staging of plays and musicals. She remembered that she never had a problem with Meghan, who was 'spot on, learnt her lines' and was 'very dedicated, very focused.' Because of Meghan's dedication, she 'knew she would be something special.'

Meghan, however, wanted to be a star both on stage and off. By the time she was a teenager, she had had enough attention from boys to know that they found her attractive and that she liked them as well. Thereafter, she would be the female lead in many a real-life romance, starting out simply enough with the boys from the masculine counterpart of her school: St. Francis High School in nearby La Cañada Flintridge. Founded by the Capuchin Friars of the Western American Province of Our Lady of Angels in 1946 on lands bought from the Flintridge Country Club, its students interacted with the Immaculate Heart girls on the basis of equality. Like most institutions whose ambition was to turn out a superior form of human being, both schools were eager to restrict the activities of their students so that they focused on what was desirable and life-enhancing, rather than opening them up to undesirable influences. Chief amongst these restrictions was fraternisation with anyone who was not a peer. It was an accepted feature of both schools that their students could mix with each other, but that they should exercise caution with outsiders. There was something old-fashioned about their desire to protect the students against undesirable influences. While this played well in a society like America, where there is frank acknowledgement of the desirability of people of status sticking together as they assist one another on the path to greater success, in Europe such attitudes were already viewed as not only dangerously old-fashioned and damagingly restrictive, but as snobbish. It really was a case of a new society keeping up the lines of demarcation while an older society was intent on bringing them down, at least enough for there to be greater mobility between the classes. This difference in cultural attitudes would prove to have a defining effect upon Meghan and Harry's relationships not only with each other, but also with everyone else.

In the meantime, the young Meghan availed herself of a series of willing beaux from St. Francis, and at the age of sixteen, narrowed them down to Luis Segura, her first serious boyfriend. A Latino who had a reputation as a natty dresser, they were together for two years. She was friends with the whole Segura family, and was encouraged by all of them to put herself forward as St. Francis's Homecoming Queen. Although unknown in Britain, in the US Homecoming Queens were and remain big deals in high schools, and Meghan went all out to win, writing an essay on her work at the Hippie Kitchen and charming as many people as possible to vote for her. She won, and, bedecked in a pale blue strapless satin gown and tiara, Queen Meghan was accompanied by a phalanx of courtiers to the ball by Luis's younger brother Danny, natty in a tuxedo with a wing-collared shirt and a ready-made black bowtie.

Meghan took her success in her stride. Some girls might have changed their demeanour, but she remained the same sweet, charming, accessible but refined girl who was fun to be with and nice to all. According to friends, it was almost as if she was using this success as practice for what was to come, as if it was no big deal, because it was really what she deserved and was entitled to. She intended to be a great star, and this was but the first taste, and therefore of no real significance.

In the 1997 programme notes for Stephen Sondheim's musical *Into the Woods*, in which Meghan played Little Red Riding Hood, she also stated that she wanted to attend Northwestern University outside Chicago as it would be a first step on her journey to Broadway. In her final yearbook, she went a step further and described herself as 'classy', a word which would remain a firm favourite of hers, and whose meaning meant much to her in practical as well as philosophical terms. To underscore her ambition and self-belief, she illustrated her photograph with a quote from Eleanor Roosevelt: 'Women are like teabags; they don't realize how strong they are until they're in hot water.'

None of Meghan's peers thought her immodest or pretentious. Although she was already prone to quoting aphorisms - something she still does - as far as onlookers were concerned, she was a jewel in search of the right setting so that she could shine even more brightly than she was shining at the moment. Ambition was good. She and her father had done, and would continue to do, whatever it took to enhance her prospects, from having expensive orthodonture so that she would have a perfect smile, to having the bulbous tip of her nose refined via plastic surgery. This was a fairly common procedure amongst aspiring actresses in Hollywood. Even the fabled beauty Elizabeth Taylor had done it in her teenage. It was a simple procedure. Cartilage was removed so that the tip of the nose was sharper than nature had intended. In Meghan's case, however, the procedure would become more noticeable with the passage of time as the cartilage between the tip and the bone drooped, giving her nose a ski jump effect which, ironically, Harry had naturally.

When Meghan graduated from Immaculate Heart in June 1999, her academic and personal attributes were apparent for all to note at the Hollywood Bowl, where the ceremony was held. As well as her graduation certificate, she was presented with the Notre Dame Club of Los Angeles Achievement Award, the Bank of America Fine Arts Award, a commendation in the National Achievement Scholarship Program, and an award for mentoring younger students.

Although Meghan had won three scholarships and could have entered several colleges either as a scholarship or a paying student, the thought had never entered her head that she should go anywhere but where she wanted. She had been brought up by her parents to have her desires fulfilled, and what she wanted was to attend Northwestern University.

This institution was and remains one of the most prestigious private research colleges in the United States. Fees were over $50,000 in today's prices. It is ranked 9th amongst the American universities and has the 10th largest university endowment in the country, valued at more than $11 billion. Based at Evanston, Illinois, its main campus covers some 240 acres, while its secondary campus in Chicago covers 25 acres. There is a third campus in Doha, Qatar. The university's former and present faculty and alumni include 19 Nobel Prize laureates, 38 Pulitzer Prize winners, 16 Rhodes Scholars, 6 MacArthur Genius Fellows, 65 American Academy of Arts and Sciences Members, 2 Supreme Court Justices, and its School of Communication is a leading producer of Academy Award, Emmy Award and Tony Award directors, playwrights, writers, actors, and actresses. Although Tom had lost a large part of his lottery winnings, he was still a highly successful lighting director, and he took out bank loans and put in the extra hours necessary to raise the money needed to send his treasured Flower to the university which would be but a stepping stone on her journey to ever increasing success.

Considering Meghan's stated purpose in attending Northwestern was to become a Broadway star, the fact that she chose to major in English, rather than acting, suggests that she was either not quite as confident as she seemed to be, or then that she was so confident that she didn't feel the need to specialise in her chosen field. Leaving the protection of home is challenging for any youngster, but Meghan had both greater advantages and disadvantages than most of her peers. Being a child of Hollywood, she was far more sophisticated than her fellow students on the Eastern Seaboard. She dressed better, had more style, knew how to present herself better than they did, and had more confidence than most of them. She made friends with both boys and girls as soon as she burst upon the Evanston campus. She had pared down her look to what she regarded as monochromatic chic; she now wore much more make-up than she had been allowed to in California, and even took to highlighting her hair. Always deliberate, measured and calculating in the positive sense of the word, she also watched and waited before deciding which sorority to join. Once she made up her mind, she went straight for her target, turning on the power of her personality in an irresistible onslaught, and not surprisingly got initiated into Kappa Kappa Gamma with its clutch of intelligent and hot girls. 'The thing we all have in common,' according to fellow member Melania Hidalgo, 'is that we're all all drive, intelligent and ambitious.' They were also avid party girls, hitting the bottle more than their books, networking in the belief that who you met might well prove more useful in the future than what you knew. So successfully did Meghan fit in, that she would ultimately be elected to chair recruitment for the sorority.

As Meghan tells it, she had one disadvantage most of her sisters did not. Northwestern was primarily Caucasian. Most of the students came from white environments. They were not used to inter-racial interaction, and, by her own account, she found one of the reactions stifling. She recounted to *Elle Magazine* how she had to navigate 'closed-mindedness to the tune of a dorm mate I met my first week at university who asked if my parents were still together. "You said your mom is black and your father is white, right?" she said. I smiled meekly, waiting for what could possibly come out of her pursed lips next. "And they're divorced?" I nodded. "Oh, well that makes sense." To this day, I don't fully understand what she meant by that, but I understood the implication. And I drew back: I was scared to open this Pandora's box of discrimination, so I sat stifled, swallowing my voice.'

Someone who knows Meghan well from childhood warns against taking these defining moments too literally. She has always had a propensity to embellish, to draw dramatic lessons out of the most anodyne events, and, especially since she became a public figure, to use poetical licence to highlight a point she wishes to make but which might not actually have happened the way she recounts it. Since investigation has never been able to turn up this racist dorm mate, notwithstanding the fact that there are records of which students shared quarters, it seems likely that this story is apocryphal rather than reminiscent. Her friend explains, 'The way to tell is how neatly they [Meghan's reminiscences] fit the story. Meg's inventions are too tailor-made to be reliable. People just don't act the way she says. Once you know her, you can tell which stories are Meghan and which really happened.'

Such incidents, whether actual or embroidered, were fortunately few and far between. By her own account, Meghan's sensitivity regarding her race followed her from inclusive California to exclusive Illinois, despite no one noticing how affected she was by it. Since there are no contemporaneous accounts of her experiencing any actual racial difficulties, and her lifestyle suggests that she was fully accepted by all quarters, and indeed that she flourished in a way any girl with real problems would not have done, this suggests that she encountered no significant or actual prejudice. It also suggests that she had transcended such internal racial uncertainties as she would later claim to have possessed, so well that they did not prevent her from achieving all she wanted. Of course, we must take her word for the fact that they remained internal sources of discomfort, but the degree of acceptance also reflected positively upon her classmates at Northwestern, two of whom would remain her friends into the present time.

As her freshman year got underway, Meghan partied up a storm, was popular with the girls as well as the boys, and got herself one of the hottest boyfriends on campus when she paired up with a white, 6'5" basketball player from Lakewood, Ohio named Steve Lepore. He was on the basketball team in his sophomore year, and would prove to be as disciplined and focused as she was. But he was more interested in fitness than partying, intending to qualify as a pro, and made all the necessary sacrifices, such as foregoing female companionship the night before a game in keeping with standard practice amongst basketball, baseball, football, and hockey players. At the end of that academic year, he transferred to Wake Forest University in Winston-Salem, North Carolina, where he became a stand out player. At the time of writing, he is an assistant coach on Eastern Kentucky University's men's basketball staff, and, with his wife Carric, is a proud parent to their young daughter Giuliana Rudi.

Patently, the relationship was not serious enough for Meghan to follow him, and she lost no time in replacing him in her affections, though for the remainder of her time at Northwestern she was never again one half of such a dynamic duo.

This had no perceptible effect upon the pleasure Meghan was having at college. She developed three friendships which went some way towards replacing the gap left when geography separated her from Nikki Priddy. Although the childhood friends kept in touch, Meghan now found a substitute of sorts in Lindsay Jill Roth, the attractive blonde daughter of Jewish lawyers from the prosperous Long Island village of Lattingtown within the town of Oyster Bay in Nassau County, New York. With a population of less than two thousand, of whom 94% were white, it had no real parallels with Woodland Hills save for both areas being predominantly white and both having median incomes above the regional averages, with Woodland Hills being a bit less than $100,000 per annum while Lattingtown was half again as much. The two girls now became fast friends after meeting in a Toni Morrison Literature class in their first year at Northwestern. They drank together, partied together, studied together, and later on, when they left college they kept in touch as Lindsay became a producer for *Larry King Now*, *The Real Girl's Kitchen*, and *Queen Boss*, as well as publishing *What Pretty Girls Are Made Of* in 2015. Meanwhile, Meghan struggled until she got the role of Rachel Zane in Suits.

In 2016, when Lindsay married an Englishman named Gavin Jordan, Meghan was her Matron of Honour. This is revealing, for when Meghan married Trevor Engelson in 2011, she chose Nikki Priddy to be her Maid of Honour. Despite this, the bond between Meghan and Roth was strong. 'We're the kind of friends' she said, 'who can be 3,000 miles away and still be talking about or thinking the same thing, and even texting each other the same thing at the same time miles away. I don't know many people who are as generous and supportive as Meg is. I think people assume that when someone gains notoriety that they change. But she's still the same girl I met years ago, with the same values and priorities. She's selfless, and that's just a part of who she is and who she was raised to be. There's a motto that Meg and I have consistently come back to throughout the years: "I choose happiness." It's a constant reminder to be self-aware, be uniquely you, be happy and to treat people with respect; to be kind, empathetic and to really learn from those around you in any circumstance. Meg does that. Meg has especially developed into an extraordinary businesswoman, actress, writer and advocate for women and children.'

Meghan had made another girlfriend with whom she would keep in touch. This was Genevieve Hillis, her sorority sister from Kappa Kappa Gamma, but her other closest friend at the time wasn't Genevieve but an African-American named Larnelle Quentin Foster. He was a gay but heavily closeted son of pastors who he felt would be disappointed if they knew of his sexuality. He studied acting at Northwestern and would ultimately become a professor of drama. He is now openly gay. In college, though, he lived locally with his parents. He and Meghan became something of an item, often going to *avant-garde* theatre shows or 'just hanging out. We were very social. We were always doing different things, having fun. She was ambitious to be an actress, but we didn't want to be in rehearsals all day like a lot of the others. We would much rather watch a show than be in one.'

Meghan often joined the Foster family for meals on weekends, and was so much a part of the family's activities that she would attend services at their church with them. She and Larnelle also enjoyed cooking together: her specialty at the time was Indian cuisine. Larnelle would later describe Meghan as being 'very kind, very genuine, someone who cares deeply about her family, her friends and the world'.

Having turned down three scholarships to attend Northwestern and study English, Meghan had not been at the university long before she realised that she had made the wrong choice of major. She therefore opted to change to theatre arts and international relations. Although she still aspired to stardom, she was now broadening her horizons to include the possibility of the *Corps Diplomatique* as a stage. 'At no time did she consider that hers would be an ordinary life,' one of her old time friends, who asked to remain anonymous, said. 'She intended to be a high flyer, no matter what she did. She could envisage herself as a Broadway or film star, or an Ambassador or a diplomat whose actions would change the world while improving the lot of humanity.'

With that in mind, Meghan approached her father's elder brother Michael, a State Department operative whose specialty was US Government communications systems. Within the family, it was accepted that he was CIA. He had been posted to such disparate places as Berlin, Guam, Bucharest, and Ottawa, with his wife Toni, who would die in 2012. He was known to be popular and well-connected within the State Department. Meghan wanted him to find her an internship with a US embassy abroad. She explained that she was considering a career in international relations, and wanted to test the water with some practical experience of the diplomatic life to see if she would like being a diplomat. The difficulty was, she had left it so late that getting her what she wanted would mean calling in additional favours from friends.

'I knew the (American) Ambassador in Buenos Aires,' Michael Markle said. 'I personally talked to him and got her fixed up with the internship she wanted.' As a result of her uncle's string-pulling, she was offered a six week long internship as a junior press officer at the American Embassy in Argentina's capital city. While there, her duties were those of any other junior press attaché. She answered enquiries, drafted letters, shunted paper from one department to another, generally making herself useful doing what was effectively donkey work. But she struck her superior, Mark Krischik, as both efficient and ingenious. 'If she had stayed with the State Department, she would have been an excellent addition to the US diplomatic corps. She had all that it takes to be a successful diplomat.'

Attitude and personality, however, were not sufficient to enter the State Department. One also had to pass the Foreign Service Officer Test, which Meghan sat while in Argentina. To her chagrin, she failed it. However, she had planned to fly to Madrid at the end of her internship, under the International Education for Students Program, to take their six week course in Spanish. She adhered to that plan, and would later on find the knowledge she gained useful.

She was not tempted, however, to resit the exam. Unused as she was to failure, she decided that her future lay in acting. Diplomacy had only been a pipe dream. She had become aware that that career path would be strewn with too many difficulties. Not only would she have a longer and harder road to travel before she became the star she wanted to be, but the rewards, close up, seemed less attractive than being a star of stage or screen. In that, her assessment was accurate, for no matter how high flying a careerist diplomat is, the top of the *Corps Diplomatique* simply doesn't have the pizazz or the allure that becoming a stage or screen star does.

This taste of failure, however, was but the first gulp of a potion that Meghan would have to swallow time and again throughout her twenties. Shining brightly in high school and university is not always a precursor to worldly success. In fact, those who sparkle in such safe and structured settings often fail to light up the real world, while those who were more mundane students soar to greater heights once they're released into the hurly-burly of the real world. So it would prove with Meghan when she graduated from Northwestern's School of Communication with a Bachelor of Arts degree in theatre and international studies.

While Meghan shone at school and university, Harry, who was born three years and one month after her on the 15th September 1984, did not. If their scholastic records would prove to be as opposite as it was possible to be, their entry into the world had parallels. The Prince and Princess of Wales's marriage hit the rocks shortly after Harry's birth, and while they remained together for the next eight years, before he was even a toddler, the marriage was in reality over. For the next eight years, the Waleses' relationship was a study in a couple avoiding togetherness except on official occasions. Charles based himself down at Highgrove in Gloucestershire, the house the Duchy of Cornwall had bought for his use from Viscount and Viscountess Macmillan of Ovenden in 1980, prior to his marriage in 1981. According to Charles's then valet, Stephen Barry, who used to ferry Diana back and forth between Buckingham Palace and Highgrove for midnight assignations with the prince, she had a great deal of input with the decoration. Once the marriage foundered, however, she opted to remain in London at Kensington Palace during the week, while Charles based himself down at Highgrove. The couple was seldom together even on the weekends. Whenever Diana was going to be in residence at Highgrove, Charles would frequently visit friends. So civilised was the arrangement that he allowed her to entertain her lover James Hewitt even in the country. A noted equestrian, with Charles's blessing he also taught Diana and the boys to ride.

Although there was a similar lack of congeniality between Charles and Diana and Tom and Doria, both couples had found a way to navigate around the shoals of disappointment to the extent that their children were able to have good relationships with both parents. Superficially, both sets of parents might have aimed for an absence of overt hostility, but only the Markles were successful in maintaining this consistently. This was largely due to Diana's emotional state. If she was happily distracted by a lover, she and Charles would have a relatively civilised, indeed settled, relationship. Sometimes it was even affectionate, in the way a brother and sister who are not particularly close but have a basic fondness for each other, would behave towards each other. This was especially true throughout the second half of the eighties, when Diana's affair with James Hewitt was flourishing. However, whenever her love life was not satisfactory, she would turn a fully loaded fusillade on Charles and blow serenity out of the water.

At times like these, everything was his fault. He had ruined her life by being the man he was and not being the man she had wanted him to be. But for him, her life would have been perfect. The scenes were traumatic for all concerned, including the children, for, while Charles was non-confrontational and would do everything in his power to avoid an argument, Diana was the antithesis. When she was spoiling for a fight, she made sure she got one and that everyone knew about it. She would scream the house down. She would be on the rampage for hours. She would hurl abuse and objects and always reduce herself to tears of frustration and hysteria. Because Diana was never faithful to any one lover, including James Hewitt and Hasnat Khan, the two men she later claimed she was truly in love with prior to Dodi Fayed, and because she was always on the lookout for the perfect man who would make her life complete, her love life was volatile even when it was relatively settled. There was always an unpredictable element as to what would set her off, for the triggers had nothing to do with her husband or even her lover's behaviour, but her inner need to feel loved: and to feel that that love was something she could rely upon. Always careful to direct her eruptions in her husband's rather than her lovers' direction, this did not make for a stable or happy atmosphere at home. Then, when things settled down, she would revert to being serene, accommodating Diana who understood that she had to remain married to Charles and the best way forward was for them to continue leading separate but civilised existences, he with his mistress, she with her lover.

As Diana approached thirty, however, she began to question why she had to remain married to Charles. She was frank about wanting a loving marriage and a daughter. This introduced a whole new level of volatility into her family life. No longer was the trigger solely when she was dissatisfied with her love life. Now, whenever she was so satisfied with it that she fantasised about divorcing her husband and marrying whichever of the lovers she wanted to marry at that moment - the main candidates were James Hewitt, Oliver Hoare, and Hasnat Khan - she set about tearing the place apart in her quest for her liberty.

Diana had an advantage over Charles that neither Tom nor Doria had over each other but which Meghan shares with Diana. Both women, from early childhood, were products of broken homes. Both learnt from an early age how to navigate between opposing factions, how to play Peter off against Paul so that they would get what they wanted. Both were soft and sweet but both were also tough beneath the ostensibly vulnerable exterior. Both had developed the tactical abilities unique to the children of broken homes. They had learnt at an early age how to palliate, negotiate, and use whatever tools worked well for them, to achieve their goal: whatever that goal might be.

Although Meghan was brought up in a more superficially peaceable environment, Diana, for all her volatility, was a loving and obliging mother. She was also the ultimate authority figure in the Wales nuclear family. She was insistent that her children would grow up to be spirited. She decreed that they would not be so disciplined, the way other royal children were, that they would have the spontaneity drained out of them. Charles was not allowed to interfere and there was never any prospect of the Queen intervening.

Although titular head of the family, Elizabeth II, known in the family as Lilibet, was not its *de facto* head. That was the Duke of Edinburgh, whose role was consistently challenged and often undermined by Lilibet's powerful mother, Queen Elizabeth the Queen Mother. Lilibet was therefore used to two dominant figures in her immediate family, her husband and her mother, neither of whom liked the other and both of whom she assuaged in her desire to have a happy and harmonious family life. Her attitude only further eroded the influence she and her husband had with their eldest son, and, by extension, his wife.

Although Philip tried as best he could to lay down the ground rules within his own nuclear, Mountbatten-Windsor, branch of the family, the Queen Mother was a constant source of opposition where Charles was concerned. She had always been, ever since he was a toddler. She never caused problems with the three youngest royal children, leading more than one royal relation to observe that the only reason why she meddled with Charles was that he was going to be king one day. She had made sure with her daughter the Queen, and now with her grandson the future King, that she would leave her imprimatur on the Crown by way of her influence over them. Her avowed reason with Lilibet had been and remained that she knew best what the Crown needed, and with Charles it was that neither of his parents 'understood' him the way she did. She felt that it was her right as a grandmother and queen consort to encourage him and give him all the love and direction she discerned he needed.

Being supportive of a man who will not stand up to his wife is no way to solve the underlying problem of how children should be disciplined. The Queen Mother was therefore inadvertently reinforcing the vacuum of influence Charles had within his own nuclear family. A vacuum which was also fostered by his hands-off parents whom he viewed with antagonism, for by this time Charles's relationship with both the Queen and Prince Philip was anything but warm.

As William and Harry grew up, becoming ever wilder, word began to spread in aristocratic circles how out of control they were. The late Kenneth Rose, one of the best connected journalists of his day whose personal friendships with several of the royals was an open secret, wrote in his diary, following a weekend with Philip's first cousin Lady Pamela Mountbatten and her husband David Hicks, how thirteen year old 'Prince William is tiresome, always attracting attention to himself. Hardly surprising when he is so spoilt by the tug-of-war of his parents, and by courtiers, servants and private detectives.' Harry was even more spoilt.

Although Prince Philip was the paterfamilias with a huge amount of influence where his three other children were concerned, his lack of influence with Charles was noteworthy. He and the Queen's position as parents to Charles had been so undermined over the years by the Queen Mother that parents and son were virtually estranged. They saw as little of each other as possible, and when they were together, they were polite the way strangers are. 'There was absolutely no warmth between them. I think the Queen and the Duke of Edinburgh would have liked things to be different, but Charles simply wasn't interested,' a prince told me. Philip therefore was not in a position to provide the critical intervention everyone in the family felt William and Harry needed, in order for them to be brought up with a sufficient degree of discipline to enable them ultimately to perform their royal duties properly. So the two boys continued to be reared in their wild way, with all the royal adults bemoaning the lack of discipline their mother had decreed appropriate.

At the time, none of the royals realised that Diana was actually encouraging her sons to be recalcitrant, or that she was encouraging Harry to develop the rebellious streak which ran throughout her nature. This the boys would inadvertently reveal later on when they said that she used to tell them, 'I don't care what you do as long as you don't get caught.' Of course, Diana expected them at all times to treat the staff well. She would never have tolerated them being rude to strangers when out in public. She never-endingly reiterated how they must always remember they were royal and therefore they should behave to the world at large in a royal manner. But, beneath it all, Diana was preaching the same lesson Joseph Kennedy had taught his boys: You can break the rules as long as you aren't found out. It isn't the rules that matter so much as making sure no one catches you out when you break them. As long as you don't suffer the consequences of the breach, it's okay. It has often been said that Joe Kennedy encouraged his sons to be amoral by instilling this code. If that is so, Diana was doing the same.

This freewheeling attitude was anathema to the Royal Family. The rules mattered. Humans being human, everyone would sometimes break the rules. But an awareness of being subject to the rules, as opposed to being above them, was an important part of being properly royal. No one exemplified this more than King George VI and his wife Queen Elizabeth. The Queen Mother had ruled her own immediate family, known to themselves as Us Four, with an iron hand in a velvet glove from the very beginning of her marriage. The king had been under the thumb of his wife from before he even slipped the ring on her finger. Their two daughters, Princesses Elizabeth and Margaret, were also reared from birth to defer at all times to their mother. The former Lady Elizabeth Bowes-Lyon had been a stickler for a happy home life grounded in good form and traditional values. These did not conflict at all with the royal regimen. Indeed, the way the future Queen Mother set up her family life reinforced it, for she overlaid iron discipline with a coating of charm and personability while adhering at all times to the traditional royal codes of conduct. Lilibet and her sister Margaret were therefore brought up to be perfect princesses and it would only be after the Queen Mother's death that Lilibet's less formal side was given vent publicly. Till then, she had to be as buttoned up as her mother required.

Considering that the Queen was in her mid-seventies when her mother died, the degree of control imposed by the Queen Mother was striking. The contrast between that royal way and Diana's could not have been more extreme. Although both Lilibet and Princess Margaret were very much their own women privately, the elder sister was by nature reserved though a fearsome mimic, while also being a wit and fun loving, though the younger was decidedly more outgoing and unorthodox, more outrageous and even more fun loving, but all within the confines of disciplined royal behaviour.

Despite their fun-loving natures, neither sister ever stretched royal boundaries when bringing their children up. All six of them - Prince Charles, Princess Anne, Prince Andrew, Prince Edward, Lord Linley and Lady Sarah Armstrong-Jones - were reared in keeping with ancient royal and aristocratic traditions. They were well behaved children who grew into well-mannered, well-disciplined and traditionally behaved royals and aristocrats. This meant that when they were in public, they conducted themselves as they were expected to behave, and not as they themselves wished, even though, in the privacy of their own homes, their standards might slacken.

This was certainly not true of Diana's children. Both boys were allowed to 'run wild', to quote Princess Margaret. By the time Diana and Charles's firstborn, William, was three, Elizabeth II was bemoaning how undisciplined he was. In 1986, when he was a page at his Uncle Andrew's wedding to Sarah Ferguson, he endeared himself to the public, though not to his own family, by fidgeting, sticking his tongue out, and generally behaving like the naughty four year old he was. Harry, at a year old, was still too young for anyone to know if he would follow in his brother's footsteps, but the harbingers, which would turn out to be only too accurate, were not good. Diana encouraged indiscipline, and wildness is what she got.

Up to that point, there had only been one wild royal child that anyone could think of in the British Royal Family. That had been the Queen's late uncle John, the epileptic and (judging from his behaviour) autistic youngest son of the late King George V and Queen Mary. Uncontrollable, his father used to say that he was the only person whom he could never get to obey him. The unruly but tragic John had died at the age of thirteen of an epileptic fit in 1919, two months after the end of the First World War. Although his parents had loved him, there was an almost audible sigh of relief that nature had come to the rescue, for there was every indication that John would have become a major embarrassment to the monarchy had he lived to adulthood.

Whether William and Harry would follow on the path of Great-Great Uncle John remained to be seen, but the question of how the boys should be disciplined was not straightforward owing to the family dynamics. Charles was Queen Elizabeth The Queen Mother's favourite grandchild. As far as she was concerned, he could do no wrong. If he wanted to turn a blind eye to the way his children were being reared, she did not feel it was up to her to interfere. Moreover, she understood Charles's predicament. She sympathised with his powerlessness as a father and husband in the face of a wife as powerfully driven as Diana.

The Queen Mother's insights into Diana's mode of behaviour came not only from what she knew through her own family, but through Diana's as well. One of the Queen Mother's Women of the Bedchamber was Diana's grandmother Ruth, Lady Fermoy, who violently disapproved of Diana's conduct, to such an extent that by the time of her death in 1993, she was no longer speaking to her granddaughter. Lady Fermoy regarded Diana as treacherous, dangerous, and irresponsible. She felt that she had been an appalling Princess of Wales, had undermined the monarchy, was a bad daughter and granddaughter, had been anything but a good wife, and moreover was proving to be a dangerously lax mother.

On the other hand, Diana thought that her own family and the Royal Family were out of touch with the mores of the time. She felt that they all needed to loosen up a bit, to be less preoccupied with good behaviour and become more in touch with their feelings. Not for her the stiff upper lip. Whether she was happy or sad, she made sure everyone knew about it. She felt it was important to be in touch with one's feelings, and to show them, rather than concealing them behind a facade of good behaviour.

In many ways, Diana's values were more in keeping with her times than either the family into which she had been born or married. She was determined that her children would not grow up straightjacketed by decorum the way royal and to a lesser extent aristocratic children used to be. The royals especially had always been isolated from everyday life and indeed from the equalising ebb and flow of ordinary friendship. Even in Charles's generation, all British royals expected their closest friends, and often their lower-ranking cousins, to refer to them as Sir and Ma'am instead of by their Christian names. All Charles's girlfriends were obliged to call him Sir, and the Queen Mother's brother, Sir David Bowes-Lyon, had to address her as Ma'am even when entertaining her at his home, St. Paul's Walden Bury, although the only other person present was his good friend and neighbour Burnett Pavitt. It was this level of formality which Diana rightly sought to change. Having lived in a less restrictive world, she was determined that her children would have upbringings that allowed them to relate to people on a human level, devoid of the crippling restrictions royal formality imposed upon royals. They were to be referred to by employees as Wills or William and Harry, not Your Royal Highness or Sir. They could go and bother the staff in the kitchen. They would be people first and princes second.

Harry, however, had one handicap that was insurmountable. He was the second son. Second sons do not count in royal or aristocratic circles except as spares. Everything goes to the first son. There can be only one king, duke, marquis, earl, viscount, baron, or baronet. Only the firstborn son can inherit the throne, palace, castle, estate and all its chattels. Second sons, of course, do inherit something. They have secondary titles, secondary possessions, secondary incomes which go along with their secondary status. But the only way to preserve the hegemony is for virtually everything to devolve upon the firstborn son.

In the world into which Harry was born, second sons are second class citizens. The phenomenon is so well known that it even has its own name: Second Son Syndrome. This does not necessarily have to be a problem. My boyfriend before marriage was a second son; I married a second son; and my longstanding boyfriend after marriage was a second son. Some second sons cope with their status better than others. My boyfriend before marriage and my boyfriend after both grappled with it well, but too many second sons are bitterly envious of their elder brothers. They resent the fact that an accident of birth prevented them from getting the lion's share of the money, status, power and privilege. They forget that their status as the scions of privilege is also an accident of birth, that they could equally have been born into penury in Somalia instead of the lap of luxury in Great Britain.

Some mothers deal with Second Son Syndrome better than others. Some bring their children up to accept that life is not fair, that you should count your blessings and be grateful for small as well as large mercies, and not covet thy brother's wife, ass or goods, in keeping with the dictat of the tenth Commandment. They point out to their second sons how lucky they are that they will not have to live up to a patrimony that might be laden with privilege, but is heavily offset by the crushing weight of responsibility for which nature might not have equipped either son, but which the first born will have to learn to bear whether he is inclined to do so or not. Other mothers make it so obvious that they prefer the child who will inherit the throne or the peerage that they mess up both the first and second sons for the remainder of their lives. Still others do what Diana did. They overcompensate. Although she always kept the boys grounded with the knowledge that only William would one day be king, she nevertheless tried to equalise an unequal situation, figuring, incorrectly, that she could redress the balance by providing Harry with additional emotional security. Darren McGrady, the chef at Kensington Palace from 1993 to 1997, recounted how she used to tell him, 'You take care of the heir; I'll take care of the spare.' She openly said that she knew that William would always be all right; Harry was the one she had to look out for. She used to say that Harry was 'an airhead like me', while William 'is like his father'. This made her more protective and indulgent of Harry.

Just as how the young Meghan felt the issue of her race impacting more acutely upon herself than those around her realised, so too was Harry aware from an early age of the disparity between himself and his elder brother. He used to complain that the Queen Mother showered William with attention while virtually ignoring him; that she had William sit close by her while he was relegated to a Siberian seat when they went to visit her. Once, he was terrifically upset when the butler brought sandwiches for her and William but none for him. I find it difficult to believe that Queen Elizabeth the Queen Mother would have countenanced such a slight, and suspect that a crucial element of the story was omitted in the recounting. Nevertheless, the fact remains, from an early age Harry was acutely conscious of the difference in importance between himself and William, to such an extent, that Diana's protection officer Ken Wharfe recounted how, when he was four or five, Harry informed their nanny, 'It doesn't matter anyway, because William is going to be king.' Wharfe found it amazing that Harry could, even at that tender age, be so aware of that fact.

The two year age difference meant that both boys were at different stages developmentally. Harry was a soft and sweet child who loved nothing better than curling up with his mother on a sofa or bed and looking at movies or shows on television with her. He was an unashamed Mummy's boy, while his elder brother made his presence felt in such an independent, indeed aggressive, manner that he was known as Basher.

Given a choice, children are much happier having fun in the country than staying in the city. Palaces are little different from ordinary houses save in scale, and both boys liked nothing better than going down to Highgrove for the weekend with their father. Contrary to the misinformation that Diana later on spread about her husband, Charles was a good and involved father whose children loved him as much as he loved them. He used to play with them the way his father, who had been a playful father, used to with him. He had a special pit built for them which was filled with colourful balls and he used to dive into it with them. He had a tree house constructed for them. He took them for long walks throughout the property, opening their eyes to the beauties of nature while instructing them on the flora which were such a passion of his. He took them to see the newly born lambs, encouraged them to keep pets - their mother was not an animal lover - and showed Harry how to take care of his favourite, a rabbit. Charles loved the countryside, and, as the boys grew up, they too developed a love for it. They learnt to shoot rabbits, to relish being out of doors, which was definitely not something their avowedly 'Metropolitan Babe' mother enjoyed.

Harry and William both had ponies, and from an early age Harry was taught to ride, first by a local instructor named Marion Cox, then by James Hewitt. The young prince was fearless and had what his aunt Anne, an Olympic equestrienne who was a Burghley gold medallist, called 'a good seat'. A love of horses, of course, ran in the Royal Family. Both the Queen and Queen Mother were avid turfites. Prince Philip had been a world-class polo player and, upon retiring, had taken up carriage-driving. Prince Charles had also been a polo player, and Princess Anne felt that Harry had such natural ability that he could grow up to compete as long as he dedicated himself to the sport.

More than horses, what Harry loved from an early age, was all things military. James Hewitt told me in the 1990s how he had mini-uniforms made for both princes, and how they absolutely adored parading around in them, especially after James taught them to salute properly. But it was Harry, not William, who truly relished the military, and even at that early age, it was apparent that his niche would be a career in the armed forces.

This was just as well, for once Harry started school, it quickly became apparent that he was as unacademic as his mother had been. At the age of three, he followed William to a Montessori kindergarten, Mrs Mynors' Nursery School in Chepstow Villas in Notting Hill, a five minute drive from Kensington Palace. Jane Mynors was a bishop's daughter whose thirty six charges started their day with a prayer, following which they moved on to singing, cutting paper with scissors and making shapes, singing, or playing out of doors. Throughout the years that the children were being prepared to begin their formal education, they were expected to learn how to paint and sing, but not how to read. Although Harry seemed to start well enough, his progress was not helped by Diana's propensity for allowing him to play truant. He preferred to stay at home with her, cuddling in her lap for hours while they watched movies, rather than attending school. Diana's friend Simone Simmons remembered how 'he used to go down with more coughs and colds than William, but it was nothing serious. Most of the time I think he just wanted to be at home with his Mummy. He loved having her to himself and not having to compete with William.'

Diana also enjoyed having him to herself. Harry's stay at Mrs Mynors' coincided with the height of Diana's love affair with James Hewitt. At various times, she would surrender to the fantasy of being married to him, creating a degree of frustration for herself that cannot have been conducive to serenity. Her children, Harry especially, were her comfort, and she derived as much emotional gratification from interacting with them as they did from her.

Once a week, on Wednesdays, Diana took the boys to have tea with their grandmother the Queen. She would warn them to be on their best behaviour, and doubtless they thought they were, but they possessed an uncontained air which was apparent even when they were being good. Harry was especially 'demonstrative and affectionate, the most huggable little boy,' according to Diana's friend Carolyn Bartholomew, which in itself indicated a degree of emotionalism that did not sit well with the royal way, in which emotional containment is prized over demonstrativeness. Already there were concerns that the boys might grow up, under Diana's ministrations, to be as hyper-emotional as she was. And that was something no one wanted, for public roles are best fulfilled with the emotions contained rather than revelled in.

At the age of five, Harry followed William to Wetherby Pre-Preparatory School in Wetherby Gardens, Kensington. This was even nearer to Kensington Palace than Mrs Mynors'. Now that Harry was that much older, staying home curled up on sofas watching movies with Mummy had less appeal, so his attendance record improved. He was a popular student, boisterous and fun-loving, qualities he would carry into adulthood, at least until marriage. When he was not at school, he would haunt the staff quarters, chatting to the staff and begging Ken Wharfe, his mother's protection officer, to set him tasks. Harry liked nothing better than being given military assignments. By this time, everyone was convinced his future would be in the military.

Harry was also a natural athlete. He was good at everything he did. Having learnt to ski at the age of six, he was fearless on the slopes, though sometimes stopping was a problem. Once, he had to be dug out of the mud when he ran out of snow and ended up in the bushes.

He would soon have greater scope for his athleticism. In September 1992, Harry was sent to Ludgrove School, a preparatory school in Wokingham, Berkshire, near Windsor Castle and even nearer to his grandmother's racecourse, Ascot. William was already a pupil. Having his elder brother there made the transition easier. For the first few weeks, Harry was, like most new boys, homesick, but he made the adjustment, partly with the help of William, and partly by discovering that he now had a host of athletic activities to choose from. Soon he was enthusiastically playing football, tennis, rugby, and cricket, his physical prowess compensating for his intellectual insufficiencies. It was quickly apparent that Diana was right. Harry was his mother's son. He had no academic bent whatsoever. This was something of a disappointment to his father and the school, for William was following in his father's footsteps and displaying intellectual interest in a host of subjects.

Later that year, the Queen would label 1992 as her *annus horribilis*. It cannot have been easy for Harry to start boarding school at the height of the War of the Waleses, as the spectacular unfurling of his parents' marriage became known. The first shot across the bow had been the publication in March of that year of this author's *Diana in Private: The Princess Nobody Knows*, which revealed that both the Prince and Princess of Wales had had extra-marital affairs, that she wanted out of the marriage, that she suffered from bulimia, and even that she believed that her late lover Barry Mannakee, formerly her protection officer, had been wiped out to prevent him from speaking out about their affair: a belief she would later confirm in print and on television. (The author never shared her belief, and always thought that Mannakee died in a genuine road accident.) The book became a worldwide best seller, hitting the New York Times and London Times Best Sellers lists. Several months later, Andrew Morton's book *Diana: Her True Story*, was published. When it became apparent that this had been written with Diana's connivance, the book made an even bigger splash, the public naively believing that its contents must be true if Diana was behind its publication. The reality was, of course, that Diana had contributed to the contents of both books, and the reason why the Morton book had come to be written was that she and this author had fallen out because of her determination to propound a version of her tale so heavily slanted in her favour that it was more propaganda than fact. From the children's point of view, however, the most excruciating incident must have been the publication of the Squidgygate Tapes on the 23rd August 1992 in the *Sun,* the best-selling British tabloid. These tapes could also be listened to for a fee, and while the most intimate minutes had been edited out, the remainder left no room for doubt. Diana had been having an affair with James Gilbey and, even more importantly, her contempt for the Royal Family was self-evident. As she put it, resentful that they were not more grateful for her presence amongst them, 'after all I've done for that fucking family.'

Worse was to emanate from the Wales quarter as Harry adjusted to his new school. In November, his parents went on a tour of South Korea. So disaffected was Diana's demeanour, so self-evidently miserable was she in the presence of her husband, that the story became yet again the disastrous state of the Wales marriage, instead of Anglo/South Korean relations, as it was supposed to be. Ludgrove School's response was to deny their students access to newspapers in the hope that Harry and William would not be affected by the public speculation about the state of their parents' marriage.

In many ways, Ludgrove's headmaster Gerald Barber could not have handled the situation better. By filtering out bad news, he created a cocoon in which his students flourished undisturbed by the ugly realities of the outside world. Harry and William were thereby protected as much as possible from the consequences of the scandal surrounding the disintegration of their parents' marriage. They would attend classes, play games, interact with the other students as if life were continuing as normal outside the school's precincts, when of course the opposite was true.

When Charles and Diana returned from the disastrous South Korean trip, the Queen consented to their separation. Up to then, she and Prince Philip had encouraged her daughter-in-law to stay within the marriage, but by now it was obvious to the Sovereign and her Consort that the only solution would be for Charles and Diana to part officially. With her goal of separation achieved, Diana arranged with Gerald Butler to meet her boys in his study, where she broke the news to them that she and Daddy would be living apart though they both still loved their boys and nothing would really change.

In truth, this was much more than a mere figure of speech. The reality is that the Prince and Princess of Wales had been *de facto* separated since Harry had been a toddler. Very little would change in terms of their actual lifestyle, except that Diana and Charles would no longer have to endure the excruciating pretence of being a couple on the few occasions that duty or convenience pitted them together. As Patrick Jephson, Diana's Private Secretary, put it, weekends had been 'a real source of difficulty for them both' and now that they were separated, it was hoped that the tug of war which, it has to be said, Diana was largely responsible for, would come to an end. It did not, at least not in the shorter term, for Diana continued to make as many difficulties as she could. Only after she had overplayed her hand in the Martin Bashir interview in November 1995, which resulted in a host of unanticipated and unwanted difficulties for her, did she rethink her tactics and become more cooperative. And by then her boys had grown up sufficiently to be expressing their desire to spend more time with their father and his family in the country, enjoying rural pursuits such as shooting, stalking, fishing, and riding, rather than remaining in London with Diana at Kensington Palace, a metropolis which she found desirable, but whose attractions had palled for both boys, though these would return once they grew a bit older and nightlife became a bigger feature in their lives than it then was.

When Diana broke the news of the separation, Harry started to cry, but William, whose age had given him more insight into the realities of his parents' lives, simply kissed her on the cheek and said he hoped she and Charles would 'both be happier now'. After Diana had left, William, playing the bigger and wiser brother, suggested the way forward for both of them: they should not take sides, should show no preference, and should respect both their parents equally. Harry agreed, and thereafter that became the *modus operandi* of both boys.

For the three remaining years that William stayed at Ludgrove with Harry, the brothers' performance could not have been more dissimilar. Harry's academic performance was a repetition of Diana's when she had been at the same school as her academically gifted eldest sister. But Diana saw no more reason for Harry's performance to bother her than it had when she was in the same boat. The message she always gave out to Harry and everyone else was that they were two peas of one pod. Look at how well life had turned out for her. You didn't need to achieve academically to flourish after school. Of course, she was right, but more than being technically right, she was playing to his strengths, and encouraging him to feel good about himself despite his poor scholastic results.

In 1995 William left Ludgrove and started at Eton. In September, Charles, Diana and Harry all accompanied him on his first day. Harry would join him three years later, by which time their mother was dead. Diana's death hit both boys hard, but Harry was hit even harder than William. He had always been a mummy's boy, and, being that much younger than William, was less well equipped to cope with the loss. By his own account, he 'shut down emotionally' and was 'very angry'. This response did not help him academically, and his stay at Eton was 'difficult'.

I know from friends whose children are presently attending Eton that, even now, the school regards it as a distinction to have educated the Heir and Spare to the Throne.

Nevertheless, Harry's Eton days were anything but distinguished. 'He would never have been accepted had he not been Prince Henry of Wales,' an Old Etonian, who still maintains good links to the school, told me. 'He simply did not possess the intelligence to perform adequately at such an academic school. He'd've been far better off attending Gordonstoun, where character counts far more than academic results.'

Another Etonian says, 'To this day, there are all sorts of stories doing the rounds (at Eton) of how the school had to alter its academic requirements so that Harry could pass tests. And even then, he'd fail them, to the despair of his masters.'

Many of these claims were borne out by the findings of an Employment Tribunal in 2005, when Sara Forsyth, an art mistress, sued Eton for unfair dismissal. She maintained that she had been asked by the Head of Art, Ian Burke, 'to assist Prince Harry with text for his expressive art project' for his Art A-Level examination. During the trial, there was evidence suggesting that Eton had not only thrashed around to find positive ways of marking Harry's entrance examinations, but that thereafter they had struggled to have him pass his further exams. The Headmaster, Tony Little, Deputy Headmaster, the Rev John Puddefoot, Ian Burke, and other members of 'staff were bluntly accused by the tribunal of being unsatisfactory witnesses whose words were unreliable' when it found in favour of Ms Forsyth. Damningly, the Tribunal concluded that while it was not called upon to find whether Eton had assisted Harry in cheating on his exams, this was because '(i)t is no part of this tribunal's function to determine whether or not it was legitimate. That is for Edexcel' - the examination board.'

By the time of Harry's arrival at Eton, William had established himself as a successful student with both masters and pupils. He had done well academically. He was athletic. He got along with his peers. Later on, he would be elected into Pop, the group of prefects who ran the school, would be chosen as Head of the Oppidan Wall, and was awarded the Sword of Honour as an army cadet. 'William was genuinely popular. He was liked by everyone. The same could not be said of Harry,' a parent of one of Harry's contemporaries told me. 'Harry was not liked. He was bumptious and antagonistic. He was a very angry young man. He swanned around rubbing everyone's nose in being Prince Henry of Wales: just the sort of thing not to do. Eton has always had royalty. The Queen's Uncle Harry, the Duke of Gloucester, was at Eton, as were his two sons, Princes William and Richard and his nephews Eddie (the Duke of Kent) and Prince Michael. So too was Queen Mary's brother Prince Alexander of Teck and his son, Prince Rupert, whose mother was Queen Victoria's granddaughter Princess Alice of Albany. The King of Nepal, King Leopold III of the Belgians...the list is fairly endless. Harry had a definite chip on his shoulder and it made him unpopular.'

Harry would later claim that he struggled not only academically, but also with sports. Although he still excelled in them, even rugby was a problem because boys 'would see me on the rugby field as an opportunity to smash me up.' This, in truth, was only part of the problem. Harry could be needlessly vitriolic, such as when he was pitted against a Jewish opponent from one of the other top public schools and hurled anti-Semitic abuse at him, a fact I received from a priest who was at school with this boy. Just as how Meghan's colour was an unseen problem for her, Harry's royal status - or at least, his perception of it - was shaping up into becoming a problem for him.

'I didn't enjoy school at all,' he admitted. His solution was to act up and act out. 'I wanted to be the bad boy.' And he was. He snuck out of school. He drank and smoked. He was abusive. And he dabbled in drugs.

People, whose children were at school with him, claim that he was 'unpopular with the boys, but the masters cut him some slack, not only because he was a prince - though that was the larger part of the reason - but also because he had lost his mother so tragically. Who could forget that poor little twelve year old walking behind his mother's coffin with the wreath spelling out Mummy?'

Fortunately for Harry, and to a lesser extent William, at the time of their mother's death they had a secondary female figure who had already been playing a significant part in their lives since the time of their parents' separation. Alexandra 'Tiggy' Legge-Bourke had been appointed Personal Assistant to the Prince of Wales in 1993, shortly after his separation from Diana. Her brief was simple. She was responsible for the welfare and, to a lesser extent, the entertainment of the two princes when they were in their father's charge. Although she has frequently been described as having been the nanny, this description is inaccurate. If anything, the old French monarchic description of *Gouverneuse* to the royal children more accurately captured her status, for she was most decidedly a member of the upper class, which nannies are not. Then twenty eight, her royal credentials were impeccable. Her brother Harry had been a Page of Honour to the Queen between 1985 and 1987. Her maternal grandfather the 3rd Lord Glanusk had been Lord Lieutenant of Brecknockshire during the reign of the Queen's father King George VI. (Lords Lieutenant are the Monarch's representatives in the various counties.) Her mother, the Hon. Shân Legge-Bourke had been a lady-in-waiting to the Princess Royal since 1987, had been appointed in 1991 High Sheriff of Powys, and would later be made Lord Lieutenant of Powys, where the family's 6,000 acre estate Glanusk Park was situated.

Tiggy's brief was simple. Keep the boys occupied. Having been appointed because she was the embodiment of the aristocratic, no-nonsense, down-to-earth way of doing things, she articulated the difference between her approach and Diana's: 'I give them what they need at this stage: fresh air, a rifle, and a horse. She gives them a tennis racket and a bucket of popcorn at the movies.'

Diana had always been jealous of any woman to whom her children warmed. When they became too fond of their nanny Barbara Barnes, she got rid of her with a speed that was truly astonishing to those who did not realise how competitive and possessive she was. However, there was little she could do once it became apparent that both boys 'adored Tiggy', as Princess Margaret and her cousin Lady Elizabeth Anson both confirmed.

The Royal Family was delighted that the boys had a more rural female in their lives to counterbalance their metropolitan mother's influence. Diana tried using Tiggy's smoking against her, demanding that her sons not be in the same room as she was when she was smoking. This, and other ploys, such as demanding that Tiggy leave the room when she was speaking to her sons on the telephone, failed to weaken Iggy's hold over the boys, and within the year Diana was obsessing about her.

Ever prone to seeing squiggles where everyone else saw straight lines, Diana told her solicitor Lord Mishcon that 'Camilla was not really Charles's lover, but a decoy for his real favourite, the nanny Tiggy Legge-Bourke', a fact he attested to during Lord Justice Scott Baker's inquest into Diana's death in October 2007.

Diana had also recounted this theory to her butler Paul Burrell in a letter she wrote in October 1993, whose contents were entered into evidence during the inquest. She had stated, 'This particular phase in my life is the most dangerous - my husband is planning "an accident" in my car, brake failure and serious head injury in order to make the path clear for him to marry Tiggy. Camilla is nothing but a decoy, so we are all being used by the man in every sense of the word.'

If, as Diana claimed over a three year period between 1993 and 1996, Charles was really in love with Tiggy and intended to marry her, and Camilla had been nothing but a decoy, that made nonsense of the public's belief that Diana held Camilla responsible for the breakdown of her marriage. However, because most of the dramas surrounding Tiggy's supposed role in Charles's life took place behind palace walls, safely out of sight and hearing of the general public, Camilla never benefited from the anomalies and the public continued to believe that Diana regarded her as the primary threat, when she did not.

By 1995, Diana had become so eaten up with the belief that Tiggy would replace her as Princess of Wales that she managed to convince herself that Charles had impregnated Tiggy. As her Private Secretary Patrick Jephson stated, Diana 'exulted in accusing Legge-Bourke of having had an abortion.' Not content to keep this information to herself, her friends, and cohorts, Diana sailed up to Tiggy at the palace Christmas party on the 14th December and said, 'So sorry about the baby.' Tiggy was justifiably furious and consulted the celebrated libel lawyer Peter Carter-Ruck. With the Queen's blessing, he wrote to Diana four days later demanding an apology and retraction. This, together with Diana's Panorama interview the month before, when she had angled to have the line of succession altered so that her son William instead of Charles would become the next king (she had also written that she believed that the Queen would abdicate the following year, so she was angling to become Regent to the next monarch), proved to be a step too far. On the 20th December, the Queen wrote to both Charles and Diana requiring them to divorce forthwith. This removed the possibility of Diana becoming Regent, even should Charles die and William accede to the throne.

Meanwhile, the public continued to believe that Diana's comment, in her Panorama interview, that 'there were three of us in the marriage' referred to Charles, Camilla and herself, when in fact it referred to Charles, Tiggy and herself.

The fallout from Diana's fall from grace came fast and furious. On the 22nd January 1996, her Private Secretary Patrick Jephson, finding his position untenable now that she had so blotted her copy that she had made her own position untenable, resigned. A day later, so did his assistant, Nicole Cockell. Diana was now a pariah in royal and Establishment circles. By the time the press got hold of the story, she was completely isolated.

Diana had badly overplayed her hand. In doing so, she had lost the sympathy of her most loyal supporters, had alienated the entire Royal Family with the exception of her two children, had also antagonised the Establishment, and found herself so bereft of supporters that she was cold-shouldered in all but her most intimate environments. Thereafter, she would have to play a serious game of catch-up to re-establish herself as a respected and respectable public figure, and by the time of her death had only partially succeeded in retrieving her position. Although the genuine tragedy of her unfortunate end wiped the slate clean, this also provided a whole new host of complications for her children, in particular her younger son.

How much of their mother's antics Harry and William were aware of as the divorce loomed, is a moot point. It is likely, off Harry's subsequent statements, that he has never delved deeply into the twists and turns of his parents' relationship, or of the tenuous nature of many of his mother's statements and positions.

What is certain, however, is that both Harry and William remained devoted to Tiggy. Indeed, in 1996 William refused to have either of his parents at the Eton Fourth of June celebrations, inviting Tiggy instead. And when Diana died, Tiggy immediately flew to Balmoral to be with the boys. Harry did not leave her side until he left the castle, and, according to Liz Anson, 'The boys were always welcome at her house in Norfolk. They loved being with Tiggy's entire family. There were a lot of weekends when the boys were at a loose end after Diana died. They got bored with being at Highgrove and it had a lot of memories of Mummy.'

Harry's half-term holidays in October 1997 coincided with Prince Charles's scheduled trip to South Africa. This was only six weeks after Diana's death, so he decided to take Harry along with a school friend, Charlie Henderson, and Tiggy. This was an inspired choice. Not only was Harry distracted, but he was being introduced to an entirely new world: one which would hook and inspire him in equal measure. He met President Nelson Mandela and various tribal chiefs and elders, went on his first Safari, saw the Spice Girls, and was given a vivid description of the Anglo-Zulu War of 1879, in which the Prince Imperial, heir to the Emperor Napoleon III, died.

In 1999, Tiggy married Charles Pettifer. She stepped down from her role of *Gouverneuse* but not from the continuing friendship with William and Harry, both of whom went to her wedding. She, of course, attended theirs, and has remained a close friend of the family. She also attended the Sovereign's Parade at Sandhurst in April 2006 for Harry's passing out as an officer in the Blues and Royals, the prestigious Household Cavalry regiment of which the Queen is Colonel-in-Chief and Princess Anne is Colonel.

By this time, Harry was well on the way to finding himself. His teenage had been something of a wasteland. The loss of his mother had caused him to shut down emotionally, although it is arguable he would ever have grown up without some emotional baggage, considering his parents' troubled marriage and his mother's ever-shifting perspectives as well as the way she spoilt him. He had also inherited her unacademic but highly emotional tendencies. This legacy caused him as much conflict as Diana's own unresolved issues arising out of her parents' divorce had caused her. Like his mother, Harry grew into a sometimes volatile, unpredictable, antagonistic, aggressive, but also charming, endearing, and energetic personality. When *The News of the World* published a lurid account of his drug-taking and underage drinking at Club H, the black-walled nightclub Charles had allowed the boys to install at Highgrove, and of his incursions to a nearby pub, The Rattlebone Inn, the Prince of Wales responded wisely. He sent him to Featherstone Lodge, a drug rehabilitation clinic in the then-unfashionable district of Peckham, south-east London, where he sat in on therapy sessions with addicts and learnt that many of the former heroin addicts had started out on cannabis. Harry was accompanied by Mark Dyer, a former Welsh Guards officer whom Charles had appointed as equerry in 1997 and who had accompanied Harry to South Africa, acting as Tiggy's male counterpart. By this time, Marko, as Harry called Dyer, had become something of a male role model for him, and though Harry was hardly teetotal after this episode, it was enough of an eye-opener for him to avoid surrendering entirely to the lure of drugs.

Instead, he surrendered to the embrace of the Army. 'Since I was a kid, I enjoyed wearing the combats, running around with a rifle, jumping in a ditch, and living in the rain and stuff,' Harry said. He intended to enter The Royal Military Academy Sandhurst to train as an officer in the Army, but first he headed for Australia in September 2003 for the first leg of his gap year. This was at the behest of his father, who had himself spent a year at the Timbertop campus of the Geelong Grammar School in the south-eastern state of Victoria while he was a teenager. Harry had actually proposed spending his time playing polo in Argentina and skiing in Klosters, but Charles, mindful of the dangers of too much partying, had insisted that Harry follow the example of William, who had gone to Belize and Chile, where he did humanitarian work for the sustainable development charity Raleigh International. Charles therefore organised for Harry to work as a jackeroo at Tooloombilla, a 400,000 acre sheep station in Queensland, after which he would go to Lesotho, to work with children in emulation of his mother.

The Australian part of the gap year was not altogether successful. Although Harry took to the hardy outdoor life of a jackeroo, rounding up animals from horseback from dawn till dusk, and was popular with his fellow workers, he had a more checkered relationship with the press, whom he regarded as intrusive. It did not help that he was fulfilling no official engagements but the Australian public purse had to foot a portion of the $1.3m cost of his protection officers, or that he went to Sydney to watch the Rugby World Cup and was tactless enough to wear an England shirt and cap with the Cross of St. George. The Australian press felt that he owed it to them to give them some access, but rather than oblige,

Harry retreated, making such pictures as they got all the more precious. To defuse the situation, Harry invited the press to come and photograph him at the ranch, but rather than answer questions, he simply issued a statement, 'I have had a great time working out here, meeting people, and learning a bit about how it is to be a jackeroo. And of course the rugby was absolutely fantastic. It's a great country.' However, as he made it clear that he was extremely angry with what he regarded as their intrusiveness, the press were not palliated.

Nor, it has to be said, did things improve when he returned to London prior to going to Lesotho. He was photographed lurching from nightclub to nightclub with a series of women, a drink ever-present in his hand. There was a *contretemps* with a photographer outside one club, and by the time he departed for Lesotho, for the second leg of his gap year, he was well on the way to reinforcing his reputation as a drunken and awkward Lad. Although it was not obvious at the time, this aspect of his personality, while causing adverse comment in the sanctimonious portals of the tabloid press, would work in his favour down the line.

Lesotho came into Harry's life as a result of Mark Dyer. Dyer was friends with Damien West and his brother Dominic, star of the American TV series *The Affair*, who had attended Ampleforth College in their native Yorkshire with King Letsie III of Lesotho and his younger brother, Prince Seisso. Having been to South Africa with Harry, and having seen how he fell in love with Africa, when Dyer was told by Harry that he wanted to return there and follow in his mother's footsteps by doing humanitarian work during his gap year, Dyer arranged for Dominic West to introduce Harry to Prince Seisso. Both men had lost their mothers, Queen Mamohato having died shortly before they met in London. She had been a revered figure in the high-altitude, landlocked kingdom which is entirely surrounded by South Africa, having been Regent three times and having dedicated herself to humanitarian works. Lesotho had the second highest HIV infection rate in the world. Some thirty per cent of the adult population was infected with the virus, life expectancy had dropped from sixty to the thirties, and in 2000 the King had been forced to declare HIV/Aids a natural disaster. Lesotho was also an impoverished kingdom where thousands of children were sent into the mountains to tend herds of cattle and sheep from the age of five, living in wholly masculine environments with neither creature nor emotional comforts.

Taking inspiration from his mother's attitude to those who suffered from poverty as well as Aids, Harry saw this as an opportunity to make a contribution. He leapt at the chance to spend time in Lesotho.

For the first few weeks, Prince Seisso played host, taking him around and enlightening him to the tremendous problems the people of his impoverished nation faced. 'We have shown him all sides of life in Lesotho. He has seen people dying of Aids, showing very severe symptoms such as blistering and lesions and with only a few days to live. Harry was very much taken aback. I think it really brought home the whole issue to him. He seems to have a genuine concern to play some role during his stay.'

Harry moved on to work at an Aids orphanage called the Mants'ase Children's Home in Mohale's Hoek, planting trees for shade, building fences and generally mucking in doing whatever was required to lend a hand. He has always been good with children, as I can attest to, having seen the patient way he and William played with my sons, despite a decade's age difference, at polo when they were all much younger. He had brought out footballs for soccer and rugby from England, and used to organise games with the kids. He also developed a touching relationship with a four year old orphan named Matsu Potsane, who refused to leave his side and with whom he has remained in contact over the years.

Despite his antipathy to the press, even at that early age Harry knew how to use it to garner attention for causes dear to his heart. He therefore got Mark Dyer to invite Tom Bradby of ITN to make a half-hour documentary of his time at the orphanage, stating, 'This is a country that needs our help.' He also explained, 'I've always been like this. This is my side that no one gets to see.' The documentary raised $2m for the Lesotho Red Cross and alerted the world to the desperate straits in which Lesotho's many victims of the Aids epidemic lived.

The documentary also proved to be a turning point in the public's perception of Harry. Up to then, the British public had only known of his troubled, troublesome and laddish side. Now they could see for themselves that here was a prince with a heart, a man who loved children, who did not care about colour or class, who wanted to make a difference. This endeared him to the British public, who have a very kind and compassionate dimension. They now began to take him to their own hearts in a way they had done only when he walked behind his mother's coffin. It was just as well, for Harry's conduct had provided rich pickings for the press to criticise him. He had appeared at his friend Harry Meade's twenty second birthday party in the Nazi uniform, complete with swastika, of Hitler's favourite Field Marshal Erwin Rommel's fabled Afrika Korps. Then his gap year was extended, supposedly owing to a knee injury, to twenty three months, during which time he went to Argentina and was fit enough to work on and play polo at El Remanso polo farm, before taking off, again for Africa, this time to stay with the family of a girl he had started dating. Despite the patina of controversy his publicity generated, Harry was actually becoming ensconced in the public's affections as one of their favourite royals. From this time onwards, until after his marriage, his popularity would only increase until he was the most popular member of the Royal Family after the Queen.

This process was fostered when Prince Charles married Camilla Parker Bowles on the 8th April 2005. Harry and William's evident pleasure in their father's marriage did much to increase the public's regard for both boys, while also deflecting the jeremiads who had tried in every way to prevent Camilla from playing any part in Charles's life. Had the press known that for most of the last four years of her life Diana had viewed Tiggy and not Camilla as her threatened replacement, they would have understood why the boys had a more nuanced view of their parents' marriage than the public did.

One calendar month later, Harry finally entered the Royal Military Academy Sandhurst as Officer Cadet Wales. He joined the Alamein Company, ironic considering the Allied victory at El Alamein had been the beginning of the end for Field Marshal Rommel, who would ultimately be forced by Hitler to commit suicide. The way Harry had breezed through the Regular Commission Board's intensive and difficult three day entrance examinations showed that he was truly like his mother: unacademic, but when his interest was engaged, bright enough, focused, determined, and possessed of genuine leadership qualities. Ken Wharfe had predicted to Diana, 'here was a boy destined for a career in the army. It was always where he wanted to do.' This time he sailed through all the tests, including the leadership and physical tests which could not have been fudged irrespective of any amount of assistance or coaching such as he had received at Eton.

The officer training course at Sandhurst is intended to instil confidence and bring out the leadership qualities in officers. According to Major-General Paul Nanson, Commandant of The Royal Military Academy Sandhurst since 2015 and General Officer Commanding Recruiting and Initial Training since 2018, it's about 'teaching new habits and hopefully helping you shake off old ones'. The simplest things are transformative. If you are made to get up early, make up your bed properly, keep your room tidy, iron your clothes up to a desirable standard, stand up straight, have a well-ordered environment, be on time, attend to your duties, you will become disciplined, effective, and self-confident. 'All of these skills can promote broader empowerment, self-discipline and leadership skills. They equip us for the battlefield, to fight insurgents and prepare for counter-terrorism ops.' Anyone, according to Nanson, can apply these techniques to develop 'a confidence that can radiate from our very being. It is not about being born with a silver spoon in your mouth. It's about how good you are. If you look good, you feel good. The road to greatness starts with a perfectly folded sock. It's about having a sense of pride in everything you do, an inner satisfaction in not having cut corners.'

Harry found the inculcation of discipline and good habits life-changing. 'I was at a stage in my life when I was probably lacking a bit of guidance. I lost my Mum when I was very young and suddenly I was surrounded by a huge number of men in the Army. My Colour Sergeant was someone who teased me at the right moments and gave me the confidence to look forward, to actually have confidence in yourself, to know who you are.'

In April 2006, Harry, by then considerably more straightened out than he had been when he entered Sandhurst, completed his training. He was commissioned a Cornet (Second Lieutenant) in the Blues and Royals. In attendance at his graduation were his grandfather the Duke of Edinburgh, his father and stepmother, and William, who had recently enrolled at

Sandhurst having graduated from St. Andrews University in Scotland. Also present were Tiggy, Mark Dyer, and Jamie Lowther-Pinkerton, a former equerry to Queen Elizabeth the Queen Mother who had been appointed both boys' Private Secretary on the 2nd May 2005.

Harry had finally come of age, and had finally found himself.

CHAPTER 3

Unlike Harry, who found stability when he left school and entered the Army, Meghan's experience of entering the real world after graduating from university was one of struggle and strife. She returned to California and her father, who was happy to support her while she tried to get a break in the 'industry', all thoughts of being a Broadway star replaced with the intention of becoming a star of the screen. If there was one thing she had realised during her studies at Northwestern, it was that she did not have what it takes to become a huge theatre star. She was no Geraldine Page, Patti LuPone, or Angela Lansbury. Such talent as she had equipped her for the screen, not the stage. Hers was not, by common consent of the professionals, a major talent, nor did she have the outstanding beauty of a Charlize Theron or the sex appeal of a Jennifer Lopez to catapult her to quick stardom.

To Tom and his beloved Flower, it did not matter whether she succeeded on the big or small screen, nor even whether she got her break via commercials; all that mattered was that she become as big a star as she could.

Meghan might have hoped that she would be 'discovered' the way Lana Turner or one of the Hollywood Heyday movie queens had been, but being a child of Hollywood, she was intelligent enough to realise that this was unlikely. She did not have the natural assets. Although she would later attribute her lack of early success to not being black or white enough, the fact is, her physiognomy not her race was the issue. Tyra Banks and Vanessa Williams had not found their colour a problem, but then, both women were spectacularly beautiful. Although appealing, Meghan was simply not quite so beautiful, sexy, striking, or memorable to jump out at observers the way Banks and Williams did. She did not have a breathtaking enough figure for screen stardom. Her frame was better suited to modelling, except that she was not tall enough to have a successful career as a model. Although she loved the camera, and already knew what to do with it to maximise herself, it simply didn't love her enough for her to become another Marilyn Monroe, Gina Lollobrigida, or Sophia Loren. Great female stars were either stunningly beautiful or outstanding talents like Meryl Streep, while Meghan, for all her hopes, ambition, and attributes, was neither.

What Meghan had in spades was ambition, but it was an ambitiousness way beyond her discernible attributes, meaning that any success she achieved would be down to her character more than anything else. This could have been a very dispiriting period for her as she went from audition to audition, go-see to go-see, without being chosen. According to people who knew her then, Meghan refused to give up, no matter how dejected she became at times. She firmly believed that she was special, that she was better than others perceived her to be, that she was so bright and resourceful that she would able to convert any opportunity into something more major once she got her foot through the door. All she needed was a break, any break, even a small break. Once she got that, she'd find a way of making her way into occupying the central position she wanted for herself.

Although at first it looked to observers as if Meghan might not succeed, as if she might be riding for a fall, she was intelligent and determined enough to appreciate what many others did not. Success in the public eye is not only about natural assets. It's also about perception and public relations. It's about what you surround yourself with. You don't have to be a great beauty to be acknowledged as beautiful. All you have to be is astute enough to maximise your assets: stylish enough, photographed enough, praised enough, for the general public to associate you with beauty. Diana, Princess of Wales was a case in point. A reasonably good looking woman with a nose too large, a mouth too small, cheekbones too flat, but good eyes, good colouring, good clothing, good hairstyle, and sufficient exposure for familiarity to breed acceptance of the illusion as reality, a stylish and attractive woman was accepted as the beauty she was through repetition and expert packaging.

All creatures of Hollywood know about Warren Beatty Odds. They apply as much to success on screen as to actors working their way through their address book until they hit upon the girl who will say yes to a last minute date. Rejection is meaningless as long as you accept that sooner or later, success will come your way. This was Meghan's attitude, and she deliberately chose to be happy irrespective of how long it took for her to achieve the success she wanted. What she did not reckon upon was that all that suppressed misery would have effects down the line.

Meghan's first real break came about through her connections, not through her own efforts, and there is every possibility she would not have even got a reading had she not been put up for it by her good friend from Northwestern, Lindsay Roth, who had a casting job on an Anton Kutcher romantic comedy called *A Lot Like Love*. She pitched Meghan for a one word role, which she got, though not before Meghan informed Nigel Cole, the director, that she had read the script and thought she'd be better suited for a larger role. Although she did not get the role she sought, she did get the one which Lindsay Roth had suggested, and even managed to get it expanded so that she ended up having five times as much to say as before. This did not lead, as Meghan hoped, to further success, nor did her attempt to up the ante affect her relationship with Roth, to whom she remains close, but it was the beginning of her acquiring a reputation for ballsiness amongst those who liked her, and bumptiousness amongst those who did not.

Her next role was in the sci-fi legal drama *Century City,* starring Ioann Gruffudd, Viola Davis and Nestor Carbonell. So poor were its ratings that only four of the nine episodes filmed were aired. Meghan, playing a party girl, delivered her one line in so hyper-animated a manner that she might well have been Richard Burton overplaying his early film roles until Elizabeth Taylor taught him to tone things down for the screen. A producer told me that her early desperation to succeed was one of the factors which prevented her from doing so. Later on, after she had become a duchess and narrated the Disney documentary *Elephants Without Borders,* this criticism would be echoed when her performance was slated as being over-eager to please, exaggerated, and schmaltzy. But it didn't stop the British betting company Ladbrokes giving Meghan and the programme 20/1 odds to win the Feature Length Documentary category at next year's Oscars.

Desperation can be a great motivator, especially if you use it to fuel your perseverance. Meghan was ambitious enough to try out different tactics under the premise that if one thing didn't work, another would. Keeping her father sweet helped to keep the wolf from the door, and so too did keeping her spirits up. A real party girl, she went out as often as she could, doubtless with the dual motives of enjoying herself and meeting people who might help her along the road to success. She lucked out one night in 2004 when she went to a 'happening' dive in West Hollywood where young up-and-coming producers, directors, writers, actors and actresses all congregated, in the belief that they were being more 'real' by avoiding more conventional (and expensive) establishments. Meghan heard someone whose voice caught her attention. He was bold, voluble, confident and charismatic. She also liked what she saw: a burly six-footer, with the body of an athlete and the reddish-golden locks of a surfer, whose bright blue eyes exuded certainty.

Trevor Engleson had the persona of a man on his way up. Born in Great Neck, Long Island, New York, in October 1976, he was educated in his hometown before studying journalism at the University of Southern California in Los Angeles. He was also as markedly ambitious and driven as Meghan. He had started off on the lowest rung of the ladder, informing the producer Alan Riche that he wanted to do what he did. Riche suggested that he first work as an agent, and got him a job at the Endeavor Talent Agency. Trevor, however, blew it when his boss, the film script agent Chris Donnelly, was away and he was caught sending out unsolicited scripts on the agency's letterhead. He was dismissed, but soon got another job as an assistant to his university alumnus Nick Osborne and his partner Jeffrey Zarnow at O/Z Films. He admitted they 'needed a hustler who could bring food to the table,' which Trevor did so successfully that when Osborne founded Underground Films, his assistant followed him, before finally taking the company over.

One thing led to another, and before the night was through, Meghan had hooked up with Trevor. Their romance thereafter moved at a quick and decisive pace. She moved in with him before a year was out. This suited her well. Living with Trevor, who was earning good money, took the financial pressure off her, but she couldn't live off him entirely, so she had a succession of jobs while waiting for her big break. These included acting as a hostess in a Beverly Hills restaurant, teaching gift-wrapping in a local store, and working as a calligraphist doing invitations and envelopes for special events. She was proud of doing the invitations for the singer Robin Thicke and the actress Paula Patton's wedding in June 2005, and claimed that calligraphy not only earned her good money but also gave her something to do while waiting around at auditions. It also set her apart from the other hopefuls. She felt it was a 'classy' thing to do, and by this time Meghan was well on the way to developing a 'classy' persona. Some people found her demeanour 'sophisticated', while others regarded her as 'pretentious' and 'full of crap', in an early indication of the way Meghan would divide, and has continued to divide, opinion. Although the producers of *Suits* sang her praises publicly, another Hollywood producer told me that Meghan Markle was not 'well regarded in the industry,' but now that she is the Duchess of Sussex, 'people who wouldn't give her the time of day' are now happy to consider doing business with her. Success does breed success, and I know from friends of hers that 'Meg is focused on success and doesn't really care if people don't like her. As long as she's getting what she wants, they can feel how they please.' This is not a view that others agree with. They say that Meghan loathes rejection, and while she pretends not to mind it, she 'nurses a slight like no one else.'

Trevor and Meghan ended up living in a series of elegant rental houses, including one on Hilldale in West Hollywood and a colonial-style two storey in Hancock Park, a historic area in central Los Angeles developed by the oil magnate/philanthropist George Alan Hancock. Theirs was but one of the many distinctive, architect designed 1920s houses which make the area as desirable as it is, bounded by Wilshire Boulevard on the south and Melrose Avenue on the north.

By the time Trevor and Meghan linked up, he was on his way to becoming a successful producer and talent manager. He lived and breathed work. He spent his whole life reading scripts, pushing for sales, or partying. Meanwhile, Meghan lurched from rejection to rejection, with only sops in the form of cameos and walk-on parts to provide encouragement that persistence might win the day. She 'encouraged' Trevor to put her up for jobs, but he usually refused. He would only propose her when he thought she was well suited.

In his own way, Trevor Engelson had integrity. This, according to friends, would ultimately become a cause of resentment for Meghan. She found it difficult to forgive her boyfriend when he overlooked her for roles which she thought were perfect for her. Though she was forced to respect his viewpoint that putting her forward for roles he regarded as unsuitable would result in rejection for her and undermine his credibility in the industry, he was inadvertently feeding a cold fury which would come back to chill him to his bones in the future.

Meghan's rage was something which she kept well concealed until she started writing an anonymous blog called *The Working Actress*. In it, she revealed how distressing she found it when she was turned down, or not considered, for roles which she knew she was perfect for, even though no one else agreed with her. She wrote about the distressing times she took to her bed crying her eyes out with a bottle of wine and bread for comfort, because she had not got some role she yearned for. Her hunger for success was never exceeded by the pain of rejection and the frustration of not being acknowledged the way she yearned to be, but the blog showed that it was a close-run thing. In it, she was open about her self-pity and pain, and while she did not spell it out, beneath that lay fury.

2006 was a dispiriting year for both Trevor and Meghan. He had been the Executive Producer of *Zoom*, a $75.6m budget superhero action movie/comedy starring Courtney Cox, Chevy Chase and Rip Torn. Despite their high hopes, the film took the princely sum of $12.5m at the box office, was universally panned as being dull and anything but funny, and had the further distinction of its lead actor, Tim Allen, being nominated for a Razzle Award in the Worst Actor category.

At this time, Meghan had landed a role as a briefcase girl on the game show *Deal or No Deal*. This brought her a steadier and larger income than she had ever had, but was, by her own account, a daily reminder that she was nowhere near where she wanted to be professionally.

By the following year, things were looking up for Trevor once more. He co-produced *Licence to Wed*, a romantic comedy starring Robin Williams, then started work as Executive Producer on the Sandra Bullock/Bradley Cooper comedy *All About Steve*. Meanwhile, Meghan bounced along on the bottom of the barrel, getting yet more bit parts until in 2010 Trevor landed the job of producer of *Remember Me*, a melodrama starring British heartthrobs Robert Pattinson and Pierce Brosnan. Finally, Trevor offered her a part, and while it was not a large one, she nevertheless had hopes that it would lead to bigger things. It did not, and not because the film was panned for its ending, which involved 9/11, but because Meghan's attributes remained unacknowledged.

Despite this, she remained hopeful, and her relationship with Trevor was stronger than ever. According to Nikki Priddy, who remained Meghan's closest friend while also having become a close friend of Trevor's, they were so completely in love, so well suited, that she could never have imagined either of them with anyone else.

Time, however, was running out for Meghan. She was approaching thirty. She had not yet made it. She had no ambitions to become a character actress though she hankered after having her acting talent recognised as if she were one of the greats like Eleanora Duse, Anne Bancroft or Patty Duke. She wanted to be a star. And she was no nearer achieving her objective than she had been when she had started out acting in school. Then along came the part for which nature, nurture, and her own character and personality made her ideal. Rachel Zane was a tough, ball breaking, bold, elegant, standoffish, competent, intelligent, but flawed paralegal at an upscale law firm. She had to be good looking, but not so good looking that she stole the show. She had to be sexy enough to capture the love interest of one of the stars, Patrick J Adams, who was playing Mike Ross, but not so sexy that she came across as tarty. She had to be refined enough to convey a background of privilege. She had to be cool and convincing, for Rachel had garnered the respect of her colleagues, all of whom admired her legal ability even though she could not pass her law exams.

Meghan's agent Nick Collins of the Gersh Agency had put her up for the role, and while she thought her reading had gone so badly that she asked him to arrange a second one, it had actually gone well. 'They loved my take on Rachel and they were putting together a deal for me. It was a really good lesson in perspective. I think we are always going to be our own worst critics,' she said, an observation she would have done well to remember when she became the Duchess of Sussex and things started to go badly awry for her.

According to Jeff Wachel, co-president of the USA Network, 'One of the things that we needed at the beginning of *Suits* was Patrick's character to come in as the hottest thing in town: he's brilliant, has a photographic memory and fakes his way into being a lawyer and then comes up against this girl who turns out to be the love of his life. We needed somebody who had a real authority to shut him down and still be the coolest thing around.' Finally, Meghan's characteristics in all their contradictory complexity had come to her rescue.

When Nick Collins rang Meghan to tell her that she had got the part, she was ecstatic, but reservedly so. She had previously had her hopes dashed when stardom had seemed assured and, lest history repeat itself, she now refused to let her expectations run away with her the way they had in the past. Nevertheless, she looked forward to the filming of the pilot in New York in autumn. Neither she nor Patrick J. Adams could be sure whether it was a good omen that they had once worked together on another pilot: one which amounted to nothing. This time, however, all the ingredients for success were there.

Nor was success limited to what was happening on the screen. At the end of the shoot, Meghan and Trevor flew to Belize, where he asked her to marry him. She accepted without demur. She was 'marrying up', her brother Tom Jr observed approvingly, but Trevor was also nailing her down in case she became the star she had always wanted to be.

Between the proposal and the marriage, Meghan received the news that filming for the first series of *Suits* would begin in Toronto on the 25th April 2011. The only downside was that she and Trevor had to commute between there and California, but she was intent on making her relationship with him and the series work, and happily threw herself into both. The show aired on the 23rd June to a positive reception from the critics and audience. It was stylish, entertaining, and sophisticated, and amongst the many elements that played well was her passionate on-screen relationship with Patrick J Adams. Meghan the woman was sweet and vulnerable superficially while being tough beneath the surface, and this combination of softness and hardness gave her an authority that was perfect for the role. She and Patrick definitely had chemistry together, both on screen and off, and he explained that he and Meghan were extremely close 'because we were the youngest people in the cast and both came in with the least experience. We grew up together over the course of the show.'

Meghan would later recount how stressful but satisfying she found the demands placed upon her in this, her first successful show. She was growing not only as an actress but also as a budding star. There were the demands of publicity, hair, make up, wardrobe, interacting with the cast and crew as well as everyone else whose path crossed hers. She deliberately retained a certain reserve behind a friendly and approachable facade. She was intent on being acknowledged as a team player, and made sure that her charm was never superseded by displays of ego.

In the midst of all this activity, she was also planning her wedding to Trevor, which was due to be held on the 10th September 2011 at the picturesque Ocho Rios hotel, Jamaica Inn, whose main feature is one of the finest beaches on the island. Although Meghan availed herself of the services of its in-house wedding planner, she kept her finger firmly on the pulse. 'She is a control freak,' a member of the staff said. 'She was **very** exacting in her demands.' Although she was perfectly pleasant, she left no room for doubt. What she wanted, she intended to get. Because the Jamaicans were more used to being micromanaged and challenged than the staff at Windsor Castle, her conduct was not viewed as being out of line, so she did not ruffle feathers the way she would later on do with her second wedding. She and Trevor had taken over the entire hotel for a four day blast, paid for in part by Tom Sr. The least part of the event would turn out to be their wedding ceremony, which 'took all of fifteen minutes.' The rest of the time was dedicated to hard partying and fun activities such as wheelbarrow races.

Both Meghan and Trevor were now earning good money. *Suits* had been commissioned for its second series and while Trevor was treading water with *Amber Alert*, a film that would go nowhere, Meghan was thrilled to be marrying him. The wedding she was planning would be a reflection not only of the closeness of their bond but also of their success.

Although Meghan had always aimed at presenting herself as both cool and classy, she very nearly came a cropper when she had the bright idea of distributing ganja spliffs in specially-made crocus bags inscribed with *Shh....* to all of her guests. Notwithstanding its reputation as producing the finest marijuana in the Western Hemisphere, Jamaica had an ambivalent attitude to its main export. There was considerable pressure from the American authorities upon the Jamaican Government to stamp out the ganja trade, and using, possessing, distributing or trading in the drug was punishable by a long prison sentence. They were very lucky no one reported them to the Police, otherwise their festivities would have come to a quick halt and they would have ended up in a Jamaican jail. Moreover, Meghan was so cool that she didn't bother to tell her guests what was in the crocus bags. She expected them to know. Not all of them did, and one of them took it back to the US. Only after getting through customs did they discover how Meghan had inadvertently made them into drug smugglers. They were anything but amused.

That aside, Meghan and Trevor's wedding was a success. It established them among their circle as 'cool, happening, and classy' hosts, and as Trevor returned to LA and Meghan to Toronto, Nikki Priddy and all their other friends confidently expected them to remain married forever.

During the filming of the second series of *Suits*, however, Meghan's life experienced another upgrade. Toronto is a much smaller and more cohesive city than LA. It also offers tax breaks to the film industry, so has a vibrancy out of all proportion to its location. An ensemble actress in a burgeoning cable series such as *Suits* is of far greater consequence there than she would be in the film capital of the world. If she is so inclined, she will soon be mixing with all of Canada's elite. And Meghan was very much inclined. By the third series, she had met and become friends with Jessica Mulroney, stylist wife of Ben Mulroney, whose father had been Canadian Prime Minister Brian Mulroney, and Jessica Gregoire and her husband Justin Trudeau. His father had been the former Prime Minister Pierre Trudeau and his mother Margaret Sinclair, the hippie First Lady whose widely reported affairs with Ted Kennedy and Mick Jagger took place against the drug-addled backdrop of Studio 54 and scandalised Canadians and Americans in equal measure, while her fling with Fidel

Castro has haunted her son Justin, whose resemblance to the Communist dictator has been much commented upon. Nevertheless, Margaret Trudeau would end up enjoying the distinction of being the only Canadian woman to have been the wife and mother of Prime Ministers, for Justin, who had been a Member of Parliament for Papineau since 2008, became leader of the Liberal Party in 2015 and Prime Minister in 2017.

Meghan 'was very impressed to be mixing with' people of that stature. Not only was she becoming a celebrity in her own right, but she was now socialising with a 'better class of person than in LA', where her and Trevor's friends and associates were successful but not of the top rank. As Canadian columnist Shinan Govani observed, Meghan's success in life owed more to the people she cultivated than her accomplishments on screen. She was a canny operator, and took full advantage of any opportunity that presented itself, sometimes even creating opportunities when none was apparent.

It was at this juncture that Meghan spotted how politics could further her trajectory to ever greater success. Canada is a more left wing society than the United States. Although Hollywood paid lip service to leftist causes, its primary aim was success through film. Compared with even the most right-wing of Canadians, woke Hollywood seemed curiously right of centre, to such an extent that the former Conservative Prime Minister Brian Mulroney seemed frighteningly leftist to even the most left of American Democrats. If you consider that Meghan's Canadian circles now consisted of members of the political elite of both the left and right, and that there was a consensus amongst Canadians of all political hues that humanitarianism was a social obligation, it becomes obvious that Meghan would be incentivised to resume the humanitarian activities which she had abandoned once she started making her way in the world. During the years that she was struggling to achieve as an actress, she could have volunteered had she been inclined to do so. Often time had lain so heavily on her hands that she had taken to her bed with a bottle for comfort, but the truth is, she was too focused on realising her ambitions, and was also too intent on having a good time, travelling the world with Trevor, visiting places such as Vietnam and Central America, or just partying with him and making herself as visible on the social scene as she could, to bother with humanitarianism.

Now, however, that she was in an environment where such conduct would elevate her from being just another actress on the make, to a caring person whose tender sensibilities for the less fortunate would earn her the respect of her new associates, Meghan reconnected with the altruism that had gained her the approbation of her theology teacher at Immaculate Heart, Maria Pollia, all those years ago when she had volunteered at the Hippie Kitchen. She asked her newfound friends to refer her to a community project, and was duly introduced to the St. Felix Centre, earning the regard of those she helped as well as those who had helped her with the placement.

Meghan's good works with the centre might have gone unnoticed by the world outside of St Felix Centre and her circle of friends and colleagues from that time, if the Duke and Duchess of Sussex had not chosen the Centre as one of the 12 charities which they highlighted in December 2019 on their Instagram for the good works each charity does to help 'the lonely, hungry and homeless.' St. Felix Centre then published the sole photograph which had been taken of Meghan while she was volunteering with them, and issued a statement:

"We feel very grateful to have been highlighted by the Duke and Duchess of Sussex, Prince Harry and Duchess Meghan Markle, as one of the 12 charities doing important work worldwide.

"This photo has Meghan volunteering in our kitchen.

"Meghan Markle was an active supporter and volunteer of St Felix Centre during her time living in the city working on *Suits*.

"She volunteered on a regular basis in our kitchen as part of our Community Meals Program.

"The Duchess also donated food from the set of *Suits*, and on one Thanksgiving she brought all the food, turkeys and the fixings for over 100 people."

The charity ended their proclamation stating what 'fond memories' they had of 'lovely Meghan', providing an insight not only into the way Meghan functioned, but also why people such as the Mulroneys and Trudeaus held her in such high regard.

It was in the third of the seven seasons during which Meghan played Rachel Zane, that her marriage to Trevor started to unravel. In his biography *Meghan: A Hollywood Princess,* Andrew Morton implies that Meghan began to despise Trevor because she had started looking down on him now that she had moved up in the world. He wasn't doing as well as she'd have liked, and moreover his exuberant personality had started to grate now that she was mixing in a more refined circle.

Trevor had always been laidback where she was controlled and controlling. He would arrive for appointments slightly late and dishevelled, his shirt out of his trousers and maybe a spot of food on his lapel, while the perfectly contained and self-possessed Meghan was always immaculately turned out, Mixing as she now was in a world where people were more restrained than in Hollywood, Trevor's New York enthusiasm came across as tacky, his enthusiasm crass, and his breeziness off-putting.

As Meghan had become more and more successful in *Suits,* he had started travelling to Toronto every few weeks to be with her, even doing as much of his work there as he could. By then he had also opened an office in New York, as much to be closer to her as for commercial reasons. While he thought being with her in Toronto would improve their marriage, in reality his presence had the opposite effect. Moreover, his career was going nowhere and that, added to his stylistic deficiencies, lessened his appeal. He had gone from being Trevity-Trev-Trev, without whom she could not imagine life, to someone she had grown beyond. 'Meg used to tell me she couldn't imagine a life without Trevor. She said if anything were to happen to him she wouldn't be able to go on. He cherished her too. You should have seen the way he used to hold her face in his hands. We all felt he was her eternal love,' Nikki Priddy said, struggling to reconcile Meghan's volte face concerning Trevor.

This change of heart, which struck Trevor as coming like a bolt out of the blue, had actually been brewing for some time. Success had had an effect upon Meghan. It had liberated all sorts of feelings she had that had been lying latent, including the grudge she had harboured against Trevor for failing to help her when he could have and refused to do so, putting his precious integrity before her needs. Even more importantly, success had empowered her so that she had connected with her inner strength and no longer needed to depend on anyone else but herself.

Nikki took a more negative view and thought that Meghan had become harder and more opportunistic with the passage of time. 'I think Meghan was calculated - very calculated - in the way she handled people and relationships. She is very strategic in the way she cultivates circles of friends.'

According to Nikki's interpretation of Meghan's motives, having found herself a new and more 'classy' circle of friends, she did not wish to be bogged down with her embarrassing misfit of a husband or even her old and less Establishment circle of friends. 'Once she decides you're not part of her life, she can be very cold. It's this shutdown mechanism she had. There's nothing to negotiate. She's made her decision and that's it,' Nikki said, explaining how Meghan dropped the axe on Trevor as well as on her old circle of friends. Having achieved a new and more elegant circle and a degree of renown in a successful TV show, 'It was like a light switched off. There's Meghan Before Fame and Meghan After Fame. After three seasons of *Suits,* she called me to say the marriage was over. Maybe she had started to change before then, but I was refusing to see it.'

Of course, people change with time, and Meghan was no exception. As she grew into the stardom she had worked so hard to achieve, she developed new aspects of her personality. To her longstanding best friend Nikki, it seemed that her 'tone of voice, her mannerisms, the way she laughed' had changed to such an extent that they 'didn't seem real to me anymore. Even by season two of *Suits,* she was turning down lunch with us because she said she'd be recognised. I felt if I questioned her behaviour, I'd be left on the outside.'

Moving up in the world can come at a price. Some are willing to pay it, others aren't. Meghan clearly was. Her new status meant that she had changed from unsuccessful actress to successful. She was happy with the changes and expected those who loved her to be happy for her too. According to Nikki, 'When she was in town, she'd want you to drop everything to see her. If I was busy, it would be, "Why don't you want to see me? I'm here. Let's hang out." However, if she wanted to cancel an engagement, she would do so and expect the friend to understand that she now had demands on her time so they should accommodate her. This age-old conflict between those who are left behind and those who have done the leaving might have been resolved with a bit of goodwill on both sides. It is impossible to say, from this vantage point, whose lack of flexibility resulted in a severing of ties, but Nikki decided that Meghan had developed a sense of entitlement because of the show, that success had gone to her head, and that she was severing ties with her past now that her old friends were no longer on a worldly par with her. Tellingly, it would turn out to be Nikki Priddy who dropped the axe on her friendship with Meghan, which gives us a wealth of information about how both women functioned, and what they valued.

It takes a lot to break the back of a lifelong friendship, but there were two straws that did it for Nikki Priddy. The first was when Meghan fell in love with a rescue dog and tried to wrest it away from someone who had displayed interest in it before Meghan did. She emailed the pet people asserting that the dog would have a better life in the *Suits* family than it would with the other prospective owner. Nikki felt she was playing the *Suits* card to gain an advantage to which she had no entitlement, and 'it left a sour taste in my mouth.' Meghan, of course, had another take entirely. She wanted the dog and was prepared to do whatever it took to get it. She would never have thought she was being ruthless, just clever in using everything at her disposal to get her own way. Being a winner.

The death knell of the friendship became the way Meghan behaved at the end of her marriage with Trevor. Nikki was bemused with the way she ended the relationship, simply posting him back her wedding and engagement rings without any explanation, leaving him feeling 'like something stuck to the bottom of her shoe.' Although there had always been 'fights' between them, there had been no warning that the relationship was even under threat, much less that it was in danger of coming to an end. Nikki, who was friendly with both Meghan and Trevor, telephoned her lifelong friend to speak to her about it, after seeing Trevor and learning what she regarded as being the callous and brutal way in which Meghan had ended the marriage. But Meghan refused to impart any information to the best friend she had had since the age of two. Nikki felt that she had not only changed personality but, having developed a new circle, really couldn't be bothered with her old one any more. 'It was obvious to me that she wasn't the friend I'd grown up with,' Nikki said, and decided to cut her out of her life entirely. People who have known Meghan all her life, believe that Nikki was wise to jump. Had she not done so, she might well have been pushed, so she at least had the comfort of doing the dropping. This was not a consolation her father would have.

If the loss of her closest and oldest friend bothered Meghan, she gave no indication. This was a time of great change for her, and the likelihood is that she was so busy growing into her new life that she barely had time for that alone, much less regrets about those she had left behind or who had dropped her. From January 2010 she had been writing a revealing blog called *The Working Actress*, about her experiences being unemployed then employed. It was time and emotion consuming. She graphically described the anguish she had suffered as she failed to land parts. 'When it's good, it's fucking awesome. The other 300-plus days of the year, it's harder than most would think. Humbling. Gruelling. Sometimes mind-numbing. But at the end of the day it's all worth it. People often describe actors who pop onto the scene as "overnight success stories". Here's the reality - it's more like years of hustle...welcome to the hustle.'

Meghan imparted penetrating insights into her psyche and the effect her years of rejection and occasional dollops of success had had upon her, writing about how she tricked herself via self-hypnosis into believing that she would succeed, endlessly repeating the mantra 'I'm a booker. I book all the time' in an attempt to give herself enough courage to audition and face failure again and again. 'Point is: sometimes when you trick yourself, it actually works. I believed my silly little mantra and well...it came to be.'

During *Suits'* first year she continued pouring her heart and soul into the blog, inadvertently giving the reader insight into how success was changing her. In March 2010, before her breakthrough, she confided that 'I loathe walking the red carpet. It makes me nervous and itchy, and I don't know which way to look. I just revert to this nerdy child that I once was. I hate it. I get off the carpet and have to shake it off. Sounds dramatic, but it's really nerve-racking for me.'

Meghan remained an unspoilt hopeful appreciative of a chuckle from Donald Sutherland when her path crossed his during her half minute appearance on the Jennifer Aniston 2011 black comedy *Horrible Bosses*. But success was having an effect. Although she was by no means a major star once *Suits* was underway, she was already positioning herself to cope with fame in such a way that Meghan the Individual would not be swamped by the demands of fame. To do so, she had to adopt an attitude of disdain, so she started to denigrate fame and its demands from the lofty height of self-awareness. She wrote, 'I am part of the horse and pony show this year. The scruffle has already begun with production and PR - the outfit I will wear, the hotel I will stay at, the parties I will attend.' She also alluded to 'the first-class flights the studio sends me out on,' as if she had been brought up in a world of private jets and first class travel was an inconvenience to be decried rather than a luxury she was barely used to. Instead of frankly embracing the whole experience the way she had embraced the pain of failure, she distanced herself from the very thing she had sought all her life by disdaining the perks and demands of success. 'They roll out the red carpet in a major way because they want me ('the talent' as they call us) to show up looking and presenting in the best possible manner. This is the ultimate "dance monkey, dance". Now let me say this - as much as some people might hear this description and feel nauseated by it (that inner monologue of "but I am an artiste") I say this to you, dear friend: Get over yourself.'

The difficulty with that admonition was, the audience to whom she was speaking was in reality an audience of one, and her injunction was nothing but one part of herself speaking to another. It was obvious she adored being on the road to fame, and was mesmerised by her new-found success. She had striven for the better part of a decade to get where she was, and who could begrudge her how she felt about her success? 'This is part of the job, and it's fucking awesome. It's fancy and it's cool, and it's the business of what it takes to make it in this business.'

However, Meghan's next statement showed that somewhere in the deep recesses of her being she had not entirely given up on her old dream of being a Broadway star or a serious actress who was way above movie or, God-forbid, TV stardom. 'If you are pursuing television, then realise that you have already sold out, and take your big fancy pay check to produce your "artiste"-driven plays on hiatus. Because you can now. '

She then revealed how she could not help intermingling delight in her good fortune, self-congratulation and disdain as she continued, 'Because flashing those pearly whites (ahem, veneers) and working the red carpet with your sexy little body (ahem, Spanx) is part of the job description you jumped on board for when you were lucky enough to sign on the dotted line that day you were testing.

'This is what we call a high-class problem. And compared with the problems of what feels like many moons ago (not having money to fill up my gas tank, Scotch-taping my headshots as CVs because I ran out of staples, crying because I couldn't get a call back, or even an audition - when I knew in my core that I was the best possible one for the part), I will take this any day.'

As if that had not been revealing enough, she also gave the first hints of the schizophrenic attitude to recognition she would later exhibit once she became truly famous. When the handyman who came to fix her dishwasher recognised her and asked her to pose for a selfie 'to prove to his brother and dad that he'd met me', she complained about having her private space violated. She also demonstrated the early sproutings of the exacting demands she would become known for once she became a member of the Royal Family. In the blog, she bemoaned the conduct of the driver who collected her from the airport. He had committed three cardinal sins. Firstly, he brandished a sign at the airport with her full name. This the discerning and authoritative Meghan tut-tutted was 'kind of a non-no, usually it's just a first initial and last name'. Secondly, he had the temerity to invade her personal space and show her photographs on his iPhone as they waited at the carousel for her luggage. Thirdly, he exasperated her when he delivered her to the wrong address.

This was the first recorded instance of the newly-privileged Meghan seeking the sympathy of her audience by demonstrating how hard done-by she was by the ineptitude, insufficiency, or plain, plumb insensitivity of people who were there to make her life easier but somehow managed to become a problem to her. The only difficulty with this scenario was that drivers are given their destination by their controller. The fault was therefore not the unfortunate Jim's, at least not on that front, but the controller who had given him the wrong address.

Meghan also admitted on the blog that she had been ignorant of 'what being a working actress would entail. I work long hours, I travel for Press, my mind memorises. My mind spins. My days blur. My nights are restless. My hair is primped, my face painted, my name is recognised, my star meter is rising, my life is changing.'

To capitalise upon those changes, Meghan stopped writing *The Working Actress* in the summer of 2012. She would wait two years before starting another blog. *The Tig* was an altogether more professional enterprise. Created by a successful Toronto digital agency named Article, it derived its name from Tignanello, a wine created in 1970 by Piero Antinori of the eponymous winery dating from 1385. This was a lifestyle blog which cleverly and self-consciously traded upon her success as an actress while at the same time earning her some $100,000 a year and ratifying her aspirations to being perceived as a classy and authoritative figure or, as Meghan put it, the 'hub for the discerning palette - those with a hunger for food, travel, fashion, and beauty. I wanted to create a space to share all of those loves - to invite friends to share theirs as well, and to be the breeding ground for ideas and excitement - for an inspired lifestyle.' Meghan was positioning herself to be as much an authority figure off screen as Rachel Zane was on it.

Make no mistake about it, Meghan is clever. She intended to use the blog to boost her profile as well as her bank balance. Thereafter, she approached celebrities who crossed her path and offered them a platform to air their views. It was a masterful move, one which elevated her and gave her ballast, for while the stated objectives of the blog were lightweight, she also roped in writers, artists, activists as well as celebrities. It quickly became successful, and by the time she ended it in 2017 just before her marriage to Harry, it had some 2m followers.

Because Meghan was intelligent and a quick learner, absorbing as if by osmosis all the lessons gleamed from the talented people who crossed her path, she was polishing her act at the very moment that the blog was growing in importance. Being a lifestyle blog, it covered everything from tennis with Serena Williams to stars like Elizabeth Hurley and Heidi Klum, with just enough coverage of serious issues such as gender, race, activism and poverty, to balance the overt superficiality of its otherwise aspirationalism.

The Tig proved instrumental in another area of Meghan's life. She had fancied the celebrity chef Cory Vitiello ever since she had first seen him in his downtown Toronto restaurant, *The Harbord Room*. He was a highly desirable man-about-town who had enjoyed a series of high-profile romances, including with the former Member of Parliament, businesswoman and philanthropist Belinda Stronach, whose billionaire father Frank is one of Canada's richest men, and television personality and humanitarian Tanya Kim, who co-hosted a popular talk show with Ben Mulroney. Cory would be a feather in her cap if she could somehow contrive to bag him, which she did through the simple expedient of publishing a glowing review of his restaurant in *The Tig* which contained an even more glowing regard for the chef himself.

According to one of Meghan's childhood friends, who wishes to remain anonymous, she is extremely seductive when she targets people she wants to impress. 'It doesn't matter whether it's a man or woman. If Meg wants to suck you into her orbit, she pulls out all the stops. She learnt a long time ago that flattery works, especially if it's dished out with lashings of self-abnegation along the lines of, "You're so marvellous, everything you do is so great, I want nothing from you except to admire you." She's wonderfully spontaneous. No one is more enthusiastic, especially when she wants to ensnare a man. She envelopes him in a miasma of adoration. She makes out that his every mundane action is a unique gift to humanity. Few people and even fewer men can resist an onslaught of such positivity from someone as appealing as Meghan. 'This makes her very seductive. Men don't want to resist the outpouring and, because she seems so sincere, they end up hooked on her.'

Meghan has tremendous charm, apparent vulnerability, sweetness, and personability. She has a great deal of sex appeal, most of which emanates from her personality and those big brown eyes which beam with delight when she wants to bedazzle. She is also highly intelligent and excellent company. Above all, however, she is self-confident. By her own account, she found leaving Trevor behind an 'empowering' experience. Once she shed that skin, and discovered how strengthening it was to be liberated from many of the anxieties and insecurities she had suffered from previously, she became a far more potent and powerful person than she had ever been. 'She knows her power and she enjoys wielding it,' someone who knows her well told me.

Meghan believed that once she got her foot in through the Vitiello door, the establishment was hers for the taking. And so it proved. Before too long, Cory had moved into the three bedroomed house at 10 Yarmouth Road in Seaton Village where Meghan had replicated the stylish pale colours, modern paintings and contemporary furniture of the cosy, yellow-painted marital home she had shared off Sunset Boulevard with Trevor. 'She lived here very quietly,' said Bill Kapetanos, a Greek native now in his late seventies who was her next-door neighbour. They had a cordial relationship, and he occasionally helped her out when she needed neighbourly assistance. When he met Doria, she did not merely thank him for being such a good friend to her daughter. She thanked him for helping out 'her angel', which shows the level of parental adoration Meghan was used to receiving.

Meghan's quiet lifestyle lasted 'until Harry came on the scene.' Only then did she start to entertain, having dinners, throwing large parties, and generally having a social buzz going that was actually uncharacteristic of the way she normally functioned.

In reality, Meghan was a homebody who loved hunkering down with her man when they were not out on the town partying. Her main company on a day-to-day basis was her two rescue dogs from LA, Guy the beagle and Bogart the Alsatian/Labrador cross and, ironically enough, her blog, to which she dedicated so many hours that it was like a living companion.

This homely, loving side to Meghan's personality meant that the parents of the men with whom she was involved invariably liked her. Trevor's parents David and Leslie Engleson had treated her as their own daughter, which was quite something when you stop to think that Jews often want their sons to marry Jewesses. So too did Gerry and Joanne Vitiello, who described her husband as 'my high school sweetheart' and declared that 'family is everything.' They hosted their son and Meghan, whose relationship Joanne Vitiello would later characterise as 'serious', during Christmas 2015, at their home in Brantford, two hours outside of Toronto. She believed that Meghan 'was very interested in being with the people she was with. She has a good sense of humour and is very personable.' Meghan and Cory 'were living together. They were in their thirties. They weren't kids,' and while she never actually said it, she intimated that marriage was a possibility.

Not everyone, however, had a rosy view of Meghan as she was ascending the greasy pole. The social columnist Shinan Govani regarded her as 'just a cable actress' who 'didn't mean much' when she met Cory Vitiello. He, on the other hand, was a huge star locally. He was known by everyone and well liked too. 'Within the confines of the city, being with him was definitely a useful platform for her.' He was much bigger 'in terms of the Establishment in Toronto. He was leverage for her.' He was also friends with people like the Mulroneys and Markus Anderson, global membership director of the elite private club Soho House, which has a branch in Toronto. Although Meghan's path had crossed theirs, she now became close friends with all of them. Their homes, and Soho House, became like her second home. Govani believed if she had never come to Toronto, she would never have married Prince Harry. 'There was something about coming to Toronto, becoming friends with the Mulroneys, and having a high social cachet. It was the perfect storm that created the opportunity.' Govani thought that there was an element of deliberateness about the way Meghan advanced herself socially, and that 'she took advantage of the opportunity that came her way.' He also felt that she 'wasn't content with just being an actress. I mean, what would happen after *Suits*? She wasn't getting any younger.'

Through Cory, Meghan's star ascended exponentially. Not only were they a glamorous couple who functioned in the most elevated circles, but the power of two, and the connections she made through him, allowed her to spread her wings in a way that a cable show like *Suits* never could have done.

While Cory was vital to Meghan's progress, it would be a mistake to ignore the role her effort and ambition played in her growing success. *The Tig* was her creation. It was, in some ways, her baby as well as her platform, and it was proving invaluable in raising her profile while giving her *gravitas* and access that she would otherwise not have had. She ensured this by shoring its content up with features that were heavyweight as well as aspirational.

According to Meghan, a part of her new-found ascendency was the realisation that she had been standing in her own way by failing to jettison her misgivings and just let herself rip. She had decided to do just that and had, in the process, strengthened herself. Having consciously resolved to let go of all the negativity that had been holding her back, she began embracing aspects of herself that had previously been problematic. Chief amongst these was her racial identity.

In Canada, Meghan had been discovering that being bi-racial was more advantageous than it had been in the US. Canadians are much more relaxed about issues like race and status than Americans, and aside from using her race in a way she had never done before, she began using her sex through the blog to branch out into areas where race, gender, and activism could be utilised positively. Meghan was on a mission, and the mission was to 'thrive rather than survive'. She would use everything she had to make her life better and richer. She would flourish.

In September 2014, Meghan was due to have a week off work. She decided to offer her services as a volunteer to the United Nations in New York. There are few bigger names in the humanitarian world, and Meghan rightly saw that if she could associate herself with that organisation in some capacity, considerable benefits would accrue to her down the line. She was careful with the UN to utilise such starriness as she possessed – and there really wasn't very much: *Suits* was still a relatively minor cable TV show – in such a way that she came across as modest and willing. She therefore told them she would be happy to serve coffee and answer 'phones, though once she was there, she shadowed Phumzile Mlambo-Ngcuka, the Executive Director of UN Women, and Elizabeth Nyamayaro of the HeForShe movement, for the one thing above all that Meghan had going for her was her dynamic personality. Within moments of meeting her, people realised that she was exceptional, and while this did not appeal to all tastes, it was enticing to sufficient for it to work in her favour.

Having put her charm and networking skills to good use and acquired a reputation for brightness and cooperativeness, the following year, Meghan was back at the UN, this time giving a speech before the Secretary General of the UN to a packed house as the United Nations' Women's Advocate for Political Participation and Leadership. For nine and a half minutes she spoke eloquently, engagingly and movingly about the airing of the now-infamous Ivory Dishwashing Liquid commercial, telling how it had set her on the path of feminist activism. Her speech was a tour *de force* which garnered her much respect in the political circles in which she now moved. It reinforced her aim of being taken seriously, not only as an influencer through her blog, but as a political activist. To the *Suits* audience she might have been merely Rachel Zane the ballbreaker who couldn't pass her law exams but nevertheless had the legal practice and Mike Ross eating out of her hand, but to the Mulroneys and Trudeaus, who were the audience she really wanted to impress, she was growing into a heavy-hitter whose humanitarian credentials established her as worthy of their attention and friendship.

Despite the spectacular way her public profile was progressing, Meghan's need to be noticed was beginning to affect her relationship with Cory. Although Cory has always been careful to only say positive things about his ex-girlfriend, friends of theirs, who did not wish to be identified, said, 'She was extraordinarily pushy beneath the soft and sweet exterior. She was always angling for the best table in a restaurant, wanting to sit in the best seat, reminding everyone not so subtly that she was this huge star, when she really wasn't. *Suits* wasn't that big a deal and Toronto is full of actors and actresses. The city gives tax breaks to film companies, so film and TV stars of a far greater stature than Meghan Markle are two a penny. It was just embarrassing. Cory's not that sort of guy, and I think after a while it began to get on his nerves and he started to lose respect for her.'

Although Meghan could be very loving, she was so impassioned that she sometimes came across as a prima donna. Friends believe that Cory had become increasingly disenchanted as a result of that aspect of her conduct, but what 'did it for him' was when she started snatching credit from him for recipes that he had created. 'Meghan is a good cook, but she's also extremely vain and always wants praise,' one of the Vitiello circle said. She and Cory had hosted a dinner party at which she had served pasta with courgette spirals. Upon being complimented on the dish, she tried to take credit for its invention. However, it was Cory's creation, and 'this pissed him off royally. No matter how loving you are, once your boyfriend realises you're a phoney, that's it,' someone who liked him but had never liked her, said.

Shortly after that incident, Meghan left for England to watch her friend Serena Williams play tennis at Wimbledon. One of the attributes which friends of hers find endearing is her willingness to cross the world to support their efforts. Her detractors do not regard this as a virtue, suggesting that she promotes herself under the guise of supportiveness. They question why her support is always for the very rich or the very poor, and defile her motives with the observation that a camera is often present to record how marvellous Meghan is. One person who had no such reservations was the tennis ace. They had met in February 2014 when the satellite television channel DirecTV threw a huge, televised party on a man-made beach, created out of a million tons of sand, in a heated tent at Pier 40 on the Hudson River in Manhattan. According to Meghan, 'We hit it off immediately.' On *The Tig*, she described their first meeting, 'Taking pictures, laughing through the flag football game we were both playing and chatting not about tennis or acting but about good old fashioned girly stuff.' Serena confirmed that their friendship had grown from strength to strength by saying, after the royal wedding, 'We have known each other for a long time, but we really kind of are relying on each other a lot recently.'

Meghan's relationship with Serena would prove to be pivotal in more ways than one. Aside from the fact that she would never have met Harry had she not gone to watch her friend play at Wimbledon, it was the tennis star whose dextrous use of the media inspired her to develop *The Tig* in the way she did, and even more importantly, whose presence in her life helped Meghan overcome the hurdles she had faced all her life concerning her racial identity. Had Meghan not become as friendly with Serena as she did; had she not seen how positive an advantage being a woman of colour could be if she embraced her African-American identity the way Serena did, she might well have continued sitting on the fence, the way she had done all her life.

It was fortunate that Meghan had finally made the leap from the areas of uncertainty which she characterised as 'greyness' to embracing her bi-racial identity, for this would prove to be yet another of the pivots which saw her make an even more important leap, from actress on a cable television show to member of the British Royal Family.

There is some doubt as to whether the relationship between Cory and Meghan had actually ended before Meghan met Prince Harry. Although Meghan would later claim it had, Cory has refused to be drawn, which leads one to suspect that it had not. Overlap or not, it was definitely limping to an end and if Meghan was fortunate enough to replace one handsome and celebrated Adonis with an even more famous and important hunk, she would have been crazy not to seize the moment.

Amongst the many things Harry and Meghan had in common was a checkered romantic past. Shortly before entering Sandhurst, he had started a romance with Chelsy Davy, a bright, bouncy, blonde Zimbabwean whom he had met the year before through Simon Diss, one of his Gloucestershire friends who formed the circle known as the Glosse Posse. She had been educated in England at Cheltenham College before transferring to Stowe School to do her A Levels, but, when they met, she was about to return to South Africa, where her family lived, to read PPE (politics, philosophy and economics) at the University of Cape Town. It was while he was in Lesotho and in need of diversion that Harry reconnected with her.

Chelsy Davy is a very attractive girl and bouncy, as I can attest, having met her at polo. She is bright and sociable. Harry joined her and a group of her friends for a night out at a nightclub called Rhodes House, and the evening went so swimmingly that they ended up spending most of their time on the dancefloor, entwined in passionate embraces. It was the beginning of a romance that would last, on and off, for seven years. They had much in common. Both were fearless physically. She was a superb horsewoman who could ride bareback and had been known to wring the life out of a snake with her bare hands. Both she and Harry loved Africa, whether it was going on safari in Botswana or just chilling at her family properties. Her father Charles Davy was one of the largest white landowners in Zimbabwe, with properties covering 800,000 acres, while her mother Beverley nee Donald had been Miss Rhodesia in 1973. Upon discovering that Charles Davy was also in business with Webster Shamu, Minister of State for Policy Implementation, at a time when Robert Mugabe's government was being reviled internationally for its policy of land grabbing, not to mention the intimidation and abuse of power which were characteristics of the Mugabe regime, the British press created such a monumental hue and cry that Davy ultimately had to sever his connections with Shamu. This cannot have been easy for either Chelsy or Harry, who were innocents caught up in a game not of their own making. Once news of their relationship broke in the *Mail on Sunday*, with staff at the lodge in Argentina where they had gone for a romantic weekend tipping off the newspaper that 'Harry and Chelsy were like any young couple in love, kissing and holding hands, and he seemed quite besotted. They looked madly in love and at one point Harry admitted that she was his first true love', the publicity proved an unwelcome pressure on the relationship.

Of course, the press can never get enough of a good romance, and once Harry turned 21 and gave the customary interview to mark the occasion, he was inveigled into commenting, 'I would love to tell everyone how amazing she is. But, you know, that is my private life and once I start talking about that, then I've left my own self open, and if anyone asks me in the future, then they'll say "Oh well hang on, you told them but why aren't you telling us?"' This was just enough to satisfy the newspapers, whose absorbing interest in the Harry and Chelsy affair seemed never-ending.

In the beginning, though, the real strains between the couple were their youthfulness and the enforced separations they had to endure. Chelsy remained in South Africa for the first two years to obtain her BA from the University of Cape Town in 2006, while Harry entered Sandhurst, completed his officer training course, before being commissioned into the

Blues and Royals. Although royal protocol deemed it inappropriate for her to be in attendance at his graduation ceremony, she flew in for the graduation ball.

In 2006, Chelsy moved back to England to take the LLB law degree at the University of Leeds. Harry, meanwhile, was flourishing in the Army. It was announced that his unit would be deployed to Iraq the following year, which created a tremendous kerfuffle, with the Defence Secretary agreeing with Harry, who wanted to be sent to the front line. 'If they said "no, you can't go front line," then I wouldn't drag my sorry arse through Sandhurst and I wouldn't be where I am now,' Harry announced, gaining the admiration of the public. The Queen, who had previously allowed Prince Andrew's life to be put on the line during the Falklands War just like every other serving soldier, sailor, and airman, agreed with her grandson. Although Harry would ultimately not be sent to Iraq, because his presence would provide a magnet for insurgents, endangering the lives of the other men, he was sent instead to Afghanistan for two separate tours of duty. This gained him the respect of the public in a way nothing else could ever have done. The fact that he was brave, determined to do his duty, happy to muck in with his cohorts and expect no special treatment, gained him a regard which he had hitherto not had. Even when he did silly things, such as being photographed cavorting nude in Las Vegas with a group of drunken friends, including his 'Wingman' Tom Inskip, the respect he had earned remained intact. Indeed, the public admired him all the more for being a 'bit of a lad'. It showed that he was not only a brave man, but a prince who was fundamentally just another accessible and likeable human being.

If Chelsy was prepared to cut Harry slack where his drinking was concerned, she was not so willing to overlook what she regarded as being taken for granted. When Harry chose to attend the Rugby World Cup final in Paris rather than be with her for her twenty second birthday, she dumped him. This was but the first of the endings that led to reconciliations, but by 2009 she was sufficiently resolute, after Harry had decided to embark on a two year training course to learn to fly helicopters for the Army Air Corps, to alter her online Facebook profile to 'Relationship: Not in One'. She knew it was only a matter of time before the news leaked to the press, but she welcomed the respite, as by then she was heartily sick of the media intrusions, and also looked forward to a break from the strains of a long distance relationship.

For the next two years, Harry and Chelsy's relationship was on and off. There was genuine affection there, but their youthfulness and Harry's career in the Army meant that she had to endure the same sacrifices that other Army wives and girlfriends do, all the while running the gauntlet with the press, who followed her every move. By the time of William's marriage to Catherine Middleton on the 29th April 2011, their status remained unresolved yet the trust between them was so strong that Chelsy not only helped Harry to write his best man's speech, but was also his plus one for the wedding and the events following it.

By 2012, Harry and Chelsy were definitely headed in opposite directions. Princess Eugenie knew that her first cousin wanted a girlfriend and that her good friend Cressida Bonas had recently split up with boyfriend Harry Wentworth Stanley. They had been an item at the University of Leeds, but when Wentworth Stanley took off for his gap year on his own, the relationship came to an end. So Eugenie introduced them and Harry and Cressida hit it off.

For a while, it looked as if they were ideally suited. Both were athletic, good looking, bohemian, and she had the advantage of being resolutely British upper class, with a family that was as colourful as Harry's.

Unlike the Davy family, Cressida's was used to the press. Her mother and aunt had been It Girls in the 70s, when we were all young and few weeks went by without all of our names featuring in the gossip columns. Her mother Lady Mary Gaye Curzon was the elder of two daughters of the 6th Earl Howe's second marriage. Her aunt Lady Charlotte Curzon was a year younger, and in the 1970s the Curzon sisters were such social luminaries that you couldn't go to a party anywhere in London or the shires without running into one or the other of them.

At the time, Mary Gaye was married to her first husband, Esmond Cooper Key, who was even better connected than the Curzon girls, if such a thing were possible. His maternal grandfather was the mighty press baron Esmond, 2nd Viscount Rothermere, and his uncle the Hon. Vere Harmsworth's wife Pat was one of the most outstanding figures in Society. While Vere was so laid back that he was almost reserved, with a delightfully droll sense of humour, Pat, who relished becoming the 3rd Viscountess Rothermere in 1978, was an unpredictable firebrand, perennially bedecked in Lacroix, a large bow in her curly chestnut-coloured hair styled like Shirley Temple, her ears and hands weighed down with stones the size of almonds, the inevitable pair of sneakers contrasting with the whole costume, which was finished off with a glass of champagne in one hand and a dazzling swizzle stick in the other. Pat drank only champagne, but hated bubbles. Hence the gold swizzle stick and the ironic nickname Bubbles, which she loathed and friends hesitated to use to her face.

By the time Cressida was born in 1989, Mary Gaye was on her third marriage, to an Old Harrovian businessman called Jeffrey Bonas. His family had once had a lot of money but no longer did. Cressida was their only child, but she had seven half-siblings: three paternal half-brothers from her father's first marriage, a half-sister from Mary Gaye's marriage to Esmond, and two other half-sisters and a half-brother from Mary Gaye's second marriage to John Anstruther-Gough-Calthorpe.

Fortunately for her parents, Cressida was athletic and won a sports scholarship to Park Prior College in Bath, after which she attended Stowe before heading to one of the aristocracy's favourite universities, Leeds, where she studied dance. She was a beautiful girl, which was just as well, for she wanted to become an actress.

The years between Cressida's birth and her introduction to Harry had seen profound changes in British society. These had loosened up everyone, including the royals and aristocracy, with the result that everyone now had greater choice as to what they could do with their lives. This was as a result of the flipping of the hierarchical ladder, which had once defined the social order from the bottom to the top, from vertical to horizontal. The divisions between the classes still existed, but they were now perceived as being surmountable. Although the aristocracy still had a degree of influence, in national terms it had ceased to be the oracle it had been in the days when deference had accompanied vertical hierarchy. British society no longer being deferential, this gave everyone the freedom to explore their desires and ambitions in a way that had been unthinkable in a previous generation. Cressida and Harry, who were exploring the possibilities of what their lives could be - whether together or separately was beside the point - were therefore typical of the open-endedness that now characterised British society.

In many ways, Harry and Cressida seemed ideally suited. They were a good match not only physically and in terms of background, but also in terms of interests and outlook. The word in aristocratic circles was that Mary Gaye was keener on her daughter marrying into the Royal Family than Cressida was, but since Cressida and Harry seemed to be so well matched, and so good together, everyone crossed his or her fingers and hoped there would be no slips between the cup and the lip.

Cressida, however, was struggling under the harsh glare of the press's attentions. When she appeared on *Woman's Hour*, she highlighted some of the difficulties. 'I think it's that thing of being pigeonholed. Especially in this country, I find that people are very quick to put you in a box, or put you in a corner, and think "Oh, well you're that so you must be this". It's incredibly frustrating.'

She was confronting the reality that friends of mine, who could have married into the Royal Family when they were her age, had also faced. Unless you were so gut-wrenchingly in love with the man that you would sooner be pilloried than live without him - and unless you knew with complete certainty that you would remain so in love with him that the torture of being royal would be endurable - or you were so ambitious that you'd endure the heat no matter what - you had your day in the sunshine, got scorched, and headed for shelter and the Camomile lotion.

By 2014, Cressida was ready for the shade. She and Harry parted on amicable terms, just as he had with Chelsy, both of whom would be asked to his wedding. She then quietly returned to her previous boyfriend, Harry Wentworth Stanley, another tall, good looking second son, whose mother is the present Marchioness of Milford Haven, wife of the head of the

Mountbatten family, of which Prince Harry's line, Mountbatten-Windsor, is a distaff branch. She remained on such good terms with the royals that she attended Harry's wedding to Meghan and Princess Eugenie's to Jack Brooksbank last year.

By this time, Harry was something of a hero with the public. His first deployment to Afghanistan, as a Forward Air Controller in Helmand Province, had come to a sudden end when the German newspaper *Bild* and the Australian magazine *New Idea* had breached the embargo concerning his presence. Disappointed that he was being forced to abandon his men, but understanding of the danger his continuing presence would place them in, he was airlifted out before the Taliban had a chance to attack. Frustrated and disappointed at how his posting had ended, he was nevertheless pleased to be presented with the Operational Service Medal for Afghanistan by his regiment's Colonel-in-Chief, his aunt Anne the Princess Royal, at Combermere Barracks.

Aside from loving the structure, discipline, and camaraderie of the Army, one of the greatest delights of that life for Harry was that he was just another human being. His royal status made no difference, except occasionally as a preventative, stopping him from being assigned postings, or being able to accept assignments, that would endanger his fellow-troops if it became known that HRH Prince Henry of Wales were involved. The challenge, for him and his superiors, became how to carve out a meaningful role for himself which would give scope to his abilities without exposing his fellows to increased danger.

Like his father, brother, and uncle, Harry then became a helicopter pilot, which is how he came to be posted to Afghanistan a second time. This time, there was no secrecy, his assignment being announced beforehand in an act of confidence and defiance by the British authorities. His arrival at Camp Bastion, for a four-month posting as a co-pilot and gunner for an Apache helicopter, was greeted by the Taliban, whose spokesman Zabiullah Mujahid told Reuters, 'We are using all out strength to get rid of him, either by killing or kidnapping. We have informed our commanders in Helmand to do whatever they can to eliminate him.'

It was obvious that there was little likelihood of the Taliban succeeding. Camp Bastion was as secure as Fort Knox. By making the announcement the way they did, the Taliban had set themselves up for failure. The British and American press thrilled to Harry's presence, which did as much for morale amongst the Allied troops in Afghanistan as it did for Harry's reputation in England.

Harry's status as a brave soldier consolidated his popularity and helped to enlarge his options both as an Army officer and a prince. These, however, did not include more tours of duty in battle zones. His presence was too risky for all concerned, so to his disappointment he was quietly transferred to a staff officer's role at Army headquarters in London. His office was in Horse Guards, and his duties included helping to coordinate Army significant events in London. This might have been a disappointment to someone who liked getting himself dirty in the trenches, who loved nothing better than mucking around with the men, but it was also an opportunity to leave his mark in a creative way. Unlike Charles and William, whose position as immediate heirs to the throne made their roles relatively easy to define, Harry, being a second son, had more scope. Within reason, he could do what he wanted. The role of spare could provide opportunities that an elder son could not have, if only he had the imagination and commitment to avail himself of them.

What Harry did next covered him in glory, and showed that his humanitarianism was not an empty drum to beat for his own glorification, but a genuine and deep seated desire to create opportunities for those who lacked them. He created the Invictus Games, a Paralympic-type sporting event for wounded, injured or infirm soldiers of either sex, launched officially by him, in combat gear, at the former Olympic Centre in Stratford, East London, in March 2014. Inspired by the highly successful 2012 London Olympic Games, and by the Warrior Games which had been created by the United States Olympic Committee in 2010, these games would take place that September.

By this time, everyone understood that Harry truly felt for those less fortunate than himself. He had been a patron since its inception of Walking With The Wounded, founded in 2010, had walked to the Arctic on their behalf in 2011, and would walk to the South Pole in 2015. He also beat the drum for Sentebale, putting both the charity and its country on the map in a way no one and nothing ever had done before. His sense of humour also garnered him many admirers, such as the time in 2012, when, on an official visit to Jamaica, he 'beat' the fastest man on earth, Usain Bolt, by out and out cheating, running to the finish line before the race had begun. When Bolt then did his characteristic Lightning Bolt movement, Harry was right there beside him, doing it as well. 'The Jamaicans loved him,' the Jamaican High Commissioner told me. 'They couldn't get enough of him. He was just such a delight.'

In March 2015, the palace announced that Harry would leave the Army in June. The constraints he had had to endure would help in his personal life, should he find himself a girlfriend or wife. Whether the lack of structure he would have to cope with in civilian life would be beneficial to him personally, was another matter. All his life Harry had needed to be kept occupied. He had flourished in the Army, because he was the sort of personality which needed structure to bring out the best in him. Even as a little boy, he used to beg Ken Wharfe to give him assignments. He had leadership ability of the median rank, was also good at taking orders, had energy and courage, and he loved being surrounded by the men and mucking in with them. He was the perfect Army man, but he did not possess the inner spark or self-discipline that enables people to flourish in an unstructured environment.

To further complicate matters, Harry was headstrong and had been brought up by Diana and, to a lesser extent his father, to overestimate his importance in the scheme of things. He was a second son, whose role could never be as well delineated as his elder brother's, and, with the passage of time, that role would become of increasingly less consequence constitutionally. It was inevitable that he would suffer the fate of Prince Andrew, who had started out as second in line to the throne and found himself being pushed further and further down the table of succession with the birth of each child who supplanted him. There were doubts that Harry had the internal resources to realise his full potential without the clear boundaries that an institution like the Army provided, but the enthusiasm with which he embraced royal projects in civilian life heartened observers.

Maybe he did have what it took to become a successful civilian prince after all.

In contrast to his public life, privately Harry struggled to find a girl who wanted to take him on full time. No one wanted the job. Although he was a nice enough guy, and undoubtedly physically appealing, with the robust athleticism of a fit soldier, he had emotional problems. He was often unjustifiably angry. I know of one instance when he tried to attack a contemporary of his father's for no reason at all. He was dragged off by his protection officers and is only lucky that nothing was made of the incident. He could be churlish and placed many demands on those closest to him. He could be overly clingy while being out of touch with his emotions. He seemed to believe that his troubles all stemmed from his mother's death, but people who knew the family well, disagreed. Relations of his tell me that he was always going to be trouble, 'Because Diana simply refused to provide consequences.' Patrick Jephson, her Private Secretary, bore this out when he recounted the three year old Harry deliberately riding his tricycle at full speed into the shins of a senior cavalry officer who had come to pay his Colonel-in-Chief an official call. Although Diana scolded him, she did not punish him, and Harry rode off without contrition or consequences.

Such a joke did Harry's quest for a girlfriend become that his sister-in-law Catherine even gave him a Grow-Your-Own-Girlfriend kit in 2016. It was no secret in aristocratic circles that he desperately wanted to marry and start his own family. Unlike many men, who want to sow their wild oats and will flit from woman to woman with no thought of emotional involvement, Harry had an almost feminine attitude to relationships. They were more about love than sex. And while he could get sex easily, lasting love had proven so far to be depressingly elusive.

Indeed, Harry's quest for love had become almost pathetic. He would ask friends to set him up with girls who were well bred and attractive, and, to ensure that they wanted him for himself and not for his name and rank - the very things, ironically, that turned off most well-bred girls - he would pretend to be someone else. He did this with a friend of my children's, Baroness Jessica Heydel, who found the whole experience so bizarre and discomfiting that she was hamstrung into stupefaction. How does one of the most famous men in the country expect a well-educated, well-bred, intelligent girl to react when he tries to start off a relationship incognito? Is she supposed to go along with the deception, or is she supposed to call his bluff? Why would he think she would care so much about his rank, style and title that he had to pretend to be someone else? How does a girl begin a real relationship with someone who isn't who he says he is? Crazy, just crazy.

Although Jessica thought Harry was a perfectly nice person, she couldn't see herself having a relationship with anyone who started out on that footing. The loss, I can tell you, was Harry's, not hers. She is a beautiful, blue-eyed blonde with a perfect figure. She is stylish and tasteful and, more to the point, the real article. She would have made the most wonderful Duchess of Sussex.

Then Harry met Meghan.

As stated earlier, Meghan had flown to London to watch Serena Williams play tennis at Wimbledon. This trip would be pivotal and the way it came about gives a real insight into how Meghan has scaled the heights she has.

Nearly two years before, she had acquired a powerful British manager named Gina Nelthorpe-Cowne, who had been upping her profile and getting her assignments while making connections Meghan would never have been able to make on her own. Because Meghan would never have met Harry without Nelthorpe-Cowne's assistance, and the business manager is one of the few people who were witness to what actually happened, her input is vital, not the least of which being that her outstanding success in her chosen field indicates that she is an authority on the traits that make for success or failure in public life.

It is through Nelthorpe-Cowne's observations that we can verify the qualities that made Meghan the success she became. The main tools, she decided, were a charming, seductive and charismatic personality allied to physical beauty and powered by a fierce intelligence and a unique determination to succeed.

The two women met in Ottawa in 2014 when the managing director and co-founder of the prestigious Kruger Cowne Talent Management company was in that city to promote the One Young World Summit, a conference for 18-30 year olds opened by Prime Minister Justin Trudeau with such stars as Emma Watson and Kruger Cowne client Cher in attendance. Meghan was there not only as a successful if still minor actress, but also as the founder of *The Tig*. On the blog, she wrote about how she had come to be a Counsellor and how "One Young World invites young adults from all over the world who are actively working to transform the socio-political landscape by being the greater good. They are delegates who are speaking out against human rights violations, environmental crises, gender equality issues, discrimination and injustice. They are change."

The two women had spoken on the 'phone and emailed each other a number of times before meeting in person. They had already 'clicked' with 'an instant connection' before the South African-born, London-based Nelthorpe-Cowne had even set eyes on Meghan, whom she first met when she showed up at the hotel room in Ottawa that Meghan was sharing with Cory Vitiello for the duration of her stay. 'I could immediately tell she was special, that she had star quality. I've been in the business a long time and I know that's not something you can train someone to be. You've either got it or you haven't. She just has it.'

Had Nelthorpe-Cowne considered the circumstances of the meeting, she might have understood that Meghan was inadvertently giving her an insight into how she viewed others relative to herself. Cory is the one who opened the door while Meghan, unprepared for her pre-arranged appointment with her visitor, was dressed in a towelling bathrobe with her hair tied back. Without displaying any compunction for what could have been interpreted as a discourteous display of disrespect, Meghan advanced effusively and 'we hugged as if we had known each other for ages. She was delightful: warm and personable and hugely charismatic.'

Meghan's social skills now completely sucked Nelthorpe-Cowne in. She made perfect 'eye contact and then the connection. She instantly brings you right into her world.' She also makes you think that there is no one else in the world with whom she would rather be. 'What people don't realise about Meghan is that she is ferociously intelligent.' And so ambitious that she is in a class of her own.

Frank about the desirability of capitalising upon every opportunity, Meghan used the Summit and her blog to advance both *The Tig* and herself while also giving it the attention it deserved. She had done her homework so knew that the Kruger Cowne Talent Management company represented 300 top names, in more than 70 countries, including Cher, Bob Geldof, Sir Richard Branson, and Elle Macpherson. Their specialty was drumming up corporate bookings, public speaking and appearances for their clients, while negotiating literary, publication and brand endorsement deals in areas as disparate as sport, design, fashion, media and broadcasting. If Meghan could get Nelthorpe-Cowne to take her on, she would have climbed the next rung on the ladder to becoming the towering success she wanted to be. Moreover, she would have made the leap from North America to England, which, she would later confide to the English socialite Lizzie Cundy, was where she wanted to go.

Meghan and Nelthorpe-Cowne immediately became what Diana Wales used to call 'fast friends'. The business manager soon asked Meghan if she would like to be represented by her. Meghan's technique, as described by others and confirmed by Nelthorpe-Cowne's account of how they came to be involved both personally and professionally, is to make the first move, go in gangbusters, let everyone realise how marvellous she is, then step back and let them make the running. It is a brilliant way of operating, for the other person thinks they're in control, while in fact Meghan has been the driving force and remains in control.

Nelthorpe-Cowne 'became her commercial agent, helping her obtain endorsements and sponsorship deals with leading brands.' In her opinion, Meghan 'is first and foremost a businesswoman. She was razor-sharp - creative and meticulous, with a good business brain and an American entrepreneurial attitude towards life.' As the two women developed 'an easy friendship after only a few meetings,' Nelthorpe-Cowne developed 'a deep affection for her and was under the impression that she felt the same: she said as much.' They even travelled together, enjoying their time as more and more recognition came Meghan's way.

In June 2016, Meghan flew to London for a PR junket which allowed her to watch her friend Serena Williams play at Wimbledon. She struck up one of those immediate friendships, which are a talent of hers, with Violet von Westenholz, the well-connected director of public relations at Ralph Lauren. Violet was a childhood friend of Prince Harry's, her father Piers, Baron von Westenholz being a former Olympic skier who is one of Prince Charles's oldest and closest friends. As a result, Violet and her siblings Frederick and Victoria grew up with Princes William and Harry. The families had remained close and Violet knew how desperate Harry was to meet someone. A royal told me, 'she set him up on a blind date with Meghan Markle. The rest is history.'

Violet has never confirmed that she played Cupid, but then, as the royal says, 'she wouldn't, would she?' By the time the public found out about the relationship, the word in aristocratic circles was that the Royal Family was tearing its hair out as a result of the background checks having provided very mixed feedback, with some people praising her and others suggesting that Meghan Markle was known in Hollywood and Toronto as an 'operator *par excellence*'. 'It was like introducing Typhoid Mary to New York.' But Meghan had one redeeming feature: her bi-racial identity was an answer to the family's prayers.

As Nelthorpe-Cowne has stated, Meghan is 'ferociously intelligent' and she played a flawless hand from the time Violet suggested introducing her to Harry until they were about to be married. By Meghan's own account, 'When she wanted to set us up, I had one question: is he nice? Because if he wasn't kind then it didn't seem like it would make sense.' Meghan was displaying just the right degree of reluctance, and it reassured Violet that she was truly the lovely, sweet, personable and loving young woman that she appeared to be. She continued to be seen like this until she and Harry were about to get married. It was only then that cracks began to emerge in the perfect facade she had hitherto presented to the royal world, but no one is perfect and few people believed that Meghan would be anything but a positive addition to the Royal Family, while none could have imagined that within a year of matrimony she was laying the ground for her and Harry to step down as senior royals.

Beyond the royal world, however, the fissures were forming as Meghan and Harry's romance gathered pace. The first to fall through the cracks was Piers Morgan, whom Meghan had cultivated on earlier visits to London. They had a last drink before she left for her first meeting with Prince Harry, and, as Piers says, thereafter she 'ghosted' him. While she doubtless felt the need to err on the side of caution and protect her budding relationship from the prying eyes of the press, the fact remains, she made a tactical error. Piers Morgan is an honourable man. For all his rhetoric and controversialism, he would never have betrayed her confidence. By behaving as she did, she was laying the ground to make herself an enemy if anything went wrong. And when it did, the chickens came home to roost.

Another of the friends Meghan had made in the last couple of years, as she jetted back and forth while Nelthorpe-Cowne raised her profile and added to her bank account, was the former WAG, model, television presenter and socialite Lizzie Cundy. They had become friendly enough for Meghan to confide that she wanted to leave *Suits*, move to London, join the upper-class cast of the reality show *Made in Chelsea*, and marry a Brit. The fact that she was neither upper class nor British seems not to have entered into Meghan's calculations as she confided her ambition to join the cast of the reality show about upper class Brits living in Chelsea, and before long she was imploring Lizzie to find her a 'rich and famous Englishman'. Lizzie suggested introducing her to the multimillionaire footballer Ashley Cole, but Meghan declined the offer once she realised who he was. Lizzie thought it might be because both their marital pasts had been checkered, but one of Meghan's critics suggested that 'it was because Meghan's taste doesn't run to men of colour. You only need to look at her history to see that all her significant others have been Caucasian.' There is, of course, no reason why a woman of colour should limit herself to men of colour, and one of Harry and Meghan's English circle believed that Lizzie's suggestion would have offended Meghan, who was sensitive about her racial identity. Was Lizzie trying to say that she was fit for fixing up with only mixed race men? To Meghan, that would have been a putdown, but she met Harry shortly afterwards, so had no need of any further fixing up. When Lizzie heard the news, she texted Meghan saying what a 'catch' he was. Meghan replied, 'Yeah, I know!!' then ghosted her too.

The next to be cut out of her life was Nelthorpe-Cowne. Despite being such close friends that they confided in each other about their personal lives, had travelled together and formed what the business manager though was a genuine bond, when Meghan informed her after her third date with Harry that they were 'serious', that they were planning a 'future together, and that she and Harry had said to each other, "We're going to change the world." Nelthorpe-Cowne tried to warn her of the reality of being a member of the Royal Family. 'I had real misgivings when I realised she wanted Harry to propose to her. It wasn't just the media attention. I distinctly remember explaining as we sipped wine in London's West End that she must cope with the enormous expectations of the British public, the Royal Family and their courtiers. I told her, "This is serious. This is the end of your normal life, the end of your privacy: everything."' Meghan's reaction was to hold up her hand and silence Nelthorpe-Cowne. '"Stop," she said in a steely manner I had not noticed before. "I don't wanna hear any negativity. This is a happy time for us."' The end had begun. It arrived shortly afterwards, a week before the news about Meghan and Harry's relationship became public. She wrote an email 'saying that she was giving up her career and we had to terminate our contract.' Thereafter, Meghan ignored Nelthorpe-Cowne's existence, acting as if they had never had a productive professional relationship or a close personal friendship, or indeed had even ever met.

For all her 'fierce intelligence', Meghan seems not to have realised that cutting people out of her life the way she was doing made them feel that she had been using them and, when they had ceased to be of use to her, she had discarded them as if they had never existed. One can make a case for the fact that Meghan was being cautious and self-protective, but the fact remains, she was building up trouble for herself. She was arming people who had been her friends, who had wanted to continue to be her friends, and no matter how successful she was or how grand she became should her relationship end in marriage, as both she and Harry already felt it would, the day would come when those chickens would come home to roost.

And roost they did. Although Meghan would later claim to Tom Bradbury during her controversial South African interview, that she had been 'naive when friends had warned her against the dangers of the media,' Nelthorpe-Cowne regards her as being anything but naive, and made a point of letting the world know it. 'She is a very ambitious woman, and when it is time to move on in her life, Meghan has a way of closing the door on the past, as she did with her father, her siblings, her first husband and me.' Although she has tried to present herself as an innocent, 'she was no ingénue, but a worldly-wise woman on the mission of her life, the mission to bag not any old prince, but **THE PRINCE.'** Nelthorpe-Cowne stated that her experience of Meghan was that she is 'disingenuous' and has no compunction about spinning the greatest yarn so that she can hide her calculatedness behind a veil of non-existent innocence. She rejects Meghan's assertions of purity of heart and purity of purpose when she met Harry. Meghan claimed that 'being American, she didn't even know who Harry was.' This made Nelthorpe-Cowne 'laugh out loud', for not only did the young Meghan have books about Diana and she had watched her funeral repeatedly and thereafter used her as a role model, but Meghan had confessed to her when they were having a drink at the Delaunay the day she was due to meet Prince Harry for the first time that she had googled him. She not only knew exactly who Harry was, but had been very excited to meet him, knowing that he would be her ticket to international fame if they clicked. 'I looked at how stunning she was and I just thought: 'There's no way he's going to be able to resist her.''

Of course, Meghan would've had to be blind and stupid, neither of which she is, not to have seen how Harry could change her life for the better should they bond. But what really made her irresistible to the lonely prince wasn't really her looks, though they helped, but the fire which burnt bright within her. She possessed a warmth and determination to make her mark that scorched the earth as she travelled over it to her destination. With each rung that she had scaled up the ladder of success, her personality had become stronger, her social skills greater, her presentation more polished. As it did, her patina of softness and vulnerability shone evermore brightly.

In the nearly seven years that she had gone from failed actress to being on the cusp of worldwide celebrity, Meghan had indeed shed all the 'negativity', as she put it, which had once held her back. Nowadays, whenever she turned on the heat of that outstanding personality with the goal of melting someone's defences, she usually managed to do so. She was utterly convincing in her displays of care and sincerity. If there was a hint of the steel beneath the surface, that was a positive, not a negative, for it indicated her tremendous strength of character and purpose. Meghan was so open about being ambitious, about her desire to put her imprint on every situation that was to her liking, about her ethics, that people supposed that the gentleness which she displayed was the only Meghan, and that all the evidence of toughness masked a soft and noble heart. While those Meghan left behind had a cynical view of her, those with whom she remained involved were convinced that she was a truly wonderful, selfless, delightful, loving and giving person, as friends such as Jessica Mulroney have stated. And strong. 'She is the strongest person I know,' Serena Williams said.

Upon meeting Harry, and deciding that she liked him, he became the latest in a long line of people to experience her gravitational pull.

They first met for a drink in early July 2016 at Robin Birley's private club, 5 Hertford Street in Mayfair, and clicked. Harry said, 'I had never even heard about her' until Violet von Westenholz mentioned her name. He asked that Violet give him 'a bit of background. I had never watched *Suits*. I had never heard of Meghan before, and I was beautifully surprised when I walked into that room and saw her and there she was, sitting there. I was like, okay, well I'm going to have to up my game.'

If you analyse what Nikki Priddy and others, who have known Meghan well over the years, have said, a pattern emerges. Meghan is so controlled but so vivid, even when she is silent, then so enthusiastic and apparently spontaneous and warm when she is not, that she brings out the best in everyone she wants to impress. But her control conveys the unspoken message to men that they have to 'up their game', as Harry put it, without realising that he was confessing that from the very beginning he understood that the name of the game would be pleasing Meghan. She is proudly and overtly a feminist, and one who not only advocates the joys of empowerment but also makes no pretence about wishing to retain control over her destiny. This is not possible without commanding her relationships as well as the other circumstances of her life.

When Meghan had said, after leaving Trevor, that she did not find separation frightening but empowering, she was actually saying that she would never again be involved with a man who didn't fulfill her demands as and when she wanted them to be fulfilled. All those years of swallowing her resentment while Trevor clung to his integrity and refused to find her parts, had taught her that a man was worth having only if he gave her what she wanted in the here and now. If he couldn't, or wouldn't, she would move on to someone else who could and would. This attitude gave her a degree of autonomy that was attractive to men who like powerful men. They interpreted it as strength and independence, not callousness or opportunism.

This was not the only aspect of Meghan's personality which captivated Harry right from the outset. She was open about her need to have 'a voice', not only with the man in her life but with everyone else. He was transfixed by how opinionated she was. She also made it clear that she must remain in control, and that she had no time for those who do not please her. 'I think very quickly into that we said, "Well, what are we doing tomorrow? We should meet again,"' she said. Not for a nanosecond did she convey the slightest degree of deference. To a prince used to it, but hungering to be accepted as a man, this was an extremely attractive quality. It was, ironically, the very quality that had won Wallis Simpson the former King Edward VIII's heart. It had also worked for Richard Burton when he treated Elizabeth Taylor, who was used to being revered as a movie goddess, as just another woman.

Harry and Meghan both left 5 Hertford Street knowing that something special had happened. The following evening, an excited prince, flying high with anticipation as only someone who is genuinely emotional can, met up with the supremely confident but very warm and responsive Meghan at Soho House. Her friend Markus Anderson had arranged a discreet space for them where they could knock back the wine undisturbed.

'Back to back, two dates in London,' Harry said. 'It was three, maybe four weeks later that I managed to persuade her to join me in Botswana, and we camped out with each other, under the stars.' They were together 'for five days out there, which was absolutely fantastic. Then we were really by ourselves, which was crucial to me to make sure that we had a chance to get to know each other.'

Meghan said, 'Everything that I've learned about him, I've learned through him, as opposed to having grown up around different news stories or tabloids or whatever else. Everything that I learned about him and his family was what he would share with me and vice versa. So for both of us it was a very authentic and organic way to get to know each other.'

Although Meghan's critics would accuse her of being disingenuous, in that she had done her homework and knew much more about him than she claimed, the fact remains that they jelled. If her motives were more mixed than his, it does not alter the fact that they patently had something special between them. This they now set about nurturing, creating a bubble which allowed the relationship to develop with speed. It was after the third date that Meghan told Nelthorpe-Cowne that she and Harry were so serious about each other that they were already plotting their future.

The couple would later claim that they had five or six months of privacy before their relationship went public. That was not so. They had met only a handful of times over a period of less than four months before the news of their relationship broke. This shows the intensity which they shared. Meghan was filming *Suits* in Toronto, so Harry flew out to see her a few times. She also came to London once or twice, staying quietly with him at Nottingham Cottage, which was then his home in Kensington Palace.

This cottage is small and quaint, and used to house retired Private Secretaries such as Sir Alan 'Tommy' Lascelles, whom Princess Margaret rightly blamed for destroying her chances of marrying Group Captain Peter Townsend. Whenever PM saw him walking in the Kensington Palace complex, she would tell her chauffeur to 'run the bastard down', an instruction he wisely avoided implementing. But the cottage was discreet, so Meghan and Harry were able to have the privacy they needed to take their relationship to another level.

Then, on the 30th October 2016, the *Sunday Express* blew the lovers' cover. The world now knew that Prince Harry had a girlfriend called Meghan Markle. He was actually staying with Meghan in Toronto when the story broke. Within hours, she had become a household name for the first time in her life.

Meghan had finally arrived where she wanted to be and the fun had really begun.

CHAPTER 4

Nowadays, news travels almost at the speed of light. Pre-internet, stories that broke on a Sunday had to wait until the Monday for other newspapers to pick them up. Afternoon papers were never published on weekends. The result was that the public always had to wait until Monday morning for the full account only newspapers provided. This was true even when a major event, such as the death of the Princess of Wales, occurred.

The internet changed all of that. Within hours of the *Sunday Express* revealing Meghan's existence in Harry's life, all the major publications had cobbled stories together and posted them on to their web pages. The degree of information, all positive, was impressive. At the time, no one thought anything of it. The producers of *Suits* were expected to have an efficient publicity department, and Meghan had positioned herself with the practised eye of the true professional in such a way that she would emerge glowingly. Nevertheless, publications as disparate as *People* Magazine in the US and the *Daily Mail* in England had access to such flattering, in-depth information about Meghan within moments of the story breaking that it begged the question: Who was fashioning the narrative behind the scenes?

The existence of *The Tig* did not trigger the suspicion that Meghan herself might be pulling the strings for the marionettes to jump the way she wanted. Most journalists assumed that actresses are too dumb to write their own lines, much less fashion their own narrative. *The Tig*, they assumed, was written by someone else, and always had been.

Yet there were clear clues that the timing might not be completely accidental. Meghan had dumped Nelthorpe-Cowne the week before, and Monday 31st October 2016, the day after the *Sunday Express* leak, the *Vancouver Sun* ran a story about her promoting her five-piece collection of spring dresses, all items under $100, for the Canadian chain-store *Reitmans*. Although Meghan was too canny to mention Harry by name, her profile had surged so exponentially in the previous twenty four hours that when she said, 'my cup runneth over, and I'm the luckiest girl in the world', she was verifying her status as Harry's girlfriend. This point was driven home that same day by *People* magazine, which would soon be revealed to have special access to her, as it delivered the message to the world that 'Prince Harry is so serious with actress Meghan Markle that an engagement could be in the not-so-distant future, insiders suggest.' The headline stated, 'Prince Harry Has Already Introduced Meghan Markle to Prince Charles…' meant that the information could only have come from Harry or Meghan or someone very close to them.

The question to ask was: Whose interests were best served by confirming that Meghan was Harry's girlfriend and they were involved in a serious relationship? Having myself been a victim of leaks to the press, and having lived through the extraordinary nineties when Diana Wales would tip various writers off, then present herself as the victim of hounds, I have developed a nose for a plant. Sometimes, the information imparted in a story is so personal that it can only have come from one of the people involved. As soon as I saw the personal details in those stories, I could tell someone very close to the couple had been the source. Knowing how Harry hates the press, whom he blames for his mother's death, and knowing that he had no motive for leaking the news of his relationship with Meghan, I tried to get to the bottom of things. I therefore rang up Adam Helliker, then the social columnist of the *Sunday Express* and someone I have known, liked and respected for decades. Adam told me, 'the tip off came in the age old way. From a servant.'

This did not explain the detail in the other stories, but for the moment I was content to let matters rest. Until you have enough information to come to a considered conclusion, it is always best to keep an open mind.

Unsurprisingly, Harry and Meghan's romance became worldwide news, with publications everywhere digging for the nuggets which would give each of them an edge over their competitors now that the *Sunday Express* had broken the story.

There can be no pretence that some countries looked more favourably than others upon the potential of a mixed-race American actress marrying into the British Royal Family. Her colour was always going to be an issue.

Even though it was a plus in Britain, the US, Canada and many other Commonwealth countries, in other, less progressive states, especially in cultures where there was little intermingling between the colours, classes and creeds, it was always going to be viewed through another prism.

There was also the issue of Meghan's past as well as her position as an actress. Although the British press chose to present her as a major star, and one moreover covered in respectability, the press in many other countries took a more jaundiced view. Their reservations might have seemed outdated to us, but to them, they were valid. These were based upon the traditional values they still held dear, even if we no longer did. In their scheme of things, it was unseemly for a man of one class to consort with a woman of another, unless she is a tart with whom he is having an affair, in which case it is conducted out of sight. Anything more serious would be unacceptable. If you added the difference in colour into the mix, this created a whole new dimension.

While we in the West took the view that these were old-fashioned and offensive viewpoints, and that relationships such as Harry and Meghan's could only advance the cause of interracial inclusivity as well as social cross-pollination, the more bigoted view was that there were disparities beyond class and colour which the Western media were obfuscating. There was also the issue of status. According to this line of reasoning, Meghan was not a major star. She had not been a household name. Two weeks before, no one had been able to identify her as a star even of *Suits*. That show was of such minor significance that even now, few people knew the names of any of the other cast members despite hers having become so memorable. Why did the Western media have to exaggerate her status if she was truly a suitable match for a British prince?

Journalists from these sceptical societies soon discovered a wealth of treasure about Meghan that lay scattered, like so many disused relics, on the plains of her past. In this hunt, they were joined by many of their British and European colleagues from countries such as Germany, whose media have a vigorous tabloid element. These are not tame publications. They never were. Although in tone and content some of them are akin to *The National Enquirer* in the United States, many others are more serious and solid publications. The very word tabloid connotes something of the sleazy supermarket variety to Americans, but in the rest of the world, it lacks those pejorative overtones and is simply a description of the more has popular end of the press. Nevertheless, all these publications share one aim with the sleazier element of the American market. They aim to unmask, and will stop at nothing to get to the bottom of a story as long as it is topical enough.

Meghan was in her mid-thirties. She had lived a full life. She had had a series of men. She had tried her hand at many different activities. There was never any doubt that there would be layers to unfold, newsworthy stories to dig up. The only question was, how dirty would the dirt be?

Speaking as someone who has had to sue every major newspaper company in Britain for libel in the course of the last forty five years, I can confirm that even relatively reputable publications seldom resist the temptation to put a sensational spin on perfunctory incidents in a celebrity's past, so that the most anodyne features are represented as appalling flaws. Alan Frame, onetime Deputy Editor of the *Daily Express,* sister paper of the *Sunday Express* which broke the Meghan story, once told me that his paper had received so many contradictory accounts of my past, from so many people claiming to be my best friends, that he would have thought me the most popular woman on earth had they not been so vitriolic. Many of the informants, naturally, wanted financial recompense for their tales, tall though they were.

The corrupting influence of filthy lucre also travels in the opposite direction. British newspapers especially are renowned for paying handsome sums to informants who might, but equally might not, have a firm handle on the facts. Many publications are cynical enough not to let the truth get in the way of a good story when they wish to present east as west and north as south. It takes no imagination to see the meal journalists of this persuasion will make of sensational and verifiable facts.

It took very little digging to discover that the beauteous, A-lister of the 30th and 31st October had a back story, and one, moreover, that there was no need to embellish. Before the week was out, half of Fleet Street knew through their investigations in Hollywood and Toronto that Meghan had a history of cultivating, captivating, denigrating, and discarding both men and woman in her ascent to the top. A *Mail* journalist told me, 'As she climbs up the next rung of the ladder, she plants the soles of her shoes on your head. And, when you wipe your face off, you see that it's covered in cow dung.'

Meghan, in other words, had discarded a whole load of friends of both sexes, aside from men with whom she had been involved, and done it in such a way, that they had become enemies. These people were happy to talk to the press and, when they were not, to direct journalists to someone else who would. Throughout the first week of November 2016, reporters from all over the world were offering huge sums of money for some of these discards to talk. And some did. Even when they did not, a capable journalist would have enough of a whiff to know that there was a body buried somewhere nearby.

So rich were the pickings that the *Mail* journalist told me, 'It's not often that we find ourselves having to downplay instead of exaggerate. But with Meghan, that's what we had to do. From the outset. It was the only way to get stories past the legal department.'

There was another and rather more touching dimension to the way the British press approached this scenario. A journalist from the *Mirror* encapsulated the whole thing perfectly by saying, 'No one wanted to hurt Harry. He was truly popular, and if that was the girl he wanted, and if she could make him happy, which she certainly seemed to be doing, no one wanted to rain on his parade. Almost by common but silent consent, we all took a soft line.'

The line, however, wasn't soft enough for Meghan, who wasn't used to an enquiring press but to a tame one which slavishly reported whatever she or her representatives fed them. By the end of the first week of real fame, she was so perturbed over the possibilities of what might be said that Harry issued a statement:

'Since he was young, Prince Harry has been very aware of the warmth that has been extended to him by members of the public. He feels lucky to have so many people supporting him and knows what a fortunate and privileged life he leads.

'He is also aware that there is significant curiosity about his private life. He has never been comfortable with this, but has tried to develop a thick skin about the level of media interest that comes with it. He has rarely taken formal action on the very regular publication of fictional stories that are written about him and he has worked hard to develop a professional relationship with the media, focused on his work and the issues he cares about.

'But the past week has seen a line crossed. His girlfriend, Meghan Markle, has been subject to a wave of abuse and harassment. Some of this has been very public - the smear on the front page of a newspaper; the racial undertones of comment pieces; and outright sexism and racism of media trolls and web article comments. Some of it has been hidden from the public - the nightly battles to keep defamatory stories out of the papers; her mother having to struggle past photographers in order to get to her front door; the attempts of reporters and photographers to gain illegal entry to her home and the calls to police that followed; the substantial bribes offered by papers to her ex-boyfriend; the bombardment of nearly every friend, co-worker, and loved one in her life.

'Prince Harry is worried about Ms Markle's safety and is deeply disappointed that he has not been able to protect her. It is not right that a few months into a relationship with him that Ms Markle should be subjected to such a storm. He knows that commentators will say this is "the price she has to pay" and that "this is all part of the game". He strongly disagrees. This is not a game - it is her life and his.

'He has asked for this statement to be issued in the hopes that those in the press who have been driving this story can pause and reflect before any further damage is done. He knows that it is unusual to issue a statement like this, but hopes that fair-minded people will understand why he has felt it necessary to speak publicly.'

This statement was a masterstroke. Not only did Harry breach boundaries, but he also waded in to protect Meghan in a way he had never done with Chelsy Davy or Cressida Bonas, both of whom had had to endure years of press attention with never a word from him to protect them. This revealed that Meghan was in a class of her own. The statement also showed both of them in the most positive of lights, garnering them sympathy from the legions of romantics and admirers who were rooting them on to long- term happiness. Furthermore, it stymied further enquiry. In so doing, it muzzled not only unfair critics but also fair ones, who could thereafter be unfairly accused of racism if they did not back off. It brilliantly confused the role of valid enquirer with the trolls, by the expedient of apportioning equal blame between those who write valid stories and those who use the internet as a forum to vent their dubious opinions.

Speaking as a public figure that has many friends in the public eye, I can tell you that no one ever reads the comments made about them on the internet unless you're in the mood to have a good laugh. All public figures are regularly trolled. It goes with the territory. Only when there is a genuine legal issue do publications monitor their comments' sections. Otherwise, everyone takes the view that the crazies who haunt the internet are such a tiny albeit vociferous proportion of the newspaper-reading public, that they should be dismissed rather than acknowledged. But in his statement Harry had conflated responsible writers with crazy opinionists, using the latter to silence the former. It was a commendably effective technique, and certainly bought him and Meghan enough time and space to develop their relationship in peace.

Sexism was another red herring thrown into the mix to useful purpose. By this time, the press had discovered that Meghan was indeed personally responsible for content on *The Tig*. In it, she regularly beat the twin drums of racism and sexism. In the context of the blog, sexism might have made sense when it prevented women from achieving their full potential, but in the context of the British press reporting on the relationship between one of its princes and a love interest, there was no sexism when they tried to garner further information about her past. They had been merely trying to substantiate the rumours swirling around about her activities. Bringing up sexism not only muzzled the press but also diverted them away from the knowledge that Meghan will have known they would alight upon sooner or later: How appropriate is it for any member of a royal family in a constitutional monarchy, which has to remain politically neutral and respectful of the opinions of all its citizens, to take up with an aggressive, proactive, ambitious, opinionated, left-wing political activist? *The Tig* was visible proof that her beliefs and personality were incompatible with the royal role which she would inevitably have to fulfill if her relationship with Harry should end in marriage. The valid question which she and Harry managed to divert the press away from was a simple one: How will someone as vociferous as Meghan Markle, whose posture is that she needs to use her voice, fit into a role that requires the silent acceptance of viewpoints which do not accord with her own? It is interesting to speculate upon whether much trouble would not have been avoided if such issues had been addressed from the outset. But, by issuing the statement that Harry did, he and Meghan avoided the inherent problems until after they had married and it had become apparent to her that she preferred utilising her voice to a life of silent service.

By buying themselves time the way they did, Harry and Meghan were actually only postponing the inevitable. They actually believed that they had successfully silenced all those organs of the press which might have been gearing up to shut their romance down. Each of them clearly failed to understand the importance of immutables: in his case, her; in her case, the role the press plays in Britain.

By incorrectly assessing the extent of their success in seeing off negative publicity, Harry and Meghan were opening themselves up to a host of misconceptions regarding their control over the press. It is a pity Harry was too young when his mother was alive, to appreciate how utterly her attempts to influence the press had rebounded to her detriment. As for Meghan, she was utterly ignorant of the way the British press works. She was confusing American and Canadian publications which had given her publicity, with an entirely more subversive, inquisitorial, irreverent, and chippy lot. She was like a child whose beloved pet is a docile and loving Cavalier King Charles Spaniel walking into a lion's den thinking that she can train it. She tweaks its nose, pulls its cheeks, threatens it with her fists and orders it to sit still. She walks away confident that she has it under her control, little realising that it simply can't be bothered to show her who's boss. But the next time will be different.

No public figure in Britain can function without an in-depth understanding of how the British press works. It is unique. There is no other press like it in the world. It is so radically different from the North American press that Meghan was used to, that she was totally unprepared for what living with its attentions would mean to her life. Had she and Harry not bought themselves the respite they did by issuing that statement, she might have understood before her marriage that she was like a swimmer used to a well heated door pool being plunged into the icy chill of the North Sea in winter.

The press worldwide is tame compared with the British. This is as true of the American and Canadian as it is of the European, Middle Eastern, Asian, or Sub-Continental. The only press that has faint echoes of the British is the Australian, but even so, it is a very muted affair compared with Fleet Street. This is largely because in Britain we have a tradition of robust iconoclasm dating back to the eighteenth century. At a time when monarchies in Europe were both secure and autocratic, with the press rigidly controlled and public opinion shaped by the Crown, the British monarch was a usurper, invited by Parliament, to sit upon the throne while the real king stewed in exile across the water. This inevitably led to instability and the possibility of regime change, causing divided loyalties which drove dissent and gave a voice to those who would not otherwise have had one. The world's freest press was born. No one thereafter would be impervious to the reach of journalists: no king, prince, aristocrat, government, official, public figure or even private individual who caught the attention of scribes.

By 1714, the first club of satirists had been formed. The Scriblerus Club's members included two of the age's most powerful writers, Alexander Pope and Jonathan Swift. They paved the way later in the century for William Hogarth, the social critic, pictorial satirist and editorial cartoonist whose best known works are *A Rake's Progress* and *A Harlot's Progress*.

By the end of the century, satirists such as James Gillray were so well established as social commentators that they could get away with poking the most outrageous fun at all public figures, including King George III and his family, especially his heir the future George IV. To his credit, the Prince Regent had enough of a sense of humour to frame some of the cartoons which mocked him, and Farmer George, as his father was known, also embraced the affectionate ribbing.

It was against this bedrock of satire that the British tabloids (so called because they were the popular press, despite some being of broadsheet size) were born in the twentieth century. My sister-in-law's grandfather Lord Beaverbrook and his competitors Lords Northcliffe and Rothermere were the titans of the popular press. Through their efforts, the satirical tradition was converted into something equally populistic and insouciant, but more palatable to a vast reading public. They were soon joined by other newspaper magnates such as Cecil Harmsworth King, maternal nephew of both Northcliffe and Rothermere, and Sir William Emsley Carr, who edited the *News of the World* for fifty years. To them, no story should be written exactly as told by the subject of an interview. A journalist's role was not to report uncritically what the subject of an interview said or did, but to portray the subject without deference and with enough sensationalism to bring the story alive while bringing the subject down a peg or two. It was taken for granted that public figures always take themselves more seriously than others are willing to take them, so a dose of irreverence was healthy. Even when these publications were writing flatteringly, they managed to include just enough pokes to make the point that everyone and everything was imperfect and it was their duty to balance the positive with the negative. Their message was: we are no respecter of persons. This has remained true till now.

Despite this, the more upmarket broadsheets such as the rightist *Times* and *Telegraph*, or the leftist *Guardian* and its sister paper, the *Observer* (the oldest Sunday paper in the world), were not iconoclastic. They did not seek to reduce everyone or everything in the self-conscious way their more populistic peers did. When writing their articles, they did not puncture people's balloons for the mere sake of it. If denigration was beside the point, they did not gratuitously include it the way the popular press did. This remained true even after the arrival of Rupert Murdoch in England in the last two decades of the twentieth century. Although he altered the tone and content of the most august broadsheet in the country, making the *Times*'s content *akin* to what you could read in middlebrow papers such as the *Mail* and the *Express*, one fundamental difference remained. The *Times* was still not iconoclastic. It remained like the other upmarket broadsheets, each of whose coverage was free of the snide tone of the tabloids. In 1977 when I was the Private Secretary to the Libyan Ambassador, I always placed stories with broadsheets, because only they could be trusted not to twist and turn what you told them. In that, they were like the North American press Meghan was so used to.

Her failure to appreciate these important differences would lead her down a very slippery slope. Had she tried to understand what she was dealing with, and why it functioned as it did, she might have stood a chance. But in her ignorance she lost the ability to cope.

Britain has more national newspapers than any other country on earth. There are too many to enumerate, but aside from the ones listed above, the most popular are the *Sun*, the *People*, the *Star*, and the *Mirror*. No other country has a freer or more vigorous press, and none has as many titles fighting for a share of the available readership. The result is that competition is fiercer than it is in any other territory in the rest of the world. In the United States, for instance, there really is not one significant daily newspaper that is read by the broad mass of people nationwide. There is the *New York Times*, the *Washington Post*, the *Los Angeles Times*, and their more downmarket brethren such as the *New York Post*, all of which are locals. Nowhere is there a major national publication to compete with them. In any given area, therefore, the competition is less intense than in England, where each paper has to fight its corner against the incursions of its competitors.

The combination of competitiveness and iconoclasm is exacerbated by another feature unique to Britain. The United States, Canada and most of the European nations long ago acknowledged the levelling of their societies, either because they became republics, or, if they remained monarchies, their royal families were perceived as being powerless and purely ceremonial representatives of the state. Despite the fact that Britain is at least as egalitarian and meritocratic a society as any other Western democracy, and is more so than many others, the fallacy persists in many segments of British society that the old hierarchy remains in place, powerful and obstructionistic as ever. This misconception gives added bite to many a transaction in daily life, because several organs of the press, whether popular or broadsheet, pander to outdated prejudices as if they were still relevant today. In doing so, they perpetuate damaging and misleading myths about the structure of British society.

Of course, there are sound commercial reasons why various publications behave as they do. By playing upon the prejudices, envy, fears, hopes and dreams of their readers, they sell their papers to readerships whose opinions they shape as well as reflect. A more dispassionate take would result in commercial failure, so they justify their actions and sometimes even convince themselves that they believe the fantasies they purvey.

Beyond the infighting, there is also the courtesy one shark has for another. Like many politicians and lawyers, they recognise that, irrespective of which side they're on, they're all in the game together. I have seen many a journalist best of friends with an adversary whose every principle is antithetical to his own. I know of cases where they've knowingly destroyed the lives of innocent people to achieve what they regard as a more important objective, such as the unseemly display in 2016 when certain publications set out to ruin the reputation of someone I know in the hope of bringing down the Secretary-General of the Commonwealth. When I intervened on this individual's behalf with one of the publications, I was told that they had nothing against him personally, but the destruction of his life would be a small price to pay if they got rid of Baroness Scotland.

Harry, of course, knew only too well what a viper's nest the British press can be. He had a real hatred of it born of his belief that they had killed his mother. In fairness to them, they had done no such thing. Diana would have survived that car crash had she been wearing a seat belt. She was also responsible for the press following her that night. She had telephoned journalists before leaving Sardinia to tip them off about her arrival in Paris. She continued tipping them off once she arrived in that city. If you are being chased by people you have encouraged to chase you, you surely bear responsibility for creating the chase.

Of course, Harry was only twelve when his mother died. He was too young to have a mature judgement about her as an individual. By his own account, when he met Meghan he had still not worked through the trauma of her death. This was not necessarily a failing on his part. There have been reams written on the emotional impact, to children below the age of fourteen, when a parent dies. *Failure to Mourn, and Melancholia* by Jonathan R. Pedder (1982) carried on from Sigmund Freud's *Mourning and Melancholia* (1917) and Erna Furman's *A Child's Parent Dies* (1974) which was informed by her own experiences at Theresienstadt Concentration Camp when her mother died there. Harry's failure to grieve was therefore a natural part of the phenomenon of a child losing its parent. But that does not mean the press were to blame.

Most people in Britain with positions that warrant press attention have a healthy suspicion of the media. Sadly, most of them also have an exaggerated fear that triggers hysterical and irrational responses at the very moment level-headedness is called for. In this regard, I speak from a lifetime of experience. I was fortunate enough to spend the first twenty four years of my life cosseted by the attentions of a tame press. For the next forty six years, I have had to endure the unwelcome attentions of the British tabloids. I therefore understand where both Meghan and Harry have come from as few others can, if only because most people have never experienced the full horror of British media intrusion, while I have.

If you look at how open Meghan was in her two blogs, it is obvious that she committed the most cardinal of all errors for anyone in public life. She revealed too much of herself. While she thought she was gaining admirers through her openness and honesty, she was also giving potential detractors information that they would ultimately be able to use against her. I can think of few people in public life who have exposed themselves to the extent that she did. One of the cardinal rules is that you batten down the hatches when journalists or servants are present. You dole out information about yourself, about your feelings and activities, as if you are a miser being forced to make a donation to a cause for which you have no regard. If you need publicity for a valid reason, such as for a charitable or commercial purpose, you put on your glad rags and monitor every word you say. You do not tell reporters what are your greatest hopes, fears, desires, ambitions, or any of the myriad of things Meghan revealed on her two blogs. You do not write articles that are so revelatory you might as well be talking to a psychiatrist. In interviews, you project an open personality while keeping your trap shut about all but the subject you are speaking about. When you see reporters out and about, you are pleasant, anodyne, uninformative, and discreet. You do not leak stories about yourself or anyone else you know. There are, of course, such things as ethical journalists, but it does not behove you to test the water unless you are sure it's not going to chill you to your bones. Princess Grace of Monaco, for instance, was such a close personal friend of the former women's editor of the Evening *News*, Gwen Robyns, that she used to stay with her at her flat in London when she wanted to escape from palace life in Monaco. I have enjoyed personal friendships with journalists like Sue Douglas, former editor of the *Sunday Express*, and freelancer Catherine Olsen (Lady Mancham in private life). Nevertheless, these are the exceptions, not the rule, which was best laid down by Sir John Falstaff in Shakespeare's Henry IV Part I: *The better part of valour is discretion.*

Many celebrities and royals have good working relationships, as opposed to friendships, with select journalists. Before meeting Meghan, Harry was chummy with Rebecca English of the *Mail* and one or two others, establishing human links with them which benefited both him and them. In that regard, he was following in the footsteps of his mother. Diana used to cultivate relationships with journalists such as Richard Kay and Sir David English, Editor of the *Daily Mail.* These were not personal friendships, but expediencies through which she would manage her public profile. The fact that Harry was doing the same suggested a level of maturity which was commendable. Nothing is more uncivilised than a public figure who cannot treat a pleasant journalist in a friendly manner.

In the week between the *Sunday Express* revealing Meghan's presence in Harry's life, and his issuing the statement which effectively warned the press off, she woke up to the difference between the tame press she was used to in the US and Canada, and the British. Up to then, she had managed her profile with admirable dexterity. She had never had negative publicity, notwithstanding the fact that the landscape traversed by her was littered with the remnants of former relationships. The reason why was simple. Up to then, she had simply not been famous enough to warrant negative attention. This comes about only when someone has a sufficiently high profile to attract unsolicited publicity. Until the 30th October 2016, however, all Meghan's media coverage had been solicited either by herself or through the studios. She had in reality been a column filler, the sort of semi-celebrity that journalists use to pad out the pages when there's nothing worth reporting upon, or when they have to pay back film companies in a quid pro quo way.

Now Meghan had arrived and the press were eager to flesh out the picture. The first wave of stories had been so positive that the tabloids wanted to redress the balance with a touch of sensationalism. Their first port of call was anyone from her past who could inform them of what she was really like. To their credit, none of her formerly close friends, boyfriends, ex-husband or even family went on the record spilling secrets. They all maintained a dignified silence when they had nothing positive to say. And when they did not, they were so measured in their statements that they could not be accused of rubbishing her. In large measure, that was because Meghan has always had the good sense to associate with decent people, or, as she put it to Violet von Westenholz, 'Is he nice?'

Even so, there was deafening silence from some of the people journalists would have expected to comment positively. This was unmistakable evidence that something was afoot. So they tried people she had known less well, people who would have less loyalty. Sure enough, there was less reticence. The picture that emerged was a mixed one. Some people, like her neighbours, had nothing negative to say, while others confided that she was 'a piece of work' and 'an operator' who was 'ruthless', 'ambitious', and practised at 'dumping people past their sell-by date.'

It might be surprising to outsiders to learn that the British press will sit on incendiary stories. But they do, as their behaviour now proved. Harry had asked for a break and, because he was so popular and because even those segments of the media that were not particularly royalist could see the merit of a woman of colour being the girlfriend of a senior member of the Royal Family, and even more importantly, because none of them wanted to be accused of being racist, they all decided to back off and give the couple space.

Although Harry and Meghan might have thought the clear run they had been given was the sole result of their statement, this was far from the truth. The reasons were more complex than that. Despite the press and the palace knowing that dirt existed that could damage Meghan, fear played a smaller part in backing off than a combination of expediency and enlightened self-interest. The uninitiated might believe that there is a total disconnect between the palace and the press, but the reality is otherwise. Both entities have a symbiotic relationship. The palace needs the press to publicise the activities of the royals and keep the public's interest in them alive, while the press needs the royals because they are the world's mega-celebrities and, as such, reliable fodder.

Beyond that, the newspapers provide a valuable function for the palace. They assist it in gathering information which is useful to the maintenance of the monarchy and the protection of the Royal Family's interests. Because journalists are obliged to ask the Press Office at the palace for a comment before publishing a story, they are a rich and frequently inadvertent source of information. Many a royal has tried to conceal his or her activities from the family and the courtiers, only to be rumbled by an inquisitive reporter asking an awkward question of a press officer.

The Royal Family had actually known of Meghan and Harry's relationship before the press did. When it became apparent that it was developing into something more than a three night stand, the palace did what it always does. It launched its own investigations into Meghan's background the way it always ascertains the back story of everyone who becomes a close associate of any member of the Royal Family. I was told by a courtier that there was 'concern' about Meghan's 'past' but because it was 'just an affair the view was: don't cross the bridge in case we don't come to it.' Nevertheless, there was anxiety at the palace about the press 'wading in, though it was my view that that would've been the best thing they could've done. It would've stopped the affair in its tracks before it had a chance to develop into something more serious. It was fairly obvious from all we discovered about her past that she might be trouble with a capital T.'

The palace, of course, was not about to convey any of its concerns to the press. No competent press officer would do such a thing, but the hope was that the romance would run its course, Harry would meet a girl with a less complicated background and a more pliable character, then everyone could breathe a sigh of relief.

As we all know, the press did not break ranks nor did anyone close to Meghan for the next six months. The first person to wade in was her half-sister Samantha, who announced in April 2017 that she was writing a book called *The Diary of Princess Pushy's Sister*. At that stage, her criticisms were implied rather than asserted, but this did Meghan no harm and Samantha no favours. She came across as a jealous attention-seeker intent on muscling in on her younger half-sibling's success, but I learnt that there was actually a more poignant reason. Although neither sister had ever been close, they had always had a cordial relationship, but when Samantha reached out to Meghan to congratulate her on her success, she was iced.

Meanwhile, the romance continued to flourish. In September the Invictus Games were held in Toronto and for the first time Meghan and Harry officially appeared in public as a couple. She was chic in an oversized man's white shirt tucked into fitted blue jeans, while he was equally informally attired. In breach of royal protocol, they held hands, something they would continue to do thereafter. Throughout that appearance, they continued to be overtly physical, their hands and legs touching in a very public display of attraction, generally conveying the message that they were a hot couple completely besotted with each other.

It is said that everyone loves a lover, and this certainly seemed to be true of Harry and Meghan. They were seen as a breath of fresh air, a good-looking, delightfully informal couple who seemed to be totally in love. In Establishment circles in the UK, people were generally pleased that Harry had found himself such a beautiful girl who seemed as much in love with him as he was with her. Her colour was much commented upon, not as a drawback but as an attribute. The timing of the romance was regarded as being particularly propitious with regards to the Commonwealth of Nations. For some time now, the Headship of that august institution had been a feature of discussion amongst the 53 member states. The position is not hereditary. King George VI had been its first Head, followed by his daughter Queen Elizabeth II, whose love of the Commonwealth is superseded only by that for the country of her birth. She is respected greatly amongst the many Heads of Government representing the other 52 formerly British colonies, with whom she has worked throughout her long reign. There had been many occasions, such as the crises involving Rhodesia and South Africa, when the Commonwealth had come perilously close to fragmenting. The Queen was credited with having kept it together, her commitment, wisdom and colour-blindness the glue that had held it together. But she was now over ninety, and the subject of her successor had been mooted for at least a decade. Some of the countries wanted one of their own to be appointed the next head, while others, being mindful of the self-interestedness of some states and the dangerous corruption of others, thought the neutrality of the British monarch would safeguard its integrity in a way no one else could. The troublesome issue of race sometimes reared its ugly head, with some of the black nations querying why an institution with a larger black than white population should be headed up by the head of a family that was exclusively white. However, if Harry should marry Meghan, the British Royal Family would no longer be purely white. That would play well throughout the Commonwealth, especially as how the process of designating its next Head was due to come up for discussion at the next meeting of the Heads of Government in April 2018.

Buckingham Palace announced Harry and Meghan's engagement on the 27th November 2017. The news was greeted with genuine enthusiasm publicly. There was even more excitement than when William became engaged to Catherine Middleton. For all its overlay of tradition, British society had jettisoned snobbishness and embraced inclusiveness. Both engagements confirmed this. Catherine's solidly middle class background and Meghan's colour and class were seen as confirmation that the British monarchy had become like the American presidency. Anyone, irrespective of background, can aspire to it.

On the 20th April 2018, the Queen got her fondest wish when Prince Charles was named as her successor to the Headship of the Commonwealth. Several of the Commonwealth High Commissioners told me that there was little doubt that Harry's engagement to Meghan had made the appointment easier for all the states involved.

Between the announcements of the engagement and of Charles's appointment to succeed the Queen as Head of the Commonwealth, the most glorious cock-up concerning colour took place. Only Princess Michael of Kent, a woman universally deplored in royal circles, could have orchestrated something so pointlessly self-defeating. At the Queen's annual luncheon party for all the members of the Royal Family at Buckingham Palace a few days before Christmas, she was photographed wearing a blackamoor brooch on her coat. She is not someone people in their right mind would aspire to emulate. She is vain and tiresomely affected. I would stake good money that she wore that brooch to garner the attention she seeks at every turn. Although she would later issue a statement claiming to be 'very sorry and distressed for any offence caused,' I for one could not help feeling that she had deliberately set out to knock the newcomer off the front pages: which she did. And while she did it with a flourish, it would be doing her an injustice if I did not point out that the brooch she was wearing cannot fairly have been regarded as possessing racist overtones, for it did not represent a Sub-Saharan black slave but a North African aristocrat. It was a Moretto Veneziano, as the figures are known. These originated in Venice and have been made there from the dawn of the Modern Age until today. Alberto Nardi, the Venetian jeweller who created the brooch, took strong exception to the way ignorant commentators in Britain and America jumped on the racist bandwagon to condemn an item of jewellery he had made, without even being aware of its cultural significance in its place of origin. 'A whole lot of nonsense has been written, and I wish to defend an object that is rich in history and unique to Venice. The brooch depicts a Moorish Venetian prince.' This was verified by the jewellery historian Anastazja Buttita, who explained, 'The blacks in these pieces were essentially being depicted as aristocrats. And over the years, these objects became one of the city's most important symbols, symbolizing to Venetians their openness to other cultures.' Not only are such items not racist in origin, but they give off the most powerful message of inclusivity. Could Princess Michael have actually been conveying a positive message rather than the negative one she was accused of? If so, it would have behoved Meghan to note that it is always dangerous for public figures to ignore public misconceptions, even when they are more knowledgeable and in the right. She too would soon hurl herself into the pit of public disapproval the way the Princess Michael, who is as over-confident as Meghan and equally blind to the effect she has when choosing between her own desires and the sensitivity of others, did.

No sooner did the furore caused by Marie Christine Kent's choice of brooch die down than Harry committed an equally injudicious *faux pas*. Sadly for him and for Meghan, his would have rather more devastating consequences. It began innocently enough, following a successful

Christmas at Sandringham. The Queen had broken precedent. For the first time ever, a fiancée had been asked to join the Royal Family for the sacrosanct Christmas celebrations. Meghan could not say, as Diana had and Catherine could have but never did, that she was not welcomed with open arms before the wedding ring was on her finger. Not only was she treated by everyone as if she were already a member of the family, but the press had gone wild when she, Harry, William and Catherine had walked to church from the big house. The Fab Four were born that day, heightening expectations and raising Meghan's stock exponentially. It now really looked as if she was on her way to becoming one of the world's most famous women as well as a beloved part of the Royal Family.

On the 27th December, Harry guest edited BBC Radio 4's *Today* programme. He was not its first guest editor. In fact, the tradition of Christmas guest editors had begun fourteen years before. Nor was he the first royal editor. That had been Sarah, Duchess of York in 2004. William and Catherine had also been invited by BBC Radio 1 earlier in the year to speak about the *Heads Together* mental health campaign which they had started with Harry. This was now his opportunity to showcase 'a range of topics, including youth violence, conservation and mental health,' according to the announcement the palace had made.

Harry acquitted himself admirably. He was warm, concerned, considered, charming and interesting. He came across as a genuinely nice and kind man. Like his mother, he was no intellectual, but like her, he had emotional intelligence in spades. Then he committed the solecism to end all solecisms. Speaking about how successful Christmas at Sandringham with Meghan had been, he said that she had finally got the family she had never had.

My sons are friendly with Meghan's nephew following their appearance with him on MTV's *The Royal World*. He and his mother have stayed with us as guests at our castle in Sussex. I do not think I am breaching confidences to repeat that the whole family was upset when they heard Harry expunging them out of existence. The fact is, both branches of Meghan's family had been close to her. Tom Sr had literally bankrupted himself supporting her. By her own account, he had been an excellent father. Her uncles had done whatever they could to help her. 'Everyone was there for her.' Tom Sr 'was a wonderful father and grandfather. Nothing was too much trouble for him. He is a truly kind, decent man, just as Meghan said on her blog. She wasn't lying when she said all those things about him.' According to Meghan, Tom Jr, Samantha, Tyler and his mother Tracey Dooley, Tom Sr is a generous man who would give you the shirt off his back if he thought you needed it. The Markles had played a far larger part in Meghan's upbringing than the Ragland family. Her mother had been away for large stretches of time. Although the Ragland family also emerged as warm, by the account of Doria's own half-brother Joseph Johnson, the times they spent together were not so frequent, but nevertheless 'it was always nice for family to get together. It was always a good time. We've got a little, small family: not a lot of cousins, uncles and that kind of thing that we know of. So when we got together, we were always happy to see each other.'

Samantha was the first off the mark. She waded in accusing Meghan of being a 'shallow social climber' and said their father had always given 'Meg everything.' While the public might have thought that Samantha was just a jealous sibling, their father hinted that the reason might have something to do with Meghan ignoring Samantha's approaches. The two sisters had never been close, but nor were they estranged. They simply lived in different parts of the country. Meghan spurning Samantha's approaches was therefore surprising. It caused hurt, and the wounded party struck out. Nevertheless, they were family, and families might have their ups and downs, but they still remained family. Or so the Markles believed.

The wedding was scheduled for the 19th May 2018. As the day neared, both the Markle and Ragland families were humiliated 'in front of the whole world' when only her mother and father received invitations. Her paternal uncle Michael, who had organised the internship for her with the American Embassy in Buenos Aires, was perplexed. So too were her maternal uncle John Johnson and his wife. Her nephew Tyler, whom she used to babysit when they were young, wished her well and wondered why she wasn't inviting everyone. They were certainly a small enough number to take up very little space. Although they had all scattered to the wind, living in different places - some in Florida, Mexico, California, Oregon etc. - they had all been on good terms with Meghan. Even Samantha had.

None of them had fallen out with her, though some, such as her brother and sister, did not speak to each other. Up to the last moment, several members of the family hoped that their invitations were on the way.

When it became apparent to the whole family that they had been deliberately overlooked *en masse*, some of them became angry. Although some refrained from going public, Tyler's father Tom Jr wrote an open letter to Harry, stating in part, 'As more time passes to your royal wedding it becomes very clear that this is the biggest mistake in royal history.'

Such conflict brought no credit to anyone. Although the press loved the drama of it all, the reality was that the whole thing was just embarrassing and uncalled for. While some commentators thought Meghan's siblings behaved badly by berating her, others thought that they were justifiably outraged. Whatever people's points of view, the one unarguable fact was that failing to invite her family had rebounded badly on Meghan, who was barraged with bad publicity.

What the public and the press did not know was that the anger of not being invited to the wedding was not limited to the paternal and maternal branches of Meghan's slighted family. Practically none of the European royals was invited either, nor were the many royal cousins in England who are normally asked to the weddings of the Royal Family. This was in defiance of the established custom whereby even third and fifth cousins are asked, weddings and funerals being the two occasions in life when royal and aristocratic clans gather together in tribal affirmation.

Although the public were never privy to this, anger amongst the relations turned to fury when it emerged that Harry and Meghan had not filled St. George's Chapel to capacity. Aside from the hundreds of empty seats in existence, there were the hundreds of charity workers, strangers all, who had been asked. But most offensive to the many relations who had been overlooked was the presence of celebrities Harry and Meghan barely knew. 'Pray tell,' said a cousin who would ordinarily have been present, 'why are we not there but George and Amal Clooney, Oprah Winfrey, and the Beckhams are? The invitation list smacks of a career move.'

Behind the scenes, an even worse scenario was unfolding. This played right into the hands of the British press, who were delighted to be released from their self-imposed restraint. Although Meghan's failure to invite either side of her family led both the Markle and the Johnson/Ragland clans to feel that they had been cast in the role of pariah in front of the whole world, the British media were careful not to mock the Raglands presumably because they feared accusations of colour prejudice should they do so. But they had no such compunction where the Caucasian Markles were concerned. The whole Markle family felt that Meghan had set them up for ridicule by not inviting them, a view which was confirmed as accurate when the British papers set about making them all look as ridiculous as possible. There was a cruel and inhumane element to the reportage which was the British tabloids at their worst. They behaved as if they had a right to mock the family because Meghan and Harry had such scant respect for them that they had not even condescended to acknowledge their existence with invitations. Although Tom Sr exceptionally had been the only one to be asked, this did not stop them from portraying him up as a sloppy, sleazy slob. He was pictured in the most unflattering poses, the implication being that he was a drunkard as well as a dolt and an oik. Because his whole life had been spent in television, Tom Sr knew that they were making a fool of him, so he agreed to stage some photographs with what seemed a friendly paparazzo. When he realised that he had been set up and had been made to look a complete idiot, he was so distressed that he suffered a heart attack and was hospitalised in Mexico. The *Mail on Sunday* then ran an expose presenting him in the most unflattering light, after which he had a second heart attack. This time, he was taken to the Sharp Chula Vista Medical Center in California, where he had stents inserted to open up his blocked arteries, running up a bill of some $130,000. He was discharged on the 17th May and warned that he could not travel.

Although Tom Sr and Meghan were in touch after the first heart attack, and she encouraged him to come over and not pull out of walking her down the aisle, as he had said he intended to do, so great was the embarrassment, once he had his second heart attack, that she declined to contact him and refused to respond on the many occasions he tried to get in touch with her. Harry, on the other hand, did text Tom. He berated him for upsetting Meghan, while failing to ask the man who was about to become his father-in-law how he was following his second heart attack.

Wounded feelings and poor judgement were about to make what the press had already dubbed the Markle Debacle into something which was not only damaging and destructive but would cause unnecessary damage and pain to all the parties involved.

CHAPTER 5

As marriage loomed for Harry and Meghan, the Markles and Ragland/ Johnsons were not the only families whose equilibrium was dashed along with their hopes and expectations. So too were the Royal Family's, though for them there appeared to be compensations which would balance the downside.

Despite the considerable advantage that Meghan's colour was, and the demonstrably apparent love between the couple, there was the inconvenient fact that Meghan had a past that could damage the prestige of the Royal Family if the press did not remain on side. As stated elsewhere, no one associates closely with the Royal Family without their background being investigated by the palace. I know of many examples where the royal concerned has been quietly informed that it will not be appropriate for him to continue seeing so and so. The palace broke up Prince Andrew and Koo Stark and tried to break up Charles and Camilla. They would have succeeded, too, had the Prince of Wales not informed the powers-that-be that she was a 'non-negotiable' part of his life.

The interventions have not been limited to royals' personal lives. Sometimes it has been someone with whom a royal is involved professionally. As long ago as the 1970s, Princess Alexandra's husband the Hon. Sir Angus Ogilvy was made to resign his directorships and cease functioning as a businessman in the light of the Lonrho scandal, when that company was discovered breaking sanctions against Rhodesia.

Not even charity provides a sanctuary. Because it is deemed to be a valid professional part of a royal's life, and there are many donors who have made fortunes dubiously then tried to gain respectability by donating large sums to royal causes, the fundraising activities of royal charities, or of charities involved with the royals, are closely watched. I know of one case, which has never been made public, in which one of the most senior royals was banned from taking further sums on behalf of his primary charity from a particularly generous donor who was reputed, whether fairly or otherwise is beside the point, to have murdered two spouses. The ban extended to that individual being admitted into any royal palace in any capacity whatsoever.

Because the palace has always functioned under the premise that there are times when the *quid* simply isn't worth the *pro quo*, intervention never comes as a surprise to royals who are intent on pushing the boundaries. They know that these lines of demarcation have been drawn to preserve the integrity and reputation of the monarchy. It is rare indeed when a royal does as Prince Charles did when he refused to give up Camilla.

Meghan's colour was an advantage that gave her and Harry flexibility they would never have otherwise had. There is little doubt that there would have been behind-the-scenes manoeuvres to break up the relationship before it could lead to marriage, had she been white. The objections lay with the tales of her past which Harry referred to in his statement at the time their relationship went public, as well as Meghan's open advocacy of political causes which could politicise the apolitical character of the monarchy. There was also her unpopularity amongst the people she had crossed in the past, some of whom would inevitably come out of the woodwork if she married into the Royal Family, and brief journalists against her. But even worse than any of that were the hard-core porn tapes purporting to be Meghan Markle performing *in flagrante delicto*. I have seen the tapes. We all know that nowadays it is possible to convincingly doctor tapes so that what looks like one individual is actually two, with the head of one superimposed on the body of another. Maybe the woman in the tapes is Meghan's doppelganger. Maybe the face is Meghan's, superimposed onto someone else's body in a cynical money making exercise. Either way, there is no doubt that someone who looks exactly like Meghan is being robustly penetrated by an immense penis belonging to a stud of the first order, and that the Meghan character is groaning in a manner reminiscent of her performances in *Suits*.

The supposed Meghan's body looks very much like what we can imagine hers to be, except that the breasts are mercifully larger than the ones Meghan presents us with nowadays. This, however, did not deter her detractors, because if one examines photographs taken of her in her early twenties while she was starting out in the industry, one observes her breasts in halter necklines being much fuller towards the armpits than they are nowadays. This suggests that she might well have had her breasts augmented, then had them reduced once she became more successful, as Victoria Beckham did. Because the timeline of the sex tapes dovetails with Meghan's penurious period, doubting Thomases took comfort from the coincidences which allowed them to remain convinced.

This was anything but a desirable scenario for any respectable institution, much less a royal family. In some ways, it didn't even matter whether the tapes were authentic or fabricated: their very existence was a problem. The idea, that any member of the British Royal Family could have had a past that permitted a sex tape, real or fake, to exist, that it was out there on the internet for all to see, and that there would always be a percentage of people who believed it to be genuine even if it was not, was anathema. The one thing that kept all critics of the marriage at bay was Harry's determination to marry Meghan, no matter what.

Nevertheless, there was great concern because Meghan herself is the sort of personality who people either love or loathe. While some people, such as the Archbishop of Canterbury, and Harry himself were convinced of Meghan's sincerity, others worried that she might be an opportunist who trots out the lines that work to her advantage. Was she just too glib, too practised in the art of conveying convincing vulnerability, too adept at portraying herself as Little Ms Wonderful, for red flags not to be raised? One critic noted that her performance was uncomfortably 'like all genuine phoneys, she has perfected the art of projecting a convincing display of sincerity. That in itself would've raised hackles even if we didn't have access to all the other information' emanating from those she had crossed over the years, 'not to mention the gobbledy-gook she'd been spouting for years. Many of her statements were all the evidence we needed. Those blogs hoisted her on her own petard.' Meghan's statements about how desirable self-love was, about how you could be anything you wanted to be, about how it was okay to lie to yourself as long as you were doing it to achieve your ambitions, rang loud bells of caution. 'She's obviously never heard the maxim: A word once uttered cannot be recalled. Nor the one about never putting pen to paper. She definitely raised our hackles.'

Her avowed humanitarianism, mixed up as it was with political activism, also caused pauses for thought. The British Establishment is one of the most sophisticated in the world. Its more intelligent members are infinitely less gullible than most of their counterparts situated elsewhere. Although these people are often highly principled, their guiding light is realism. They are refreshingly free of prejudice, very up-to-date with the zeitgeist, interested in workable solutions rather than cant and hypocrisy. They know that humanitarianism is often a mask put on by hypocritical attention-seekers to disguise their true intentions as they seek to gain approbation through pretending to be more wonderful than they are. To use an example, I witnessed Sir David Eady, the senior judge of the Queen's Bench Division who used to preside over defamation cases, dismiss the attempt of a billionairess to impress him by declaring her occupation as 'philanthropist' when in fact she is known as a rampant social climber. 'Philanthropist?' he said bitingly, conveying in that withering question what he thought of her pretensions and, by implication, her character.

No one actually cared whether Meghan's humanitarianism was genuine or not, as long as she was prepared to do the job of royal consort as and when she was required to do so. But her avowed politicisation was a real worry. It could taint the Crown if she and Harry married. The British monarchy, like all the other constitutional monarchies in Europe, is resolutely apolitical. All of them appreciate that their survival depends upon absolute apoliticism; their very *raison d'* être rests upon their ability to provide society with the protection only apolitical heads of state are capable of giving against the encroachments of ambitious politicians. Privately, it is no secret that most of the royals are either extremely centrist or slightly left of centre politically. They are, in reality, liberal conservators. This has come about in the last century because reigning royal families appreciate the need for change. They desire the improvement of their citizenry's lot. However, they also appreciate that it is necessary to retain elements of the past if a society is to remain stable. Change, to be truly effective, has to be measured and gradual. The lesson learnt from revolutions has been that throwing the baby out with the bathwater renders people childless, even when it clears the bath. Meghan's advocacy of change as if it were inevitably a positive indicated a degree of naiveté which could be dangerous once she had a royal platform, for she was clearly ignorant of the destabilising aspects of change.

Insofar as anyone could tell, Meghan's political sentiments were also resolutely American. America is a young country while Britain and all the other European monarchies are ancient. In the last two centuries, European society has undergone extensive changes as all the states have democratized and some have become republics. The present-day monarchies are often more stable and meritocratic than their republican counterparts, with the result that contemporary constitutional monarchies regard themselves as not merely a form of government, but as the best form of government. In their opinion, their system of government protects the welfare of all in society, not only as a bulwark against power grabs by ambitious politicians, but also by representing all the citizens of their country irrespective of their political persuasions. Republican government only ever represents those citizens who voted for the party in power. There was concern in palace circles that Meghan was not experienced enough to appreciate the subtleties of the world she would be joining, and that Harry would not assist her in seeing the light.

In the year between the Sunday *Express* exposing Harry's relationship with Meghan and their engagement, the powers that be had been able to get what they believed to be an accurate measure of her. Although she had endeared herself to the Prince of Wales by smoothing out some of the ruffles in his relationship with Harry, and the Queen liked her because she likes anyone who is bright, vivacious and has a sense of fun such as Meghan conveyed, the feeling amongst dispassionate observers was that she might turn out to be more troublesome than they hoped. This was because she was so strong-minded, had such pronounced political bias, was so strident where silence would be desirable, and was so upfront about having to have her own way, that an air of confrontationalism followed her wherever she went. At the palace, where an atmosphere of agreeability has always been valued above any one person getting his or her own way, this made people pause for thought and question whether Hurricane Meg wouldn't be blowing down all sorts of edifices which everyone wanted to remain upstanding.

What also perturbed observers was the control Meghan exerted over Harry. Admittedly, he was happy. Indeed, both he and Meghan seemed to be flying high as they sparked each other off to ever greater heights. Their relationship also seemed to be fairly layered, with Harry strutting around playing the Alpha male protecting the hyper-feminine flower against potentially adverse elements, while she stroked his back and clucked after him like a Mother Hen with her chick. So what if she did most of the talking, and even when he wanted to make a point, she would either talk over him or finish what he was saying? She was extremely feminine while he was extremely masculine, on some level playing out the Yin and Yang almost stereotypically. But some people who were concerned about Meghan being the stronger, more intelligent and capable partner, noted that hers was the femininity of a strong and assertive matriarch, not of the obliging and docile Little Woman. They questioned, possibly unfairly, whether she wasn't too dominant for everyone's good, her own and Harry's included. 'The surprising thing was that the only person who couldn't see it was Harry,' someone who has now left the palace told me, quite missing the point that if Harry was happy to follow in Meghan's wake, the dynamic suited him.

Putting the relative strengths of the couple aside, 'She and Harry were tripping,' someone close to him told me. 'He is a very emotional guy, and she knows just what buttons to press to get him going.' While admirers felt that she was very much in tune with Harry emotionally, and managed him well, detractors felt that 'she'd slam the physical button, wrapping herself around him like bindweed, stroking his back as if she were his nanny and he a vulnerable six year old in need of reassurance. I for one felt that she was manipulating him emotionally. Undermining him by playing on his vulnerabilities. Doing so under the guise of caring for him when in fact she was really gaining power over him. The way he used to look at her when she was on the other side of the room was painful to see. He was like a puppy looking adoringly at its master. His eyes would swivel in his head as his gaze followed her around the room. But she's clever. She would be constantly reinforcing her control over him by agreeing with him, indicating how clever he was, how wonderful. Laying on the adulation with a trowel. It was pure treacle and I wonder if he would've seen through it if the sex hadn't been so good. You could tell it was fantastic. He couldn't keep his hands off her. She also touched him a lot, though I felt that she used touch as another device to control him. I got the distinct impression that she'd reward him with pats when he was good: shades of nanny. She'd also snap at him if he stepped out of line. She did it at Princess Eugenie's wedding in full view of everyone, and I've seen her do it on many other occasions. But if he moved too much out of her orbit, or was in danger of eluding her, she'd re-establish contact physically. This would have the effect of sucking him in again. There really was no escape from her. Not that he seemed to want to escape. On the contrary.'

A controlling, dominating ultra-feminine woman playing upon the masculinity and weaknesses of a handsome and vulnerable prince is one interpretation. Another is a couple so in tune with each other, so absorbed in each other, so in love with each other, that one finishes the sentences of the other because they have ceased to be two individuals and are now functioning as a unit. Certainly, Meghan had a lot of time for Harry. It didn't seem to be a sacrifice for her to be with him. Yes, he was in her thrall, and seems to have been from very shortly after they met, but like many Alpha males, he had found himself an Alpha female who was a stronger personality than he was, and he was happily enchanted by her. The fact that Meghan was also far more intelligent than him, and more worldly-wise than any prince, who has spent his whole life being cosseted by nannies, servants, private detectives, staff and courtiers, could ever be, might well have been a plus where Harry was concerned, even if critics felt it should be otherwise. Hungry for love, feeling love and believing that it was reciprocated, he was placing his fate in her hands. To those who questioned her motives, this was frightening, not only in practical terms, but in emotional ones as well, but to those who did not, their relationship was something to celebrate.

Because Harry was so far down the line of succession to the throne, no marriage of his would ever possess such importance constitutionally that it would threaten the fabric of the monarchy the way the direct heir's could. It was therefore safe to leave the problem, should there really be one, for family and friends to solve. The first person to try to try to influence Harry into taking things at a more considered pace was William. By this time, it was obvious to everyone that Harry and Meghan were hurtling at great speed towards matrimony. By their own admission, by their third date they were planning their future together and even telling each other how they would change the world together. Harry had never before shown such a predilection to make his mark on the world at large, and observers became worried that such potent headiness could lead to problems unless he took a step back and pursued the relationship at a more considered pace. These concerns would have existed even had Harry and Meghan's worldly positions been more equal, but the fact that they were not, raised a red flag. When one had so much and the other so little in comparison, the question that Meghan might be using Harry was bound to arise. But Harry himself had no such reservations. He might have been blind to the dangers of the adage, 'Marry in haste, repent at leisure', just as how I was until I found a wedding ring on my finger and a millstone around my neck, but William was only too aware of the possibilities. He tried to introduce an element of caution into Harry's reckoning, even warning his brother how their mother had always preached the virtues of longstanding relationships rather than sudden passions. Harry, however, had already burnt his bridges emotionally, and now started burning them personally as well. His response to William was aggressive, unappreciative, and resentful. He even accused him of being jealous and trying to deprive him of his right to happiness, which really was ridiculous, as William has always loved his brother and had always sought his happiness. But that still did not stop Harry from resenting his brother's intrusion and putting a wholly personal and somewhat irrational spin on his motives.

It was relatively easy for Harry to burn his bridges with William, because he was now one half of a couple who were both at one remove from everyone else. Meghan has always been one of those women who backs up her man fully, who displays loyalty so utterly that she always takes his side against everyone and everything, with the result that there were elements of an 'us against the world' posture. One only needs to look at the almost identical black and white photographs she had both husbands pose for following their weddings to see that she has a vision of her husband and herself, arms intertwined, their backs to the world, as they jointly gaze upon a distant but unseen horizon, entwined together but apart from everyone else.

This 'us against the world' attitude has powerful appeal to men who want to shelter and protect the woman with whom he is involved, which is why Alpha males are ideal partners for women who want to be protected. And Meghan is undoubtedly a woman who wants to be protected. Such a dynamic has great appeal for the couple involved, but it can trigger concern in loved ones, especially as how there are elements which can be evocative of paranoia. As the couple becomes increasingly detached from the world around them and they become more and more intertwined with each other, loved ones can begin to feel that they are becoming unhealthily wrapped up in each other. The couple might then become hyper-sensitive to what seems to them to be attacks upon their relationship, but are in fact mere attempts to maintain a healthy equilibrium, which is what happened when William tried to get Harry to take things more slowly.

No one likes to lose a loved one to a burgeoning romance which has exclusionary overtones. It is therefore understandable that William would have been concerned that he was in danger of losing the brother he loved, as indeed he did. While cynics may take the view that Meghan set out to detach Harry from his family and friends, Harry was always going to be susceptible to a powerful, dominant woman because he was the Mama's boy of just such a woman. For all her warmth and affection, Diana was obsessively jealous, possessive and dominating. She was also a very strong personality. Like Meghan, she appeared to be soft and sweet and vulnerable when in fact she was all of those things as well as all of their opposites. She could be charming, captivating, and fun, just like Meghan. In fact, there were so many similarities between the two women's characters, personalities, *modus operandi* and performance, that it was almost inevitable that Harry would quickly and irrevocably fall under Meghan's spell. There is nothing more appealing to a Mama's boy than a woman who is like his mother. It is said that most men marry their mothers, and while I would dispute the accuracy of such a blanket statement, the truism is that men who love their mothers gravitate towards women who are like their mothers. They are the most devoted of spouses, because there are few things more potent that a man replicating his mother in adulthood.

To understand Meghan's hold over Harry, and why he was so eager to place his fate in her hands, one has to appreciate how his mother primed him for just such a woman. Diana was a very contradictory personality. For every virtue, there was a corresponding vice. She could be warm and kind and natural and affectionate then, when she wanted to turn, she would be cruel, cold, and vengeful. She was extremely manipulative and definitely did not hold by the maxim that 'charity starts at home.' She frequently cut out friends and family for little or no reason then, if it suited her, picked them up back again as if they were a toy. As a child, she had been badly damaged emotionally by her parents' divorce. It left the most dreadful imprint upon her, and was responsible for much of the misery that dogged her into adulthood.

According to people who know her well, Meghan displays many of Diana's personality traits. This includes the positive ones as well as the negative. Diana isolated Charles from all his friends in the early days of their marriage, and Meghan was already shaping up to be the sort of person who would be so engaging that Harry had little time, energy or desire for anyone else. Meghan never forgives nor forgets a slight, real or imagined, which was classic Diana, and, like the mother-in-law she never knew, when she decided to charm, she would charm, but when she decided to discard, she would drop someone as if they were a leper in Biblical times. Being as powerful a personality as she is, she also has the ability, whether she wishes to or not, to instil real fear in men who fall in love with her. If they are anything less than completely enthusiastic about providing her with the response she requires, she will let them know that they were letting her down. In a variety of ways, the mature, post-Trevor Meghan has made her men aware that they'd better give her what she wants if they want to keep her. Trevor's failure to give her the breaks she wanted from him taught her never to 'sell herself short again', as she told a friend. In Meghan's scheme of things, couples are meant to fulfill each other's requirements. Her talent ever since the collapse of her first marriage has been to make them want to, or, as Harry put it, 'what Meghan wants, Meghan gets'.

The psychotherapist Basil Panzer once said that men are much more fascinated by women who challenge them than those who don't. They think they want all sweetness and light, but in reality what they want is some of that and being kept on their toes at the same time. Meghan, like Diana, learnt the art of variable reinforcement. In common with her mother-in-law, Meghan also possessed a cold fury when she did not get her way that made it impossible for others to disagree with her and maintain a pleasant relationship in which adults agree to disagree, while also maintaining a healthy degree of personal autonomy. Those who did not please her were in danger of losing her, which could create a terror of losing her in people - not only men but parents and friends as well - with whom she was involved.

Although Diana could equally instil the terror of loss in those with whom she was involved, hers was anything but a cool technique. She used to get so caught up in her own emotions that she would have to disentangle herself before she could detach herself from someone. This meant that Diana's relationships seldom ended without a bang, while Meghan, who was far more self-possessed, had perfected the art of terminating hers so silently that there wasn't even a whimper when she dropped the axe. Yet the parallels between the two women's *modus operandi* were so pronounced that onlookers feared that Harry, familiar since childhood to the terrible consequences of going against his mother's will, had been so primed that Meghan has been able to obtain a hold over him that has made her power invincible. Whether that is a fair assessment only time will tell, but what is undoubtedly certain is that Meghan is the dominant partner in their union, and she tolerates no threats from any quarter.

A case in point was Harry's reaction to William's suggestion that he should take things at a more measured pace. His reaction had been so adverse that the brothers fell out in a wholly unnecessary way. Catherine was caught up in the crossfire. Meghan could now appeal to Harry's protective instincts as she capitalised upon the family's reservations about the speed with which the relationship was hurtling towards permanence, detaching him further from his old support network. Rather than loosening Harry's connection to Meghan, William's intervention had tightened it. In doing so, Meghan's influence over Harry had increased. This caused concern not only within the family but amongst the courtiers, all of whom only wanted a marriage if it would work, but were nervous of one that might not. Then Harry brought things to a head by asking to see his grandparents and told them that he wished to marry Meghan.

Any family, confronted with the possibility of a union which had the hallmarks of becoming problematic, would try to delay the ultimate commitment in the hope that time might bring insight and it would collapse under the weight of its unsuitability if that turned out to be the case. Both the Queen and Prince Philip had a good relationship with Harry. Philip is known within royal circles for being an accommodating pragmatist who will always try to find a way that reconciles royal duty with personal urges. In his eyes, there would be no better outcome than Harry and Meghan pursuing their relationship without matrimony until all the doubts were cleared up. And if they were not, Harry could still remain with Meghan, but without the ultimate commitment.

Harry knew that his grandfather was of a generation and persuasion in which marriage was not only about personal fulfilment but also about dynastic obligation. In the past, paramours had been people's private business. A man could sleep with whomever he pleased, but marriage was another matter entirely. Issues such as duty to the nation and the family, as well as suitability, must be factored into any marital equation, and if you could not guarantee a positive outcome, you must resist the urge to marry. History was littered with awful warnings, such as the marriage of Prince Philip's cousin Princess Ena of Battenberg to King Alfonso XIII of Spain, which ended in predictable misery and helped to undermine the Spanish Crown. But when a man gets the bit between his teeth, and wants to marry a woman, caution doesn't always prevail.

It has been widely, and I gather accurately, reported that, when Harry brought up the subject of marriage to his grandparents, Prince Philip, already up-to-speed about why Meghan Markle would find it impossible to fit into the role of royal duchess without a personality transplant, pointed out to him that 'we step out with actresses; we don't marry them.' This was not snobbishness on his part. The qualities that make an actress successful are the absolute opposite of those which make a good royal duchess, and there was no doubt in his mind that it would be unfair to both Meghan and the monarchy to expect her to fulfill a lifetime of royal duty with a fully developed personality at odds with the requirements of the royal role.

What has not been reported is the remainder of the conversation, which came to me via two different sources, one a close friend of the Queen, another a prince. Harry, desperately in love with Meghan and willing to do anything to keep her, discounted his grandfather's suggestion with the intensity of an addict being threatened with deprivation. He informed his grandfather that he would be marrying Meghan no matter what.

In fairness to Harry, Meghan also wanted to marry him. She had also closed her eyes and ears to all warnings, such as given by Gina Nelthorpe-Cowne, about why she would find it impossible to make the adjustment from television actress to royal duchess. No one had actually envisaged a scenario in which she could marry Harry and, rather than adjust to her new situation, she would convince him to create a new one that suited her better, by abdicating their royal roles. So the three participants to the conversation had imagined only one possibility, namely Meghan adjusting to the royal role, when in fact there existed an alternative, Meghan and Harry abandoning their royal roles and inventing new ones for themselves.

A material fact in agreeing to the marriage was Harry's place in the line of succession. Harry, the Queen and Prince Philip were aware that he would shortly be slipping down to sixth place once the Duchess of Cambridge's third child, due in April 2018, was born. This position was crucial, for, following the repeal of the Royal Marriages Act of 1772, which was replaced with the 2013 Succession to the Crown Act, Harry was peripheral in the true meaning of the word. The likelihood of his succeeding to the throne was now so remote that withholding permission for any marriage, even one which might be problematic, would seem like an act of spite, or worse, prejudice.

The Queen likes consensus and is always extremely well briefed as to what is going on in the world as well as within her own family, so when Philip's interdict raised the temperature, Elizabeth II intervened with the intention of lowering it. Harry did not even let her finish what she saying. He cut her off mid-sentence with the imprecation that he was 'going to marry her and if you don't like it, you'll just have to suck it up.' The Queen had never heard the expression before, nor indeed had I until the conversation was recounted to me, but I fully identified with her comment that 'I didn't need any explanation as to what it meant. As soon as I heard it, I knew.'

That, however, was not the end of the matter. The prince who recounted the conversation to me said that Harry then issued the *coup de grace* by telling his grandparents that they would be accused of racism unless they agreed to the marriage. Of course, Harry knew only too well that Meghan's race was not a negative to the family, but a positive. But the public would not know that, so this was his ace in the hole. Faced with what the Queen's grandmother Queen Mary called 'a fine kettle of fish', Elizabeth II and Prince Philip had no option but to give way to their determined grandson. 'We all only hope to God it doesn't turn out to be the catastrophe everyone fears it will be,' the prince said.'

The family's great fear was that, aside from Meghan's unsuitability for the royal role, she loved what she could achieve as a result of being Harry's wife, and that, rather than love of him, was her motivation. Although they hoped that their doubts were unfounded, her track record made them unsure, which was unfortunate, for they had been sure that Catherine loved William and Sophie Wessex loved Prince Edward. They hoped that with time their fears would be dissipated.

Ironically, the one unexpurgated consolation, acknowledged by everyone within the family and at the palace, was Meghan's bi-racial identity. It was the single most important aspect of her identity that overrode all the reservations created by her dominating personality, political inclinations, and past conduct which had generated such mixed reports. As the prince told me, 'Had Meghan not been a woman of colour, they would never have allowed the marriage. It was the only thing that was unreservedly in her favour.' It reinforced the diversity of British society and was viewed as an updated version of Queen Elizabeth's statement when the Germans bombed Buckingham Palace during the war: 'I'm glad; now I feel I can look the East End in the face.'

With the die cast by Harry's determination, everyone tried to be positive. Meghan definitely had many virtues. She was beautiful, stylish, vivacious. She was bright and energetic. She had a good work ethic. She was good company if you agreed with her. She had set out to charm Charles and the Queen, and to an extent she had succeeded. Everyone hoped that such misgivings as had arisen would be laid to rest when she became a member of the Royal Family. 'The Queen and Prince Charles were particularly delighted with her virtues, not the least of which was her colour,' a European royal told me.

To show how welcome Meghan was, the Queen even included her in the Sandringham Christmas house party in 2019. Although everyone did their utmost to make her feel welcome, although she responded with the charm and grace which she possesses when she wishes to respond positively, there was nevertheless an undercurrent emanating from her that some people picked up as disdain or disapproval. One of the British royals told a European counterpart that she made it clear that she disapproved of hunting and shooting and would therefore not be hanging around to participate in the traditional Boxing Day shoot. 'I suppose it's to her credit that she has the strength of her convictions, but what worries me is this: Why can't she be like my cousin's wife, who would sooner die than kill a fly? She doesn't make a point of disapproving of us. She has her ways and we have ours. We all rub along happily despite our differences of opinion. I'm just worried that someone who is so dogmatic that she makes it clear that hers are the only opinions worth having isn't going to fit into our world, or indeed, into any world at all where anyone disagrees with her. What gets me is the underlying disrespect she seems to have for anyone who doesn't agree with her. I hope I'm wrong, but I can't shake the feeling that young Harry's picked up a right little madame. I only hope Havoc isn't her middle name.'

Havoc comes in many forms and is precipitated by many things and, in the run-up to the wedding, the white side of Meghan's family proved a rich hunting ground for the British tabloids. The black side of the family was deemed to be off limits, not through any humanitarian sentiments, but because the British public would have attacked the press for being racist. But the Markle family was seen as rich pickings, to be got at at every turn. Tom Jr, Samantha, Tyler and his mother Tracey were all made to look ridiculous, their every action picked to pieces as the tabloids competed with each other to relate how un-English, how working-people American they were. What hicks. There really was no excuse for such conduct. It was unedifying and unconstructive, but the price you sometimes have to pay for a free press is injured feelings. These are infinitely preferable to politicians who can't be called to order owing to a toothless tiger which has lost the ability to inflict damage when it bites, but that did not help the unfortunate Markle family. All of them were pilloried in varying degrees, very occasionally with some merit, but largely without any whatsoever.

Embarrassing though the Markles found the way they were being represented in the British tabloids, it was nothing compared with the way they now started to portray Tom Sr. He has rightly stated that they made him look like a slob, like white trash, like a drunkard. They hounded him day and night for the six months from the announcement of his daughter's marriage until the week before the wedding, when he fell out of view following his heart attacks. Tom Sr has spoken on television about how embarrassing it was to be made to look like a dolt in front of the whole world.

From morning till night, his every action was observed, his ever movement commented upon and decried. Harry and Meghan's advice to him was as impractical as it was impersonal. 'Don't talk to the press at all,' they said. When, at the beginning of the couple's romance, Doria had been given the merest hint of what Tom Sr had been having to endure for months, Harry had waded in, specifically complaining about the tabloids' treatment of his future mother-in-law. Now that his father-in-law to be was being dished up an even more intensive dose of the same poison, he was left to fend for himself with what was really ineffectual, even silly, advice. If they did not realise how unrealistic it was to tell him not to talk to the press when every day his every action was dogged by them, they should have. If you are a man on your own, living in a house in the middle of a populous town, you are exposed as you come and go on a daily basis. You can't stay holed up like a bear in its den. Whether you want to be or not, you are accessible. Even if you don't speak to the press, they will still follow you, photograph you, and make you look ridiculous if that is their intention. Which it clearly was, even when he did something as innocent as shop for food in his local supermarket.

Harry and Meghan seemed to have no empathy for the mortification Tom was facing as he was portrayed on a daily basis in the most unflattering light. They could have hired a media advisor to run interference for him. They should also have done the same for Samantha and Tom Jr. Such basic consideration would have been humane as well as clever, for it would have assured Meghan of positive responses from her relations and the negativity which emanated from her spurned relations would not have existed. Instead, she and Harry decided to blank out what was happening, which was somewhat perplexing. Harry had always had such sympathy for his mother's plight, despite the fact that she usually tipped off her supposed pursuers, and had also expressed concern when Doria was subjected to undue attention, but Tom Sr was given neither support not consideration beyond the repetition of empty platitudes.

To the embarrassment of the palace and the astonishment of the public, 'the Markle debacle', as it was soon called, intensified as the wedding date approached. It could not have been more obvious that Meghan's family was unsophisticated with regard to the press, but why would they have been otherwise? They were not public figures, nor were they aristocrats or royalty. They were simply American working people, and if they were looked at askance in America, they would soon gain admirers in Britain for what was regarded as their forthright and unpretentious honesty.

Nevertheless, the situation as it developed became increasingly embarrassing for all the Markles, who were held up to ridicule, the tabloids feeling that they were fair game for mockery as the message Meghan had given out was that they were such undesirables that they couldn't even be included in her wedding. Tom Sr's response was to fall for the line of a journalist who suggested that they stage photographs of him pursuing more upmarket activities than the resolutely downmarket ones he had so far been pictured enacting. Instead of buying beer in his local deli, he should be measured for a suit, should be looking at computer images of his daughter and her fiancé, and what about doing gentle exercises while jogging up a hill with weights in his hands? Tom Sr was undoubtedly naive in thinking that such activities would improve his image, or that other journalists wouldn't find out what he and one of their colleagues had cooked up between themselves, but who can blame someone who is being pilloried for trying to regain a bit of dignity?

The week before the wedding, his unfortunate attempt to divert the narrative into something more presentable was exposed in the *Mail on Sunday*. Stripping him of whatever remained of his self-respect, the paper revealed that he had cooperated with a paparazzo, staging photographs for a vast sum of money, which was not accurate. The tabloids being the tabloids, exaggeration was the order of the day. Tom's humiliation was so complete that he not only had a heart attack, but also offered to withdraw from the wedding.

To their credit, Meghan and Harry declined his offer, and insisted he fly over and give her away. However, they lost patience with him when he had his second heart attack shortly after being released from hospital in Mexico following his first. Meghan stopped speaking to him, while Harry berated him by text. Tom told them that he suspected they were really sorry he hadn't died, so that they could pretend to be sad and not have to bother with him. Their response was a complete lack of response to him and to all subsequent messages and 'phone calls from him.

The palace's worst nightmare, at least until Meghan and Harry bolted, had now begun in earnest.

CHAPTER 6

To the hundreds of millions of people who watched Harry and Meghan marry at St. George's Chapel on the 19th of May 2016, theirs was a fairy tale come true. The bride looked so beautiful, so demure, so modest, so radiant, while the groom seemed so happy, so handsome, so proud. She was the apex of femininity, he of masculinity. Theirs was not merely a love story, but one with a message, the most important part of which was that the glass ceiling had now been removed for people of colour. The formerly marginalised could now aspire to anything. One of their own had achieved the greatest height apart from the presidency of the United States of America. She was now a royal highness, and not just any old royal highness either, but a fully paid up member of the most prestigious family on earth: the British Royal Family.

Meghan had now become the embodiment of hope and accomplishment for people all over the world, a beacon of light for billions who could thereafter look at her and think: If she could achieve this, maybe my children can scale great heights, even if I can't. Meghan had reached a pinnacle that no other woman of colour ever had before. It was, by any measure, a tremendous accomplishment. It was also a great responsibility, and those of us who were aware of how many people's hopes were vested in her, hoped and prayed she would have the attributes to live up to it.

The American entertainer Pharrell Williams summed it up well when he told Meghan and Harry, 'I'm so happy for your union. Love is amazing. Love is beautiful. Don't ever take it for granted. But what it means in today's climate, I just wanted to tell you it's so significant for so many of us. Seriously. We cheer you guys on.'

Harry and Meghan's response was indicative of their attitudes. While she nodded graciously, completely in tune with the sentiments, she said, 'Oh, thank you,' before stating that her critics 'don't make it easy.' She had missed the point entirely, which is that she now had a sacred duty to live up to, and no matter how difficult it was, she would be dashing the hopes people everywhere if she should fail. It was therefore beside the point whether her critics made it easy or not. Indeed, the mere fact that they did not was all the more reason to ensure that she succeeded in the role she now embodied.

Of course, it is not easy to live up to the expectations of others. Being royal is in many ways a thankless task, rather like being a secular nun, albeit one who is called upon to be a style icon. The personal rewards are there, but not in the emotional way that Meghan was used to either as a volunteer serving in soup kitchens or in the applause she would receive from a good performance in front of the camera or an audience at the UN. There is a very self-sacrificial aspect which is never entirely offset by the superficial glamour surrounding the high-profile aspects of royal life. Meghan was something of an expert on Diana, Princess of Wales. She will therefore have been familiar with Diana's complaint to Princess Grace of Monaco on the occasion of her first official engagement with Prince Charles at the Royal Opera House, Covent Garden. As Diana bemoaned how 'horrendous' she was finding all the public attention - attention, incidentally, which she ensured she maintained till the very end of her life: attention, in fact, which actively contributed to her death in that it could not have existed without the participation of the press, and this Diana was careful to nurture despite her protestations to the contrary - Grace said with equal parts of wit and truthfulness, 'Don't worry, dear. It will only get worse.' And it did, though it never got so bad, for all Diana's complaints to the contrary, that she swapped the approbation that came her way as a result of being the Princess of Wales, for a more retired way of life.

Plainly, Meghan was taking a leaf out of Diana's book, resenting the demands and intrusions while contradictorily fulfilling the glamorous aspects the press and public demanded of their new style icon. Like Diana, who was also very in tune with her feelings, Meghan had conflicting attitudes to the pros and cons of being royal. Had she had a more open and less personal approach towards her new role of royal duchess, had she focused less on the sensations it generated within her and accepted the rough with the smooth in a more comprehensive manner, she would have been entirely in tune with what Pharrell Williams was saying. She would have realised that when the going gets tough, the tough get going - towards success, not towards complaints or self-pity. One way or the other, you are obliged to pay for your privileges, and though the downside was disagreeable, the upside should have been well worth the effort, especially if she hoped to undertake the massive humanitarian role she and Harry had indicated they intended for themselves.

Meghan's adjustment to her royal role would have been more successful if someone close to her had pointed out that she had been perfectly happy to pay the price for being a cast member of *Suits*, and now that she had an even bigger role, with greater potential and more rewards, she should be focusing on the positives rather than wallowing in the negatives and jeopardising her chances of success as a result of her attitude. She had had no problem with keeping her feelings in their rightful place when she had been a working actress. She had willingly hung around the set waiting for her three minutes of filming while she shot the breeze with the film crew for hours on end. She had not objected to the hours of primping and priming when her hair and makeup were being done, when her costumes were being fitted, and she hung out affirming her status as a down-to-earth team player with the crew. She had willingly allowed herself to be used on publicity junkets and, when none was in the offing, had volunteered for others under the aegis of humanitarian work. Now she had well and truly arrived. Now she had the platform from which she could undertake all the philanthropic projects which had seemed to inspire her, and it was disappointing to learn that she seemed unable to realise that there was still a price to be paid.

In some ways, being royal was not that different from being an actress in a television series. Yes, there were differences. There was more scrutiny and you were expected to conform to entirely different standards, but if she had moved on to playing another role in another television show, she would not have expected, now that she had a new role, to call all the shots with scriptwriters, producers, directors, gaffers, cameramen, and everyone else associated with the new show the way she had been doing with everyone at court.

Having moved up in the world from minor to major stardom, her head seemed to have been turned and her sense of proportion displaced. Diana Wales had suffered a similar fate when she had married Prince Charles, but she had been half Meghan's age and she at least had had the good grace to keep her struggles quiet until she was ready to bolt. Yet here was Meghan, barely married, already bemoaning her lot and wanting to be taken for a hardship case while also demanding that everyone do everything her way.

Success as a royal duchess was only possible if she remained a team player, if she understood that the game had changed, that she had a new role and a part to play, but that there were still boundaries, and in this bigger, much expanded role, the approbation she yearned for she would receive only if she understood that it would take an entirely new form from what she was used to. She couldn't expect emotional gratification the way she had got it from the crew or cast of the show, or even from the occasional reviewer. She would have to settle for an entirely different sort of gratification, this time a more intellectualised, spiritual version that would be less obvious but no less real or significant. The hyper-emotional interchanges upon which she had relied had to be a thing of the past. Instead of twenty indigents or a camera crew, she would be interacting with tens and hundreds of thousands of people on an annual basis, some for no more than thirty or fifty seconds, others for only a matter of minutes, and all within a more formalised, less emotive setting. There would seldom be the opportunity for people to express the approbation they felt, for the life of a royal on public duty is so transient, so busy, the interactions with people so fleeting, that there simply is not time to get feedback the way she was used to from the lightning engineer or the cameraman with whom she had interacted on a daily basis for hours on end on set. However, if she gave herself the chance, with time she would come to appreciate that there was feedback: it was simply more subtle. But the rewards nevertheless existed, and they were profound.

There was also the issue of discipline and control, and here the balance was radically different from what she had been used to. Had Meghan and Harry exercised the patience and diplomacy that his grandparents the Queen and Prince Philip did at the time of the accession, laying down their imprimatur slowly and cautiously rather than stating, as Meghan did, that she intended to 'hit the ground running' upon marriage - thereby conveying the message that everybody had better watch out, as the new broom intended to sweep clean - she would have received a more positive response.

Meghan was used to a structure on the *Suits* set whereby she could interact with the producers, directors, and script writers. Prior to that show, she had had very little luck in influencing anyone to expand her role, but, by her own account, on it she had had so much success that she had got them to tone down the sex scenes and build her character up into something even more potent than the powerhouse they had originally envisaged Rachel Zane as being.

Royalty has a different structure. The courtiers organise and advise. The royals perform, but do so within well-defined boundaries. Royalty is an ensemble act. Each player exists to enhance the Crown. The monarch is the chief player. The importance of each player thereafter is determined by their proximity to the throne. After the monarch comes the immediate heir. After him comes the next heir in line, and so on down the scales of precedence. If you are the sixth dancer in the chorus line and you are supposed to kick after number five and before number seven, you screw up the whole routine if you do so out of time. In royal families as in Broadway shows, each player needs to know his or her place. If you break ranks, you are damaging the show. You are especially destructive if you break ranks in such a way that you make it clear to the audience that you are a better player than all the other members of the ensemble. In doing so, you are not only boosting yourself at the expense of the whole show, but you are also showing up the other players adversely.

Since the whole purpose of a royal family is to represent its nation as a whole, there is only ever one game in town for each royal family. An undisciplined and destructive ensemble player who breaks rank will therefore ultimately be nothing but a force for destructiveness where the royal family is concerned. And the idea of setting up your own dance routine, separate from the one everyone expects to see, was so beyond all comprehension that no one conjured it up as a possibility. With the exception of Meghan, who plainly had contemplated just such an eventuality, for why else would she have failed to disband her Hollywood team when she got married?

It was against this backdrop that the wedding took place. Behind the scenes, it was a massive relief that the day itself went off as well as it did. Aside from the unfortunate publicity involving Meghan's father and the rest of the Markle family, her own conduct and that of Harry in the run-up had created fear rather than comfort. With his backing, she had demanded control of the wedding, notwithstanding neither of them having any financial responsibility for it and despite her being a newcomer to the royal scene and him acting as if she should be allowed to break every existing precedent and rule. Meghan had never been disruptive or disrespectful of the parameters laid down by the producers of *Suits* to ensure that it was a success. She had been happy to fit herself into that scheme of things. Yes, she was known to have been demanding and challenging, to push for better lines for herself, to want to expand her character, but all of this had been done in a professionally respectful way. If she could understand and respect those parameters, why would she and Harry seek to disrespect and disregard the parameters of the royal world?

It was no secret in royal circles that Diana had been a maverick who had often not only disrespected but also denigrated the royal world, despite it being her platform for greatness. Harry had also from time to time shown himself to be inclined to kick over the traces, quite mindless of the fact that he was rebelling against was the very thing that gave him any degree of greatness that he possessed. Could it be that the combination of Meghan and Harry, with his emotional issues and maternal heritage, and her dominating and exacting nature, might result in a challenge to the very way the monarchy expected the royals to conduct themselves?

As far as everyone in the royal circle was concerned, Meghan and Harry's demands to be allowed to do as they pleased without very much regard for past practices did not bode well for an easy adjustment for Meghan as an individual or for them as a couple. In royal and aristo-cratic circles as in any other establishment, newcomers are expected to have some respect for the values and traditions of the world they are joining. This would be so whether the establishment is a company, a law firm, a television series, or anything else. Newcomers are not expected to demand fundamental changes to the lifestyle until they have had time to adjust to it and see what suits them. Everyone has quibbles over certain things, and is given latitude to ignore minor rules that are not fundamental to the existence of the institution, but the idea that someone at entry level will impose a new way of doing things on an old order is unthinkable. The idea that an establishment figure like Harry would consider it acceptable to expect everyone to fall into line as he and a newcomer like Meghan flouted tradition at every turn would never have entered into anyone's head until it happened,, and when it did, it received the expected reaction. This is because there was a genuine conviction that the values adhered to in a royal or aristocratic lifestyle are laden with wisdom gleamed over hundreds and sometimes a thousand years of trial and error. The British actor Larry Lamb once observed to me and the late Elizabeth Steuart Fothringham, the chatelaine of two stately homes in Scotland, 'There seems to be a rule or at least a guideline for everything in your lives, but I've come to realise that a lot of it makes sense. It's the wisdom of the ages. Even the way you drink soup is practical. You scoop it up away from yourselves unlike all of us, but that's so, if it spills, it doesn't spill on you. I bet you've never realised how clever little things like that are.'

Aside from the practicality of many of the modes of behaviour, there is also the underlying code of conduct in which duty, honour, reliability, decency and all the other sterling virtues are living concepts to which one is expected to aspire. Nobility is not just a matter of rank, but a way of being, which is why one of the biggest insults in elite circles is to accuse someone of not knowing how to behave.

It therefore came as something of a surprise for Meghan to indicate, with Harry's full backing, to many of the people she was now associating with, that she regarded their way of life, their values and their codes of conduct as way beneath hers. 'She almost spelled it out that she was here to rescue us from our pathetic way of doing things,' a courtier said. 'She is so breathtakingly sure of being in the right at all times that she is beyond arrogant. I've never seen anyone in my life so entirely lacking in self-doubt. She is so upfront about it that she is beyond shameless. She walks into a room, takes over, tells everyone how she wants things to be, and sashays out expecting everyone to fulfill her demands. She is beyond dominance, beyond being a dominatrix. She fancies herself a force of nature, and a perfect one at that.' And Harry considers her perfect.

One of the royals bore this out, stating, 'She is so self-confident it's frightening. I used to think Queen Elizabeth (the Queen Mother) was the most self-confident person I'd ever encountered. Meghan puts her in the shade.'

It is here that we see the line going back into previous generations. Meghan is not the first of the powerful personalities to have been absorbed into the British Royal Family. The Queen Mother was the first. Admitted into the family as the Duchess of York in 1923, she was such a force of nature, so determined and strong-willed, so wily and effective an operator, that even Hitler felt compelled to describe her as 'the most dangerous woman in Europe'. Her husband Bertie, better known to history as King George VI, was as besotted with and entranced by her as his brother David, then Prince of Wales and afterwards King Edward VIII and Duke of Windsor, was by Wallis Warfield Simpson. I knew the Duchess of Windsor slightly, but will save my comments regarding her for later. Suffice it to say that Meghan and Harry are continuing a long tradition of powerful women captivating the House of Windsor's princes, many of whom seem to have a susceptibility for placing their fate in the hands of these women, each of whom has been treated as the Delphic Oracle by her prince. All three were frankly ambitious, but only two of them actually ended up getting what she wanted, the third living out her worst nightmare.

With hindsight, it is obvious that Meghan had an agenda where her wedding was concerned. She wanted it to be the most beautiful and glamorous occasion. It must be the perfect setting for her introduction to the world at large. It would establish her as a beautiful, desirable, 'classy' woman of style and taste, as someone who had everything, every virtue, from superficial style and beauty to profound depth of character. She was a jewel that the Royal Family was lucky to have in its Crown and the world must see this. She did not want any of her family, with the exception of her parents, there. She wanted none of them or her oldest friends raining on her parade. She was flying high and didn't want too many links with the past she had left behind. Then, she had been an ordinary girl on the make. Now, she had made it. She was now an extraordinary woman, and one moreover who conveyed the message that she was full, complete, and as perfect as it was possible to be. This was the beginning of a new life, a glorious life, a life where she would enjoy the approbation she had sought all her life and had been gaining in increasing measure for the past seven years. Her wedding was also an opportunity to cultivate people she'd barely met but who were potentially useful in the future, such as Oprah Winfrey. She would hereafter be an A-Lister, and she intended to reinforce her status by having real A-Listers such as George and Amal Clooney there, notwithstanding knowing them only slightly.

By Meghan's own account, she is supremely aspirational. Quite how so still remains to be seen, though the past two years have shown that she is a woman of boundless ambition and vision. 'No one actually realised just how ambitious she is, nor how financially-driven,' a royal cousin told me. However, once she and Harry announced that they were retiring from royal life to make their fortune financially, it became clear that being a senior royal, having one of the most eminent positions on earth, was not sufficient for her. It was too limiting, and rather than adjust herself to it, she had decided to have it adjust to her. In doing so she demonstrated to what extent she is a true game changer. This is something which her admirers applaud, and ironically, one of the people who have been most supportive of her has been the Queen. Elizabeth II and Philip were, in their day, game changers too, but they did it in such a way that they did not rock the royal boat. The Queen still hopes that Meghan and Harry's float into the future will allow them to function in such a way that they make their way without damaging their royal heritage while creating a new way of being from which future generations of spares might benefit.

Although Meghan and Harry emphasised when departing from the Royal Family that their goal was financial independence, not everyone thinks that her ambition is limited to lining her pockets to the full extent of her capacity. 'I've heard that she intends, down the line, to run for President of the United States,' one of Harry's old friends told me. 'I believe she's using [her royal status] to improve her chances. Let's see if she achieves her objective.'

Long before the public knew that Meghan was encouraging Harry to step back from his royal role, she was laying the ground for them to do so. She did it in a variety of ways, one of which was to convey the message to everyone with whom she came into contact that she had no awe for the monarchy. As his friend said, 'One thing's for sure. She's never had any respect for the institution she married into. From the word go, it was obvious that she felt she knew better than we did, and could enlighten all us poor slobs in how we should be living our lives.'

While Meghan's supporters will consider it admirable that she could be so rock-solid in her beliefs and attitudes that she remained unmoved and unimpressed by her inclusion into the world's most eminent family, those who crossed paths with her were astonished by what they took to be disrespect for themselves. Her conduct in the run-up to her marriage was an illustration. From the outset, she bucked royal tradition with the full backing of Harry, who went around saying, 'What Meghan wants, Meghan gets.' There were incidents such as Meghan reducing Catherine Cambridge to tears over Charlotte's dress; Meghan virtually calling a member of staff a liar when the woman was patently telling the truth (which resulted in Meghan being advised that royals do not speak to staff like that); and the kerfuffle over the supposed mustiness of St. George's Chapel, which had resulted in Meghan being blocked from spraying scent all over the ancient chapel so that it would smell like the ladies' room at Soho House.

I have attended many events at St. George's Chapel over the years, including Prince William's Induction as a Knight of the Garter. I can tell you, it has the reassuring bouquet of the ancient, well-tended and clean chapel that it is. The pews glow with the patina of centuries of beeswax, which also gives off a subtle but delightful fragrance. This was clearly anathema to someone as 'classy' as Meghan, who by this time was viewed by her followers as not only the Petronius Arbiter of 'classiness' but as its quintessential embodiment. Despite having had some exposure to what passes for antiques in America by way of her grandfather's antique shop, Meghan was still not *au fait* with an older way of life, so would not have known that what passes for antique in America, i.e. something older than 75 years, is almost new in Europe. She would not have been familiar with the aroma of furniture well-polished over centuries. Rather than recognising the appealing fragrance of a well-tended building like St. George's Chapel, she found the scent alien and therefore off-putting.

People do not enjoy a newcomer telling them, in word or deed, that their way is not as good as the newcomer's. This causes especial offence when the recipient of the criticism believes that his way is the better one and moreover has proof of that fact in the thousands of compliments he has received over the decades from compatriots of the critic which run absolutely contrary to the critic's criticism. Since Meghan was accusing the chapel of malodorousness when it is often praised for its subtle and ancient scent, this caused offence. It also resulted in many people at Windsor coming to the conclusion that she had a lot to learn and Harry would be wise to inform her of that fact instead of acting as if everyone else was ignorant but the two of them. A good starting point, in their view, would have been the couple understanding how limited her knowledge of their world was. Instead, she was so supremely self-confident that she gave the impression of being a disdainful know-it-all.

And where the wedding was concerned, she knew exactly what she wanted, and they both intended that she get it.

'Harry and Meghan were throwing their weight around in the most extraordinary fashion,' a royal said. 'Their conduct did not bode well for the future.'

'It's our wedding and we want it done our way,' Meghan said, but since Harry had little or no input beyond repeating the mantra, 'What Meghan wants, Meghan gets,' no one was deceived into thinking that her use of the plural first person pronoun meant anything but the singular. The invitation list was the first of the many traditions that were jettisoned at Meghan's command with Harry's full backing. Hundreds of people associated with charities were invited, which ratified their credentials as humanitarians who think in terms of charity. They also weighted the list heavily in favour of every celebrity she had ever crossed paths with and was still speaking to. Some she had barely met, others only two or three times, but she and Harry asked them all and they all came, adding glamour to the occasion while embarking on what Andrew Morton observed was a clever career move, for once they had been asked, they were thereafter in the couple's debt.

Marrying into the British Royal Family was not an everyday occurrence. It was a once-in-a-lifetime occasion. For Meghan's family, it was more than that: it was a source of great pride that had turned into worldwide humiliation. Prince Philip especially understood how painful it is when relations are not asked. His three sisters had been excluded from his own wedding because their husbands had been German officers during the war, which had ended only two years before his wedding. This had caused him pain and Princess Gottfried von Hohenlohe-Langenburg, the Margravine of Baden, and Princess George of Hanover tremendous embarrassment. Meghan and Harry, however, were indifferent to the effect of their actions upon her family. As far as they were concerned, she had a new family, one which he was now gravitating towards. This was not the royals, who by this time they were already resiling away from despite Harry's comment over the radio that she had bonded so well with his relations that they were substitutes for the family she had never had. No, this new family was the many showbiz or celebrity-related representatives from a life which seemed to have begun, with few exceptions, only after Meghan had gained her role in *Suits*. This new family included what Meghan and Harry called her *Suits* 'family', all of whom were out in force at the wedding, as well as friends like Jessica Mulroney, Markus Anderson, Oprah Winfrey, Gayle King, and Amal and George Clooney.

To everyone at the palace, Harry and Meghan's management of the invitation list seemed inappropriate as well as dangerous. Royal and aristocratic weddings are not occasions for the bride and groom to ratify their humanitarian credentials before the eyes of the world or to include celebrities who are actually thrilled to be admitted to royal circles and are not ordinarily asked to such family occasions but to other, less personal, events, like premieres and parties. Weddings are meant to be celebrations of union, with all branches of the bride's and groom's families being asked, as well as all close or longstanding friends. By excluding her family, Meghan and Harry had not only harmed them, but themselves as well, Meghan herself especially, for the conclusion most people would draw would be that Meghan more than Harry bore primary responsibility for the exclusion. The one thing the palace didn't want was someone entering the Royal Family as damaged goods, but as Harry and Meghan's wedding was not a state occasion, no one at the palace had the right to intervene.

There was another dimension to Meghan and Harry's approach which also seemed destructive. To justify the exclusion of Meghan's relations, they had also neglected to invite what one royal, who expected to be asked and was not, called 'the wider cousinage'. This caused no end of offence, all of which was totally unnecessary, especially as how there were hundreds of available seats in the chapel. Although everyone put a good face on it, it rankled. The Duke and Duchess of Kent's grand-children Lady Amelia Windsor, Lord Downpatrick and Lady Marina Windsor were but three of the many glaring omissions. So too were all the European royals. Although Harry's marriage was not an affair of state, hence why no heads of state or government were asked, it was a family affair. Everyone in royal circles knows how important such occasions are as bonding exercises. On a human level, they were even more important to the royals who had lost their thrones. Such occasions as marriages and big birthdays are a rare form of ratification of their once-glorious and now lost status. Confusing family occasions with social networking events or career moves not only deprived these people of a meaningful opportunity, but also led many to conclude that Harry and Meghan were being heartless.

What was also viewed as cruel was the way some of Harry's oldest and most loyal friends were brushed aside. They had been true to a fault. People like Tom 'Skippy' Inskip had taken flack for Harry when he had been caught taking drugs. Tom had allowed the press to pillory him unfairly, accepting blame that was rightly Harry's, remaining silent to save his friend's skin. It was beyond belief that Tom and Lara Inskip were excluded from Frogmore House. His offence? To warn Harry against rushing into marriage.

Harry had been an usher at Tom's Jamaican wedding to Lord St. Helen's daughter the Hon. Lara Hughes-Young at Round Hill in 2017. They had been such good friends that he and Lara made the ultimate sacrifice to satisfy Meghan's desire for privacy by preventing their guests from using their mobile 'phones throughout their marriage celebrations. This had not gone down well with many of the guests, but best friends are happy to accommodate other best friends even to the inconvenience of lesser friends. Yet, once Meghan knew that Skippy had been less than enthusiastic about her existence, he was given the deep freeze treatment and excluded along with his wife from the holy of holies, giving out the message to everyone, including the world's press (which picked up on their humiliation), that the Inskips had been demoted from first to second class.

'All the score settling Meghan and now Harry are involved with is just pathetic,' a royal cousin said. 'Totally uncalled for and so much the opposite of life enhancing.'

The Inskips, however, would get their own back. Normally, royals are invited to be godparents of their friends' children. Failure to issue such an invitation can be interpreted as a snub. With Lara about to have a baby, their friends wanted to know if they'd be inviting Harry to be a godfather. They said they would be doing no such thing, and said it so often that the slight ended up in the *Mail on Sunday*'s gossip column.

Royal weddings are memorable occasions not only for those who watch them on television, but those who attend them, and those who do not. There were so many surprising omissions at both St. George's Chapel and Frogmore House that several people asked the question: What is going on? Had Harry and Meghan abided by royal and aristocratic tradition, all the relations whom custom decreed should have been invited, would have been. Very few invitees would have declined, so the chapel would have had a plethora of obscure royals and fifty or so attendees from Meghan's past. These would have included people like her paternal Uncle Mike Markle and her maternal Uncle Joseph Johnson and his wife Pamela. They most likely would not have made the cut for the evening celebration at Frogmore House, but honour would have been served all around and Meghan would have shown the world that, proud as she was of her ascent in the world, she was not ashamed of her roots. This would have enhanced her reputation, instead of which the omission called her values into question. It was a fatal error on her and Harry's part.

Admittedly, Meghan and Harry had sufficient supporters who would have behaved exactly as they did, for their viewpoint to enjoy merit in some quarters. But the controversy they created meant that they started their marriage in a maelstrom and, once that tone was set, it became difficult to alter it. Nevertheless, the church service, the reception at Windsor Castle and the subsequent black tie celebration at Frogmore House were great successes. According to one attendee, 'it was a lovely party,' a 'very happy occasion.' The couple was obviously 'very much in love though they spent quite a lot of their time posing for photographs.' Despite this, the absentees generated a great deal of talk and an even greater deal of speculation. Because such exclusionary conduct seemed atypical of Harry, people asked whether Meghan could have got such tight control of him so early in the game that she was already freezing out his friends?

To the older generation, this was reminiscent of the way Harry's mother had used the invitation list to her own wedding, and the wedding breakfast following it, to wield power. She had struck her step-grandmother-in-law Dame Barbara Cartland's name off the list on the grounds that she would garner too much attention from the public, thereby stealing thunder that Diana reserved for herself. The diarist Kenneth Rose wrote how Diana's father 'Johnnie Spencer tells me that he wanted to wear his Greys uniform when Diana marries the Prince of Wales, but that Diana herself objected. She thought it would detract from her own appearance. This is most extraordinary, like something out of *King Lear.*'

Showing that she could embody both Goneril and Regan, 'When Johnnie Spencer showed Diana his draft list, she crossed out all the family who had not bothered to come to the weddings of her sisters! One day she will be very formidable.' In fact, Diana was already formidable at nineteen, and she had used the occasion of her marriage to deliver messages to many of her husband's circle, as well as to the world in general, in much the same way that Meghan and Harry did. She had even tried to prevent Charles from asking many of his closest friends such as Lord and Lady Tryon, and when he had dug his heels in, she had insisted that they could only attend the church service and not the wedding breakfast at Buckingham Palace. In doing so, she had made the point that they had been demoted, a tactic her son and his wife would deploy with people like the Inskips.

People who noticed the parallels between the way Diana and her son and daughter-in-law behaved started asking the question: Will the axe be falling in a discomfiting echo of the way it had fallen on staff, friends and relations once Diana joined the Royal Family? In 1981, within months of being married, she had insisted that Charles get rid of his loyal valet, Stephen Barry. She then forced out his Private Secretary, the Hon Edward Adeane, son of the Queen's former Private Secretary Michael, Lord Adeane, despite the fact that Edward Adeane had given up a highly successful career at the Bar to work for the Prince of Wales. She also shoved out her own Private Secretary Oliver Everett because he had kept on giving her briefing papers she didn't want to be bothered to read, even though he too had given up a successful career as a diplomat to take up the post with her. Were the parallels with Diana coincidental, or should people steel themselves for an onslaught like Diana's?

The answer was not long in coming. Three days after the wedding, Harry and Meghan attended the garden party at Buckingham Palace celebrating Prince Charles's 70th birthday in the presence of representatives of his many charities and associates. Meghan looked beautiful as she and Harry stepped out onto the lawn. They plunged in, glad-handing those who had been selected for introductions. She charmed everyone. Fifteen minutes into the event, she turned to Harry and said, 'Harry, this is really boring. Let's leave.'

To his credit, he informed her that they would have to stay. 'But Harry,' she said, 'this is so boring. We've done our bit. Everyone knows we've been here. Let's go.' Harry asserted that they had to stay, and they moved on.

As mentioned in Chapter 1, I was having dinner with a scion of the aristocracy with impeccable palace connections the following evening. The main subject of conversation was Meghan's desire to bolt once she had taken her bow and boredom had set in at the garden party. Formal events stultified her. If she could not be emoting she had no interest in being present. The individual who had overheard the exchange between her and Harry had been so gobsmacked that he could not keep it to himself. We all agreed that this was a very bad sign. Meghan had patently believed that it was enough for her to doll herself up, radiate delight and glamour as she posed for the cameras, then depart after fifteen minutes once boredom set in. She clearly did not appreciate that the civic duties of royalty and aristocracy involve meeting and greeting as many people as you can on occasions such as these. In our world, there are no short cuts. You either fulfill your duties to the full extent of your capacity or you are a failure. Much of the goodwill that is generated does not take place in front of a camera, but off it, when you're interacting with people who have come great distances to meet you, sometimes at considerable expense and with great inconvenience. She clearly did not understand the difference between a movie star's appearance and the reality of a royal appearance. 'She thinks life is a photo op,' the scion said. 'She has a lot to learn,' I added. It then emerged that 'they've started taking bets at the palace as to how long the marriage will last. Most people opt for two years, the optimists say five.' A third party gave it eighteen months, while I refused to bet at all. Aside from not possessing enough knowledge to make an informed guess, I also hoped 'she will realise how important a role she has been assigned.' I wanted her to live up to it. I saw it for what it was, a unique place in history.

The conversation concluded with the information that the recently created Duke of Sussex had gained himself a new nickname at the palace. He was now known as Blow Jobs Harry because people there were convinced that his brains had been addled through mind-blowingly good sex. 'It would be touching if it wasn't so dangerous,' a royal cousin told me. 'His eyes follow her around the room as if he's a devoted puppy and she's the most marvellous master that ever existed.' It was David and Wallis (the Duke and Duchess of Windsor) , or Bertie and Elizabeth (Albert, Duke of York, King George VI and Lady Elizabeth Bowes-

Lyon, Duchess of York then Queen Elizabeth) all over again. Yet Harry had stood up to Meghan when she wanted them to shun what he knew to be their duty though she hadn't understood the importance of it. That in itself was a promising sign. It meant that where his duty was concerned, he might fulfill it, and moreover might encourage her to do likewise. As long as that continued, there was hope for Blow Jobs Harry and Me Gain, as people such as the writer David Jenkins, partner of former Vogue Editor Alexandra Shulman, had already started calling the newly minted Duchess of Sussex.

Little did any of us know, but in less than two years, Meghan and Harry would chuck the royal way of life, stating that they wished to make themselves 'financially independent.' Since Harry had never given any indication of being financially driven prior to meeting Meghan, it seems safe to conclude that she was the driving force behind that decision, and that Gina Nelthorpe-Cowne had been right all along. Meghan Markle is a businesswoman first and foremost. While there is nothing wrong with that if that's what you are, it does strike me as a significantly lower calling than being the altruistic and living embodiment of the hopes of billions of people.

Maybe, just maybe, Meghan really had been truthful when she had said in her first blog that she wasn't interested in fame for its own sake. Maybe her true purpose was a combination of activity and the rewards that go along with success. She had indicated that she loved the perks of celebrity: the primping, priming, promoting, titivating, and money. It wasn't the money alone that counted, but financial recompense was an integral part of her reckoning. And since royalty is compensated for its activities by respect rather than being rewarded financially for them, the business of royalty, of duty done without financial profitability, wasn't for her.

CHAPTER 7

In the immediate aftermath of Meghan and Harry's marriage, no one had any idea that her ambitions exceeded the platform of royal duchess. Everyone in royal circles believed that she had acquired the greatest role of her life, that, being the actress she was, she would play it to the hilt. To quote her, she 'hit the ground running' following her marriage. She was an exemplary performer, and at first it looked as if her acting skills would be successfully deployed onto the wider stage that she had acquired along with the title when she became Her Royal Highness the Duchess of Sussex.

Meghan has great charm. At first, as she performed her royal duties she came across as warm, kind, down-to-earth, sweet, modest, and eager to please. Her first post-marital engagement without Harry was to join Queen on the royal train to Chester in the northwest of England. The monarch had a full schedule of engagements, from unveiling a plaque declaring open the Hatton Bridge which crosses the Don River, to inspecting a group of Syrian refugees doing traditional craftwork, a dance performance by a group of local recovering addicts called *Fallen Angels*, performances of set pieces from a production of *A Little Night Music,* local primary school children performing songs alongside actors from the 2016 film *Swallows and Amazons* which was first published by Arthur Ransome in 1930, at which point the Queen unveiled the second plaque of the day before the two women headed into lunch at Chester Town Hall as guests of honour of the Chester City Council. They also went on a walkabout, the Queen working the crowds to the right while Meghan was instructed to walk to the left. Royal aides informed the press that Elizabeth II had asked her new granddaughter-in-law along specifically to show her 'the breadth of work the Royal Family carries out.' Meghan said how pleased she was to be there, and the Queen, notably undemonstrative as a matter of course, was unusually animated, smiling up a storm and laughing at Meghan's asides when they were seated together.

Although the press judged the event a great success, those who were more dispassionate queried Meghan's boycotting of royal attire. The Queen was dressed in one of her typical outfits, a mint green Stewart Parvin coat over a silk floral dress with a matching Rachel Trevor Morgan hat and the inevitable white gloves, pearls and diamond brooch. Meghan wore an off-white Givenchy dress with a black belt, black clutch bag, and black shoes. While she looked chic, she did not look royal, and, to those in the know, she had broken several sartorial guidelines:

1) She had worn no hat when the custom is for royal women to wear hats on such occasions, especially when accompanying the Queen;

2) She had worn black and white, which are two of the royal mourning colours, along with mauve;

3) She had worn a French designer, not a British, which was in breach of the protocol whereby British royals wear British designers to drum up support for British trade when on royal duties. While it had been just about acceptable for her to wear a wedding dress from the French couturier because its designer was British, the same did not hold true for everyday attire.

While it was some comfort that the press did not revile Meghan for the breaches, they did notice that she had ignored royal protocol for what was her introductory engagement with Her Majesty. This was hardly the way to garner praise, yet Meghan seemed so eager to please that she was given the benefit of the doubt. Behind the scenes, however, those of us in the know soon learnt that Angela Kelly, the Queen's dresser, personal designer, and even more importantly personal friend, had rung Meghan up and informed her that the Queen would be wearing a hat, which was palace-speak for you are to wear one too. Meghan had informed her that she would not be wearing one, and that was that. Was this a sign of a policy of deliberate disregard on her part for the traditions of the institution into which she had married, or was it an unintended slight born of ignorance? Since Meghan was known to have always fulfilled the sartorial demands of the producers of her television shows and films when she was promoting a product on their behalf, could this be an early display of independence, and a message that she would not be abiding by the traditions of the monarchy but would be making up her own rules as and when she wanted? Recently, there had been so many little signs that she did not feel it necessary to be constrained by any rules of conduct but her own, chief of which had been her failure to curtsy to the Queen on her wedding day following the signing of the register at St. George's Chapel.

Soon it emerged that Meghan had indeed chosen to devise her own protocol where attire was concerned. Despite being undeniably stylish and chic, her choice of colours was more New York Seventh Avenue than House of Windsor or, come to it, Houses of Orange, Saxe-Coburg-Gotha, Bernadotte, Lichtenstein, Luxembourg-Nassau, Schleswig-Holstein-Sonderburg-Gluckstein, Bernadotte, or Grimaldi. As she appeared in public more and more, it was as if she were starring in her own interpretation of a sit-com in which a chic American woman decides that she is too stylish to be bothered to respect the sartorial mores of the institution into which she has married. Not surprisingly, the British press noticed. They knew only too well that royal women usually wear coloured garments so that they will stand out in a crowd. It is deemed polite that you make yourself visible to those who have taken the trouble to come to see you. It is one of the many minor and unspoken protocols, based upon consideration, under which all royal women function. It is a form of respect for the public, and disregarding the protocol disrespects both the public and the sentiment behind the custom.

Although colour suits Meghan, her concept of chic is very French *bourgeois*: a mode of attire that crossed the Atlantic seventy years ago and has become engraved on the hearts and minds of those fashionistas whose taste is circumscribed by safety and a reverence for any colour as long as it is black. She was seldom seen in anything but a mourning colour, black being her favourite, but grey and white also featuring as variables.

It was only a matter of time before Meghan's choices began attracting press attention. Although she was so beautifully presented that practically everything she wore looked wonderful on her, and anything that wasn't couture sold out so rapidly that the Meghan Effect became a phenomenon, she was nevertheless building up a bank of hostility which seemed counter to her efforts. She so obviously cared about looking as good and as glamorous as she could that it was inconceivable she would deliberately seek to bring criticism down on her head. Yet some of her choices so flagrantly breached the rules of what constitutes acceptable attire for women of rank that she either had bad advice or refused to take any at all. For instance, her tendency to wear cocktail attire during the day meant that she was either ignorant of what was acceptable attire in certain situations and at certain times for a woman of her station, or then she cared more for looking good than she did for dressing with appropriate respect for the customs of her adopted land, and was thumbing her nose at British customs at the very moment she wanted everyone's approbation for her beautiful she looked.

There were one or two examples which demonstrate the mistake she was making. On one of the few occasions upon which she wore a multi-coloured print on a cream background rather than her inevitable black or grey, the dress was made from a transparent material lined on the body but with sheer long sleeves and a square neckline front and back which was so scooped that there was barely an inch between the bodice and the sleeve. In one fell swoop, she had breached two dictats: 1) you do not wear transparent sleeves during the day except with formal morning wear; they are cocktail wear, to be worn only after sundown, and 2) you do not wear necklines that are so scooped out during the day, unless the fabric of the garment is clearly daytime attire, such as opaque cotton.

Worse was to follow when Meghan joined the Royal Family for her first appearance on the balcony at Buckingham Palace following the Trooping The Colour ceremony at Horse Guards Parade in 2018. Although she wore a beautiful pale pink Carolina Herrera dress with huge covered buttons that screamed couture, it sported an off-the-shoulder neckline as if the dress code had been cocktail or evening attire, not formal day wear. She complemented the dress with a fetching Philip Treacy hat of the same colour, though her choice of handbag was also unorthodox: a white Carolina Herrera clutch bordered in gold metal. One does not wear gold accessories in the day. They are regarded as vulgar and inelegant, or what the interior designer Nicky Haslam would dismiss as 'common'.

A month later Meghan was back in cocktail wear during the day on the Buckingham Palace balcony, wearing yet another couture dress by yet another foreign designer. Yet again the dress, by Dior, was beautiful, but once more it was, in British terms, inappropriate for the occasion. It was of black silk with a bateau neckline: a style that is only ever worn after dark or with informal attire such as beachwear, except for wedding dresses. Her hat was another stylish concoction, mercifully by another British milliner, this time Stephen Jones. But again her handbag was an evening bag: now a black silk clutch that was luckily more discreet than the gold metal chosen the month before.

To the sartorially knowledgeable, what made this *faux pas* even more undesirable was that Meghan had chosen to attend church in cocktail wear. The occasion was celebrating the centenary of the founding of the Royal Air Force on the 1st April 1918. It had started off with a service at St. Paul's Cathedral commemorating the many members of the RAF who had endangered or sacrificed their lives for the nation. Princes Harry and William being helicopter pilots, the event had personal significance for them. Following the service, there was a flypast of 100 aircraft over Buckingham Palace. The Royal Family watched it from the balcony, Meghan enjoying pride of place immediately beside the Queen.

One princess said, 'I only hope the press doesn't notice her breaches of the dress code. We don't want them criticising her. I gather she is extremely sensitive to criticism. In fact, she requires constant adulation. Presumably that's why Harry keeps his mouth shut.' I could not help pointing out that Harry might well have remained silent through ignorance, for prior to Meghan's arrival in his life, he had invariably looked unkempt. Fashion was clearly not his forte.

Unfortunately, Meghan's inappropriate attire was not the only thing exciting comment. The *cognoscenti* also noticed that she had no idea what constituted good British form when greeting strangers. Again, it was hoped that the press would not pick up on her approach. Whenever she was greeting strangers, she would inform them how pleased she was to meet them. For a plethora of good reasons, the standard greeting has always been, 'How do you do?' Firstly, it is friendly and neutral while covering a multitude of possibilities without opening you up to criticism. While that might seem reserved to those of a more effusive nature, the reason why it has always been standard is simple. You cannot know that you are pleased to meet people until you have met them. You are therefore laying claim to a sentiment you do not yet possess if you tell them how pleased you are. This is at best insincerity and is tantamount to hypocrisy, as in the original meaning of the word, which is lack of critical faculty. Avoiding insincere and hypocritical conduct is a matter of principle as well as policy, for a) insincerity is a mark of bad character and b) hypocrisy is indicative of weakness as well as duplicity. If you really want to stretch the boundaries and show strangers how warm and friendly you are, it is acceptable to say, 'Thank you so much for coming,' though the old standard royal questions such as 'Have you travelled far?' or 'Have you been waiting long?' are equally cordial without running the risk of overstepping the mark and inadvertently descending into either insincerity or hypocrisy.

Within the Establishment, people regretted that Harry, who had grown out of his schoolboy tendency to antagonise and had become a popular public figure, was not pointing out to Meghan how some of her modes of conduct jarred. In fact, rather than tucking her under his wing and steering her in the right direction, he either ignored her breaches or then backed her up, even when she was being injudicious or unreasonable. This was counterproductive, for Harry could not expect a whole institution much less an entire nation to alter its modes of conduct to facilitate a woman who, either through ignorance or because she honestly thought her way was the better way, wanted to do as she pleased, and, if she ruffled feathers, the failing was not hers but the owner of the feathers.

By taking the stance he did, Harry was losing respect left, right and centre. This was a pity. He had gone from being a trying teenager to a respected young man who had the common touch and was popular with everyone he came into contact with, from those with whom he worked closely to strangers. His conduct when he had been with Chelsy Davy and Cressida Bonas had been so markedly different from what it was with Meghan, that observers surmised Meghan must be responsible for the changes within him. With Chelsy and Cressida, there had been no awkwardness with anyone except the press, except when he was in his cups, feeling lonely, and subject to striking out angrily at the nearest onlooker. Otherwise, he had fitted in with both girls' circles, and they had fitted in with his. They had all had vibrant social lives, with everyone rubbing along well. Harry has always said he wanted nothing more than to be just a person, just Harry and, with them, he had shared equal footing with their peer group. They had been just another couple, maybe more glamorous, maybe more high profile, but nevertheless equals.

By the early days of Meghan and Harry's marriage, this had changed. Harry and Meghan were no longer just another couple amongst friends. There was an aura of specialness that now emanated from them jointly. They were more evolved, more mindful, more conscious, more woke. They were no longer ordinary human beings but extraordinary people whose awareness of their destiny to change and save the world separated them from mere mortals like Harry's friends.

As they settled into marriage, Meghan's 'us against the world attitude' began to predominate. They had been putting distance between Harry and some of his oldest and closest friends, whom she clearly thought were too frivolous or too traditional for an aware and enlightened couple like Harry and herself, and he had adopted her attitude as well. Not only was there payback time for those who had done as William and Tom Inskip did when they had advised Harry to take things more slowly and who now found themselves being marginalised, but those who remained in favour began to notice that Harry was no longer as open nor as much fun as he had been. Under Meghan's influence, he was far more serious. Where before he was up for a good laugh, now he had to save the world with her. Woke rhetoric, hyper-political attitudinising, yoga and meditation had replaced the fun sessions the couple had enjoyed prior to meeting each other. The Meghan who used to knock back the booze with Lizzie Cundy, who was a girly girl with Serena Williams, might still maintain the structure of her A-List friendships, and behave in such a way that they could truthfully say that she hadn't changed at all, but with Harry's friends, she couldn't even be bothered to be friendly, nor did she make any attempt to fit in the way she had done while she was on the up and up in Canada, New York and London prior to meeting Harry. Now that she was a Princess of the United Kingdom, she had a gravity to match, and, to the regret of his old friends, so did Harry, who had become as heavy going as Meghan.

Even when Harry remained in touch with the few old friends from the past who had somehow miraculously escaped the cull, Meghan made it clear to them that she had nothing in common with any of Harry's friends, or their wives and girlfriends, with very few exceptions. Nowhere was this clearer than at the wedding of Harry's Ludgrove schoolmate Charlie van Straubenzee to Daisy Jenks. Held in a field adjoining the family home, where dogs and other animals came and went and bales of hay were everywhere, the atmosphere was typically English upper class. Everyone was relaxed. Most people knew one another well, and had done so for many years. These were the *crème de la crème* of English society, people who were warm, friendly, without side. Those on the periphery who did not know Meghan were delighted to meet her. Contrary to what foreigners often think, the British are very friendly and forthcoming, at least in the upper classes. It was therefore entirely within expectation when a girl went up to Meghan, introduced herself, and said how beautiful she thought she was. She said she knew it was Meghan's birthday and wished her a happy birthday. Meghan looked at her as if she had committed a great *faux pas* by speaking to her and, without saying a word, walked off. 'It was so cold,' someone who witnessed the exchange told me. 'Really rude.'

One can only hope that Meghan was under the impression that people aren't supposed to speak to royalty first, otherwise her reaction was inexcusable. Even if she believed that, no such rule applies within Harry's social circle. If it did, royals would have very lonely lives indeed, for no one would be able to go up to them and initiate a conversation. But even if the rule had applied, none of the other royal women would have behaved as she did, with the exception of Princess Michael of Kent, who takes herself as seriously as Meghan does.

Worse followed during the wedding breakfast. Another girl told Meghan how much she admired her, and how wonderful she thought it was that she and Harry were married, and how well she thought she was doing. She told her she was rooting for them, and wished them well. Meghan's response? She looked her up and down, turned away without saying a word, and froze her out for the rest of the wedding breakfast.

'She was beautifully turned out,' one of the guests told me. 'I was surprised at how small she is. But she is undeniably good looking. She was really well dressed, but more for a town wedding than one in the country. She had on high, high heels while everyone else was in espadrilles. I mean, the wedding was in a field. You don't wear high heels to a wedding that you know is going to be in a field. You could see she wasn't comfortable around us. It was your typical English wedding. Everyone knew everyone else and everyone was bright and bouncy. Maybe she felt like a fish out of water. Harry was the best man, but when he wasn't performing his best man duties, he and Meghan kept themselves to themselves.' Someone else told me Meghan actually walked off and went to sit on her own on more than one occasion, and that Harry joined her every time he noticed that she was missing. This has the ring of truth. I was told by many different sources that Meghan has a habit of walking off from big groups. If she doesn't feel comfortable, she doesn't make any effort to fit in. She removes herself from the scene. However, she only does this when she is with a man or when there is a man around on whom she has her eye. He then has a choice. He either leaves her to stew on her own, or he goes and joins her. 'That way, she detaches him from the group and has him to herself,' a Canadian who has observed her over the years explained. 'She is very good at getting men to dance to her tune.' This technique is one that Meghan has been using since childhood. She used to withdraw from Nikki Priddy whenever things weren't going the way she wanted them to. As Nikki observed, she is stubborn, she would not relent, and if you didn't go to her, she'd never come to you.

By this time, Meghan's various techniques had worked so well with Harry that he was happily, willingly, and entirely in her thrall. While his friends were pleased to see him happy, they were perplexed as to how anyone could have undergone such a complete change of identity that he was now virtually a new individual. Putting aside the leaden quality that had crept into the newly serious, world-changing Harry's behaviour, there was a new and disturbing dimension that worried his friends. He and Meghan had begun to behave as if they functioned in a bubble, with no thought or care for how their actions impacted upon their associates. Although they could be perfectly charming when they wanted to be, they often crossed a line where the traditional modes of behaviour with which most of his friends conducted themselves. This was nowhere more apparent than when they attended dinner parties. Their public displays of affection were so ostentatious that onlookers found their conduct embarrassing.

Firstly, they would huddle together, putting up an invisible barrier between themselves and everyone else, as if they were the only couple who had ever been in love, and that everyone present was of such insignificance that they had no time for them. Rather than partake of the occasion by fitting in with the group, they would be completely absorbed in each other, whispering into each other's ears as if they were the only two people who existed. Whispering is bad manners; it excludes others, but Harry and Meghan seemed to have no awareness of the offence they were causing as they froze everyone out from their hallowed communion. While this was going on, they would be pawing each other and, if that wasn't enough of a display of how much they desired each other, they would periodically kiss like teenagers on a fifth date.

Distasteful as such displays were to people who had been reared from childhood with the injunction No PDAs (No Public Displays of Affection), what catapulted their conduct into insupportability was the havoc they created when it came time to be seated for dinner. The custom has always been that married couples are never seated beside each other. Engaged couples yes, but married couples, no. There are sound reasons for this. Aside from the fact that people who live together will ordinarily have less to say to each other than to those they see less frequently, the main purpose of a dinner party is for people to mix, have good conversations and a good time. This is not possible unless couples are dispersed around a dinner table. Hostesses take seating arrangements seriously because *place à table* is not only important in terms of creating good interchange, but also for other reasons. The most honoured man is placed at the right hand of the hostess, the next at her left, while the rule is reversed for the host and women.

Harry and Meghan ruined several dinner parties by refusing to be separated. Someone who witnessed them in action told me, 'Rather than take part in the occasion, they behaved as if they were new lovers on heat, exhibitionistically asserting their absorption in and sexual desire for each other.' In the process, they created embarrassment for everyone present, and while there is little doubt that they did not intend to convey disrespect or create an obstruction around which conversation had to flow, the effect of their conduct was nevertheless disrespectful and obstructionistic. A royal cousin told me, 'Unsurprisingly, people stopped asking them to dinner.'

Another complaint about the newlyweds was that they had become heavy going. Conversation was no longer the pleasure it had been before they had discovered each other and set out on the journey to reshape the world. Gone were Harry's light banter, Meghan's giggly wit and girly charm. On the few occasions they actually gave anyone space to enter their magic circle, their conversation was intense and leaden. While Meghan could still be personable with her own friends, with Harry's she created a chasm of disinterestedness deepened by her flamboyant wokeness, and he mirrored her.

To people who knew Harry's parents, Meghan was doing with their son and his friends a variation of what Diana had done with Charles and his. Diana had been a metropolitan babe who had found country life boring. Charles and his friends had been country-lovers. Although she was more of a naturalist than Diana - for instance, she used to fish with her father - Meghan was so pointedly anti-everything that the royal world represented, that people feared that she intended to detach Harry from his roots. And he seemed to be so completely under her spell that there was no point in trying to intervene, especially as how everyone who had previously tried to intercede had been frozen out.

'Everyone who cares about him simply hopes that Harry won't be too hurt if things go wrong, which, by the look of it, has become an increasingly likely scenario,' one of his friends said.

The old Harry had ceased to exist and a new Harry had taken his place, but, despite the reservations his circle now had about the effect his marriage was having upon him, in the wider world, he and Meghan had become global superstars. She was revered as a style icon while he was admired for being the down-to-earth charmer that he had once been. Word had not yet got out that his personality had undergone a change. Her untraditionally British and, in British terms unsophisticated, demeanour was not apparent to her admirers, even while style arbiters such as Nicky Haslam started to condemn her as 'common'. This was ironic, because Meghan considered herself 'classy', little realising that in Britain anyone who is too self-consciously 'classy' is automatically dismissed as being anything but.

It is possible that Meghan did not appreciate that she was behaving in a way that would trigger opposition. Display of willingness to be harmonious as opposed to the overt assertiveness which some interpreted as aggressiveness, would have won her supporters instead of gaining her detractors. Softly softly might have bought her and everyone around her time to make the adjustments necessary to a positive accommodation, but, by declaring that she intended to 'hit the ground running' when she became royal, then doing it with the expectation that everyone should appreciate her different ways, without her appreciating that others too had a point of view and there might be room for mutual respect rather than everyone having to defer to her superiority, made waves where a more gentle approach would have created something more constructive.

Meghan is indubitably strong-minded and upfront about her beliefs. She expects others to admire them and brooks no opposition. She is also a very sensitive person who basks in the appreciation of others and withdraws when she fails to get it. Then she nurses her wounded feelings as she takes deep and personal offence at not receiving what she regards as her just deserts. Someone who knows her well told me, 'If you don't appreciate her, she doesn't waste time trying to win you over. She excises you. She has no time to waste on what she calls naysayers. She's on a mission to change the world, as she sees it for the better, and to achieve what she wants, and if you don't sympathise or agree with her, she can't be bothered to waste her time or energy on you.' While her supporters regard this as proof of her strength and integrity, such decisiveness does not always make for a smooth ride. By 'hitting the ground running' at the time of her marriage, she was not only asserting her postures, positions and beliefs, but also managed to get the backs of many people up by riding roughshod over them. Forces of nature who advocate change and militantly declare their intention to alter scenarios others might want to remain intact inevitably face a backlash. It would not be long in coming as Hurricane Meghan, as she was sometimes called at the palace, blew through the corridors of power with Harry's full backing.

Within months of their marriage, it was apparent to both Harry and Meghan that their desire to initiate profound change was not being received with the enthusiasm they had imagined it would be. Meghan's naiveté as to how real power actually works amongst institutions which possess it, and Harry's expectations were not so easily explained away. He had spent his whole life as a royal. He should have understood that reform cannot be sudden or dramatic, and certainly not as frequent or 'impactful' as they now both desired it to be. Impactful was one of Meghan's favourite concepts, and he had adopted it along with her zeal for constant change. Neither of them could see that constant and relentless alteration had the potential to precipitate instability. They regarded themselves as humanitarians who should, on a daily basis, seek out areas that needed improvement, shine a light upon them, and set about implementing the modifications they deemed desirable. They had come to the conclusion that their role in life should be to call out each and every area throughout the world that required change, and refused to see how damaging 'shining a light', to use another of their favourite expressions, could ultimately become.

Rather than accept the dangers inherent in their postures, Harry and Meghan decided that those who preached caution to them should be dismissed as traditionalists who simply didn't 'get it'. They decided that 'tradition' was the problem. The word tradition, as used by them, became a catch-all for any aspect of the *status quo* with which they did not agree. Soon they were complaining that they were being hemmed in by tradition. Tradition became a dirty word which they used to pour scorn on anyone who stood between them and what they wanted to do as they extrapolated their concept of this bright new world where they would lead everyone into the light. Both Meghan and Harry had always had excellent social skills. They shared the gift of being able to articulate their points of view with such conviction that even those who disagreed with them could not deny how heartfelt they were about the positions they adopted. They also used buzz words to annihilate their adversaries. Whether it was a hostess trying to seat them where she wanted to at her dinner table, or a courtier wanting Meghan to respect the dress code of royalty, or Harry dismissing the concerns of courtiers who were trying to rein him and Meghan in as they bombarded their staff with twenty and fifty new ideas every few days, they dismissed all concerns about potentially undesirable consequences as if nothing untoward could ever come of their good intentions, and blamed 'tradition' for standing in the way of 'change', which was another of their favourite words.

It was now apparent to everyone surrounding them that Harry and Meghan were feeling aggrieved about what they saw as unnecessary restrictions being put in their way. They were both so impassioned, so Messianic, about their need to change the world for the better, that they were soon complaining that their 'efforts to modernise the monarchy were not being acknowledged or rewarded', that 'no one appreciated their talents' or knew how to 'exploit' their 'special qualities'. They openly disparaged other members of the Royal Family for their style of doing things, disdaining it as being 'stiff', 'out of touch', 'traditional', 'uptight' and 'old fashioned'. They criticised the courtiers for being 'hopelessly out of date and inefficient', declaring that they weren't 'savvy' like Meghan and her Hollywood colleagues, who really knew how to 'get the message out there.' When this criticism did not gain them the latitude to function with the freedom they desired, they looked around for who was behind the restraints being placed upon them. They concluded that 'everyone' in the Royal Family, with the exception of the Queen, was 'jealous' of them, of their popularity, their star quality, their unique gifts which, if properly exploited, could change the monarchy and the world for the better. This was taken to mean William and Catherine, and sure enough, it was only a matter of time before they started making it clear that they believed that William and Catherine were indeed jealous of them and their greater star quality.

These complaints did nothing to improve the atmosphere surrounding the couple, but some of the wording was so alien to anything royal or aristocratic, and so characteristic of someone of Meghan's type and background, that listeners concluded that she was writing the script even though both she and Harry were voicing identical concerns. A few words, in particular, were viewed at the palace as giveaways as to who was really the architect of the dissatisfaction. Meghan and Harry were vociferous in using the word 'exploit' to describe the failure of the palace to capitalise upon what they described as their 'unique' or 'special gifts' and 'star quality'. Aside from the fact that the deployment of terms such as 'unique/special gifts' and 'star quality' are redolent of Hollywood but alien to the British tongue, Harry and Meghan were using the word 'exploit' in a purely American way. In Britain, the word exploit has pejorative connotations that include taking undue or unfair advantage, being mercenary, or milking something to excess. Had Harry and Meghan complained that the palace were not 'utilising' their talents, the question of who was the source of the dissatisfaction might have been blurred, but their deployment of so many Americanisms led everyone to suspect Meghan.

Both Meghan and Harry are headstrong. There was no doubt at the palace that they were both sincere in their desire to achieve their goals, but there was also no doubt that they had become troublesome. He has always taken skilful handling. Volatile and emotional, he is very much both his parents' son, for Charles and Diana shared explosive and at times doggedly temperamental personality traits. Meghan was equally impassioned and determined. Even in Hollywood, where pushiness is often regarded as a virtue and being called a hustler is complimentary, Meghan had acquired a reputation for being in a class of her own. While her admirers commended her for her tenacity and toughness, one producer told me that he regarded her 'an odiously pushy, voracious piece of work'. She was 'greedy', had 'far too high an opinion of herself', and was 'a player who has a compulsion to always push for more. If you offered her California, she'd demand Arizona as well, and, if you didn't give it to her, you were victimising her.' Meghan was proud of living by her mother's advice, 'Don't give the milk away for free', but she had now reached the stage in life where her old habit of requiring more and more might have outlived its usefulness as a tool for further success. Such conduct only got many people's backs up unnecessarily, and made them question her suitability for the role of royal duchess or even as a Hollywood sophisticate.

It seemed to those of us who were rooting for Meghan to be a huge success that she and Harry were throwing up obstacles, instead of keeping them to a minimum. One hurdle which they had introduced to keep everyone at arm's length, and which began to acquire a life of its own, was their ever-increasing demand for privacy. As this was often directed at the most surprising and unexpected of sources, it caused consternation within their social and family circle. It was also articulated against a backdrop of conflict and controversy in such an inconsistent manner that those close to them were left wondering against whom they were protecting themselves, and to what purpose. A case in point was the way they behaved at Princess Eugenie of York's wedding to Jack Brooksbank, brand ambassador of George Clooney's *Casamigos* tequila. 'Who knows whether there was an element of payback because Meghan hadn't been allowed to *pinch* Grand Duchess Xenia's tiara from Eugenie for her own wedding, or whether they were now so wrapped up in themselves that they couldn't think beyond their own immediate concerns,' a royal cousin told me. 'But they found the perfect way to steal Eugenie's thunder', and to drive home the point that they were a unit beyond the reach of everyone else. 'They spent the whole time going from person to person *sharing* the news that [Meghan] was pregnant. This from the couple who had only a few short months before caused grave offence, when, asked how their honeymoon had gone and where they had been, had responded, "We're not telling anyone. We're keeping that *for* ourselves."'

It was as if Meghan and Harry had decided that they had to protect themselves against all sorts of people who wished them well and were cheering them on to success. By creating walls, they were deliberately excluding people, who were deeply offended to be shut out.

This created antagonism, and the royal cousin observed, 'You should've seen her expression (when they refused to say where they'd spent their honeymoon). She was just so *smug*, like a twelve year old in the school yard scoring points over everyone else by keeping secrets from them. Just preposterous.' Since Meghan and Harry had been married for only a few months, and the first year of marriage is customarily viewed as a period of adjustment, everyone erroneously marked down the increasing signs of alienation to something it was not. Had they known that Meghan was either unwilling or unable to make the compromises necessary to fit into her new role as a royal, they would have been horrified. But no one knew.

What was rapidly becoming apparent, however, was how trying the situation had become for all concerned. Despite the increasing hostility that seemed to be emanating from Meghan and Harry's quarter, the palace remained eager to take full advantage of their attributes, hers in particular. Both she and Harry were outstandingly popular. Even before their marriage, plans had been afoot for them to open the Invictus Games on the 20th October 2018 in Sydney, following which there would be a sixteen day tour of Australia, New Zealand, Fiji and Tonga. There were high hopes for it as it was being organised, to include Meghan and Harry doing so well that they would be pleased by their place in the scheme of things.

On the 15th October, three days after Eugenie's wedding and just before they were due to fly out of Britain, Kensington Palace announced, 'Their Royal Highnesses The Duke and Duchess of Sussex are pleased to announce that The Duchess of Sussex is expecting a baby in the Spring of 2019.'

There was genuine delight that the Royal Family would soon possess progeny of colour.

Before their 'plane had even taken off, Meghan and Harry had the world at their feet. They landed in Australia to mass adulation. They drew huge crowds wherever they went. Unlike Harry's previous visit, when there had been friction with the press, this time there was nothing but approval. It has been said that every time there is a royal visit, the cause of republicanism is set back years in Australia. Their popularity bore this out. The only red flag throughout the whole of the tour occurred in Fiji, where Meghan gave a speech to youngsters, ostensibly inspiring them to educate themselves. She used the occasion to take a swipe at her father. It rankled with her that Tom Sr and sister Samantha from

Trevor Engelson was the tall, brash, brawny movie producer who became Meghan's first husband. They were so in love that she used to tell her best friend Nikki Priddy that she would not survive if anything happened to him. Then she outgrew him.

Before competitiveness and jealousy tore the Fab Four apart, there were high hopes that they would become the new and exciting face of monarchy. Here they are, two months before the wedding, introducing Meghan as the latest member of the Royal Foundation under the theme Making a Difference Together. Only Prime Minister Boris Johnson's sister Rachel struck a discordant note, stating, 'I fear Meghan's a bit out of tune already'.

In the run-up to the wedding, Thomas Markle Sr was humiliated by the tabloids and ill-advisedly tried to restore his dignity by cooperating with a paparazzo. Exposure would lead to two heart attacks and his daughter and son-in-law, whom he has yet to meet, severing contact with him.

FREE **LONDON** TUESDAY 15 MAY 2018   24/7 ONLINE NEWS STANDARD.CO.UK   **WEST END FINAL**

Evening Standard

MY WEDDING AGONY BY MEGHAN'S FATHER

» **DAD'S 'POPPING VALIUM'**
TO COPE WITH THE STRESS

» **ANGRY AT ELDER DAUGHTER**
AFTER STAGED PHOTOS ROW

» **SAYS HE HASN'T SPOKEN TO**
BRIDE SINCE SCANDAL BROKE

upset: Thomas Markle said today he feared he might have to return to hospital after suffering heart problems

Robert Jobson and Jonathan Prynn

MEGHAN MARKLE'S father today spoke of the emotional and physical agony he has suffered following the scandal over staged paparazzi pictures. Thomas Markle, 73, indicated last night that he would not attend his daughter's wedding to Prince Harry in Windsor on Saturday following the furore over his alleged deal with a photographer. The former Hollywood lighting director, who reportedly checked himself out of a Mexican hospital after suffering a minor heart attack six days ago, told celebrity news website TMZ he was "popping Valium" because of chest pains triggered by "emotional upset" and could return to hospital because he fears another coronary. Mr Markle specifically mentioned his elder daughter, Samantha Grant.

Continued on Page 4

Tom 'Wingman' Inskip was one of Harry's oldest and closest until he tried to dissuade Harry from rushing into marriage. Meghan ensured that he and his wife Lara, seen here walking to St. George's Chapel, suffered for the slight, though they would later get their own back.

CBS TV talk-show host and comedian James Corden and his TV producer wife Julia Carey were two of the many high-profile acquaintances asked by the royal couple to their wedding.

The inimitable Oprah Winfrey was another of the heavy-hitters from the world of entertainment who were asked in preference to family, causing Meghan's biographer Andrew Morton to observe that the guest list was a 'career move'.

Doria Ragland was a huge hit with the public as well as the Royal Family for her quiet and dignified manner, but she cut a very lonely figure at her daughter's wedding, being the only representative of the bride's family. Seen here descending the steps of St. George's Chapel with the Prince of Wales and Duchess of Cornwall after the ceremony.

Having signed the register, Harry and Meghan rejoined the congregation followed by their pages and flower girls as well as her mother Doria Ragland and his father Prince Charles and step-mother the Duchess of Cornwall. Note the spectacular but simple floral decorations.

The Queen asked the newly-wed Meghan to accompany her on a typical away day series of engagements. The normally deadpan monarch was noticeably responsive as she interacted with her vivacious grand daughter-in-law, but behind the scenes trouble was already brewing, as astute observers would have noted from Meghan's attire.

Harry and Meghan were now one of the world's most glamorous couples, and their presentation became all important. Here they are at their first Trooping the Colour, Harry in uniform and Meghan in a stylish, off-the-shoulder Carolina Herrera cocktail suit with a Philip Treacy hat.

Meghan, in Dior couture cocktail wear with a Stephen Jones hat, had pride of place beside the Queen on the Buckingham Palace balcony to view the flypast celebrating the 100th anniversary of the Royal Air Force in July 2018. Here she is with l to r: Princes Charles, Andrew, Camilla, the Queen, Harry, William and Catherine.

Meghan's habit of keeping her hands on her bump came in for so much comment that Harry approached Prince Charles and the Queen and tried to get them to muzzle the critics.

Master Archie Mountbatten-Windsor was officially two days old when his proud parents presented him to the public in a carefully orchestrated news conference at Windsor Castle, following which they introduced him to delighted his great-grandparents, whose regret is that they have not been given the chance to see as much of the baby as they would have liked. (l-r)Meghan and Harry proudly holding his son.

Meghan created a storm when she turned up at Wimbledon in June 2019 to watch her friend Serena Williams play tennis. Aside from breaking new ground by clearing out the forty surrounding seats, she was attired in jeans and a Panama hat, both of which are forbidden. She was accompanied by her Northwestern University friends Genevieve Hills (l) and Lindsay Roth (r).

In late September 2019, the very tactile Meghan and informal Harry endeared themselves to South Africans by jettisoning protocol and hugging their way through the tour. They turned triumph into sensation the day before their departure by attacking the British press and announcing a lawsuit against the Mail on Sunday.

Meghan is a great believer in the virtues of monochromality. In January 2020, she chose shades of brown as she and Harry paid a courtesy call on the Canadian High Commission and the Mission staff to thank them for the hospitality Canada was giving them while they used it as a temporary refuge prior to moving to their real destination: California.

time to time gave interviews stating that he had been a good father and had paid for her education. She disliked the implication that she was an ungrateful daughter who should be mending fences with him rather than a put-upon VIP whose public profile was being sullied by her garrulous relations. She had also contradicted Tom Sr and Samantha's version of events privately, including with Harry. One of the things he especially admired about her was how she had pulled herself up by the bootstraps from a life of little into a world of a lot. He not only took pride in how she had surmounted the many obstacles she had told him about, but how pained she was that her father and sister would proffer an alternative version of her history which effectively denied her claimed accomplishments. Fed up with her image being defaced the way it was being by them, she took advantage of the opportunity the speech in Fiji gave her, to shoot down her father's claims of having put her through Northwestern University. She categorically stated that she had done so herself, by taking part-time jobs and resorting to student loans. Honour and her image were restored.

Depending on your point of view, this was either a terrible mistake on Meghan's part, or it was a tactically clever move which went some way towards shoring up the sympathy she deserved and thrived upon from her supporters. Nonetheless, royals do not use official tours to further their own personal vendettas. They are there to represent the nation, and to further its objectives, not their own. Mixing up the roles pollutes the pond and distracts attention away from the true purpose of the visit. Which is what Meghan now did.

Although it was not yet generally known, her father had the bills to prove that he had put her through college. All he would need to do, and as he would ultimately do when she embarked upon her lawsuit against *The Mail on Sunday*, was to give a newspaper sight of them. This would prove that Meghan's struggles, though real enough, were mostly within herself and not external the way she was claiming they were. That, of course, is not to denigrate them. A woman who struggles with her identity the way Meghan has confirmed she struggled with hers is deserving of sympathy, and the fact that she surmounted her complexes and achieved what she did was commendable in anyone's language.

But, by mixing up the struggles, she opened herself up to all sorts of interpretations and misinterpretations, few of which were comfortable to hear. By far the most unfortunate consequence was that she had reopened an old wound that was best left to heal on its own. Most of the damage to her reputation had been caused by her troubled relationship with her father. Although the consequences seemed to have been very slight in the United States, where pride in Meghan as an American princess was still pronounced, and few people seemed to understand why she was not being relished in Britain the way she was on the other side of the Atlantic, here her estrangement with her father had been particularly damaging. Her critics were noisome in their assertion that everyone makes mistakes. They expected her to forgive her father for what, after all, struck them as a relatively trivial offence; a source of embarrassment rather than something serious. Failure to forgive a stranger was one thing, a friend another, but a parent? That degree of harshness did not sit well with the average person in Britain, and, unsurprisingly, sister Samantha then waded in, accusing Meghan of being a liar and an ingrate for having denied their father's generosity. The internet came alive with what they had dubbed the Markle Debacle, and while Meghan's failure to respond might have come across as quiet dignity to her admirers, to her critics it was affirmation of callousness allied to haughty indifference.

It was not yet as apparent as it would subsequently become, but a turning point had been reached. No matter what Meghan did thereafter, her troubled relations with her father had put her in such an unflattering light that, as far as half the internet and a goodly proportion of the general public in Britain were concerned, she was now singing to the deaf and dancing for the blind. This was not an enviable position to be in, and one would have had to possess a heart of stone not to be concerned for Meghan, Harry, and her father, as well as for her reputation. Could the first acknowledged woman of colour in the British Royal Family have become such damaged goods that the chances were that she would fail in the role of royal duchess?

Because much of my life is lived in the public eye, and I deal with the general public with a frequency known to few private individuals, and because in Britain most people know who I am and want to speak to me about the Royal Family, I now learnt from Mr and Mrs Joe Public how catastrophic a fall from grace Meghan and Harry had suffered. People were now dismissing him as a 'pussy-whipped' 'weakling' who was 'brain dead', 'pathetic' and being 'led by the nose' by a stronger and brighter woman and by his nether regions. Catastrophically, most of them thought that Meghan was a 'phoney' who was 'on the make' and an 'avaricious opportunist' to boot. As far as they were concerned, she was a 'hypocrite', a 'sanctimonious, pretentious, affected fraud', a 'liar' and a 'hard-hearted, self-seeking bitch who had treated her father in a manner they wouldn't treat a rabid dog'. Repeatedly, they reiterated that 'they had seen through her', and 'no matter how many hoops she jumped through' or the 'cacophony of righteousness' emanating from her, people had made their minds up about her and weren't going to change them.

This was not a desirable position for any public figure to be in, especially one who embodied the hopes of hundreds of millions of people all over the world. Not only would all those who were cheering her on be disappointed, but their hopes would be dashed and a golden opportunity lost. I hoped then, and I hope now, that she will find a way to retrieve her position and with it, the goodwill and respect with which she was endowed as she stood on those steps in May 2018 and exchanged vows to become the Duchess of Sussex. But I also know from personal experience that the British public has a nose where public figures are concerned, especially after it has seen them on television a few times and had an opportunity to get their measure. While the press can bury public figures in misrepresentations which are not easily dissipated, once the British public decides that it has seen through someone, there usually isn't much that figure can do to alter their opinion, for the British public, unlike the American, do not like resurrections. As far as they're concerned, once a corpse, always a corpse. In Britain, there are few second acts in public life.

Although things had not yet come to the pass where Meghan and Harry were so unpopular in Britain that they had crossed the Rubicon and been relegated to Has Been status, they were now in danger of approaching it. Then came even more negative reports from people close to her and Harry to further lessen her popularity. It was now being whispered that she was acquiring a reputation for treating staff in a manner most Britons disapprove of.

The one inexcusable in the upper reaches of society has always been treating staff in an untoward way. No matter how charming you are to your equals, no matter how apparently philanthropic with good causes, if you get a reputation for treating employees unacceptably, it is akin to a man being known as a wife-beater. You can be as rude as you want to your friends, family or social equals. If you want to mistreat them, and they are dumb or weak enough to let you get away with it, that's between you and them. They are your social equals, and therefore they are in a position to defend themselves. However, staff are not your social equals. They are therefore at a disadvantage from the word go. Treating them indecorously breaches every code of *noblesse oblige*, and as that matters greatly to people who regard nobility as a commendable aim in life, once you acquire a reputation for mistreating those who work for you, you lose a lot of respect and are viewed with suspicion.

It had been one thing for Meghan to acquire a reputation for being unfriendly towards Harry's friends and family, but it now became quite another as word began to spread that she behaved dubiously towards people who were not in a position to defend themselves. Prior to the marriage, people had cut Meghan some slack when they heard about how she gave vent to her frustrations when her expectations were dashed. All brides lose their rag. She's nervous. She's only human. Give her time, she'll settle down. She's in a strange country.

Sometimes, the line between compassion and gullibility is a fine one. Most people prefer to give someone the benefit of the doubt. But when the doubts reverberate symphonically, the sound carries. So it now proved in Meghan's case as first the elite, then the press, got wind of various incidents which she and Harry would be at pains to deny, but which did her reputation no good.

One incident which is meant to have taken place shortly after her marriage did not bode well for the future if it was not invented. Meghan, who is well known to be something of a perfectionist, was accused of hurling onto the floor a dress that had not been ironed to her exacting standards with the imprecation, 'You call this pressed. This hasn't been pressed. I want this pressed. Properly. Now.' Could this be true? Could anyone with aspirations to civility speak to staff like that? Hopefully, this was nothing but Chinese whispers.

The next incident involving staff was even more astonishing. I only hoped that it too was apocryphal, though the more apocrypha there were, the more likely it was that the tales were rooted in the truth, even when exaggerated or twisted. This time Meghan was on tour. She lost her temper and threw a hot beverage in the direction of someone who had annoyed her. This had resulted in the member of staff resigning and being paid £250,000 to leave without disclosing the incident.

In a way, whether the incident had taken place or not was almost beside the point. If it had, it was appalling, and if it had not, it was equally appalling that stories like this were being spread about someone who had not behaved like that. Meghan and Harry were supposedly of the opinion that all the negative stories about her were racist or snobbish in origin, but this seemed unlikely for several reasons. Firstly, most of the people who were spreading these stories were not racist or snobbish. Many of them were frankly concerned with the way Meghan and Harry had been conducting themselves. They wanted them to behave in a less aggressive, assertive, and demanding manner. They felt the Sussexes' attitudes were antagonistic and patronising when not being dogmatic and insulting. They wanted Harry and Meghan to conduct themselves the way William and Catherine did. They were often and openly at a loss as to what they could do to improve the situation, but Harry and Meghan were so caught up in their own bubble that they had become unreachable.

Then the departures began in earnest. One departure that was definitely not imagined was Senior Communications Secretary Katrina McKeever. She had been the liaison with Meghan's family in the early days. She quietly left the Kensington Palace Press Office in September 2018 amidst reports of flurries of emails descending upon her from Meghan starting at 5am every morning. Meghan was a volcano erupting with idea after idea about how she wanted to shape her role. Her work ethic was formidable, and so, staff said, was she. Too much so.

Two months later, Meghan's Personal Assistant Melissa Toubati left amidst claims that Meghan frequently reduced her to tears with her endless demands. Toubati had previously worked for Robbie Williams and Ayda Field, and was so capable that a palace source was authorised to praise her performance and make special note of the crucial role she had played in helping to organise the royal wedding.

To those in the know, this was code for Meghan being impossible, though Meghan and Harry themselves believed that their demands were reasonable. They were on a quest to save the world and nothing mattered more than that cause. If people were petty and needlessly negative, they had no place in the grand scheme of things. Meghan had a strong work ethic so drove herself and everyone else hard. Harry appreciated her commitment and, by his own account, her values. She gave of her all, and expected others to do likewise. If the fainthearted wanted to discard themselves by the wayside, they were entitled to do so. But they mustn't expect her to deviate from her path of righteousness because they were too weak to stay the course.

Two months after Melissa Toubati's tearful departure, the revolving door again creaked into action when it was announced that Amy Pickerell, Meghan's Assistant Private Secretary who was often described as her 'right hand woman', would be exiting when Meghan and Harry's baby was born. She was joined by the Communications Secretary for the Sussexes and the Cambridges, Jason Knauf, who was leaving to become Chief Executive of the Royal Foundation of the Duke and Duchess of Cambridge.

The Royal Foundation had been set up in September 2009 before William and Harry's marriages as the vehicle for their charity work. Both brides had joined their husbands upon marriage, in what became known as the Fab Four.

Then, as the world awaited the birth of Harry and Meghan's baby, word leaked out that the fractured relationships hadn't been limited to staff, and that the brothers' once close relationship had also hit the rocks. There was confirmation of a sort when Harry and Meghan announced that they would be moving offices from their shared space with William and Catherine to their own office at Buckingham Palace, and moreover they would be leaving the Royal Foundation which the two brothers had set up, to set up their own charity, Sussex Royal. They would have their own public relations chief and Instagram account. They would also be leaving Kensington Palace to live at Frogmore Cottage, ironically Grand Duchess Xenia's refuge following the overthrow of her brother Tsar Nicholas II. Meghan might not have got to wear her kokoshnik, but she would be living in her house.

That Christmas, the newlyweds joined the rest of the Royal Family at Sandringham for their first Christmas as a married couple. By then, the rumours of estrangement between the brothers and their wives had gained enough traction for the press to be speculating upon its cause. The story was not going the way royalists wanted it to, and even the tabloids were at pains to put as positive a spin on things as they could. But it was proving difficult to pretend that nothing was wrong. Although there were no verified reports, 'it's no secret that the problem arose because William warned Harry against leaping into marriage, and Meghan has never forgiven him. That girl demands nothing less than total adoration, and if she doesn't get it, you're iced,' a royal cousin told me. The press, not quite sure why there was *froideur*, were full of reports of the Queen ordering the Fab Four to put on a united front, which they did as they walked on Christmas Day from the big house to St. Mary Magdalene Church on the Sandringham estate.

Although Meghan and Harry's profile in America was high, and they could often be found on the cover or in the pages of magazines like *People*, the reality was, in Britain, they were not just celebrities the way they were on the other side of the Atlantic. They were intrinsic and fundamental members of the British Royal Family, two parts of the Fab Four whom the press wanted to succeed so they could write about them *ad nauseam*. The sisters-in-law were perfect foils for each other as well as obvious evocations of their respective stances, and as the two couples gave the press the photo op they yearned for, for a few short hours, the media were able to run with the idea that the Fab Four would continue long into the future. Catherine Cambridge was the picture of traditional royal elegance in a beautifully tailored, buttoned-up, highly visible berry-red double-breasted woollen coat with velvet pockets and collar and matching hat, while Meghan wore a black coat open to reveal her bump, with a form fitting matching dress and a Philip Treacy hat.

By this time, the palace were painfully aware that they had a whole host of problems on their hands. Not only were there the tensions within the Royal Family itself, plus the wastage of Harry's friends, but the issues between Meghan and her relations had grown into an ongoing concern. Not only were the public in Britain turning against her as a result of her attitude, but people closer to home wanted to know how any daughter could have dumped her father the way she had, especially when she herself had always said that he had been an excellent father?

This is a question I found the answer to by speaking to people who know the various parties well, including relations of his and hers. I came to the conclusion that Meghan had little choice but to behave as she did. She had established common ground with Harry in the most effective way possible: she had hooked him by appealing to his emotions, by presenting herself as a person whose strength had been forged in the crucible of deprivation and pain, just like his, and that she held the keys to happiness. Because theirs was a love match, and there was nothing to hold it together but the bonds that they forged together, the relationship's very existence would be threatened if third parties began to feed him information that was contradictory to her representations.

Meghan Markle is her own creation, as she confirmed in her two blogs. As she put it, you can be anything you want to be. All you need to do is become it. Fish can become fowl, pink green, and boundless ambition caring humanitarianism. Like all fabrications, the back of the picture is never as polished as the front, but that in itself signifies nothing.

As with all self-inventions, there was a gap between the reality of what Meghan had once been and the facade she was now presenting to the world, Harry included. That was why she had not been able to maintain many of her truly intimate friendships from her past, for Meghan in the present was not the same person as Meghan in the past had been. Indeed, as one Canadian said, the only thing the two Meghans had in common was her body. Virtually everything else was different. As Nikki Priddy said, the Meghan she knew before fame was not the same person she became after it. And while she had liked the former, she deplored the latter so much she did not want to have anything to do with her.

Spoilage of friendships can be viewed as the natural process of growing apart. It's not so straightforward when parents are involved. Although Meghan had praised her father to the skies publicly, privately she had become concerned that a garrulous loose cannon like Thomas Markle Sr would cough up inconvenient facts which might cause Harry to query aspects of her past which did not accord perfectly with her present version of events. For instance, she had led Harry to believe that she had had a far harder life than she had. She had gained his admiration by making herself out to be far more self-sufficient than she had ever been, to have surmounted struggles that did not exist. She had told him how hard she had had to struggle to put herself through university when, in fact, her time there had been one long joyride on her father's bandwagon. She didn't want Tom Sr giving the game away and shining a light on those aspects of her persona which were, to put it politely, self-generated rather than organic.

These were sound reasons for not introducing Harry to her father before the wedding. The worst possible scenario for Meghan would have been father and fiancé getting along so well that Daddy would give Harry enough information for him to realise that Flower had not been forged in quite so much steel as Harry thought she had been. He loved her strength. He drew strength and certainty from it. She could not afford to have him question the authenticity of the struggles she had evoked, though, ironically, there had been challenges. They had simply been between Meghan and herself, largely based around her identity and the embarrassment she had felt as she passed for white while being bi-racial. They had not been between Meghan and a harsh, racist world, as she now wanted people to believe, for no one could identify one incident throughout the whole of her life when she had been subjected to racist prejudice, though everyone could remember many times when she had not been subjected to any prejudice at all. Such strictures as she had faced with the world at large had been based solely on her desire to be acknowledged as special, as a star, as someone who was exceptional and out of the ordinary. These were the ordinary, mundane, everyday frustrations of an ordinary but ambitious person who viewed herself as special, pitting herself against the world until they acknowledged her view of herself as being more accurate than their own. In summation, her struggles were the ordinary tussles of an ordinary woman as she surmounted the restrictions of ordinariness until she could change them for the acknowledgement of specialness. It was the conventional journey of people pre and post fame; nothing more, nothing less. It was an everyday tale told by countless people of all hues and creeds. It had nothing to do with racial or sexual prejudice. It certainly had nothing to do with a deprived background, and all to do with the deeply unglamorous strictures of ambition.

Meghan is not an actress for nothing. She understands drama and appreciates its value. She is bright and talented enough to understand that a theatrical narrative is more engaging than a pedestrian one. One plucks at the heartstrings, the other leaves the emotions cold. She had worked herself into the position of *prima donna assoluta*, and now faced the task of maintaining her ascendency without having inconvenient relations like her father opening her version of events up to inspection. Nor could she convincingly eradicate her father without arousing suspicion. So she controlled his attendance instead. It was obvious that the safest course of action had been to get Tom Sr to fly over just before the wedding. There would be so much going on then, that there would be no time for him to interact too deeply with Harry. Her devoted swain would continue to believe that she was this brave lioness who had fought her way up in a cruel world, instead of being the pampered Flower who had been nurtured the way she really had been.

Harry is a very emotional person. He has great emotional intelligence even though he is not outstanding in its intellectual equivalent. Meghan, on the other hand, is highly intelligent, highly skilled socially, and highly effusive. She functions at a fever pitch of passion, enthusiasm and spontaneity that come across as warmth, though people who have been dumped by her regard her as insincere and opportunistic to a fault. Whether they are right or wrong, she is superficially appealing and captivating, has a talent for making people believe that she is what they want her to be, knows just what note to strike to gain the regard of those she wants to impress, and possesses *sang froid* in its fullest meaning.

According to people who know them well, Meghan won Harry by appealing to his genuinely humanitarian instincts. She did this by demonstrating her own humanitarian credentials, articulating philan-thropic values which she knew he possessed, while making herself vulnerable in his eyes. She endeared herself by appealing to his sympa-thies, by mirroring them, by making him aware of how much she had suffered at the hands of a cruel world while gaining his admiration for the brave and noble way she had coped. She could not have Daddy blow this touching picture of suffering, which she had never actually experi-enced, out of the water by shooting his mouth off.

There is much evidence to suggest that Meghan is by far a stronger and more forceful individual than Harry. Beneath the blustering Alpha male lies a sensitive boy who identifies and sympathises with those who have suffered. For all the good works Meghan has done, she has never really suffered loss and therefore does not possess a similar degree of empathy. She is also more strategic than Harry. Like many Army officers, he is good at giving orders, but he is also good at taking them. He functions best in an environment in which he can flex his muscles while having the cover of a safe roof. This the Army used to provide. Now, Meghan does. She, on the other hand, hates taking orders. If necessity requires it, as occurred when she was in *Suits*, she will cooperate, but only to the extent that it is expedient. And while she's cooperating, she also negotiates and haggles, making it clear that her cooperation is a sign of strength, not weakness, and certainly not mindlessness. In other words, Meghan is a dominating personality who only surrenders control when she has to. At all other times, she insists on being in the driver's seat.

Because she has a nurturing, considerate side to her personality, she makes an ideal mate for a man who loved his mother. She makes an even more ideal mate for one who loved and lost his mother. Her dominance comes across to him as caring. He thinks he's being mothered when in fact those who know and question Meghan's motives believe he's being controlled. One indication that there might be some substance to that suspicion is the vow Meghan wrote into the marriage service. She swore to 'protect' Harry. How she came to position herself as the protector of a prince is what fascinates. She was able to convince him that she had successfully survived so much pain and suffering, that she had the strength to protect him, a boy who lost his mother and has suffered thereafter. Because her suffering had transformed her from an ordinary woman into an extraordinary human being, he, ordinary man that he is, needs her protection.

People can say what they want about her, but Meghan is truly an amazing woman. Only someone with her remarkable gifts, uniquely imaginative personality, and undoubted cleverness could have forged the bond she did with Harry.

CHAPTER 8

Although Harry truly believed that Meghan and Meghan alone knew the route to the Holy Grail, and she still had her admirers, as she and Harry settled into marriage, an uncomfortable and growing percentage of the populace as well as the press in his native country were coming around to the distressing viewpoint that she was a pretentious piffler with the depth of a teaspoon, the sincerity of a phoney, and the trustworthiness of a fraudster let loose in a roomful of cash. This was disastrous for anyone who had hoped that she would turn the role of Duchess of Sussex into a glorious one. To those of us who understood that she represented something no amount of money could buy, the tainting of her image was laden with long term repercussions. These had the potential to affect race relations negatively, for her supporters might not realise that her detractors' objections were based largely or entirely upon her performance and what it said about her character, and might instead erroneously conclude that colour prejudice was motivating her unpopularity. This would do no one any good, no one, that is, with the possible exception of anti-monarchists and Meghan herself, who would be given a free pass if she could behave in an inappropriate manner without suffering any adverse consequences and indeed, be taken to be a victim when she was anything but one.

As the situation deteriorated, those who believed that Meghan was a non-contributory victim to her worsening reputation began questioning whether the negative attention might be due to covert colour prejudice, while those who saw her as a contributory factor to her reputation's demise became increasingly perturbed that they were being accused of racism when in fact her race had nothing to do with her unpopularity. A courtier said, 'No one [at the palace] believes that either the Duke or the Duchess of Sussex deludes themselves into thinking that racism plays any part in this. But we're all aware that they're not above playing the race card if it works to their advantage. They did it before [at the time their affair became public knowledge] but we're all hoping they won't ever do it again. It would be too damaging to the national interest. Prince Harry will see that [and will hopefully prevent it from being played]. But it will nevertheless be damaging to the national interest if they remain silent and allow their supporters to continue blaming racism for something any fool knows has nothing to do with it.'

Because Meghan and Harry's conduct was creating divisions instead of being the unifying force the monarchy is meant to be, and because the issues being thrown up were larger than simply their personal popularity, the press were on heightened alert. Controversy is always more newsworthy than dullness. A mixed narrative is always more interesting to the media than a straightforward one. Whether Meghan fully realised that her actions were geared towards gaining her ever-increasing amounts of press attention, or she was unintentionally blundering into being a newspaper's dream figure - with equal parts of glamour, controversy, conflict, conciliation and opposition all heightened with a massive question mark over what lay beneath her buffed surface - the fact is, the move she made shortly after returning from the Antipodean trip which had ended in such drama over her family background, catapulted her further into the forefront of media attention.

On the 11th December 2018, barely a month after a lithe and svelte Meghan had returned to England from their tour, she dramatically burst onto the stage as the unexpected guest of honour at the British Fashion Awards at the Royal Albert Hall. She was there to present an award to Clare Waight Keller, the artistic director of Givenchy who had designed her wedding dress. Depending on your opinion, Meghan either showed what a wonderfully warm and natural human being she was, or the actress turned on the charm which had started to wear thin with many of her critics, striding out onto the podium, her beautifully and professionally made-up face beaming brightly as only hers can, radiating delight and projecting joyousness as only a professional actress occupying a stage can.

Royalty is not known for its surprises, its predictability and reassur-ing lack of Eureka moments being two of the features its supporters find so welcome in this age of hype and unpredictability. Glamorous to a fault, but in the estimation of her critics in too Tinseltown a way as opposed to the regality royalists require, Meghan was yet again in a black dress, this time a sleek, elegant, one-shoulder figure hugger from the award winning couturiere's foreign atelier.

Her demeanour was pure Hollywood, that purveyor of glamour where bighearted immediacy cannot be bested though, to contrarians, it is a centre of artifice where everyone smilingly walks over the carcasses of their discards as they project apparently sincere hearts of gold along with equally real white veneers. Meghan could not have been more gracious or indeed loving towards Clare Waight Keller. As her friends have often said, she is a truly loving human being who never fails to give expression to her loving nature, though her critics decried her displays of affection with the jaundiced comment that they wished she could summon up something approximate for her father or the members of her husband's family with whom she was now known to be on cool terms.

In reality, both sides had a point. Meghan had been declaring behind the scenes that she felt hemmed in by royal protocol. She thought it was 'nonsense', 'cold', 'stiff', and 'inhibiting'. She wanted to be free to indulge the love she felt for people. She believed in 'hugs' and thought nothing was better at letting someone feel welcome than enveloping them in a huge embrace. She did not wish to be limited by dictats of how she should behave. Whether it was a friend, lover or stranger, if she wanted to show love to someone, she should be able to do it. She had made it clear that she would not be allowing 'all that royal protocol nonsense' to stand in the way of demonstrating how loving she was. Whether in private or in public did not matter, nor did whether she was functioning in an official or a personal capacity. Her heart was too big, her light too bright, for either to be hidden under a bushel. So she enveloped Clare Waight Keller in the most massive bear hug, all the better with which to let the critical world know that they were meanies and her display of affection signified a warmer heart and truer nature than they possessed.

Behind the scenes, Meghan had been greatly taken aback by the adverse reactions she had been generating. Like most actresses, she thrives on public acclaim and approval. The slightest criticism disconcerts her, so the level of hostility she had been receiving had rattled her to the very core of her being. Her response was to continue holding her course, projecting the image of the warm and wonderful woman she was, while also letting her friends leak stories to the press about how down-to-earth she was. Proof of this now surfaced in accounts of how she functioned as her own stylist despite being the worldwide style icon she had become, how she did her own makeup up to a professional standard even when she did not have her favourite make-up artist on hand, and how she often did her hair as well.

While such information added to her lustre with her fans, with her critics it was beside the point. They did not care about such superficialities; they were more concerned with the profundities. And, following Meghan's appearance at the Royal Albert Hall, they had alighted upon a profundity of great importance. The *Daily Express* summarised this phenomenon best when it howled, **Pregnant Meghan Markle shows off PROMINENT baby bump at Fashion Awards.**

When Meghan had stepped out onto the stage to present the award, the hall exploding in cheers, what people noticed more than the award this latest royal was handing to the designer, or the hug she enveloped her with, or even how loving she was, was the dramatic way in which her pregnancy had progressed. In four short weeks, she had gone from flat as a pancake to what one journalist described as 'the size of most women at seven months'.

Nor was Meghan content to let the immense and unexpected development speak for itself. It should have been obvious that she was so thrilled to be pregnant that she was mesmerised by the life within her. Being the sort of personality who must convey what she is feeling not only in word but indeed, before and after handing over the award, she clutched her belly. And continued clutching it. And clutched it some more. And some more still, her hands rooted to the bump in a display of such delight at the happy condition she found herself in, that she had to draw the whole world's attention to it. There was something so frankly exultant about the display that it was akin to sharing a secret of which one is inordinately proud with the whole world.

Not everyone accepted such an ostentatious display in such a flattering light. To her critics, Meghan was simply confirming that she was actressy, attention-seeking, attention-demanding, and attention-creating. One fashionista told me that she had never seen such a 'palaver' before, and questioned whether Meghan was afraid that people would miss that she was pregnant if she didn't clutch her belly like a lizard clinging to a tree, or did she fear it would jump off her body if she didn't hang onto it? Some people unkindly asked whether she was so proud of having royal seed growing in her womb that she had to draw constant attention to her condition? Or was she so full of herself and her own importance that she had to remind everyone that she was now a duchess and on the way to being the mother of a royal baby?

Counterbalancing this viewpoint were those who defended Meghan's conduct. There was much speculation that someone as new wave as her might believe that the foetus flourishes better when its mother communicates with it from outside the womb. Let Meghan do what she pleased, was their message. Leave her alone. So what if she wants to clutch her belly. She's not harming anyone.

Nevertheless, the turn the pregnancy had taken opened up other questions. How many months gone was she? Because the due date was being kept secret at the insistence of the couple, in defiance of accepted royal practice, there was speculation that she might be approaching her seventh month and the baby would arrive in March. This at least explained the Vesuvian explosion that had erupted abdominally.

The anomaly inherent in all of this was too good for Meghan's growing band of detractors to ignore. The belly clutching and the sudden growth of the bump fed right into their incredulity. They quickly leapt to the conclusion that she wasn't pregnant at all.

The internet now came alive with speculation. While all reasonable people accept that it is a forum where conspiracy theories proliferate and crazies have their say without anyone taking them too seriously, events such as the Arab Spring have also shown that it can be a platform for the dissemination of factual information that established circles, including the press, can and do suppress. All political institutions, including royal ones, monitor the internet. Their survival depends on it. Some ground-swells can wash them away unless they are careful.

Underlying the more bizarre speculations, however, was a message that Meghan might well have profited from, had she cared to listen to it. This was that too many people didn't believe that she was what she was projecting. She did not ring true to them. She did not convince them. Despite the decades she had spent acting up a storm, they were simply not buying her act. Since much of royal life is about getting the tone and content right, of projecting the appropriate image and doing so in a believable and constructive way, Meghan would have been well advised to have listened to some of the criticism.

Beneath this, there was another issue. Royalty doesn't act; it is. The message being delivered was that she should stop projecting and start being. She should be more like the Queen, or Princess Anne, or the Prince of Wales, or Camilla, and less like Princess Michael of Kent, whose affectations and pretentiousness had made her a mockery which her detractors asserted Meghan was quickly matching and now in danger of exceeding.

In fairness to both sides, Meghan is an actress and actresses act. Asking someone whose whole life has been about performance to unlearn the art of projection is a tad optimistic. This, of course, is one of the reasons why Prince Philip did not think Harry should marry Meghan. He foresaw the problems she would have as she went about her royal duties, not only in terms of executing them behaviourally but also in the discomfiture she would endure as her performance was rated. With rating inevitably comes slating, which no one as thin-skinned as Meghan would find tolerable. The Queen and Prince Philip had been friendly with Princess Grace of Monaco. They knew the struggles she had had before she was taken seriously. And how, once she had settled into the role of ruling princess and been accepted in it, she had chafed against its restrictions. Moreover, Grace had taken the whole business of royalty far more seriously than Meghan did. She had been highly motivated to fit in, and had made the sacrifices even when she was tempted to do otherwise. But that hadn't made them any the easier to bear. By the time of her untimely death, she had taken to poetry readings as a means of satisfying the undying yearning to be on stage. Would Meghan have the motivation to do something similar, or would the actress within her prevent her from adjusting to royal demeanour while also propelling her to make a hash of a role which, with a bit of willingness on her part, she might be able to master successfully, to the benefit of herself, the monarchy, and her ethnicity.

Although the public will have thought nothing about the struggles of an actress adjusting to a role that requires the absolute opposite of projection, Meghan's actressy demeanour was turning out to be both a plus and a minus. Being a more polished and dramatic performer than any of the other royals, she wowed where they did not. But this, for many, was a part of the problem. Only time would provide a solution, for, until people got used to her and realised that her actressiness might not be a sign of insincerity but merely the manifestation of an innately dramatic personality, they would continue to look askance. In the meantime, they would be faulting her on the grounds that she was a little too conscious of what she was doing, that she deliberately projected just that little bit more than they were used to with the other royals. In reality, there was an exact corollary between Meghan when she was starting out as an actress and Meghan when she started out as a duchess. In both situations, her eagerness to project what she believed the role required was so excessive that she did not strike the right note. It was for that reason that she took so long to achieve success as an actress, and it was the same reason why she got some people's backs up.

Putting the admiration of fans to one side, public figures are most convincing when they are not focused on their performance, nor on conveying any message except authenticity. When a public figure is so busy enacting an underlying message that onlookers are made to feel they are being railroaded into sidings not of their own choosing, they rebel against the celebrity's message and come to their own, oftentimes entirely opposite, conclusions. They feel that they are being manipulated, and they do not like it. This, of course, is the failing of all hams. This is why the Queen has declared that she will not act. This is why royalty and aristocracy are brought up from the cradle never to simulate, but to be authentic, even to be perceived as inadequate rather than false. To avoid anything that will smack of manipulativeness. To be forthright or at least bland rather than hypocritical. Even to be considered rude rather than insincere. To avoid pretending, but to *behave* properly and authentically.

Meghan's projections by now were proving to be her undoing, for too many people who wished to be convinced by her but were not. These projections, ringing the hollow note they did, now added fuel to the fire where her expanding bump was concerned. The result was that she, and by extension the monarchy, became involved in one of the most distasteful stories since 1688.

Not being a conspiracy theorist, I was prepared to consider that Meghan's conduct as she drew attention to what she called 'the bump' owed more to her actressiness than to anything else. However, the word had spread on the internet amongst an uncomfortably large number of contributors that she was attempting to con the world into believing that she was pregnant when she was not. While it was possible to discount some of the contributors as crazies, or something even more odious, like racists, there were just too many people piling in, some quite sane-sounding, for the problem to be dismissed out of hand. Plainly, there was a problem, and it needed to be addressed respectfully and, if possible, learnt from.

According to the doubters, Meghan had got too big too quickly. She had then continued to grow at a pace that was more in keeping with a woman having triplets than one who was having one child or even twins.

Soon, I had journalists approaching me every time I attended an event in public. Then they started ringing me up. Did I know what was going on? What was the inside story on how the palace was coping with the deluge of internet stories about the bump being a prosthesis? The palace was stonewalling them, as it ought to have been doing.

The speculations being fed to Fleet Street for Meghan's conduct would have been entertaining, had the matter not been so serious. A *Mail* journalist told me that there was a persistent rumour that 'the reason she's always clutching the bump is because she needs to keep it in place.' This journalist also said that there were stories circulating about the bump slipping; about photographers having taken pictures of

Meghan when the bump had slipped; about the bump being sometimes too high, sometimes too low, other times just right.

Although all segments of the mainstream press, from the respectable broadsheets to the most downmarket tabloids, avoided reporting on these stories, their very existence was an embarrassment to the monarchy as well as a concern that these rumours might gain further traction. Also embarrassing and of growing concern was Meghan's increasingly flamboyant conduct as she answered criticism of her belly clutching by clutching her belly ever more resolutely.

This was not the sort of story people who wanted Meghan to succeed cared to see. It was at best distasteful and more realistically damaging, not only to her status but to the aspirations her supporters had for her. Aside from the occasional woke journalist, the only other category of individual in society who seemed to commend her rebellious flamboyance as she met criticism with further ostentation was minor celebrities who were pregnant. I attended several premieres where some virtual unknown would encircle her unborn child in front of the cameras. None, however, did what Meghan did. Only she kept her hands firmly planted on her protuberance after the flashes had faded. Although there were simple explanations, ranging from rebelliousness to New Age Communication, which could explain away Meghan's determination, as far as many of the people who came into contact with her were concerned, the belly-clutching really was too much. The chief ground for criticism was that ladies simply do not clutch their bellies, pregnant or otherwise. No one except the New-Agers were buying the line that Meghan was soothing the baby, and as the pregnancy progressed and the bump grew apace while her hands continued to hover over it, the criticism grew louder because there has always been a generally accepted viewpoint that modest women simply don't clutch their pregnant bellies. Doing so draws undue attention to a fact which all societies have traditionally treated with respect and circumspection, irrespective of class or colour, whether one is in the US, Canada, Britain, Europe, Africa, Asia, the Middle East, the Far East, the Sub-Continent, South and Central America, the Caribbean or the Antipodes.

Another consideration from the point of view of Meghan's critics was the fact that, until fairly recently, pregnant royal women were so discreet that they did not draw attention to their condition or even say they were pregnant. Some might allude to being *enceinte*, while in the aristocracy women might 'breed', but they would not 'make a spectacle of themselves' by wearing clothes that accentuated their condition, nor would they flaunt their pregnancy the way Meghan was flaunting hers.

Once more, people in certain circles began to query why Harry was letting this groundswell of criticism grow. He knew what was acceptable behaviour to the British, and what was not. Pregnancy is a fact of life, but one which has personal connotations. Like all bodily functions of a personal nature, it is treated with *finesse* irrespective of class, colour or creed. Just as how British men do not advertise their private parts through their clothing, nor do they scratch or make adjustments except out of view, nor does anyone go around belching and farting as if the public arena is a private lavatory, pregnant women do not draw undue attention to their condition. While it is acceptable for a pregnant woman to fleetingly pass her hand over her bump occasionally, accentuating it the way Meghan was doing was exceptional, and her conduct was not only exciting comment amongst all classes of people, but doing so without merit.

This was not a good scenario where Meghan and Harry were concerned. However, rather than respond to the sensitivities of those whose feathers they were ruffling, they dismissed them out of hand by refusing to alter conduct which a too large percentage of the population found objectionable. Their attitude was: Meghan can do what she wants. If you don't like it, lump it. However, some of those sensitivities were not stylistic, but went to deeper fundaments within all societies, civilised or otherwise. Pregnancy touches upon many invisible strands and, as Harry and Meghan's roles within British national life were as representatives of the very people whom she was offending, they were in effect abnegating their responsibilities and coming across, whether thinkingly or otherwise, as arrogant and uncaring.

What also lost Meghan and Harry admirers was that, as the bump got bigger and bigger, her dresses got tighter and tighter. Possibly this too was an issue they did not understand the significance of, living as they were doing in a mutually admiring bubble where Meghan could do no wrong and Harry backed her up uncritically at every turn. However, skintight clothes on pregnant women are a breach of the code of ladylike conduct by which vast swathes of the British public, irrespective of class or colour, live. Just as how modesty forbade the extreme public displays of affection to which Meghan and Harry were prone until they ceased being invited to dinner parties, so too did the wearing of extremely tight clothes when pregnant except in the confines of one's own bedroom and bathroom. The question to be answered was: Why was a royal duchess wearing thin, stretchy fabric pulled tight over her bump, her belly button displayed for all to see, in defiance of all accepted custom in her adopted country? To show how wide a spectrum of objection there was, a black West Indian said, 'It's not seemly;' a duchess said, 'This is exhibitionism run riot;' while a young Nigerian woman put it slightly differently, 'I would be stoned back home if I went out in public dressed like that.'

In the light of such disapproval, it was symptomatic of the deference and latitude with which Meghan was being treated, that no one in the Royal Family or at the palace read her the riot act. This had not been the case when Diana and Sarah York used to step out of line. They would be called to order by the Queen's Private Secretary, who was the brother-in-law of the former and the first cousin once removed of the latter. Diana Wales once complained to me about how Bobby Bellows, as she called Sir Robert (now Lord) Fellowes had carpeted her for not wearing tights. Although times had changed, society's concept of decorum had not to such an extent that Meghan's sheer attire was broadly acceptable to the average Briton. Because I was rooting for her to succeed, I felt that it would be in her best interest if someone pointed out to her that this was causing disquiet where one would have hoped to find approval. I therefore suggested to a royal cousin that someone sympathetic have a quiet word with her and point out how important it was that she clean up that aspect of her act, if none other. I was told that that would never happen. She was so opinionated, so calculated and deliberate in all her actions, so sensitive to criticism, so resentful of anything but the most fulsome praise and displays of approval, that she would 'eat off the head' of anyone who 'dared' to say anything to her. Then she'd 'dump' them.

This was sadly reminiscent of the past. 'It's Diana all over again,' I said. To which the royal cousin bitterly replied, 'You said it, not me.'

Knowing that the Queen had once invited the Fleet Street editors to Buckingham Palace when Diana was pregnant with William to ask them to lay off her, and that the press had also kept its distance from William and himself when they were growing up in a compact agreed between the editors and the palace, Harry approached both his father and grandmother. He wanted them to intervene on Meghan's behalf, to put an end to the critical commentaries. She was very upset about the backlash her behaviour was causing. She was especially put out about the comments about her belly clutching. She felt everyone was being 'mean' and 'cruel' to her and wanted a stop put to it. It hadn't occurred to either herself or Harry that the way to achieve closure was to stop behaving in the way that was triggering the objections. They genuinely felt that Meghan should be able to clutch her belly as much as she wanted, and that the entire British press should be muzzled rather than she desist from the practice that so many found noteworthy.

As far as Harry was concerned, it was his duty to 'protect' his wife, who was very 'sensitive' and 'took things very much to heart'. He had become as obsessed with the concept of 'protection' as she was, and they used the word all the time. It was one of the catch-alls, along with 'change', 'the greater good', 'humanitarianism', 'negativity' and 'progressive' that littered their language. As far as they were concerned, if she wanted to clutch her belly till the cows came home, he would defend her right to do so to the death. No one had the right to upset her with their negative responses. Hyper-sensitive to criticism and hyper-emotional in their reactions, they claimed that their lives were being 'destroyed' by all the 'negativity'. It was up to his father and grandmother to help him 'protect her.' He really didn't know how much more of this 'torment' they could 'endure'. Unless Charles and the Queen assisted him in 'protecting' her - the word he kept on using - they would be preventing him from fulfilling his role as a husband. 'His and Meghan's lack of proportion was breathtaking,' a royal cousin said. 'The Queen and Prince Charles heard him out and expressed regret but said there was nothing they or anyone else could do. Effectively they pointed out in as gentle a manner as possible - Harry is extremely emotional, and it's almost impossible to get through to him when he has the bit between his teeth - that this is a free country and the Royal Family values a free press even when they don't like what it's saying. They made it clear that they could not interfere with the freedom of the press when it is making what it believes to be fair comment on the behaviour of a member of the Royal Family. Harry was very unhappy with their lack of *support*, as he put it. Neither he nor Meghan could see that their personal comfort did not come before the freedom of the press, but both the Queen and Prince Charles did.'

Little did anyone know at the time, but in refusing to join forces with Harry, the Queen and Prince Charles had triggered unforeseen consequences. Thereafter, Harry and Meghan would be looking for ways to break the back of their critics. And they didn't care if there were constitutional consequences either, for they were in the process of working themselves into the uniquely contradictory position of being royalty when they wished to swathe themselves in that cloak, and private citizens when that mantle suited them better.

By this time, the mainstream public were beginning to pick up on some of the concerns that were feeding the rumours at grassroots level. 'She isn't even a good actress,' the Nigerian who alluded to stoning said. 'If you've seen *Suits,* you've seen the act. Sometimes she's acting out a scene from one episode, sometimes another. There's nothing real about that woman.' I pointed out that Meghan might merely be projecting how she genuinely feels, and was silenced with, 'Then someone ought to tell her to stop all the projecting.' With that, I had no argument, though I could see how her admirers would be disappointed if she stopped beaming them her subliminal messages.

Matters of sartorial taste aside, the real danger was what would happen if the wider public came to believe, as a vociferous segment of the internet commentators and the press did, that Meghan was faking a pregnancy. Because the palace were alert to the danger, there were teams of people working behind the scenes to shut down some of the internet sites and shut up the more extreme commentators.

Buckingham Palace has traditionally had a very competent bureau-cracy. They may be colourless compared with savvy, aggressive American media management specialists like Sunshine Sachs, but they do know their business, and they go about it quietly and efficiently. The courtiers who run the monarchy direct not only royal operations but the Royal Family itself. All royal diaries are agreed six months in advance. If the Queen is doing something in Aberdeen that warrants press attention, the remainder of the family undertakes pedestrian duties that will not make the papers but will address the needs of the community the royal is serving. The same rule applies across the board. One royal does not steal another's thunder. Doing so undermines the whole system and defeats the long term goals of the monarchy, which are to further various initiatives in a meaningful way so that the public appreciates what is being done in its name. The only person who ever bucked that system before Meghan and Harry started to was Diana. She used to compete, at first with her husband, then, in the run-up to her separation and thereafter until her death, with the entire Royal Family. 'She delighted in causing discomfort up at Balmoral,' the diarist Richard Kay said, giving away only part of the reason for her mischievous behaviour. The truth is, Diana liked being the centre of attention. She was also competitive and addicted to the attention she got from the press, and the only time she was satisfied was when she rather than any of the other royals was the item of the day.

Although no one at the palace yet suspected that Meghan might be Diana's reincarnation, they did feel that there were discomfiting resonances between the two women. Both were troublesome in that they did as they pleased, refused to take direction, and had a talent for whipping up controversy. 'The bad old days are back,' a courtier said during the pregnancy. 'We waste so much time dealing with the fallout from all that's going on around the Duchess of Sussex that some of us have time for little else. There's a sinking feeling of *déjà vu*.'

One consolation was that the rumours surrounding the falsity of Meghan's pregnancy would come to a natural end once she gave birth. There was an established regimen for royal pregnancies and births, and these would silence the doubters. Royal mothers-to-be invariably used Court gynaecologists and obstetricians, leading men in their field whose reputations were beyond reproach. There would therefore be no doubt as to who was carrying the baby, or who had given birth to it, once it was delivered so transparently.

The birth of royal babies used to require the presence of the Home Secretary, who would remain in attendance throughout labour until the infant was born. This custom had arisen following the birth in 1688 of James, Prince of Wales, son of King James II and Queen Mary of Modena. Because James II and his consort were Roman Catholic, once they had a son to supplant the king's two non-Catholic daughters from his first marriage to the Earl of Clarendon's daughter Lady Anne Hyde in the line of succession, the possibility of Catholicism being reinstated as the nation's official religion became the hottest topic of the day. This was intolerable to the Protestant lobby, who overthrew the king, in what is known to history as the Glorious Revolution, by accusing him and his queen of smuggling in a male baby in a warming pan into the palace as a ploy to secure the Catholic succession to the throne. This was a farcical notion, for the custom was that all royal *accouchements* were witnessed by countless courtiers aside from physicians and family. Nevertheless, the ploy worked, James II, his queen and heir were driven into exile to the Court of his first cousin King Louis XIV in France, and a law was passed requiring the Home Secretary to be present at each royal birth thereafter, to prevent the passing off of infants. James II's elder daughter Mary was then invited by Parliament to take the throne with her husband and paternal first cousin William, Prince of Orange, who reigned as King William III, while the rightful kings of England remained in exile abroad.

The custom of the Home Secretary bearing witness to the delivery of all royal infants was only discontinued after the birth of Princess Alexandra in 1936, by which time it was deemed to be redundant, qualified Court physicians being seen as equally safe preventatives to the smuggling in of illegitimate babies.

Until the last quarter of the twentieth century, royal infants were born at home rather than in hospital. The Queen's four children were born at Buckingham Palace while Princess Margaret's son was delivered at Clarence House, home of the Queen Mother, and her daughter at her own home, Kensington Palace. There was no secrecy. The medical professionals in charge were all known to the public.

This tradition extended into the next generation but for one important difference. Royal babies started being delivered in hospitals. The Lindo Wing of St. Mary's Paddington in London became the favoured place. Once more, there was no secrecy. The royal mother was surrounded by medical staff, the senior doctors' names being made public as a way of eliminating any suspicion of subterfuge. Although it is unlikely to have been common knowledge, this was an extension of the age-old practice whereby royal births were always publicly verifiable through unimpeachable witnesses. The public, after all, had a right to know that their potential monarch had a right to the throne, and both sets of rights were respected through the reinforcing presence of witnesses. This was true even under absolutist monarchies, hence why Marie Antoinette's room was so stuffed full of courtiers at the birth of her first child that she grew faint from the lack of air, necessitating the removal of several of the witnesses. This might have been an extreme example, but the reality is, potential monarchs are living representatives of the people and, as such, a form of public property. Their provenance needs to be beyond doubt.

It was therefore contrary to all known custom for Harry and Meghan to decide that they would not be revealing the names of her medical team. This, they stated, was private. Their argument was that they were private individuals and, as such, entitled to the same degree of privacy as anyone else. This premise, of course, was simply not factual. Harry was sixth in line to the throne. A child born to him and his wife would automatically be seventh in the order of succession. William and Catherine sometimes travelled with their three children in the same aircraft something which no other heir to the throne had done before. Should the 'plane crash, Harry and Meghan would be the heirs assumptive after Prince Charles. As the Queen was in her nineties, there was the presumption that sooner or later Charles would be king. But if he should die before the Queen, and the Cambridge family had been wiped out in an accident, that meant that Harry and Meghan would become the next Prince and Princess of Wales, with their child third in line to the throne. Once the Queen died, they would become King and Queen, their child its father's immediate heir. The possibility was not so remote as to be beyond contemplation, which meant that their demands for privacy were spurious and unconstitutional.

Moreover, by creating a degree of opacity that had never before existed, Harry and Meghan were, whether through ignorance or obduracy was beside the point, feeding the rumours that she was not pregnant and that their expected child was being borne by a surrogate. Had Buckingham Palace wanted a worst case scenario to deal with, they would have been hard-pushed to invent one, and this, to the courtiers, meant that their lives were being made quite unnecessarily impossible for no better reason than that Harry and Meghan were putting their desires before the Crown and the Nation's interests.

Bad as that was, Harry and Meghan then decreed that the baby would not be born in a hospital, but at home. There had been no home births for two generations. Not only was this bucking the trend, but it was adding a whole new layer of opacity to an already needlessly dark situation. Medical wisdom was that home births might be relatively safe for young mothers, but geriatric motherhood starts at twenty eight and Meghan was a decade older. Putting aside the political inadvisability of a home birth, Harry and Meghan were putting herself and the baby in unnecessary danger. 'The whole thing was just insane,' a courtier said.

Despite all of this, Meghan and Harry had decreed how they would disport themselves and they were not prepared to countenance any opposition. They continued to insist that they were private individuals who had a right to have their baby as and when and how they pleased. They wanted this time for themselves, and could see no reason to change their minds. Britain is a free country and it is virtually impossible to force an implacable adult to do something he or she does not wish to do, even when the national interest is at stake. As long as no laws are being broken - and Harry and Meghan were breaking no laws despite flouting a whole range of protocols and precedents - the powers-that-be had no choice but to accede to their demands and allow them to proceed with the home birth they were demanding.

The way to clear up a mystery is to shed light upon it. The way to increase its power is to lure it further into opacity, as Meghan and Harry were doing. It is hardly surprising that even people who had doubted the stories about Meghan's bump being a prosthesis, who had thought that the Doubting Thomases were being silly in their suspicions, now began to question what was really going on.

In the midst of this turmoil Meghan did something which shored up the disbelievers in a way only one's worst enemy would wish. At nearly eight months pregnant, she attended a function, elegantly accoutred in the highest of high heels. She greeted a child, got down on her haunches, legs spread wide open, displayed her undoubted skill in dealing with children, then without missing a beat, bounced right back up. This was an exceptional display of agility, even for an advanced yogi like her, and it caused astonishment. Indubitably, Meghan is an extraordinary woman, and this proved it, for while most women start waddling like a duck by their seventh month, and find it difficult to walk straight in flats much less balance themselves on their haunches while wearing high heels in the final trimester of pregnancy, there she was, giving everyone sight of how truly amazing she is.

Whether it was Meghan's natural ability to gain attention, both positive and negative, or her intention to remain at the forefront of all news reports by always providing the press with some new angle or snippet with which to run, thereby knocking all the other royals off the front pages, or whether she was so naive that she honestly didn't realise that her behaviour was feeding a frenzy of her own creation, what she did next was pure genius in terms of headline nabbing. She announced that she would be retreating from public view until the baby was born, and moreover that she and Harry had no intention of revealing when the birth had taken place until they were good and ready. She would not be parading around with a newborn. She objected to the custom whereby royal women stepped out of the Lindo Wing, shortly after giving birth, with their baby wrapped up in blankets while they themselves were beautifully coiffed and attired. That sort of thing was barbaric, she maintained, yet again conveying the message that she disapproved of royal traditions and her way was the more enlightened one. As far as she was concerned, the custom put too much pressure on the woman, and being an avowed feminist, she wanted to protect herself and all royal women by changing the practice. She therefore wouldn't be playing ball. She would be enjoying being a new mother in the privacy of her own home, with her husband, as is the right of all mothers and fathers. This was 'their time', she said, and they wanted to keep it to themselves. Only when they were good and ready would they 'share' their joy with the world. On one level, her argument was sound if one accepted the premise that she was a private individual and not a constitutionally significant national figure, but on another, it was guaranteed to provoke a reaction, and sure enough, it triggered a whole new wave of speculation about the baby.

The basic theme was that Meghan and Harry had gone to ground to await its arrival, but where, the internet and too many speculators wanted to know, was it coming from? A damaging number of people were now convinced that Meghan would not be giving birth at all. Had they known about James II, Mary of Modena and James, Prince of Wales, they would have concluded that this was an updated version of the Baby in the Warming Pan. Only this time it was being smuggled in right under the noses of the world's press, according to the conspiracy theorists.

To add even more fuel to the fire, the Sussexes now issued instructions stipulating the degree of privacy they required. These were new and increased demands, coinciding not only with the impending birth of the baby, whose due date they were careful to keep secret in defiance of precedent, but with their move from Nottingham Cottage at Kensington Palace to Frogmore Cottage. An exclusion zone was declared around their new residence. Press, public and neighbours were banned from its environs. Local residents who were used to seeing members of the Royal Family out and about, such as the Queen, the Duke of York, even the late Queen Mother and Princess Margaret when they had been alive, and who were used to exchanging nods and sometimes even brief words, were informed that they must not approach, acknowledge or even look in the direction of either Harry or Meghan. Some of the strictures were so taut that the recipients interpreted them as impertinent rather than merely offensive. For instance, if the locals saw the couple walking their dogs, they were not even to look in their direction, and if one or other of their two dogs bounded up to them, they were not to pet it. This was a new way of doing things, one that the locals believed claimed all rights for the Sussexes, while stripping them of their own rights, so that they could not even be civil or respectful to the couple or neighbourly with the pets. This did not sit well with any of their neighbours, some of whom made their sentiments known to such an extent that word leaked out to the press. The reality was, Harry and Meghan had created a *cordon sanitaire* around their property, themselves, and their pets such as had never been done before. Had they been trying to make enemies and create mysteries, they could not have gone about things more efficiently. But if they were trying to protect themselves and their privacy, they had gone about their objectives so cack-handedly that they had triggered suspicion, resentment, and hostility where a lighter touch, fewer demands and some respect for the rights of others and the traditions of this country would have given them, if not the privacy of private individuals, at least the respect and admiration which they presumably still wanted from the British public.

Several journalists told me they had misgivings about what was happening, but the press nevertheless fell in with the party line. This was that the Sussexes were obsessed with privacy and were insisting upon being treated as private individuals instead of the royals they were, so, rather than the newspapers printing the suspicions that the ground was being laid for a deception on a massive scale, they ran with the story that Harry and Meghan were behaving like spoilt, demanding, hypocritical brats who contradictorily wanted to be treated as private citizens when it suited them, despite requiring at all other times that they must be accorded all the privileges and constitutional dignities that went along with being royalty.

These demands were uncomfortably reminiscent of those made by autocratic royals going back a century or two, and since Harry and Meghan claimed to be progressive game-changers who wanted to be forces for good and to leaven the inequities of society, there seemed to be an innate contradiction which got the press's back up as well as the neighbours'. Worst of all, however, was the suspicion, so far unaired in the mainstream press, that their restrictive imprecations smacked of paranoia, 'unless they have a secret they need to keep,' as a journalist from the *Mail* observed.

Quite how Harry and Meghan had worked themselves into the position whereby the choice for journalists was between spoilt, hypocritical, mentally unbalanced brats displaying signs of psychosis or an astute pair harkening back to the bad old days when royals could do as they pleased and everyone had to fall into line, was not so easily unravelled. But the fact was, their erection of an unseen fence around their new home fuelled the fires of suspicion that they could possibly be preparing to practise a massive sleight of hand on an unsuspecting public, while their excessive secretiveness further fanned the flames. From the outside looking in, it might have appeared as if the British press were carping and petty, but to those of us in the know, their restraint was surprising and commendable.

Unsurprisingly, Meghan and Harry's behaviour had the undesirable effect of increasing internet speculation regarding the impending birth. This ran to theories that the royal couple needed to create a buffer zone between themselves and the world, behind which they could have a baby delivered that would then be passed off as one to which she had given birth. Many a questioner wanted to know why couldn't the doctors' names be made public? What was the big secret? If Meghan and Harry had nothing to hide, why were they hiding away like that? What was so confidential about the names of the attending physicians? Were they afraid that a doctor might confirm that the baby had been born to a surrogate and not to Meghan? Weren't doctors' patients protected by client confidentiality as a matter of course? Since their privacy was protected by legal and professional protocols, why the secrecy unless they were covering something up? The whole thing smacked of too many cloaks and daggers, and the common thread that emerged on the internet was that only those who are intent on practising sleights of hand demand the extraordinary degree of protection Harry and Meghan were demanding. As far as far too many people now believed, the extraordinary lengths to which the couple had gone led them to believe that Harry and Meghan were not protecting their privacy but themselves against the possibility of exposure.

This was hardly a viewpoint any supporter of the monarchy wanted. It mystified many within the Establishment that Harry and Meghan would prefer to continue tripping down the path that had given rise to these suspicions rather than taking steps to overcome the suspicions. However, they dug their heels in and stubbornly refused to alter their plans. Indeed, they began to behave as if they were being victimised. They simply could not see that their own behaviour was almost entirely responsible for what was happening.

The palace would have had to be particularly inept not to understand that Harry and Meghan's behaviour was feeding rather than defeating the latter-day version of the Warming Pan rumours. 'You can imagine how people were tearing their hair out at the palace,' a royal cousin said. This was just the sort of conjecture no reputable organisation wants. But Harry and Meghan had done everything possible to increase rather than decrease the speculation with which the internet was alive. No one was pleased by what was happening, but it was impossible to get through to the couple. He faithfully backed up her demand that she was entitled to give birth however she pleased, and supported her requirements to such an extent that even people who had originally thought that the Warming Pan rumours were preposterous began to question whether there might not be some substance to them. Quite how such rumours could be in anyone's interest, much less a royal couple's, seems to have eluded them. But Meghan and Harry are a united couple, and one which adheres to its chosen path despite opposition, for the lesson Meghan had learnt over the years was to stick to her guns and do what she thought best. The lady is most definitely not for wavering.

It was amidst this extremely dubious background that the birth of the baby was first announced on the Instagram account that the Sussexes had started the month before. The announcement was simple, stylish and effective in a 'classy' way as befitted the mother from Hollywood who had recently announced to someone in the presence of a deeply insulted onlooker, 'I'm here to show 'em how things should be done. They're just not classy enough.' Certainly the account was a lot more stylish than anything any other royal had hitherto thought up, and so too was the announcement. It was nothing like the dull, conventional notice posted on an easel in a plain frame later that same day behind the railings of Buckingham Palace, when the Queen and the Royal Family announced how pleased they were that the Duchess of Cambridge, later altered to Sussex, had been safely delivered of a boy, with mother and baby both doing well.

Meghan and Harry's Instagram announcement rocked with updated glamour and contemporary chic. 'It's a BOY!', the communique rang out, the white lettering of the words tastefully contrasting with the royal blue background, beneath the stylishly regal ducal coronet and the inter-mingled H and M initials of the couple in Meghan's own calligraphic handwriting at the top of the page. Underneath those three dramatic words, was another, equally emphatic, and surprisingly revelatory hint of those aspects of the Sussex identity which were being highlighted: 'Their ROYAL HIGHNESSES the DUKE and DUCHESS of SUSSEX are OVERJOYED to announce the BIRTH of their CHILD.'

To those in the know, this slick, highly-professional, hyper-glam-orous and attention-grabbing presentation was only to be expected. According to Liz Brewer, socialite doyenne of the British aristocratic PR world, whose information came from someone at Buckingham Palace's Press Office, and according to a European prince whose information came from a British royal, Meghan had flown to LA shortly after the baby's conception with the specific objective of employing the best Instagrammers in the world. The brief she gave them was straight-forward enough:

1) I need you to create the world's number one Instagram account for me. It needs to end up having more followers than any other Instagram account on earth;

2) I want to be bigger than Diana, Princess of Wales;

3) I need you to make me the most famous woman in the world.

If Meghan was naive enough to think that the palace wouldn't hear about her plans, she was mistaken. There is very little that happens in the royal world that the palace doesn't get wind of, usually sooner rather than later. As long as she functioned within royal parameters, no one object-ed to her ambitions, though the feeling was that it is always safer to err on the side not being too driven, excessive ambition being somewhat suspect in royal circles since the days of Lady Macbeth and certainly something to be avoided since Charles I lost his head to the axe in 1649.

Although Meghan's well-wishers, myself included, would have liked her to set her sights lower, she has always been astonishingly open about her objectives and ambitions, including to the professionals she briefs. As Nelthorpe-Cowne has stated, Meghan told her that she and Harry intended to 'change the world', which she actually interpreted as meaning that Meghan wanted to 'rule the world'. While that might seem an exaggeration of Meghan's aim, the admission that she and Harry felt they could change the world showed that they both had no issues with confidence and that they were eager to wield influence above and beyond what royals are expected to possess in this democratic age. She also told her media people that she wanted to break the internet, and would later on that year be disappointed when the *Vogue* magazine issue which she guest edited failed to achieve that objective, despite her specific instructions that her American media representatives, Sunshine Sachs, should strive to achieve that objective.

For all her forthrightness, Meghan did not seem to appreciate that articulating such ambitions, when you're a member of a royal family, might be acceptable in the United States, but in Britain they leave the listener wondering whether you really have any understanding of what your role should be. It is no more appropriate for a royal duchess to want to break the internet, to be the most famous woman in the world, or to have the largest Instagram following, than for her to want to pose nude in Playboy magazine or become the Pope of Rome. Each ambition is equally undesirable, for the reasons which follow.

The royal world is not a platform for personal achievement or the realisation of personal ambitions, but a fully-established and functional organ of state. Popes, prostitutes and princesses should not aspire to certain degrees of recognition, for, in doing so, they denigrate their proper function and disparage the institution of which they are a part.

Once the palace were informed about Meghan's brief to her people in LA, they naturally worried that she might inflict damage upon the monarchy as she set about achieving such contemporary and inappropriate ambitions. Nowhere in her brief had there been the typically royal concepts of duty, obligation, unsung public service, or any of the other driving forces behind the monarchy. If the information as reported back to them really was as stated by the well-placed source - and there was no reason to doubt it, as it came from an impeccable quarter - Meghan's objectives seemed to them to be fame for fame's sake. This was truly frightening to them, for everyone of rank and status knows that the pursuit of fame as an end in itself is invariably destructive. Partly, this is because positive publicity never gives sufficient column inches to fame-hungry people. The only thing that keeps the flame of fame flickering brightly is variability. The narrative has to have twists and turns, negativity and positivity, drama and conflict, controversy and unpredictability. Without these elements, the level of fame each individual achieves is determined by the degree of interest that his or her activities and talents genuinely attract. This is true of even the most famous people in the world, for instance the Queen, the Pope, the Dalai Lama, or Albert Einstein when he was alive. The flame of publicity will flare up intermittently for them, but no matter how famous you are, unless you're actively pursuing attention, you are often out of the news. The only people who remain topical with any constancy are those who court publicity, who do what it takes to keep themselves splattered over the papers and before the eyes of the world on a daily or weekly basis.

The palace had been down this route before and they had no desire to do so again. Diana, Princess of Wales had been a fame junkie. If a day went by when she was not in the news, she could become depressed and find some way of inserting herself back into the narrative. At the very moment that she was bemoaning how the press were pursuing her, how she could get no surcease from their unwanted attentions, and how no one must let the press know that she would be attending this or that event, she herself would violate her own privacy. There is a very entertaining description, in former Conde Nast International president Nicholas Coleridge's memoir *The Glossy Years,* of Diana attending a luncheon at Vogue House under the most secretive of conditions. As Coleridge is walking her out to her car at the end of the meal, they are papped. He wonders who on earth could have betrayed their trust. Upon making enquiries, he discovers that Diana herself had rung up the press to inform them that she would be leaving Vogue House at such and such a time.

There were many different variations on this theme, several of which were known to Buckingham Palace, if only because Diana tried just about every trick in the book to ensure that she remained a figure of interest to the press. She was so resourceful that her tactics are still regarded as the ultimate manual for press manipulation. The idea that Meghan might develop into another Diana 'filled them [everyone at the palace] with terror', according to a princess who is a close friend of mine. Their reasoning was simple. Fame-hungry people are only satisfied when they are **the** story of the day. Scandal and controversy must inevitably form a major part of the narrative, otherwise there is no story for the press to report upon. Fame junkies will therefore do the most bizarre things which they would never have done otherwise, had there been no press about to report on their activities. It's what playing to the gallery is all about, and it rattles all sensible people.

If Meghan truly wanted to be the most famous woman on earth, as her brief stated, that must mean that she is a fame addict. A fame addict is like any other addict. Addicts do not play by the same rules as ordinary people. One of the first warnings the friends and relations of alcoholics receive in Al Anon is, 'Never get between an alcoholic and his bottle. If you do, you'll always end up the loser.' Addicts are notoriously ruthless in achieving their fix. Because the palace understood the consequences of Meghan's brief as it was reported back to them, there was real fear that she would deliberately stoke the fires of controversy in a quest to achieve her objective. 'You don't become the most famous woman on earth by being a dutiful duchess,' a courtier said. 'You become the most famous woman on earth by creating drama, chaos, controversy, call it what you will. You only need to look at what made the Princess of Wales and Elizabeth Taylor so famous to see that that degree of fame is a five-word letter spelt h/a/v/o/c.'

Because only time would tell whether Meghan really was as fame hungry as her brief suggested, the question remained unverified. What was beyond doubt, however, was that she had a gift for scripting her own narrative. Two days after the baby's birth, she and Harry presented him to a select crew of cameramen and journalists at Windsor Castle. They gave a brief interview while Harry held the baby, swaddled in white from head to toe, with only the tiniest glimpse of his nose and mouth visible. Gayle King voiced the complaint of everyone everywhere when she said on CBS's *This Morning* that the baby's face wasn't visible. The 'very proud mother' and 'over the top, giddy Dad', as she called Meghan and Harry, radiated joy but failed to provide the baby's name until later in the day, when they announced that he would be known as Master Archie Harrison Mountbatten-Windsor. They also posted on their Instagram page a black and white photograph of his presentation at Windsor Castle to the Queen and Prince Philip in the presence of Doria Ragland, who had been staying with them at Frogmore Cottage since April. His great-grandparents were plainly thrilled with little Archie, as they ought to have been, for he is undoubtedly an adorable baby and he was the first member of the British Royal Family who was indubitably mixed race, though the Queen and Prince Philip are descended from one, and possibly two, women of colour in the forms of Madragana of Faro and Philippa of Hainault, while Harry and William undoubtedly have Indian blood as a result of their many-times Scottish great-grand-father Theodore Forbes's progeny Katherine Scott Forbes, the daughter of his Indian mistress Eliza Kewark. Prince William even gave blood to stand up the supposition, which plainly shows that he is proud of his mixed race heritage.

Archie's name showed that Harry and Meghan's gift for surprise had not deserted them. The baby's name broke every rule in the royal book and was as maverick, unexpected, untraditional, and woke as could be. Royal children have always been named after royal antecedents. Harry and Meghan, however, proved that they so seriously took their goal of change as a perpetual precept that no area of their lives would be safe from their innovations. These might have been gratifying to their admirers and were certainly fodder for the press, who thrive on novelty, but the dizzying array of newness was starting to become disturbing to traditionalists.

Never before had a royal child been given a nickname instead of a

Christian name. Had he been called Archibald, there would have been no issue, for Archie is a diminutive of that name, though Archibald is not actually a Windsor family name, being one of the four or so names the ducal house of Argyll has reserved over the centuries for its dukes and lords. The 9th Duke of Argyll had been married to Queen Victoria's daughter Princess Louise, so to that extent there was a royal connection. But Archie? It is a name which has customarily been given to dogs belonging to the upper classes, and only latterly to working class Britons, so its choice caused consternation.

Meghan and Harry would later claim that their inspiration for the name came from the ancient Greek word Arche whose primary and secondary meanings are 'beginning' and 'origin' with the tertiary meaning being 'source of action.' It is this third meaning which they have stated led them to call their son Archie.

Their choice of name was commendably erudite, to say the least. Few people nowadays are as familiar with Ancient Greek as they are, so it shows that they really are far deeper thinkers, with far greater sensitivities and far greater vision than the other royals, who call their children such mundane names as Charles, James, William, Henry, Andrew, Edward, David, George or any of the other names the Royal Family has used throughout the centuries. It also shows how liberal Harry and Meghan are in selecting only those aspects of something which suit them, for the word Arche is not pronounced Archie as in Master Archie Mountbatten-Windsor, but Arkie, as in the Archangel Gabriel and the *ie* sound at the end Penelope.

The source of the baby's middle name was equally innovative. In British terms, Harrison is not a Christian name, but a surname, though the American custom of endowing children with family surnames as Christian names has resulted in the actor Harrison Ford possessing it as a first name. Claims that the name had been chosen by Meghan to honour the baby's father were greeted with perplexity, for no one in Britain attaches the Scandinavian suffix of son to a father's first name and uses that as a middle name, nor does it seem to be a practice followed in North America. Only in ancient times and in countries such as Denmark or Norway would Harry's son gain the distinguishing suffix and become Harrison. Even then, it was not a middle name, but a distinguishing mark which is how surnames came about.

The uniqueness of the baby's names aside, one consolation was that Meghan and Harry could not complain about being denied their choices the way the Yorks had been when they were prevented from calling one of their daughters a non-royal Christian name because there was no royal precedent for it. This was proof, yet again, that the Royal Family and the palace were tearing up the rule book to facilitate Meghan and Harry's choices.

Although the family and the courtiers might have thought they were doing the couple a favour, in reality they were not. Sufficient people in the world at large knew about royal rules, regulations, practices and customs to be alert to the possible meaning of this latest game-changer. It wasn't only the baby's unconventional names that were flying in the face of convention, but his moniker. And that could mean something huge.

All legitimate royal children, like all legitimate progeny of peers, are born with titles. If the child of a peer or royal is born without a title, the implication is that it is illegitimate. The eldest sons of dukes, including royal dukes who are the grandsons of a monarch (with the exception of the eldest son of the Prince of Wales, whose children are granted the style and title of royal highness and prince or princess) take their father's subsidiary title, and their eldest sons take the tertiary title. The style and title of the firstborn legitimate son of the Duke and Duchess of Sussex is Earl of Dumbarton, and his firstborn legitimate son would be Lord Kilkeel. When the Sussexes therefore announced on Instagram that their son would be known as Master Archie Harrison Mountbatten-Windsor, this fed the supposition that Meghan had not carried or produced the child, for he should by rights have been Lord Dumbarton, and if he is not, that means he is not legitimate in the eyes of British law.

British and American laws governing surrogacy are completely different. In Britain, a child is deemed to be illegitimate, even if it is the biological issue of a married couple, as long as it is borne by a surrogate.

The law in the US states that a child born of a surrogate is the lawful and legitimate child of the mother and father who have arranged the surrogacy. In England, however, the legal mother is the surrogate even though the legal father is the inseminator. Under English law, the woman whose egg produced the child has no legal status at all. If she wishes to be acknowledged as its mother, she has to adopt it. Even then, the child remains illegitimate at birth.

Under the laws governing titles, no illegitimate child can succeed to a peerage and no illegitimate child can therefore use the secondary and tertiary titles which customarily attach to peerages. Illegitimate children cannot have royal or aristocratic titles. Even if they are subsequently legitimised, they are disqualified from inheriting peerages, though they can acquire the style and title of second sons or daughters, i.e. courtesy titles. This puts them on a par with adopted children who, until 30th April, 2004, were prevented from using even courtesy titles. Only the persistence of the Marchioness of Aberdeen and Temair on behalf of her four adopted children resulted in a change to the law, but illegitimate children are still denied any titles at all unless they are then adopted or legitimised.

The baby's style and title were not the only indications alighted upon by the sceptics, that the internet stories about her bump being a prosthesis might have merit. Archie was allegedly born weighing seven pounds three ounces. This was hardly a huge baby. While it was impossible to discern his size with accuracy during that first interview at Windsor Castle when he was two days old, the internet came alive with comments that he was suspiciously big for a two day old baby whose birth weight had been so slight. The gist of the comments was that, unless Archie had been padded deliberately, which seemed unlikely, his size suggested an infant of his birth weight who was rather older than two days.

Harry's comments during the interview further fostered the theories about Archie not being born when and to whom it was alleged. Had Harry wanted to increase rather than decrease the rumours about his son's birth, he could not have done so more effectively than the response he gave when asked who the baby looked like. He said 'everyone says the baby's changed so much over two weeks we're basically monitoring how the changing process happens over the next month.' This was an extraordinary statement to make. Archie was two days old. Babies don't change appearance markedly and frequently in a forty eight hour period. Yet here was Harry asserting not only that his son kept on changing appearance over a two week period, but that he had done so to such an extent that it was impossible to say whom he looked like; notwithstanding the baby being officially two days old.

Any student of behaviour looking at that interview can see Harry trying to retrieve his slip of the tongue. Not only does he waffle on about monitoring the changing process over the next month, but he then slips back in that his son has been around but 'it's only been the last two and a half to three days....' Notwithstanding the fact that Archie wasn't officially more than two days old.

In reality, English and Scottish law are such that Archie Mountbatten-Windsor being the son of a royal prince makes his position very straightforward. If he is the natural and legitimate son of Harry and Meghan gave birth to him, he is not Master Archie Mountbatten-Windsor but Archie Mountbatten-Windsor, Earl of Dumbarton. By law, he would only be Master Archie Mountbatten-Windsor if he had been carried by a woman other than Meghan. Whether she is the biological mother is irrelevant under English law. A famous jurist told me, 'The father is the person who usually registers a child's birth. If the father informs the Registrar of Births, Deaths and Marriages that the baby had been born to him and his wife, the certificate would be issued without further ado. Hospitals don't register births. Parents do. And no one checks the information given.' In such an eventuality, the child would therefore be apparently legitimised but would not be able to succeed to his father's peerage. And he would have no place in the line of succession, as illegitimate children cannot inherit the Crown.

Nevertheless, Archie Mountbatten-Windsor is listed as being seventh in line of succession to the throne. This is on the strength of the birth certificate which was issued stating that Harry is his father and Meghan his mother. A royal told me, 'You see the mess.' No prominent family, royal or otherwise, welcomes speculation about the arrival of a child, and the fact that this speculation has been all over the internet has been a monumental embarrassment. While Meghan's supporters will say that she has every right to conduct herself as she pleases, and the more extreme ones will even say, 'And damn the consequences,' one member of the establishment who supports the monarchy expressed the view shared by many of Meghan's critics on the internet. 'She's the one who's caused all these problems. People pick up on her not being real. That's the root cause of all of this. She's incredibly spoilt and utterly selfish. She's also the most pretentious person anyone will ever meet. Have you seen her handwriting? **Almost** as contrived as her personality. Her whole life's an act. Like all people who are basically hollow, she covers it up with all sorts of gush intermingled with unreasonable demands, including wanting a buffer zone between them and everyone else. But he's completely captivated by her. He truly adores her and I know he honestly believes that she loves him. He'll do anything to keep her happy. He's terrified of losing her. I think his feelings are caught up with having lost his mother. Remember: death is the ultimate rejection. He can't afford to have another Mummy leave him. She mothers him as well as lays it on with a trowel being the little woman to his big man one minute, then the big bad mama to the naughty little boy the next. He goes along with everything because he's terrified of losing her. He'll do anything to keep her happy.'

What people on the outside looking in might not realise is how very much the human factor counts in this story. People close to Harry are genuinely worried that he could suffer a total mental breakdown or even commit suicide if his relationship with Meghan should be threatened or fail. A psychologist who knows him told me that he displays all the symptoms of someone who is co-dependent. If Meghan is addicted to success, Harry is addicted to her. People like Nikki Priddy believe that Meghan is tough and will sacrifice anyone or anything if they stand in her way; Harry will sacrifice anyone, including himself, to maintain her regard and remain by her side.

Because Harry's emotional fragility plays such a part in everyone's calculations, Meghan is beyond the control of everyone but herself. This is not as enviable a position to be in as it might appear to be. In fact, there is much to be said for the fact that Meghan's strength of character has isolated not only Harry but also herself. Had she had someone who could have stood up to her, who could have helped her adjust to a new way of life in a truly meaningful way instead of enabling her when he should have been informing and at times diverting her, she might well have gained greater appreciation of a way of life she was dismissive of. Everyone needs guidance at times, strong people included. They also need resistance when it is necessary. When they are making mistakes, they need someone to tell them. In situations such as Harry and Meghan's, it is fruitless to apportion blame, for Harry is highly emotional without the outstanding intellectual capabilities a woman as strong and intelligent as Meghan would require, to divert her from the path of certitude upon which she consistently treads. And without a naysayer, she has made mistakes which she could easily have avoided. These have affected her popularity, and brought condemnation down upon her.

Two incidents in particular which turned the British public against her stand out. The first was when Meghan flew to New York for a baby shower which was reported as having cost $300,000. One must remember that the press often exaggerate how much things cost, but even so, there is no doubt that the event was lavish. It was organised by her friends Genevieve Hillis, with whom she has been friendly since their days together at Northwestern University when they were sorority sisters in Kappa Kappa Gamma, Jessica Mulroney and Serena Williams. Gayle King said, 'I think her friends just wanted to celebrate her. Those were the three women who put it all together. It was a very, very small, private affair and just a very special time for her.' Held at the Mark Hotel, in its most luxurious suite, it was attended by her fifteen closest friends including Amal Clooney, on whose jet she was given a lift coming and going. For the forty eight hours that she was in New York, Meghan provided photo op after photo op for her admirers, to the annoyance of her detractors. She was a news editor's dream, her hand perpetually hovering over her bump like a helicopter above a landing pad, a faint smile playing on her lips as if she had some secret only she knew about, but wasn't it wonderful? This patent enjoyment of life appealed to her admirers but riled her detractors, who kept on saying they wished she'd look a little less smug, while the former group exulted in her open joyousness at her good fortune. While the battle raged, Meghan treated all onlookers to a fashion parade. Whatever her critics say, they cannot deny that she is a beautifully dressed, stylish woman who knows how to wear clothes and shows them, and herself, to advantage.

It was interesting to see how radically different the American newspaper and television coverage was from the British. In the US, there was universal celebration for Meghan's good fortune in not only having hooked a prince and become a duchess, but also in luxuriating so effortlessly and stylishly in a paradise only a hallowed few will ever be able to occupy. In Britain, there was universal condemnation for what was perceived as crass and vulgar wallowing in a tasteless display of conspicuous consumption. The British don't mind their grandees living in palaces and castles, don't even mind them wearing millions of pounds worth of inherited jewels and sitting upon tens of millions of pounds of chattels, but they do object to royalty cadging lifts on celebrities' private planes, staying in hotels where suites cost tens and tens of thousands of dollars a night, wearing tens and tens of thousands of dollars' worth of clothes which will only ever be worn once. To them, palaces, castles, furniture, art work, and jewels are heritage, and therefore acceptable. But putting a match to that amount of money for one night's stay, for one outfit's outing, for one party which will be over in a few hours, is offensive to them. These are fundamental cultural differences which it would have behoved Meghan to understand and Harry to explain.

I was told that Meghan was extremely upset by the criticism levelled against her. She simply could not understand why the British weren't thrilled with her the way the Americans were.

So what is she'd got a lift on Amal Clooney's aeroplane? What was all the fuss about? Amal was using it whether she was on it or not. And in any event, who flies commercial if they have the chance to go private? She found the British attitude stupid and unreasonable.

This clash of cultures could have been avoided with greater discretion, but the fact is, Harry did not help negotiate Meghan's way around the shoals. He was simply not canny enough to spot the sinkhole into which she was stepping. He also shared a damaging trait with his great-great-great-uncle David, the Duke of Windsor, who was so also enraptured by his wife that he too could never prevent her from hurling herself headlong into unnecessary pits. Like David, who thought that Wallis was a paragon of perfection, Harry thought that Meghan had much to teach his compatriots. He honestly believed that the monarchy was run by stuffed shirts and several members of his family were jealous of him and Meghan to such an extent that they all wanted to keep them down when everyone could learn so much from her. In his estimation, the monarchy could have become so much more relevant under her guidance. It could have been a force for change in a way it was not and had never been. He earnestly believed that they'd be able to show everyone how they could shake things up if only the prigs would give them free rein.

This, of course, was precisely what the courtiers and family did not want. They didn't want Meghan and Harry chucking out the babies with the bath water when, in their view, those babies were the future of the monarchy and the country. They were only too aware that only a small percentage of the country shared Meghan and now Harry's perspective. The monarchy needed to represent that vast swathe of people whom Meghan especially looked down upon for being traditional, old fashioned, politically unenlightened, sticks-in-the-mud. But then, Meghan's focus had never really been on Britain, but on the United States, and gradually she had induced Harry to share her vision.

No one knows precisely when Meghan decided that Britain would not work for her. Some of her old friends believe that she never had any intention of making the transition from the US to the UK. They posit that she is the archetypal businesswoman who saw the opportunity a takeover of Harry Incorporated presented. Being dished up with a handsome and eager prince whom she found physically and personally attractive, who was so keen to please her that he slotted into the role of adoring poodle without her even needing to train him up, was too good an opportunity to miss. They postulate that she walked into this with her eyes wide open, with no intention of fitting in. If Britain wouldn't mould itself to suit her, she would bide her time, complain about how unappreciated she was, and move back to the US with the added benefit of royal status - with or without her husband.

This, of course, is pure speculation. What is not is the fact that Harry and Meghan tried to strike out on their own by setting up their own household independent of all the other palaces, when they split from William and Catherine prior to Archie's birth. 'Going rogue' is what such ambitions are known as in palace circles. To say that their attempt was greeted with incredulity would be to minimise the disbelief felt at the palace. A prince told me that he is sure that Lord Geidt, the Queen's former Private Secretary who was shoved out in 2017 by the Prince of Wales and the Duke of York, but still has the Queen's ear, was behind the move blocking Harry and Meghan from going 'completely rogue'. He argued for their office relocating to Buckingham Palace, where the Queen's advisors could keep an eye on them. 'Otherwise they'd have been like two cars hurtling down a dirt track with no brakes, kicking up dust in everyone's eyes,' the prince said.

From Harry and Meghan's perspective, all they wanted was the freedom to indulge their tastes and values and, where they thought appropriate, to update the monarchy. They actually complained vociferously to all and sundry that their 'special talents' were not being used, that they weren't 'appreciated' enough, and that, left to their own devices, they'd be 'real forces for change'. They simply could not understand that it was unreasonable to expect any newcomer to any institution to be given the freedom to enact change the way Meghan and now Harry proposed. Insisting on being given the licence they wanted was a recipe for change, all right, but not change the way they originally intended, and certainly not change the palace wanted.

In the meantime, the turmoil continued both privately and publicly. No sooner did the furore over Meghan's baby shower in New York die down, than she found herself caught up in yet more controversy. She and Harry moved out of Nottingham Cottage at Kensington Palace into Frogmore Cottage amidst fury at the cost of the refurbishments. These came to some £2.4m and were being paid for by the state. Their critics wanted to know why taxpayers should absorb the cost when they were being given free accommodation. One could equally have taken the view that since Frogmore Cottage is a state-owned building, the state should pay to keep it updated, though the outlook that would have covered all bases, and which is what the Grosvenor Estate used to utilise with its grace-and-favour leases, was that Meghan and Harry should be responsible for the full cost of repairs and refurbishment in return for living there *gratis*. This, however, was an age-old dilemma, and Harry and Meghan viewed the criticism that came their way as unfair, for who wouldn't opt for the state paying for their refurbishments given the chance?

Within a month of Archie's birth, Meghan burst back onto the scene, displaying the remarkable aptitude she has for generating interest. A very slender and flat bellied Duchess of Sussex turned up at Wimbledon to watch her friend Serena Williams play tennis. She was accompanied by Genevieve Hillis and her other Northwestern girlfriend, Lindsay Roth. Both women were appropriately dressed, as were the men and women who accompanied the trio. The rebellious Meghan, however, struck a blow of sartorial freedom by defying yet more British traditions as she breached two of Wimbledon's cardinal rules. She was wearing jeans, which are banned, and a hat, which is never worn. She had actually taken the same hat, or an identical looking one, to Wimbledon the year before, when she sat with Catherine Cambridge. Then she had been perspicacious enough to keep it in her lap, but this time, she had it planted firmly on her head.

Although Meghan either did not know or did not care, there is a reason why women do not wear hats at Wimbledon. They have the potential to block the view of the person sitting behind the wearer. It is therefore considered 'poor form' to wear hats. But Meghan's attachment to the hat suggested that she was living out some sort of fantasy of what California girls do when they get a chance to attend Wimbledon, and, as such, one has to feel for her.

Nevertheless, Meghan's breach of the Wimbledon dress code earned her criticism, though what really incensed her critics was their perception that her conduct conveyed both contemptuousness and arrogance. She had ensured that she could wear a hat by clearing out the forty or so seats behind her. The only people allowed within spitting distance of her were her suite. Behind and beside her, there was row after row of empty seats. Outside, there were queues of people being prevented from witnessing the match, from occupying seats which they had paid for, while Meghan and her Northwestern university mates were flanked by her suite and a buffer zone of empty seats to keep her comfortable.

To the British people and to the British press, this was a gross abuse of power. No other royal had ever caused forty surrounding seats to be vacated, all of which would normally be occupied by people who had paid for them. The Queen, Prince Philip, the Duke and Duchess of Kent, the Cambridges, Princess Alexandra, even the late Diana, Princess of Wales, had never had *cordons sanitaires* created for them at Wimbledon. All the seats around them had always been filled. Yet here was Meghan surrounded by a sea of empty blue seats, attired in jeans and a hat in defiance of the established dress code.

If Meghan and her team had tried their hardest to come up with something that was unpopular, they could not have bettered what happened next. Her security people had the temerity to go up to two members of the public who were taking selfies and inform them that they could not use their cameras in the presence of Her Royal Highness, as she was attending Wimbledon in a private capacity and required privacy. Privacy in a public place, in front of television cameras which were beaming images into hundreds of millions of homes around the world, while Meghan was a guest of a national institution which she would not have had access to had she been a private individual, caused national outrage. Just who did she think she was? The respected British television presenter Eamonn Holmes gave voice to the sentiments of many people when he said that Meghan had got 'above herself'.

If Meghan's objective was to garner herself column inches, her conduct made sound sense. However, if it was to rewrite the rules regarding the conduct of the press and public when members of the Royal Family were guests in public in an unofficial capacity, she had only shown how naive she was. No one who appears in public has a right to privacy. To courtesy yes, but privacy, no. By its very definition, being in public means that you are a part of the public and therefore no longer private. If you wish to be private, you remain in the privacy of your home, or the privacy of other private places. You do not, however, go out in public, in front of television cameras which are beaming into hundreds of millions of homes, and demand that others respect your right to something you do not possess, while you are actually stripping them of their rights. The public have a right to look at anyone around them. They have a right to treat a public figure with the appropriate degree of recognition, attention, and respect that the said public figure's presence realistically generates. All civilised and well-mannered public figures understand that fact and treat the public with the courtesy they deserve. Speaking as a public figure who was born into a prominent family, married into another, who has spent her whole life surrounded by public figures, I can say with absolute authority that it is inappropriate for a public figure to think that he or she has the right to regulate the conduct of the public to the extent that people can't look at you, smile at you, or even if the moment seems right, approach you respectfully. I know that there is a category of Hollywood personality who does not agree, but in civilised circles, they are dismissed as the pretentious pifflers which they are. As for the message that any public figure is so special that there has to be a buffer zone, whether of empty seats or something else is beside the point, between him or her and the public: Since when did the odious expression 'the great unwashed' gain such acceptability that any public figure, much less a member of the Royal Family, can now claim the right to have barriers erected whereby ordinary people are kept so well away from them that the message has to be: your presence defiles me?

In fairness to Meghan, there are significant cultural differences between the British and the American ways of life. She might well have not realised how offensive a message she was relaying when she embarked upon what she regarded as 'progressive' behaviour at Wimbledon. This is where she would have been well advised to have taken the time to learn the nuances of British life, rather than 'hitting the ground running' to 'update and modernise the monarchy', as she put it. You cannot modernise an institution when you do not even understand the basics of the culture whence it emanates. Such attempts are doomed to failure. Your conduct will antagonize large swathes of people who start out being charitably disposed towards you. Whether you intend to or not, if you don't understand their culture, don't bother to learn about it, think that your way is better than theirs, you are not only telling them that you regard your way and yourself as better than their way and themselves, but you are ultimately conveying lack of respect for them and their ways.

That is not how one garners respect.

Despite the Queen and Prince Charles refusing to go along with Harry and Meghan's request that the Royal Family alter the protocols by which it and the media relate to each other, and in so doing muzzle the press so that they could no longer criticise Meghan, the hyper-sensitive and determined couple decided to begin the process of cutting the Fourth Estate down to size. Meghan had been media savvy for years. Not only had she cut her teeth on her blogs, but she also took professional advice from media managers and understood that the best way forward was to use social media to reach their public directly.

Instagram became their platform of choice. They would drip feed news as and when they wanted. This would give them total control and cut out the hated tabloids, so, on privacy grounds, they refused to allow Archie to be photographed by the press, but posted an 'artistic' black and white picture of his feet in her hand.

Whether it be a star, publicist, producer, director, agent, or wannabe, everyone knows that nothing keeps the press hotter than someone who tries to elude them. Everyone also knowns that nothing infuriates the press quite so much as public figures who bemoan intrusions into their private life, while seeking to control the narrative so absolutely that they violate their own privacy by posting precious, artsie-tartsie photographs and 'meaningful' messages on their Instagram, Twitter and Facebook accounts. As Harry himself had observed when he turned twenty one, you cannot on the one hand demand privacy from the press and on the other violate your own privacy by revealing information about your private life as and when it suits you. Yet that is now precisely what he and Meghan started doing.

As they sought to gain absolute control over the information they imparted to the public, few people outside the press and palace realised just how dangerous a ploy they had embarked upon by trying to cut the press out of reporting on them. Once more, the couple had decided to change the game, this time by excluding the press from photographing Archie. Up to then, royal babies had traditionally been photographed by a well-known photographer, whose pictures would be disseminated throughout the media. That way, the royals would get positive coverage, the press would make money, which was becoming harder and harder since the advent of the internet, and the public would be kept informed.

Because of the threat the internet has presented to the media, it had become an increasingly important duty of the Royal Family to cooperate with the mainstream on such anodyne occasions as photo sessions with royal babies and other happy royal events. As stated earlier, the British press and the British Royal Family have a symbiotic relationship. Each needs the other. The existence of each furthers the security of the other while advancing the cause of freedom in Britain, a free and robust press being a guardian of democratic freedoms, and a constitutional monarchy being a preventative to the grabs against democratic freedom to which politicians are prone. You therefore undermine the media at your own peril - whoever you are.

All enlightened people understood this, and even made personal sacrifices, such as I made when I refused the Police's invitation during Operation Weeting to complain officially against the Murdoch papers and the Mirror Group for having hacked my 'phones. My reasons for inaction are relevant to this subject. During Operation Weeting, the Hacked Off movement was launched by public figures such as the actor Hugh Grant, who had been exposed for using the services of a prostitute, and Sir Max Mosley, whose penchant for prostitutes and Nazi paraphernalia had been written about in the tabloids with the public being reminded that his father, Sir Oswald Mosley, had been the head of the British Fascists, while his mother had been the former Diana Mitford, friend and admirer of Adolf Hitler. Despite my own personal suffering at the hands of the tabloids, I took the view that Britain needs a vigorous free press. Why should a few jaundiced celebrities muzzle the media out of spite for having had their debaucheries revealed, and in so doing, put everyone's liberty at risk? I therefore told the Inspector who almost begged me to reconsider, 'The price people like me have to pay for our privileges is a free press. There are already sufficient laws in place to protect our rights. Maybe some of them need beefing up, but we certainly don't need new laws that muzzle the press so absolutely that they can't have a go at us, or at crooked politicians.'

What Meghan and Harry were in effect doing was undermining the press by trying to cut them out and deal directly with the public through social media. Royals have an even more important part to play in the functioning of a free British press than public figures like Hugh Grant or Max Mosley. Yes, celebrities are tabloid fodder, and yes, it's a two way street that frequently benefits both press and public figure. But the part the royals play is of far greater significance. I would go as far as saying that only an ignoramus, someone who is truly irresponsible, or someone who is utterly naive would seek to behave towards the press as Meghan and Harry now started to do. You do not push your hand into the lion's mouth, tickle the back of its throat, scratch its tongue, as a parting shot pinch its lips, and expect to emerge unscathed. Of course, if you have on impenetrable armour and you wish to gain an advantage out of the lion's response, that's something else. Provocation then makes sense, especially if the provocateur or provocateuse intends to flip things and emerge intact as the lion's pretended victim.

It was against this culture clash, and Meghan and Harry's refusal to deal with its causes and effects, that the questions surrounding baby Archie's arrival on earth were dealt with by both the press and the palace. There is no doubt that most British publications took a very responsible line. So did the palace. One of the royals told me that there was genuine fury intermingled with despair that Harry and Meghan's conduct had created such doubt about the baby's legitimacy. There was serious concern that the Royal Family's reputation for integrity would be damaged. There was also real fear the monarchy would suffer if it became an accepted and generalised belief that Archie had been borne by a surrogate. No monarchist wanted a situation in which a member of the Royal Family was believed to have practised a deception upon the public by pretending to be pregnant when she was not. It was felt that the honour and integrity of the monarchy could be called into question if the public believed that the Royal Family and its courtiers had colluded with faking a pregnancy when they had done no such thing. The dilemma was obvious. If the public believed that Meghan had been guilty of a sleight of hand, and that the Royal Family was innocent of any collusion, that was one thing. The public would look at the powers-that-be as innocent bystanders who knew nothing about it, but if the public believed that they had cooperated, that would be something else.

The passage of time has provided a degree of relief. Since Meghan and Harry have stepped down as senior royals and moved to California, the fear that the Royal Family itself would be implicated has receded. Partly, this is because there has been a growing awareness within the general public that Meghan and Harry are both mavericks. They are also increasingly perceived in Britain as fragile personalities whose mental health demanded that they be allowed to do as they please. In America, of course, they are celebrated as freedom fighters who have broken free of the shackles of royalty and are now at liberty to pursue the human-itarian and commercial activities they were hampered from doing in Britain. In fact, this is only partly true. There is no better platform for humanitarianism than constitutional monarchy, but there have been human elements governing their departure which have received scant attention, especially in the American press. By Harry's own account, he has struggled with mental health issues, and though Meghan has been less forthcoming in making admissions of that kind, the evidence of her blogs and their conduct suggests that she too has personality issues. It is these mental health concerns that have allowed the Royal Family and the powers-that-be at Buckingham Palace to cut them slack. What would otherwise have been intolerable has been made tolerable by these considerations, but the idea that being royal turns you into a victim entrapped in a cruel world where you aren't even allowed to make money could not be more ludicrous. Even anti-monarchists accept that being royal is a great privilege.

CHAPTER 9

The palace had known, for a year before Meghan and Harry's bombshell announcement in January 2020, that they were making plans to achieve what they would later call 'financial independence' by entering the commercial world. This was something no member of the Royal Family who was publicly funded had hitherto done, and that the possibility existed that Meghan's ultimate aim was to enter American politics, which was also incompatible with her royal status.

They found out easily enough, because Meghan had flown to the United States in 2019 and met with the three leading members of her business team from when she was a jobbing actress. They were Nick Collins, Andrew Meyer and Rick Genow.

Nick Collins is Co-Head of Talent at the Gersh Agency, Inc., a talent and literary agency ranked sixth of the top agencies in the country. It is the only agency which has never diversified from its core purpose, the representation of acting and literary talent, although in the last decade it has taken active steps to plump up its divisions, which include Talent, Alternative, Books, Branding, Film Finance, Literary, Personal Appearance, Production, and Theatre. Its primary client base is what *The Hollywood Reporter* calls 'a roster of steadily working actors whose faces might be more recognizable than their names.' It has 2,000 clients, 175 employees with 75 agents and 16 partners, with offices in LA and New York. Founded in 1949 in the golden age of Hollywood by Phil Gersh, his sons Bob and David are the Co-Presidents and the Senior Managing Partner is Leslie Siebert. It also has a reputation for an aggressive left-wing political profile, and became involved in controversy when it fired one of its best known actors, James Woods, by email on the 4th July, 2018. He accused it of political bias, stating that they had stopped representing him because he is a Republican. Their signature clients are Kristen Stewart, Kyle Chandler, Adam Driver, J.K. Simmons, Taylor Schilling, and Patricia Arquette, who has such an impeccable liberal profile that she apologised publicly for having been born white and privileged, and took part in the Women's March against President

Trump.

Nick Collins started out as an assistant to Bob Gersh in 2005, since when his rise within the company has been stellar. He became an agent in 2007, a partner in 2015, and was appointed Co-Head of Talent in February 2018. His clients include Courtney B. Vance and Eric McCormack of *Will and Grace*. He is regarded as sharp, bright, reliable, and possessing great taste - something which matters greatly to the stylish and tasteful Meghan, though she makes an exception for her husbands, both of whom have been stylistic messes.

According to *The Hollywood Reporter*, Andrew Meyer is listed, along with his partner Steves Rodriguez, as one of the top twenty five business managers in Hollywood. Meyer handles the talent while Rodriguez deals with music and production. The former's clients include Ellen Pompeo and Kathryn Hahn. They have a reputation for being good managers. Like Gersh, they are capable and reliable but their clients are not generally of the first rank.

Harvard graduate Rick Genow is listed as one of Hollywood's top hundred lawyers. He is a partner in Stone, Genow, Smelkinson, Binder & Christopher, a boutique firm specialising in the representation of actors, writers, directors and producers in the film and television industries. He also works with emerging filmmaking talent as well as established veterans, packaging, producing and setting up projects, and representing the sale of distribution rights for finished films. The firm boasts that it has a 'knack for finding exceptional projects that [are] creatively satisfying, commercially appealing and cost effective.' They 'also assist financiers seeking material.'

Tellingly, Meghan never disbanded her trio of commercial representatives when she married Harry. Then the palace discovered that pregnant Meghan had instructed them to drum up commercial opportunities for her to exploit. And not small time things either. Each project should be worth millions of dollars.

Insofar as Buckingham Palace was concerned, royals cannot be both fish and fowl. You cannot be a British royal and an American businesswoman at the same time. The word trickling back to England was deeply ominous as far as they were concerned, for it appeared as if Meghan intended to breach one of the cardinal rules under which royalty functions, namely that it cannot involve itself in commercial activity for personal gain. Not only were they being told that Meghan had articulated an interest in maximising her earning potential, but she and Harry were also rumoured to have cut deals which, if true, were decidedly beyond the ken for royalty. A princess told me in 2019, 'There are rumours - hopefully untrue - that Meghan has been entering into deals with all sorts of people on behalf of herself and Harry.' Meghan was rumoured to have even asked designers to give her credits for dresses which she had worn and which the Duchy of Cornwall had paid for. She was also alleged to be making deals with suppliers - people like jewellers - for promoting their wares. 'It is to be hoped that these stories are untrue,' the princess said. 'But the mere fact that they exist is disturbing.'

Perturbing as those rumours were to the Royal Family and the people running it, they were less shocking to Americans than to the British. Partly, this is because Americans admire an entrepreneurial approach even if it has covert elements, and partly because it is a well-known fact that Jackie Onassis used to run through her dress allowance of $30,000 per month from Aristotle Onassis as a means of 'exploiting' - again that word with such differing connotations depending on which side of the Atlantic it was being used - it to feather her nest. Sometimes she wouldn't even bother to wear an item before sending it to the resale shop. She would then pocket the money, and repeat the whole process month after month. When her husband found out, he accused her of being a 'cheap hustler' and 'little better than a thief'. This was no rumour either. Ari himself told his first wife Tina's sister-in-law Lady Sarah Spencer-Churchill, who was a close friend of mine and at whose 72nd Street townhouse in New York I used to see both Onassises, as well as Jackie alone at Sarah's Jamaican home, 'Content'.

If Meghan was doing a variation of a Jackie, the British needed to appreciate that she would not have been viewing her conduct as anything but entrepreneurial and resourceful. 'Double recovery' and 'double dealing' might be the height of dubious behaviour in Britain, but in the circles whence Meghan originated, they were commendable resourcefulness.

Nevertheless, commercialism, whether overt or covert, was anathema to the powers-that-be at Buckingham Palace. But it was nowhere near as bad as politicism. And they had been told that Meghan had let it be known that she had political ambitions. Nor were her ambitions modest. Characteristically, her ultimate goal was to be President of the United States of America. She had even told people that she saw no reason why she couldn't 'do a Reagan'.

Aside from the constitutional conflicts inherent in a member of the British Royal Family seeking political office in a foreign country, even the country of her birth, there was the question of Meghan's suitability for the American presidency. To the courtiers, with their British attitude towards political office which is at variance with the American, she was not qualified for any political office, much less one of the magnitude of President of the United States of America. She hadn't even passed her State Department examinations, yet here she was voicing ambitions to be the Commander-in-Chief. Self-belief does not have the magical quality in Britain that it does in the United States, so to them this was something to be suspicious of, rather than to celebrate. The fact that Meghan had voiced the belief that her career as an actress put her on a par with the late 40th President of America, because Ronald Reagan had been, like her, a moderately successful actor before moving on to greater things, struck them as incomprehensible.

To the courtiers, whose colleagues had had dealings with the late President and had a great deal of respect for his wiliness as well as his sophisticated overview, Meghan seemed not to realise that the limited success as actors which she and Reagan had shared was the full extent of what they had in common. She was confusing the role playing she did when she appeared in soup kitchens and gave speeches to the UN about having changed the face of advertising at the age of eleven, with actual political experience. Meghan had never held down a political role of any type, much less one of any significance. Reagan, on the other hand, had had an extensive political background even while he was a jobbing actor. He was first elected to the Board of Directors of the Screen Actors Guild (SAG), the powerful actor's union, in 1941. In 1946, he was elected their third vice-president. In 1947 he was elected president and would subsequently be re-elected six times, the last being in 1959. He successfully steered SAG through the McCarthy Era and the dark days of the Hollywood Black List, implemented the controversial Taft-Hartley Act, oversaw various labour-management disputes at a time of tremendous political and economic upheaval, during which Hollywood's studio system collapsed under the weight of television, before sitting twice as Governor of California from 1967-1975.

Meghan also looked to President Trump, for whom she had nothing but contempt, as a comparable. 'If Trump can be president, there's no reason why I can't be,' she said. Harry would echo a variation of this sentiment when he spoke to the Russian pranksters who pretended to be Greta Thunberg and her father Svante on New Year's Eve 2019 and in January 2020 and stated that if Trump could be president, pretty much anyone could be as well.

As regards Trump, Meghan was on firmer ground. Prior to holding office as president, he had possessed no more political experience than she did. He had been a well-known businessman and television personality, but there the parallels between the two of them began to diverge. While she had engaged in commercial activity as well as becoming a television personality, the degree of his renown had not been comparable with hers. Whatever his track record commercially, Donald Trump has had vast experience of deal-making. He had become a household name long before he became a television personality. Meghan had never been a household name prior to her marriage to Harry. She had never owned hotels or casinos or a successful club like Mar-a-Lago, nor had her name ever appeared on airlines, hotels, and iconic New York buildings. While she regarded herself as a businesswoman because she had agents who had successfully obtained minor endorsements for her, she was out of Trump's league both as a businesswoman and a television personality. He had fronted one of the United States' most popular television network shows, while she had been an ensemble player on a minor albeit reasonably successful cable TV show. But she was now a member of the British Royal Family, and her profile would continue to grow exponentially. Being a superb strategist, if Meghan played her cards right, her springboard could be every bit as appealing to a different category of supporter and she could be equally electable.

There was, however, an important difference between The Donald's acquisition of the presidency and Meghan's ambition to achieve it. Over the years, I have met members of the Trump family socially. Three of my oldest friends know them very well. Some like him, some don't. On one thing they are all agreed. Donald Trump fell into the presidential contest to boost his profile commercially. Being someone who likes winning, he then set out to win. But no one was more surprised than he when he was actually elected president. Accidental success is patently different from focused ambition, and though Meghan disparages him, there is no doubt that he has thrown himself into the presidential role with gusto. To his admirers, he has made a success of it. To his critics, everyone else is responsible for the successes of his administration.

As a character, Trump superficially has more in common with Diana, Princess of Wales than he appears to have with her daughter-in-law. Somehow, Diana always managed to grow into the role, whatever her latest role was. To his supporters, Trump has done the same. This is not an attribute which Meghan's critics regard her as having displayed during her brief tenure as a working royal. They would have us believe that even her supporters cannot claim that she successfully lived up to the role she then abandoned after less than two years.

But they could actually have misinterpreted her actions and ambitions. Meghan's apparent lack of tenacity allied to her unwillingness to adjust to her royal role and fulfill its requirements, filled her supporters within the Royal Family, the Establishment, and the Commonwealth with perplexity. Behind the scenes, people really struggled to understand how someone who had been made so welcome could be making her life and theirs so difficult when with slight adjustments, she could so easily succeed. I was told early on that her 'inordinate self-belief' would be her downfall unless she was careful. She was too confident, too inflexible, too convinced that her way was both the best and the only way, and that all other ways were beneath her contempt. Her attitude was that she had better things to do with her time than consider, much less negotiate with, points of view that did not accord with hers. She came across as disrespectful, narrow- minded, and self-satisfied, with more than one person who dealt with her ending up thinking that she was too arrogant, smug and sanctimonious to ever fit into a solid institution like the monarchy. Or indeed to succeed as a politician anywhere. What they seem not to have understood, was that Meghan might well have had a more sophisticated game plan than they were giving her credit for. Why adjust to something if it's only ever going to be a small part of your future goal?

If that was the case, and her real end-game was the Presidency of the United States of America, just how does Meghan propose to achieve her goal? Politicians even more than constitutional monarchists need to be pliable enough to forge alliances. They have to duck and dive, bend and weave far more than royals, because the electorate is their judge. And that electorate is even more nuanced than any royal institution. It consists of a plethora of special interest groups, some clashing with others, few of whom want to be lectured to by politicians as if they are nine year olds in Sunday School, much less by a former actress and a royal prince who preach one thing but practise another. The end result was that many of the courtiers who came across Meghan while she was adjusting to her royal role, ended up thinking that she was 'naive', 'politically inept', a 'loose and dangerous cannon' who was 'delusional about what she had going for her' and would 'muck things up' if she didn't alter her attitude. But they could have been wrong, and she right. They had misjudged Diana, and there is every likelihood that they misjudged Meghan. Both women were, so to speak, playing poker while the courtiers thought the game was canasta.

Yet many of the very people who were now perplexed by Meghan's failure to adjust to her royal role had initially been optimistic about her inclusion in the Royal Family. 'We misjudged her,' one courtier told me. 'We thought she was more open-minded than she is. She's bright, but she's not as clever as she thinks she is. She's so up her own bum-bum that she miscalculates at every turn. She has a real gift for making enemies of people who want to be her friends.' An attitude like that is not a winning formula unless, of course, victory lies in failing to adjust, in which case it is the best tactic to employ.

By the time Meghan's pregnancy had been announced, it was obvious in court circles that she was not growing into her role, but was expecting it to change for her. In short, she was not acquitting herself as successfully as her supporters, this author included, had hoped she would. There is always a transitional phase between hope and despair. In the early days, everyone hoped that Meghan would learn and adjust. They still did not understand that she might actually have no need to adjust. They still thought that she was 'in for the long haul' as a fully paid up member of the Royal Family. To many of the courtiers, who believe that their jobs serve a valuable purpose in national life, it was inconceivable that any newcomer to the Royal Family would treat such an august position as just another career move, of no more importance than a secretarial job or a role in a cable television show. This attitude was so beyond their contemplation that even when the evidence began mounting up that this is precisely how Meghan approached her royal role, they simply could not absorb the fact. They therefore continued to function in a state of suspended disbelief, and thrashed around for explanations as to why the duchess was not adjusting.

One canny courtier, however, summarised Meghan's underlying problem to me once the palace discovered that Meghan had gone to the States to consult with her agents and representatives there. If being a royal duchess was just a career move, as now seemed possible, that would explain why she could not and/or would not make the necessary adjustments to fulfill her royal role satisfactorily. 'A priest who's an atheist is always going to be problematic to the Church. The Duchess of Sussex doesn't have the subtlety, sophistication or self-restraint to be another Talleyrand: she's more like Princess Diana.' This courtier did not consider her to be a formidable adversary. He thought that she was 'too naive and unsubtle an operator to be truly effective. She's so obvious that she'll tie herself in knots rather than follow the clear lines of the turncoat Bishop of Autun. He was as self-interested as she is, but he had self-restraint and a solid enough self-regard to put success above applause. I don't see Meghan Markle doing that. Nor did Princess Diana.'

In my not-so-humble opinion, this analysis misread the skill and subtlety of both Meghan and Diana. Just because they had the gift of being able to project their feelings with the commensurate reward of gaining followers did not mean that they lacked self-restraint. On the contrary. It seemed to me that they both had a winning combination of self-restraint allied to self-projection, and by discounting one of those two elements, their detractors were underestimating them. Since their critics acknowledged that both women were wily, it seemed to me paradoxical that they would be judged only on their superficial actions, rather than on their underlying motives and ultimate achievements. Their goals, after all, were neither straightforward nor obvious, and since their journeys took place with much subterfuge and double-bluffing on their part, why fail to acknowledge their skill in playing canny hands successfully? Could it be that they were more skilful than was thought?

If Meghan and Harry's agenda was to elevate themselves using their royal status for their own material and political gain, there was no way Meghan could sustain the way of life of a British royal. The patrician world is tough. It is one which Diana rebelled against and had contrived to leave behind prior to her death. She was in the process of doing what was then known as 'a Jackie' when she had her accident. Both Diana and Jackie Kennedy had left the heavy hitting Establishment circles whence they originated, to drift off into the more salubrious climes of the ocean-going yachts and private planes of the super-rich. Both were happy to leave behind the ostensible but limited and self-sacrificing glamour of a great position for the freedom, comfort and true glamour of a richer and easier way of life. Both of them had had enough of the sacrifices that go along with grand positions, of the self-restraint, self-abnegation and discipline which are fundamental. They were happy to swap the delights of real wealth for the countless dull and worthy occasions that so heavily outweigh the occasional glamorous red carpet events that so mislead the public into believing that royalty and world leaders lead enviable lives when, in fact, dull duty is more often the case. Diana, Princess of Wales used to complain about how excruciatingly tiresome she found 'yet another lunch with yet another boring mayor,' and, while Jackie tried to explain away her flight into Onassis's world as providing her children with the safety only great wealth can guarantee, the truth was simpler: She loved the freedom, comfort and self-indulgence of great wealth. So too did Diana. She happily jettisoned over a hundred patronages following her separation, freeing up her time for long girly lunches, gym and tennis sessions, sybaritic holidays on West Indian beaches and sojourns on private yachts in the Aegean whether owned by Panagiotis Lemos or Mohamed Al-Fayed was beside the point, not to mention the pleasures of the Harrods private plane.

Although it was not tactically wise for Harry and Meghan to admit that they too liked the lifestyle of the super-rich - he has gone to some pains on several occasions to explain away his use of private 'planes as necessary for the protection of his wife and child, as if they are any safer on a private plane than they would be on a commercial flight - the reality is that both of them - she especially - are like just about everyone else. They enjoy the delights of that way of life. And while he displayed no interest in it until she came into his life, her frank lust for the best, richest, grandest, most sumptuous and comfortable that the world has to offer was already an established feature of her personality long before they met.

Prior to becoming a duchess, Meghan was completely frank about her appreciation of the finer things of life. On her blog *The Tig* she dedicated much time and space into honing the joys of wealth, luxury, and fine living. She also displayed how willing she was to enjoy the simpler pleasures of life as well. In an interview with *Vanity Fair*, she even advanced the theory that 'most things can be cured with either yoga, the beach or a few avocados.'

Nowhere in her past writings nor her subsequent conduct did Meghan indicate possessing the attitude of a Duchess of Gloucester, a Countess of Wessex or a Princess Alexandra, all of whom are classically royal princesses joyfully and charmingly fulfilling each year hundreds of unglamorous royal engagements which never make the newspapers, but which nevertheless reward ordinary men and women for their civic service. These women embrace the dullness that Meghan was so eager to avoid during her first public engagement as a royal, when she suggested leaving the Buckingham Palace garden party after fifteen minutes. These royal women are in tune with royalty's need to acknowledge the efforts of ordinary people apolitically, and to do so in environments not deemed newsworthy by the press or worthy of Instagram postings. It is understandable why an emotive activist like Meghan had no interest in doing the bread and butter stuff that has no emotional reward and will never make it into the papers or onto the net. Diana did not want to like doing bread and butter stuff either, and at the first opportunity, she ceased doing it. So Harry had a precedent which made Meghan's distaste for the mundane acceptable to him, and though he resisted acceptance at first, once the marriage got underway her deep unhappiness at having to do things she didn't want to reached him, and he gradually began to support her position of what one courtier calls 'dereliction'.

That is not to say that Meghan is lazy. She is not. But, like Diana, she prefers the dramatic stuff. She understands how important glamorous photo ops are to her legion of followers, but she also relishes popping into soup kitchens and visiting survivors of disasters such as Grenfell Tower or encouraging women who are struggling against domestic violence. She is wonderful at letting them know that she feels their pain and always leaves those she has visited with a smile on their faces.

Like Diana, Meghan's feels that her talents are unique. She has been as vociferous as her mother-in-law was in making everyone know that her natural gifts should not be wasted on the ordinary activities which she dismissed as 'petty stuff'. She indubitably had some excellent ideas, such as creating a fundraising cookbook for the survivors of that disastrous fire, but at Buckingham Palace it was an accepted fact of life that the bread-and-butter duties which Sophie Wessex and the eighty-something year old Alexandra were happy to do was essential for all royals, Meghan included. She could not expect to cherry pick her way through royal tasks, dumping the boring ones on the other royal women while reserving only the emotionally-satisfying and glamorous ones for herself.

The reality is, anybody who isn't cut out for the meat and potatoes business of everyday royal life, will struggle with the mundanity of political life as well. Should Meghan have even a passing chance of achieving her goal of becoming President of the United States of America, she will have to learn to take the rough with the smooth, the dull with the exciting, the boring with the stimulating, and not expect that she can somehow be spared the onerous bits while always benefiting from the gratifying highs. She might well succeed in the mixed commercial and humanitarian lifestyle that she has opted for - all leavened with much downtime with Harry, Archie and their friends, for she has always liked her pleasures, which is one of the reasons why she was happy to spend hours shooting the breeze with film crews while waiting for her three minutes of screen time - but a brightly-shining star like her will never succeed either as a royal or a politician unless she finds a way to tolerate the ordinary, unexciting, unemotional, dull requirements of life such as lunches with mayors, untrumpeted visits to worthy institutions, and the momentary meetings and greetings with countless strangers who will gain a high from meeting the luminary they admire, while she, the brightly shining star, will not.

Despite her failure to adjust to the royal world, Meghan has undoubtedly been successful in other areas. This success came about because she acted the part ascribed to her with a remarkable degree of élan. But she also believes it's not enough to survive: 'You must thrive.' And since she didn't like the lines or the limitations of the role that were being given to her, she did a variation of what Diana had also done: She left the stage for one of her own devising.

Of course, if Meghan was never genuinely interested in being a working royal, and only wanted the platform to catapult herself to greater worldly success, she has been achieving her objective brilliantly. But what if she did genuinely think that she might be able to adjust to her royal role? If that is the case, hers is indeed a sad story. It might have been different if she and Harry had figured out that you can't do as they have done. You can't treat an enterprise as something worth undertaking only when you're getting the rewards you require. Success as a royal has eluded her and success as a politician will do likewise unless she learns the lesson he knew before linking up with her. To succeed in those worlds, your goal cannot be to thrive. It has to be to survive, and to survive well.

While Meghan and Harry have shown themselves to be brilliant at commanding the stage, whether royal or otherwise is beside the point, her conduct to date suggests that Meghan is congenitally unsuited to a life of service, though she might well be perfectly suited to a commercial life that has a side-line in humanitarianism.

The reality is that the way of life of a constitutional royal was never going to have any appeal for someone who is as financially driven as Meghan has admitted she is. To be a successful royal, money can't be a high priority. You also have to be a true believer in something that is both intangible and greater than yourself. Whether you are born into the position, like the Queen, or marry into it, like Queen Elizabeth the Queen Mother and the Duchess of Cambridge, you need a vocational approach if you are to stay the course. If you lack that, as Meghan patently does and Diana, Princess of Wales and Sarah, Duchess of York did, you begin to question the merit of the sacrifices you are compelled to make while pursuing the life of service royals are called upon to lead. Ultimately, if you are not a true believer, you find yourself putting your personal feelings above the cause you are meant to be serving. Once that happens, you are bound to fail, for success as a royal comes by putting your sensations to one side and rising to the occasion, whatever it is and however you feel. Self-abnegation is an intrinsic part of the whole process, and if you cannot deny yourself, you cannot succeed as a royal.

That does not mean that there are not huge personal benefits and payoffs to being royal. There are, but they exist only if you respect the constraints of the system. My regret is that Meghan did not give herself enough time to discover what they were. This is a regret many of the courtiers share, though others take the view that she is better out of the picture. To them, her disrespect for the boundaries, which prevent politicisation and commercialisation, were inexcusable. To them, all individuals, whether they be political, commercial, professional, social, or royal, are expected to function within the system. As far as those courtiers are concerned, the British monarchy has spearheaded the concept of constitutional monarchy since the execution of Charles I in 1649 and the restoration of the monarchy under his son Charles II in 1660. In the 360 years since then, the Crown has learnt by trial and error what works, and what does not. The British monarchy is now a vast and highly sophisticated institution in which the Royal Family and the courtiers play equally vital roles. The royals are expected to take advice only from their official advisors and tailor their conduct accordingly. These advisors are dedicated professionals whose sole goal is to maintain the efficacy of the British political system, of which the Crown is the head. They are, in their own way, vocationalists, as dedicated to the monarchy as a priest, rabbi or imam will be to his religion.

In the circumstances, it is hardly surprising that there was consternation amongst the courtiers when Meghan, an utter novice as well as a foreigner, not only resisted all advice from her official advisors from the very beginning, but went behind their backs and appointed a whole range of alternative advisors separate from her and Harry's Buckingham Palace advisors within eighteen months of her marriage. None of these appointments was approved by the palace. All were regarded as antithetical to the interests of the monarchy.

The most contentious was Meghan's appointment of the American media management firm Sunshine Sachs early in September 2019. This followed a summer of controversy in which Meghan's micro-management of her and Harry's public profile had backfired spectacularly. There were several incidents, all of which triggered an outcry predictable to everyone but Meghan and Harry, whose earlier nous seemed to have deserted him under his wife's determination to control the press as she micromanaged her image.

All of these incidents were avoidable, the negative reactions predictable. The first of these resulted in the furore surrounding baby Archie's christening by the Archbishop of Canterbury on the 7th July at Windsor Castle. Meghan and Harry had decided to throw precedent to the wind and make totally private what had hitherto been a family event shared with the public through the presence of photographers, cameramen, and godparents. In furtherance of opacity, Harry and Meghan decreed that they would not be revealing the names of the godparents, nor would they be granting access to the photographers and cameramen who customarily covered the ceremony. They would issue a photograph of their own choice to the press, as and when they were ready to do so, and not before.

Not surprisingly, this caused a hue and cry. Adam Helliker, who features earlier in this work discussing the leaking of the news of Harry's relationship with Meghan, wrote an opinion piece in the *Sun* quoting the biographer Hugo Vickers, whose opinion neatly encapsulated the consensus. Keeping the press and public away would only 'antagonise' the world's media. 'It seems to me that the Sussexes are adopting a Frank Sinatra stance of "I did it my way" and I think it is the Duchess who prompts these decisions,' Hugo said. He also made the point that withholding the names of the godparents was in stark contrast to previous custom. Their names and photographs had always been published 'as far back as at least the present Queen's christening in 1926.' He then used the example of Queen Elizabeth the Queen Mother, a revered figure in press and palace circles, to show up the uncooperative conduct of the royal couple, stating, 'The Sussexes might do well to take a leaf from the Queen Mother's book. She would always pause for the cameras, make sure they had a good chance to do their jobs and then move on.'

To those who know code, these comments were interesting, because Hugo Vickers would not have been saying any of the things he did, had these sentiments not been shared by the palace. I have known Hugo for many years and know how well connected he is. I also know to what extent he values his palace connections. I'd go as far as saying that I wouldn't want to have a baby with him and give him a choice between our progeny and his palace connections, for I know which one he'd choose. He is not only a lay steward at St. George's Chapel, but is also a Deputy to the Lord Lieutenant of Berkshire.

The following month, Meghan and Harry found themselves embroiled in even hotter water when they managed to score a whole series of own goals with one football. Not only did they spurn the Queen's invitation to take Archie up to Balmoral for some family time with the other royals, on the grounds that the baby was too young to travel that distance, but they gave the press the opportunity to accuse them of hypocrisy by then flying, at the very time they should have been up at Balmoral, a greater distance with Archie, to stay with Elton John and David Furnish and their kids in the South of France. As the Queen was known to have been disappointed that her grandson and his family would not be visiting her at her beloved Balmoral, where she can really let her hair down and relax, this was seen as a slap to the face. When Harry and Meghan then managed to use private jets four times in eleven days, while lecturing ordinary people about the need to keep their carbon footprints small, they set themselves up for pillorying.

In for a penny, in for a pound. No sooner did Harry park Meghan and Archie at Frogmore Cottage, than he put both his hands and his bare feet in the stocks by hopping onto yet another plane to join what the

Sun called 'the hypocritical superstars travelling to the Google Camp conference in Italy in [114 separate] gas-guzzling private planes. And dozens of A-listers are reportedly choosing to stay on giant polluting superyachts' while being 'ferried to-and-fro from the tech giant's seventh annual jolly at an exclusive Sicilian resort in fuel-sucking Maseratis.' Amidst glamorous conscionables such as Stella McCartney, Orlando Bloom, Diane von Fürstenberg, Chris Martin, Katy Perry, Bradley Cooper and Leo DiCaprio, a barefooted Harry, whose feet gleamed thanks to a recent pedicure, gave a rousing speech confirming that he and Meghan were so concerned about the state of the planet and the effects of climate change that they would never be immoral enough to have more than two children.

Up to now, the British press had been having a field day condemning Meghan and Harry for inconsistency and hypocrisy. They now found a third charge to add to the roster. They decided Harry had finally joined Meghan in casting shade on William and Catherine, who had three children and were rumoured to be considering having a fourth. Competitiveness, spitefulness and point-scoring were the latest adjectives being used to describe the couple's conduct.

None of the reports credited Harry with being the instigator. They pointed to how Meghan had begun the year by leaking private information to five of her friends, all of whom remained anonymous, though there was speculation that one might be *Suits* actress Abigail Spencer. They had boosted her profile while rubbishing her father in a cover story published by *People* magazine in the first week of February under the headline *The Truth About Meghan*. She was portrayed as a 'selfless' person whose friends' sole concern was to 'speak the truth about our friend' and 'stand up against the global bullying we are seeing.' The picture these friends painted was of a simple, self-abnegating, down-to-earth girl who is so self-sacrificing that 'I'm not even allowed to ask about her until she finds out about me.' They described how 'much she loves her animals, how much she loves her friends, how much she loves feeding you, taking care of you.' They stated how worried they were that Meg's health and that of her unborn baby might suffer unless the press stopped saying negative things about her. And they plunged the knife into Thomas

Markle Sr, who had been claiming that his daughter was refusing to respond to his calls and letters. They stated, 'He knows how to get in touch with her. Her telephone number hasn't changed. He's never called; he's never texted. It's super painful, because Meg was always so dutiful. I think she will always feel genuinely devastated by what he's done. At the same time, because she's a daughter, she has a lot of sympathy for him.' Twisting the knife for maximum damage, Meghan's friends continued, 'At no point [following exposure that Tom had cooperated with a paparazzo to improve his image] was there talk of "Now that he's lied, he's in trouble." Tom wouldn't take her calls. Wouldn't take Harry's calls.' So poor Meghan was forced after the wedding to write her father a private letter, one whose contents he had never disclosed to anyone, though the ultra-private Meghan had shared these with five separate friends, providing copies for them to leak to *People*, in which she had stated, 'Dad, I'm so heartbroken. I love you. I have one father. Please stop victimizing me through the media so we can repair our relationship.' She pointed out how his every comment was 'an arrow to the heart'. And what was the response of her father, whom her friends were portraying as a cynical, publicity-seeking liar and hypocrite? According to them, 'He writes her a long letter in return, and closes it by requesting a photo op with her.'

Within days of that story being published, the prevailing opinion in the British press was that Meghan had not only got her friends to purvey an absolutely false picture of her father and of her relationship with him, but that she had done so in the belief that he loved her so much he would never expose her. The inconsistencies and plain, plumb incredible premise of the *People* story was not lost on a more incisive and questioning audience in Britain, though they seem to have eluded the American readers and, even if not them, *People* magazine. The suspicion was that Meghan had deliberately orchestrated the whole story to deflect criticism of her conduct by courting public sympathy. While the American public might not appreciate that five friends of a royal duchess would never behave as they had, without her connivance, the British public was only too aware of how public figures manipulate the press, and had no doubt as to who had caused it to be written, and why. When Meghan failed to dissociate herself from the story, her silence confirmed the suspicion that she had been complicit. Had she not been, she would not only have carpeted her friends, but would also have dumped them. Time would tell whether the more cynical viewpoint was justified, but in the meantime Meghan's admirers, especially in America, viewed any support for Thomas Markle Sr as yet more evidence that she was being bullied.

As the year progressed and so too did the couple's own goals, Meghan and Harry found themselves more and more trapped by the exclusionary way they were dealing with those who disagreed with them. All royals need No Men. In a situation such as theirs, the advice was simple. If they wanted to avoid controversy, avoid controversial actions. Do not encourage friends to brief sympathetic publications like *People* magazine, and if you haven't, take steps to dissociate yourself from the story and restore what little dignity had been left to your father, rather than colluding with your five friends' stripping him of its remnants.

The British rebel against press manipulation in a way the Americans don't. Meghan and Harry should have known that the immutable law whereby each action has an equal and opposite reaction applied as much to the press as to physics. While Harry and Meghan had no recollection of how his mother used to brief the press herself when she did not get her friends to do so on her behalf, British journalists had only too vivid recall on the subject. Meghan's friends providing America with her side of the falling out with her father might convince readers on that side of the Atlantic that she was being protected by her friends against a bullying press in Britain, but in Britain the view was that she had simply taken a leaf out of her late mother-in-law's manual of press manipulation. Rather than being convinced of her victimhood, they were now more convinced than ever that she was a pro-active manipulator who was using the press in exactly the same way that Diana had done.

Meghan now showed everyone why Prince Charles's nickname of Tungsten fitted the strength of character her friends and foes both acknowledge she possesses. Harder than nails, tougher than boots, and anything but malleable, tungsten can withstand most pressures without buckling. Someone, who has known her for a long time and spoke to me under an assurance of anonymity, explained that 'all those years of rejection [when Meghan was trying to make it] taught her to hang in there, to believe in herself, to ignore what anyone else says and stick to her guns. It took her years to make it, but she stayed true to her vision of herself. She's doing the same thing now. She thinks the palace crew are a bunch of no-hope suckers. All she needs to do is stay true to her vision and everything will come right in the end.'

It is hardly surprising that Meghan would, with a belief like that, hold her line no matter how rough the ride was becoming. Her track record also showed that she had a real talent for turning everything, whether it be an opportunity, a setback, or anything in between, to her advantage. This would become more and more apparent as she and Harry pulled further and further away from their royal moorings. In the meantime, there could be no doubt, from the comments they both made about how inept the palace were at exploiting their undoubted gifts to their full advantage, that they both disdained the advice and opinions of 'the palace crew'.

From the disdained crew's point of view, the issues looked radically different. To them, there were no relevant analogies between an actress stubbornly waiting for her big break and a royal duchess who had started out her royal life with the attitude that she knew better than they did what was in the monarchy's best interests, was persisting in denigrating the wisdom and experience of advisors who have been in the game longer than she had, was stirring up unnecessary controversy to the detriment of her royal position, and who continued to let them know that she had nothing to learn from them but all to teach.

If you know anything about how publicity works, and how the late Princess of Wales functioned, it was obvious that by this point Meghan and Harry were outmanoeuvring their palace advisors. Although the press did not yet know that their purpose was to lay the ground to expand their horizons in a quest for financial and commercial independence, they knew that something was afoot and whatever it was, it was not kosher.

As far as Meghan and Harry were concerned, they had no incentive to take any of the advice they were being given by their official advisors at Buckingham Palace, because the 'palace crew' had been functioning on the premise that this sort of publicity must be dampened down, while the Sussexes were intent on ratcheting it up. In the light of that, it was unsurprising that Meghan ignored their advice to keep her head down, but went behind their back and brought in the big guns to shoot down the British press. Her ploy was simple. Neutralise the uncontrollable British tabloids so that she would have absolute control over her public image. She therefore instructed Sunshine Sachs in the US to assist her in developing tactics to neutralise them.

Meghan could not have chosen a firm better placed to take on and crush the press and supplant the gentlemanly 'palace crew'. In making the appointment, she was making it clear that she would not be limited by anything the monarchy told her. Sunshine Sachs is headed up by Chief Executive Shawn Sachs and founder Ken Sunshine, whom the *New York Times* accused of using 'bare-knuckle tactics' on behalf of clients such as Harvey Weinstein when he was first accused of groping model Ambra Battilana Gutierez, Michael Jackson at the time of his paedophile troubles, and Justin Smollett following his dismissal for faking a racist, homophobic attack. Ken Sunshine is also known to be an avid supporter of left-wing causes and to be a personal friend of the Rev Al Sharpton and Bill and Hillary Clinton. By instructing Sunshine Sachs to act on her behalf, Meghan was sailing dangerously close to the wind in that Sunshine Sachs's political affiliations could potentially taint the apolitical stance of the British Royal Family. She, of course, had a defence against that. She was being represented at Sunshine Sachs by Keleigh Thomas Morgan, with whom she had worked when she was on *Suits*. Nevertheless, the mere act of making this extra-official appointment meant that Meghan and Harry had breached several rules at once. Firstly, no responsible national entity can have two representatives fulfilling the same function, and secondly, by appointing Sunshine Sachs without permission, Meghan was demonstrating that she intended to push an anti-press, pro left-wing, commercial agenda, irrespective of these positions being antithetical to the long term interests of the monarchy.

Any doubt about what this appointment meant was cleared up by

Ken Sunshine's comments. 'We don't play it safe. We're not genteel. We name names and battle the media when we have to.' He insisted that his clients had a 'right to privacy' and that he regards press photographers as the 'stalkerazzi'.

Because Sunshine Sachs is known within the industry for the hardball tactics it employs in maintaining its clients' privacy against their adversaries, that company's appointment was a direct challenge to the press from Meghan and Harry. While such tactics on behalf of Sunshine Sachs' Hollywood clients might work with the American press, an adversarial approach when adopted on behalf of a British royal would be unconstitutional and liable to bring the Crown into conflict with one of its lynchpins.

Nor was this the only threat the palace spotted. This was the second overtly political appointment Meghan had made that year, the first being the appointment of Sara Latham as Meghan and Harry's head of communications. A former senior advisor on Hillary Clinton's 2016 presidential campaign and special advisor to the late Tessa Jowell, Secretary of State for Culture, Media and Sport under the previous Labour government, Sara Latham was adjudged to be too party political a figure to serve in such a sensitive position.

However, Sara Latham is a respected figure, and the appointment proceeded. By this time though, the palace were so concerned that Meghan and Harry's actions, some of which were impulsive in the extreme, would damage the monarchy, if only by bringing them negative press, that anyone who could gain the air of her boss would be a Godsend. Although Meghan's critics and the American public might not realise it, the palace wanted her and Harry to enjoy the approval of the press, the British press in particular. The difficulty, so far, had been to convince the royal couple that they should modify their conduct and be more sensitive to the concerns of all segments of the public as well as the media. To ensure that the couple would not be able to run riot and damage the monarchy by overt politicising or any of the other infractions which they seemed hell bent on pursuing, a term of Ms Latham's appointment was that she was to report directly to the Queen's Communication's Secretary. 'That [term of employment] had Christopher Geidt's fingerprints all over it,' a prince told me, meaning that the recently ennobled Lord had set things up in such a way that the Queen and her senior advisors would be able to exert some control over Meghan and Harry, which really meant Meghan, for while he was an active and willing participant, she was the main tactician and architect.

Within months, the palace would learn how completely ineffectual their attempts at control were. Meghan simply went behind Sara Latham's back and brought Sunshine Sachs in to assist her and Harry in blowing the most popular newspapers in Britain out of the water.

Hard on the heels of Sara Latham's appointment came an application by Meghan and Harry on the 21st June 2019 to trademark over 100 items under their brand, Sussex Royal. They were casting a very wide net. Although they claimed to be doing this in furtherance of their humanitarian work, the categories covered were so extensive that the only reasonable conclusion to come to was that this a straightforward endeavour at commercial exploitation with possible political overtones. There were items such as materials; printed educational materials; printed publications; books; educational books; textbooks; magazines, newspapers; periodicals, diaries; art books; notebooks; greeting cards; even stationery and office requisites. On a more commercially mundane level the items included clothing; footwear; headgear; t-shirts; coats; jackets; trousers; sweaters; jerseys; dresses; pyjamas; suits; sweat shirts; caps; hats; even bandanas; socks, neckwear and sportswear. More overtly political were such items as campaigning; promotional and public awareness campaigns; organising and conducting community service projects; and a host of other activities, some specifically charitable, others less obviously so, but all 'information, advisory and consultancy services relating to the aforesaid services, all of the aforesaid services also provided online via a database or the internet.'

There was little doubt by this time that Meghan and Harry were planning a move into the world of commerce, despite such activity being strictly forbidden for senior members of the Royal Family. There was rather more doubt as to whether she and Harry understood the significance of trademarking a name containing the word royal. It is a word restricted by law in the United Kingdom. No one can use it without the permission of the Crown. The question was: Were Meghan and Harry even aware of this, or did they know it and were they canny enough to register the trademark while they were still working royals, in the hope that they had a better chance of retaining the ability to use a royal description to which they would have no right once they embarked upon commercial activity?

Even before Meghan and Harry's attempt to trademark the Sussex Royal brand was known, it was obvious to the palace, the press, and all sophisticates what Meghan's aim, and with her Harry's, was. This was summarised by the *Guardian* columnist Mark Borkowski, a PR expert and author of two books on publicity stunts, who voiced the universal viewpoint that Meghan intended 'to build a global brand'.

He also cautioned against the aggressive approach she and, through her, Harry were taking with the media, contrasting it to his mother's policy of 'charming' the press into coverage Diana had wanted. He foresaw trouble for the couple as 'American PRs don't get charm. They get size and power. And they don't understand the world outside America.'

These warnings would come true only too soon. Although it would take another few months for Meghan and Harry to sue the British press, Meghan's guest editorship of the September 2019 issue of British *Vogue* quickly resulted in yet more criticism from the British press rather than the praise she had hoped for. Sunshine Sachs had helped her with the project. On the face of it, it was a golden opportunity to shine, but once the magazine came out, becoming the bestselling issue of all time, excitement turned to disapproval, demonstrating just how totally lacking in appreciation of British culture and British sensitivities Meghan and Sunshine Sachs were. The cover, of fifteen women in boxes, with the sixteenth box left bare for the reader to insert herself in it, or anyone else of her choice, was deemed to be a good idea highjacked by superficiality and woke bias to such an extent that it had become a bad idea slickly executed.

By common consent, Meghan's editorship was judged to be too Holly-wood. Where among her choice of the fifteen most important *Women for Change* was a heavy-hitter like her grandmother-in-law, Queen Elizabeth II or the female British Prime Minister Theresa May? Why, in an edition dedicated to women who were forces for change in society, were most if not all of the women connected to Hollywood? Why were most of them actresses, models, celebrities or left-wing activists? Yet again, the clash of British and American culture was apparent. In Britain, Hollywood is viewed as the slickest and most famous source of entertainment in the world, but beyond that, it has no *gravitas*. Very few people in Britain care one iota about the opinions of Hollywood personalities. They are there to entertain, not to instruct, and those who get on the bandwagon, such as Vanessa Redgrave or now Meghan, turn the public off. They prefer to obtain their instruction, elucidation and education from more conventional sources such as educationalists, writers, politicians, newspaper editors, even television pundits. This contrasts sharply with the respect Hollywood and its representatives generate in the United States.

What further reduced the respect of the public reaction was *Vogue* editor Edward Enninful's confirmation that Meghan had approached him rather than the other way around. This immediately removed all the cachet of an invitation and replaced it with a degree of pushiness which might earn respect in the United States but did the opposite in the United Kingdom. In the British scheme of things, royalty acquiesces to invitations; it doesn't seek them out. Doing so converts those who are in a position to endow into supplicants. As such, there is a loss of stature and with it, concomitant esteem.

Also, in Britain the fashion industry is regarded with less reverence than it is in the United States. Although it is viewed as glamorous, it simply does not have the solemnity it possesses across the Atlantic. Here, it is regarded as frothy and frivolous, so dedicating an issue to a sociological subject like women who are forces for change in society became, in British eyes, a bizarre mixture of the superficial and the profound. Had Meghan guest edited a serious publication like the *Economist* or even a newspaper like the *Telegraph* or the *Guardian*, and had she chosen really hard-hitting women like her grandmother-in-law, Angela Merkel the German Chancellor, Christine Lagarde (President of the European Central Bank) or even the incoming President of the

European Commission Ursula von der Leyen, she would have gained respect rather than criticism.

Then it emerged that Enninful had offered Meghan a cover, but she had declined it on the grounds of 'modesty'. This was taken to mean that Meghan was implying that Catherine Cambridge, who had recently been on the cover, and with whom she was known to be on the outs, was vain and immodest, while she, Meghan, was retiring and modest for declining the honour. She was condemned for casting shade on her sister-in-law and for supposing that declining a lesser position, while requesting a greater one such as the guest editorship, indicated modesty.

Mr Borkowski had been absolutely correct. Sunshine Sachs and Meghan simply did not understand that what works in America doesn't necessarily work in Britain. Not only was Meghan's guest editorship mocked for being shallow and puerile, but it was also condemned for having revealed political bias, unnecessary prejudice, woke pretentiousness, and unregal behaviour. From a public relations point of view, it had been a disaster, demonstrating how out of step both Meghan and her media management team were with their target market. They had demonstrated such insensitive overkill that they had managed to turn what could have been a golden opportunity into a rout. In the process, Sunshine Sachs had made their undoubtedly intelligent and capable client look silly.

The guest editorship also confirmed the worst fears of those who believed that Meghan was intent on making herself into a global brand. There were real concerns at the palace that she would damage the reputation of the monarchy for being above commerce as well as politics unless a way could be found to redirect her energies into something less controversial.

The reasons are obvious why constitutional monarchy needs to ban members of reigning royal families from political activity as well as from engaging in commercial activity for personal gain. Yet Meghan and Harry seemed oblivious to the fact that you cannot on the one hand represent all the people of a country while on the other hand you are espousing only one political persuasion, nor can you be above the hurly-burly of finance while at the same time getting your hands grubby making deals. Even if your commercial activities are beyond reproach, the overlap between commerce and politics is self-evident. There is always a segment of the population who might disapprove of your monetary activities and in doing so, draw you into a political argument. Having politically and commercially clean hands is like being a virgin. It is an absolute. It's either/or. You can't be above the hurly-burly of trade and politics while being an entrepreneur or a politician, any more than you can be almost a virgin.

Meghan and Harry, however, were oblivious to the consequences insofar as they might adversely affect the monarchy, though they were only too mindful of things as these affected themselves. They both felt that Meghan had a right to her political opinions, that no one had a right to deprive her of her right to express them, moreover that they were such good opinions that everyone else should possess them, and those who did not, needed enlightening. Never one to hide their light or misery under a bushel, Meghan, and Harry on her behalf, complained vociferously about how her 'voice' was being 'muted' and her 'soul crushed'. She did not consider that the monarchy might be worth the sacrifice, and he backed her up in that belief. As far as they were concerned, monarchy or none, she was going to get her point across, and if she couldn't do it orally, she'd do it silently. So when President Trump, who is someone for whom she has a pathological loathing, arrived in Britain with the First Lady Melania Trump for their State Visit at the beginning of June 2019, Meghan declined to attend a reception at Buckingham Palace with the other royals, though Prince Harry made an appearance. Maternity leave was given as the excuse for her absence, though she managed days later to progress down the Mall from Buckingham Palace to Horse Guards Parade for Trooping the Colour in one of the state landaus, a veritable picture of robust good health with an adoring Harry shooting her approving looks when he wasn't beaming proudly at the assembled crowd. The press were quick to pick up on the underlying message: Meghan had snubbed Trump. This did not strike the British as a source of glee, not when the Queen had exemplarily hosted world leaders such as Presidents Xi Jinping of China, Robert Mugabe of Zimbabwe, and Nicolae Ceaușescu of Romania, and made sure that she accorded all of them the dignity their office demanded even if she might have had personal reservations about their human rights records. One person who could not condemn his daughter-in-law for her undiplomatic behaviour, however, was Prince Charles, who had snubbed President Hu Jintao of China on his state visit in 2005.

Of course, if Meghan did have long term goals where American politics were concerned, her conduct made perfect sense. Shortly afterwards, she reaffirmed her political sympathies when she asked Hillary Clinton and her daughter Chelsea for tea at Frogmore Cottage - and made sure that the world knew about the visit. It began to look suspiciously as if Meghan was playing a long game, and that she was doing it with skill.

Political ambitions aside, she and Harry remained working members of the Royal Family, so, on the 23rd September 2019, they took off on a ten day tour of South Africa. No one outside royal circles appreciated that this would most likely be their final royal tour. As far as the British press were concerned, it was once more business as usual. It needs to be emphasised at this point that everyone wanted Meghan and Harry's tour to succeed. Because a constant run of bad publicity is in no one's interest except possibly the subject who wishes to be presented as a victim, the British press were eager for the trip to go well so that they could file glowing reports and restore Meghan and Harry's popularity. One editor told me that all the papers were delighted to see that the Sussexes were greeted with joyousness, the local people taking pride in one of their own race being a member of the Royal Family. This, after all, was one of the most important attributes Meghan possessed, a veritable gift for the monarchy and a unifying link between it and the citizens of colour in the Commonwealth which, it must be remembered, is primarily a union of people of colour.

Meghan acquitted herself admirably. She was charming, gracious, affable, and delightful. She made a speech to a group of women referring to herself as a sister and a woman of colour. She was greeted with genuine enthusiasm and it was a true joy to see the pride people everywhere took in her existence. In royal circles, everyone could not have been more pleased with the reception she was getting. Meghan was fulfilling the promise which people all over the world had vested in her, and everywhere, genuine delight reigned. Many of the Commonwealth diplomats to whom I spoke felt that she was representing people of colour everywhere with true grace and dignity. They all expected her to be a real force for good as long as she continued to represent such hopefulness and positivity to the hundreds of millions of people who now regarded her as the embodiment of what people of colour could achieve.

The press also noticed, and commented favourably upon, Meghan's choice of wardrobe. Tactfully, it was more high street than couture as she downplayed amongst the poverty stricken the fashion parade for which she was so well known, and which garnered her such praise amongst the fashionistas on both sides of the Atlantic. What remained unknown so far were the furious battles that had been fought between the couple and the financial comptrollers for the Duchy of Cornwall, who were liable for the expenses of Meghan's wardrobe. In the months since her marriage, she had gone through some $2m for clothes alone. She never wore the same item twice, and virtually everything was couture. As the cost mounted and the courtiers tried to keep the tab down, Meghan and Harry doggedly refused to relent, stating in no uncertain terms that she had to look good and they weren't about to cut corners for penny pinchers.

Proving that even when she pinched the pennies, she looked good, Meghan used the visit to display not only her stylishness but also to show off her son. She and Harry introduced Archie to Archbishop Desmond Tutu and his family. The press, hungry for pictures of the baby and the happy family, lapped up every charming moment.

Harry then left Meghan and Archie on their own to visit Botswana, Malawi and Angola. While there, he retraced his mother's footsteps in the famous landmine journey she had made in Huambo shortly before her death, though by now the fields were gone, replaced by a concrete jungle. Articulating the ultimate purpose of the tour, he said, 'This is a wonderful example of how the UK, in partnership with Angola, can address the issue of landmines, bringing prosperity to an area, creating jobs, helping people access education and healthcare and making communities safer.'

As the tour approached its end, it seemed to observers as if the Duke and Duchess of Sussex had finally turned a corner. Their run of bad publicity had come to an end. All their publicity had been positive. They had acquitted themselves admirably. They had behaved in impeccable royal style and done so with all the charm, style and gloss which had turned them into one of the world's most famous couples. The trip had been a resounding success. The goodwill with which they had started their marriage, and which had seeped away in the year and a four months since it, had flooded back in. Then, the day before their departure, they took a pickaxe to the pool of wellbeing, hacked away at the accumulation of success, drained away all the positivity which had been built up in restored good relations with the press, and dissipated the very purpose of a royal tour, which is to promote harmony while turning the world's attention to the place being visited. In one fell swoop, Harry and Meghan diverted attention away from South Africa, the suffering of its people, and their own success, by issuing a statement, unknown to their official office at Buckingham Palace or to the Foreign and Commonwealth Office, which is in charge of royal tours, through their American-managed official website. It declared:

Statement by His Royal Highness
Prince Harry, Duke of Sussex
01 OCTOBER 2019

As a couple, we believe in media freedom and objective, truthful reporting. We regard it as a cornerstone of democracy and in the current state of the world – on every level – we have never needed responsible media more.

Unfortunately, my wife has become one of the latest victims of a British tabloid press that wages campaigns against individuals with no thought to the consequences – a ruthless campaign that has escalated over the past year, throughout her pregnancy and while raising our newborn son.

There is a human cost to this relentless propaganda, specifically when it is knowingly false and malicious, and though we have continued to put on a brave face – as so many of you can relate to – I cannot begin to describe how painful it has been. Because in today's digital age, press fabrications are repurposed as truth across the globe. One day's coverage is no longer tomorrow's chip-paper.

Up to now, we have been unable to correct the continual misrepresentations - something that these select media outlets have been aware of and have therefore exploited on a daily and sometimes hourly basis.

It is for this reason we are taking legal action, a process that has been many months in the making. The positive coverage of the past week from these same publications exposes the double standards of this specific press pack that has vilified her almost daily for the past nine months; they have been able to create lie after lie at her expense simply because she has not been visible while on maternity leave. She is the same woman she was a year ago on our wedding day, just as she is the same woman you've seen on this Africa tour.

For these select media this is a game, and one that we have been unwilling to play from the start. I have been a silent witness to her private suffering for too long. To stand back and do nothing would be contrary to everything we believe in.

This particular legal action hinges on one incident in a long and disturbing pattern of behaviour by British tabloid media. The contents of a private letter were published unlawfully in an intentionally destructive manner to manipulate you, the reader, and further the divisive agenda of the media group in question. In addition to their unlawful publication of this private document, they purposely misled you by strategically omitting select paragraphs, specific sentences, and even singular words to mask the lies they had perpetuated for over a year.

There comes a point when the only thing to do is to stand up to this behaviour, because it destroys people and destroys lives. Put simply, it is bullying, which scares and silences people. We all know this isn't acceptable, at any level. We won't and can't believe in a world where there is no accountability for this.

Though this action may not be the safe one, it is the right one. Because my deepest fear is history repeating itself. I've seen what happens when someone I love is commoditised to the point that they are no longer treated or seen as a real person. I lost my mother and now I watch my wife falling victim to the same powerful forces.

We thank you, the public, for your continued support. It is hugely appreciated. Although it may not seem like it, we really need it.

MEDIA INFORMATION

Her Royal Highness, the Duchess of Sussex has filed a claim against Associated Newspapers over the misuse of private information, infringement of copyright and breach of the Data Protection Act 2018.

The proceedings in the Chancery Division of the High Court relate to the unlawful publication of a private letter.

A legal spokesperson from Schillings who are representing The Duchess of Sussex said:

"We have initiated legal proceedings against the Mail on Sunday, and its parent company Associated Newspapers, over the intrusive and unlawful publication of a private letter written by the Duchess of Sussex, which is part of a campaign by this media group to publish false and deliberately derogatory stories about her, as well as her husband. Given the refusal of Associated Newspapers to resolve this issue satisfactorily, we have issued proceedings to redress this breach of privacy, infringement of copyright and the aforementioned media agenda."

The case is being privately funded by The Duke and Duchess of Sussex. Pending a Court ruling, proceeds from any damages will be donated to an anti-bullying charity.

This was throwing down the gauntlet in a major way. It was a declaration of war against the British press and while the American media might not have understood this, their counterparts on the other side of the Atlantic did. Although it isn't totally unheard of for royals to sue, it is highly unusual. And the timing could not have been worse from the point of view of the British Nation, even if it could not be bettered from the point of view of Sunshine Sachs, whose brief was not to protect Britain's interests, but to weaponise any and everything to the advantage of the Sussexes personally.

Putting aside the personalities and the personal benefits Sunshine Sachs could gain for the Sussexes by hijacking the purpose of a royal tour to the detriment of Britain's national interests and indeed the benefits that would otherwise have accrued to the people of South Africa, the announcement brought a worse than sour end to royal duties that had been a howling success. The statement eclipsed a tour that had been months in the making, had cost a vast sum of money, and had gone so well until the declaration of war had stolen the scene from South Africa and its problems. The only mitigating factor, if one existed, for stealing the tour's thunder and diverting attention away from its purpose, i.e. the South African people and their problems, to the personal interests of the Duke and Duchess of Sussex, was that Sunshine Sachs, being an American company with left-wing sympathies, had neither knowledge of nor interest in furthering the monarchic and Commonwealth agenda when they could take a wrecking ball to a royal occasion on behalf of their clients. Unsurprisingly, their timing was greeted by outrage in Britain.

There was little doubt who had advised him and Meghan regarding the statement and its timing. It had all the hallmarks of an American initiative and this smacked of interference by a foreign entity into the national life of another country. Sunshine Sachs, Harry and Meghan might not have had it to the forefront of their thinking, but the press, the palace and the rest of the Royal Family appreciated in full the constitutional significance of members of the British Royal Family taking on the press the way they had one. The statement itself was a curious blend of fact, fiction, wishful thinking, fear, loathing, and false accusation. Harry's passion and emotion were uplifting, though whether they were misplaced was another matter altogether. The fact was, when you cut through all the unfounded claims of bullying, of the wicked press manipulating a gullible public and hounding Meghan and Diana who, as stated earlier, customarily tipped off journalists and was therefore largely if not totally responsible for her own pursuit, the supposedly innocent Meghan was not suing over lie after lie, as Harry stated, but because her father had approached the *Mail on Sunday* over the use to which Meghan and five of her friends had put a supposedly private letter she had written to him the year before, a letter whose contents he had kept private until she divulged them, patently with the sole purpose of leaking its contents to discredit him. Contrary to the claims of her friends, who had quoted from the letter and could therefore have had sight of it only through Meghan, she had not tried to contact Thomas Markle on the many occasions she claimed, nor had he failed to contact her on the many occasions he said he had done. He had the telephone records to disprove her version and prove his, along with much else besides, including who had paid to put her through university: something he had done.

The grounds for action were therefore not the deviousness, manipulativeness, or mendacity of the *Mail on Sunday*, whose behaviour on that occasion had been beyond reproach. The legal and moral issues could not have been clearer. That newspaper had merely referred to the *People* article and quoted from a letter Meghan had written to her father, following her breach of her own privacy by revealing its contents to not one but at least five separate friends, all of whom had joined forces to further the breach of that privacy by revealing to *People* magazine the contents of the letter she had written. According to Meghan, she had put pen to paper to repair their broken relationship, not to lay down a paper trail in which she could bring as much ammunition as she judged necessary to blast her father into oblivion, and in so doing restore some of the damage which her icing of him had caused to her reputation. The facts spoke for themselves. If she had truly wanted to restore relations with hi, why had she failed to respond to any of his subsequent to contact her? Why had she publicised a supposedly private communication between daughter and father which he had expected would remain private but which she had revealed to not one but several of her friends? What was Meghan's definition of private? Did it extend only to her protection of her own interests? Did it have such a loose definition that she could demand silence from the recipient of a letter whose sole *raison d'être* appeared to the fabrication of self-serving proof of her side of a story? Did all rights repose in Meghan and none in Tom Sr? And what about those five friends who had violated Meghan's trust in them by repeating the confidences she had imparted for publication? Were we to accept that friends who betray your privacy are alright, because you take the view that they're trying to protect you, but the father whose privacy has also been betrayed, by you and your friends, has no right to defend himself against the violation of privacy you have instituted?

The sheer illogic of the premises being put forward by Harry for the lawsuit against the *Mail on Sunday* was untenable, not that anyone in the know expected the general public to realise that. Why would they, when they only had the merest glimpse of the whole picture?

Meghan would then stretch the bounds of credulity further by maintaining that her friends had taken it upon themselves, without her knowledge, consent or approval, to fabricate the whole thing in an attempt to protect her. Were we truly to t believe that Meghan, who has made such an issue of privacy, accepted her five closest friends breaching the confidences she had placed in them as she showed them the letter she had written to her father? As they contacted, arranged and fabricated the interview they gave, to a nationwide publication as popular as People magazine? That they were free to do so without any adverse consequences, but that the father they had pilloried did not have a right to defend his actions, his interests, and his privacy, which they had violated in furtherance of their own interests? Meghan had seemingly written the letter with the purpose of reviling her father. She had revealed the contents to her friends, who had parroted her words to *People.* She was therefore the perpetrator of the breach, not its victim. All her father had done was defend himself against accusations Meghan's friends had made on her behalf. According to the *Mail on Sunday*, which had tapes and documents to back up their claims, all her father had done was sought to set the record straight, using her own words to reveal the facts.

It is always unfortunate when families wash their dirty linen in public. The stench of grubby water sticks to all concerned, not just the guilty. Had Harry been older when his mother died, he might have understood how destructive it is to try to use the press against family. He would also hopefully have had more sympathy for those whom Diana had sullied as she poured bile over them, posing as the victim when in fact she was more often perpetrator than anything else. The place for resolving family conflicts is not in the world at large, but behind closed doors. Nor is the public arena a suitable platform for boosting oneself at the expense of family members. It always backfires, if only because with every victory, you lose a disproportionate number of supporters. The law of diminishing returns kicks in.

Meghan and Harry were aware that falling out with her father had done her image a great deal of harm. They appear to have thought that the weak link in the chain would be the *Mail on Sunday* for reasons which I will get into shortly. An American cousin of mine who likes Meghan - 'She is so beautiful and elegant' - spoke for many when he said, 'Her father is dreadful. I wish he'd just disappear.'

Be that as it may, lawyers on both sides of the Atlantic acknowledged that Thomas Markle Sr had a cause of action against his daughter for defamation. Under American law, the plaintiff has to prove malice to succeed. A top lawyer told me, 'What could possibly be more malicious than a daughter writing a letter to her father, full of misleading and inaccurate statements, with the evident purpose of leaking its contents to friends who then leak it to the media, to humiliate him and portray him in an unflattering light?'

While Meghan's US admirers might have wished Tom Sr to disappear, in Britain the feeling was more nuanced. The fact that he had chosen not to sue her, but to get a British publication to put his side of the story, showed that he did not want to hardball Meghan, though he did want to redress the balance. Had he been the money-grubbing, attention-seeking jerk that Meghan's friends had made him out to be, he could have got millions off *People*, as well as a lot more coverage than an article in the *Mail on Sunday*, by suing her and the friends who had defamed him to *People* magazine.

To those of us who know the score, Meghan's choice of publication to sue was interesting, possibly even cynical, and certainly indicative of a sophisticated and intelligent operator. The *Mail on Sunday* is owned by DMG Trust, whose main shareholder and chairman is the 4th Viscount

Rothermere, a cousin of Lady Mary Gaye Curzon's first husband, Esmond Cooper-Key. The present editor is Ted Verity, but the previous editor was Geordie Greig, now editor of its sister paper the *Daily Mail*. The royal couple might well have thought that the Mail group would be a soft touch because Jonathan Rothermere and Geordie Greig have impeccable connections within the highest levels of British society and would not want to jeopardise their connections with the Royal Family. If that is so, they miscalculated.

British press barons are vastly influential, but Jonathan and his father Vere have always been known to be have been hands-off owners. They literally let their editors and managers function with no reference to themselves. During the Leveson Enquiry into press standards, this was proven when Jonathan was shown to be so detached from the running of his mighty media empire that he had resisted the former Prime Minister David Cameron's blandishments to influence his editors over Brexit. I knew his parents, whom I first met in 1973 in Jamaica, where they had a house at Round Hill where Tom Inskip's reception was held and Harry and Meghan stayed. It was therefore only natural that once I started having trouble with his newspapers, I would approach Vere to intercede on my behalf. He told me that much as he liked me, and would love to stop his papers defaming me, he simply did not have the authority to do it. And if he made an exception for me, he would have to do it for everyone else in future. Jonathan's mother Pat confirmed her husband's detachment, and used to say that the only person Vere would ever bestir himself for was the Queen.

Geordie wielded more day to day influence as the editor of one of the country's most popular papers. He was as well-connected as the Rothermeres. His father Sir Carron Greig had been a courtier, a Gentleman Usher to the Queen for thirty-four years before being made an Extra Gentleman Usher. His eldest brother Louis had been a Page of Honour to the Queen, his sister Laura had been a lady-in-waiting to Diana, Princess of Wales, who was godmother to her daughter Leonora Lonsdale. Harry certainly knew Laura well, so the link was anything but notional.

If Harry and Meghan thought that Jonathan and Georgie could

intervene should things get dire, they miscalculated. The *Mail on Sunday* have stated publicly that they will defend Meghan's claim to the bitter end. Through friends in that organisation, I have been told privately that that is indeed the paper's intention. Thomas Markle has given statements to their lawyers, has provided evidence of the considerable financial assistance he gave Meghan over the years, to include proof that he put her through Northwestern University, has furnished medical records to substantiate that he did have the heart attacks which prevented him from attending the wedding, and has turned over his telephone records which show that Meghan and Harry never once tried to telephone or text him after their wedding, despite claims to the contrary. On the other hand, he tried on numerous occasions to contact her, again contrary to her friends' claims to *People*.

Within days, Harry would announce that he was also suing the *Sun* and the *Mirror* for hacking his 'phones many years ago. The die was now well and truly cast.

It is a very serious occurrence when a member of the British Royal Family sues a British national newspaper. It is even more serious when you not only have a weak case, as Meghan patently did, but your opponent can argue that you don't have right on your side. No royalist wanted to see either Meghan or Harry embarrassed and humiliated in a court of law. Moreover, the wisdom in established circles has always been that you sue the press only when you're on *terra firma*, occupying the high ground both legally and morally. Aside from the fact that all legal cases are unpredictable and therefore frequently less manageable than novices think they are - Oscar Wilde and Gloria Vanderbilt Sr are two cases in point - the British tabloids, despite frequent evidence to the contrary, do have standards, though these are rather higher where others are concerned than for themselves. Despite their double standards being leavened with generous doses of sanctimoniousness, hypocrisy, self-importance, self-delusion, and judgementalism, they truly believe that they have a righteous purpose in preserving liberties in our society. To an extent, they are right. They therefore have all the righteousness of Pharisees while being brutally tough, their survival skills honed thanks to the fierce competitiveness that exists between the various national publications. They hate being sued. They never forgive those who sue them, even when you are in the right and they in the wrong, as I know from personal experience. They have long memories and even longer print runs. They will punish you down the line for taking them on. It therefore does not behove you to litigate unless the issue is so important, and you are so patently in the right, and they are so patently in the wrong, that you really have no choice. It really must be something fundamental, like an honest person being accused of being a thief, but it should not be wishful thinking and pretensions to victimhood.

When Harry declared in his emotive way that he and Meghan had no choice but to sue, he was being rhetorical. Doubtless his words moved him. Doubtless they were intended to move others. Meghan is known to be a superb wordsmith who captivated millions with her blogs. It is unlikely that she would not have overseen Harry's statement, as she oversees everything else. They would have been wise to understand that in terms of suing the British press, no choice should literally mean no choice, and that though their rhetoric might move their supporters to sympathy, it would leave the press, and that segment of the British public that believes in a free press, cold.

The British press, with their skewered sense of justice and their tendency to join forces against anyone who attacks one of their own, were not about forget how the *Mail on Sunday* had been accused of being in the wrong when they were simply doing their job properly. The reckoning was inevitable, and came soon enough. On the 21st October 2019, ITV aired a documentary entitled *Harry & Meghan: An African Journey*. This was supposed to be a programme about their South African trip, with the focus being on their work, not themselves. The interviewer Tom Bradby was known to be friendly with William as well as Harry. No one could have imagined that Harry and Meghan would use the television programme as a forum for confession. Royalty, with the exception of Harry's late mother, does not treat television appearances as if they are group therapy sessions, nor are the secrets of the confessional appropriate for spilling by the subjects of an interview to millions of viewers. Yet Tom Bradby managed to get Harry to confess to a breach with his brother, well known within elevated circles, but only now confirmed to the general public when he asserted that he and William were on 'different paths' and there were good days and bad days within the relationship. Since it has been a truism of British national life since 1997 that the royal brothers were close and mutually supportive, this was a bombshell revelation.

Because Bradby can lay claim to mental health issues of his own, having experienced a serious bout of insomnia, and because Harry and Meghan were wearing their misery openly, he brought up the subject of their mental wellbeing. Harry revealed how 'every time' he sees a flash from a camera he is cast back to his mother's death. This was yet another instance of what Gayle King described elsewhere as Harry being 'over the top'. Diana had been dead for over twenty two years. Was Harry seriously expecting anyone to accept that he was such an emotional mess that flashbulbs catapulted him back to Diana's death - a death which he had implied in his October 1st statement was due to the press - or was he trying to gain the public's support by playing the sympathy card? Several journalists to whom I spoke opined that Harry was either 'losing the plot' and had gone 'bonkers' under Meghan's ministrations and 'all that yoga and meditation she has him doing', or then this was a bald attempt on his part to cynically play the card of his mother's death in an attempt to muzzle them. They did not like it.

Disapproving as they were of Harry's move, they were even more condemnatory of what they regarded as Meghan's more overt attempt to gain the public's sympathy for her hard lot. When Tom Bradby asked her how she was doing, and she bit her trembling lip, appeared to be fighting back tears, and bravely confessed that she was finding adjusting to royal life a struggle, that no one had asked her before how she was doing, implying that she was a sensitive soul surrounded by callous people, and that 'It's not enough to just survive something....You've got to thrive,' she certainly moved admirers and even neutrals in North America. One of my oldest and closest friends, whose first husband was a household American name and whose second husband is an eminent figure in New York, told me how touched she was by Meghan's struggles. In Britain, however, it was another story, with opinion divided much less in her favour. While Meghan had her supporters, a discomfiting number of people, journalists as well as pedestrians, expressed sentiments including, 'What an actress. What a phoney. What a fraud. What a spoilt, greedy, self-centred, self-pitying, entitled cow.'

They were convinced of the fairness of their conclusions because Meghan had made her discomfiture known to Tom Bradby while she was surrounded by people whose everyday life is a genuine struggle to survive. Yet here she was, pleading for the world's sympathy for her hard lot in life. To them, she did not deserve compassion for the hardships involved in her ultra-privileged existence; she should have been looking around her, counting her blessings, and thanking Harry, God and the Queen for having landed her in the hyper-privileged lap of luxury. One member of the public, who attended an event at my castle and engaged me in conversation, said, 'Meghan Markle has to be the most insensitive woman on earth. How can you beg the public to pity you because you're a royal duchess who has worn a million dollars' worth of clothes in a year? Because you've spent £2.4m on renovating your five bedroomed house on the Queen's bleeding estate? Because you have an army of staff to help you with your sprog (baby)? Where's the cause for pity? Me and my friends find it really distasteful that this woman has come over here and, rather than be thankful for all she's been given, she whines about not having enough support.' To the British, who thought not only about Meghan the person but also Meghan the royal duchess and how she had so much to be grateful for, she was not deserving of sympathy, while to the Americans, she was.

Before anyone had time to recover from the sensation generated by the airing of the Tom Bradby interview, Holly Lynch, a 33 year old Labour MP gathered together a group of 71 other female MPs, mostly Labour like herself, to sign an open letter to Meghan on the 29th October 2019 showing solidarity. On House of Commons writing paper, it was addressed to Her Royal Highness The Duchess of Sussex at Clarence House, which, ironically, was the first of many indications that the writers were neither as sophisticated nor as knowledgeable as the public might imagine. The Prince of Wales's residence is Clarence House. The Sussexes' office was then at Buckingham Palace, their home at Frogmore Cottage, so before the letter had even begun, it was setting the tone for the inaccuracies, misleading information and the genuine lack of insight into what was going on that would follow. It stated:

'As women MPs of political persuasions, we wanted to express our solidarity with you in taking a stand against the often distasteful and misleading nature of the stories printed in our national newspapers concerning you, your character and your family.

On occasions, stories and headlines have represented an invasion of your privacy and have sought to cast aspersions about your character, without any good reason as far as we can see.

Even more concerning still, we are calling out what can only be described as outdated, colonial undertones to some of these stories. As women Members of Parliament from all backgrounds, we stand with you in saying it cannot be allowed to go unchallenged.

Although we find ourselves being women in public life in a very different way to you, we share an understanding of the abuse and intimidation which is now so often used as a means of disparaging women in the public office from getting on with very important work.

With this in mind we expect the national media to have the integrity to know when a story is in the national interest and when it is seeking to tear a woman down for no apparent reason.

You have our assurances that we stand with you in solidarity on this.

We will use the means at our disposal to ensure that our press accept your right to privacy and show respect, and that their stories reflect the truth.'

Meghan, of course, was delighted to receive such overt and unprecedented support. She got in touch with Ms Lynch and thanked her.

Nevertheless, there were several problems with that letter, chief of which was the accusation that the press stories were violating Meghan's privacy, failing to show respect, and violating the truth. The press in fact had a much more accurate handle on what was going on behind the scenes that the MPs, were also confusing the more bizarre comments posted on the internet with the valid criticisms the press were making. Journalists cannot be held accountable for what takes place on the internet, but of course politicians of all complexions are always keen to muzzle the media and will leap on any bandwagon that helps to further their censoring agendas. This was therefore a classic case of politicians trying to make capital out of a situation with which, by rights, they should not have been involving themselves. The conflicts between a member of the Royal Family and the majority of the press should have been off limits to Parliamentarians, and would have been had any other member of the Royal Family been involved. Meghan Markle being an America mixed race feminist and left-wing political activist, her unique qualities were extrapolated by these MPs into giving them licence to interfere, when in fact they had neither the right nor the correct degree of information with which to intervene.

There was actually a strong case to be made that these politicians were exploiting Meghan's identity for their own benefit and to further their own political interests. The fact that they were interposing themselves when there was a lawsuit between a member of the Royal Family and the *Mail on Sunday* made their actions even more indefensible. In a democracy, the right of the press to comment freely upon the actions of public figures, especially public figures who are either politicians or royals, is a fundament which needs to be protected by everyone who understands that a free press protects a free society and vice versa. Meghan had launched a lawsuit against a publication that had a valid right of response legally, and therefore the argument could be made that these politicians were abusing their positions by writing to Meghan in the terms they did.

The timing of the letter was also mischievous. Britain was a few short weeks away from a fiercely contested general election which, without exaggeration, represented the most important choice voters were required to make in a lifetime. The very soul and future of the country was at stake. Would Britain remain a centrist democracy under the sitting Prime Minister Boris Johnson, or would it become a Marxist state under the Labour leader Jeremy Corbyn? Would it remain a part of the European Union or would it regain those elements of its national sovereignty that had been surrendered as a part of its membership of the European Union? Would Britain Brexit or would the voters opt for reversing their original vote to leave and remain one of twenty seven? Most of the signatories of the letter were Labour MPs. Many were avowed republicans. Several of them were known political agitators. The few who weren't rabidly left-wing anti-monarchists were either avowed feminists who saw misogynism everywhere, or then they were the occupants of marginal seats who were plainly jumping on what they estimated was the populistic and popular bandwagon in the hope that they would save their seats. Beneath the ostensibly noble sentiments there was therefore a tremendous amount of cynical and politicised self-interest. Which, as far as the palace was concerned, was just the sort of situation they had always sought to avoid, and which would never have occurred had Meghan and Harry not been pandering to the very political elements in the country who wanted to abolish the monarchy. This was yet another example of how dangerous it was when leading members of a choir decide that it is their personal interest to sing off key. The anti-monarchist, pro-republican Marxist MP Rebecca Long-Bailey actually said that while she wanted to abolish the monarchy, she'd like to see Meghan made queen first.

Even more offensive than the letter's rank politicisation of an issue that had nothing to do with politics, was the implication that Meghan was being victimised on racial grounds. The thinly veiled allusion to 'colonial undertones' was accusing the press of racism when they had welcomed Meghan with open arms and suppressed much negative information about her. They were not prejudiced against her on racist grounds. On the contrary, they had been prejudiced in favour of her on those precise grounds. The fact that they knew, in a way none of the MPs who had signed that letter did, that Meghan viewed many British traditions with barely concealed contempt, did not make them guilty of 'colonial undertones'. If anyone was guilty of prejudice, it was the MPs who had written the letter, or Meghan herself, for what can be more prejudicial than a foreigner disdaining national customs and institutions? It was obvious that whoever was prejudiced, it was not the press, but the authors and subject of the letter, which had been written with the specific purpose of exploiting a time of national vulnerability. It was the signatories who were prejudiced: against the monarchy, the centrist and right-wing elements of the British press. They were trying to make political capital out of something which they had no right interfering with.

The British people, however, had more to worry about in the lead-up to the election of the 12th December 2019 than any of the fanciful claims the female MPs had made. Water sought its own level and the issue floated out to sea, as everyone in Britain concentrated on the truly important issue of whether the country would remain a centrist democracy outside of the European Union or become a Marxist state, possibly in, possibly out of, the EU.

It was a massive relief to people all over the country when Boris Johnson was re-elected Prime Minister with a huge majority. Several of the MPs who had so mischievously tried to make political capital out of the conflicts between the press and the Sussexes lost their seats.

The problem of opportunistic Marxist MPs having been solved by the electorate, Harry and Meghan set about providing solutions to their own problems. They gave the first indication of what they had been planning for the whole year when they announced that they would not be spending Christmas with the Royal Family, but would go abroad with Archie to be with her mother. Although few people outside of a tight royal circle appreciated that the royal couple was taking the first step in realising their ambition to base themselves in California, safely beyond the reach of the palace and its supporters in the British media while they promoted their interests and became financially independent, Harry and Meghan had nevertheless just handed their critics a dagger and the media did not hesitate to use it. Their refusal to spend what Fleet Street and most well-informed people suspected would be Prince Philip's last Christmas with him raised questions as to just how humane they actually were when dealing with those close to them, as opposed to strangers who would give them adulation as they indulged in displays of humanitarianism. It had been an open secret in well-informed circles in Britain for some time that Prince Philip commiserated with someone with pancreatic cancer by stating that he too was diagnosed with it. Out of respect for him and the Queen, the editors in the know had decided not to break the news until the palace announced it. As no announcement had been made to date, no editor had published that fact, but anyone with a brain in his or her head only needed to look at Prince Philip to see that he could not possibly be very long for this earth, pancreatic cancer or none.

So the press waded in and questioned just how sincerely humanitarian Harry and Meghan were. While some reports did allude to the rumour that Meghan had been deliberately detaching Harry from his family, none stated that she resented her grandfather-in-law for having advised Harry not to marry her. As such, they were exhibiting self-restraint, for the word in smart drawing rooms was that Meghan had skilfully used the family's original caution about her to gain absolute control over Harry and steer him away from his family in the direction she wanted, which was worldwide celebrity based in California.

While the press marked down the couple's bolt across the Atlantic to self-indulgent inconsideration, with the more left-wing newspapers taking the alternative viewpoint that they were a young couple and should not be expected to always spend the festive season with Harry's grandparents, this book's original proposal to the publishers written earlier in the year had stated that Harry and Meghan would be seeking to lead a life on both sides of the Atlantic as they set about maximising commercial opportunities while capitalising upon their royal status and fame. The issue, as I made clear, wasn't if; it was purely when.

To that extent, the press were therefore outside of the loop. Obviously Harry and Meghan would not be considering Prince Philip's existence when their focus was on their own. Sentimentality aside, it mattered not a jot whether they spent Christmas in Canada or at Sandringham. What counted was where they would be living, and my information, which would only too soon be confirmed by the statement they made when they stood down as senior royals, was that they intended to live between Britain and California, enjoying the full benefits of their royal life when they were here, and the complete advantages of their American activities when they were there.

CHAPTER 10

As far as the public were concerned, 2019 ended on a high note for Meghan and Harry. They had announced that they were retreating from public view to spend six weeks away on a much needed break, which would be, in keeping with their previous demands for privacy, entirely private. Although one or two publications were ungracious enough to point out that Meghan had spent most of the year off, that Harry's schedule had not been exactly onerous either, and that their interpretation of privacy seemed at odds with their endless postings on their stylish website, the rumblings were focused more on their failure to be with Prince Philip than anything else.

Buckingham Palace cleared up the mystery of where the couple had retreated to by announcing that they were spending the festive season 'enjoying sharing the warmth of the Canadian people and the beauty of the landscape.' Prime Minister Justin Trudeau then tweeted, 'Prince Harry, Meghan, and Archie, we're all wishing you a quiet and blessed stay in Canada. You're among friends, and always welcome here.'

To celebrate the Festive Season, Harry and Meghan cut out the hated tabloids and communicated directly with their followers, posting on the Sussex Royal website an informal black and white photograph as they squatted in front of a heavily decorated Christmas tree smiling joyously at Archie, who was gazing directly into the camera. Beneath the ducal coronet was the message: 'Wishing you a very Merry Christmas and a Happy New Year from OUR FAMILY to YOURS.'

The problem, with taking command of their media coverage as forcefully as Meghan and Harry had done, was that they didn't only make adversaries of the people whose livelihood they threatened, but they also exposed themselves more than would otherwise have been the case had the palace press office been handling their publicity. Since it was obvious by now that Meghan herself was the sculptress moulding the clay - she is well known to micromanage everything - and since her fingerprints and Americanisms were over virtually every one of their postings, the press began drafting in experts to find out what the hidden meanings were behind the pronouncements and even the body language.

Some of the interpretations were positive. For instance, the British communications and body language expert Judi James noted that their pose in their Christmas card demonstrated 'the tight affection between Harry and his wife as they sat on the floor in mirrored poses.' She also suggested that Harry and Meghan's configuration made them seem to be 'rather lost in their own trio of love'. She thought that their position-ing gave out the message that they were 'equals', in contrast to the Cambridges' Christmas card, which was more traditional, with William at the centre of it.

To the extent that the Cambridges do have a traditional marriage, while the Sussexes have a woke one, she was right. Where things might have got confusing is that royal and aristocratic wives are traditionally the powers behind the thrones. They wield their might quietly; they do not flaunt it. But pushovers? I have seen very few in my lifetime. Most of the men have far more respect for their wives, and defer to them rather more frequently than outsiders might imagine, or might be apparent to those who do not understand the traditional world. And most of the women are far better able to shape their destinies, and those of their families, than many a feminist might imagine. In a way, these traditional wives have long since had the power feminists have been hankering after since Women's Lib came along, and they continue to wield it to this day.

Diana Wales, for instance, exercised tremendous influence in her marriage. Her mistake was to think that she could dominate Charles so completely that she would change him into the man she wanted him to be, after which he would meekly follow in her wake. Rather than lose his identity totally, he withdrew from their relationship, which happened right after Harry's birth. But even then, Diana continued to be a force to be reckoned with. She was an extremely strong personality, and the sons of strong mothers usually choose strong women for their wives, which is what both William and Harry did.

Insofar as Catherine Cambridge is concerned, those who underestimate her do so at their peril. Her sister Pippa used to go out with Billy, the son of my great friends Alan and Patrea More Nisbett, and so they had an insight into both sisters long before they became as famous as they now are. Catherine may be sweet and traditional but she has always been highly intelligent with a strong character. She does not function at a fever-pitch of hyper-enthusiasm like Meghan, nor is she a dominating personality, but still waters run deep. To imagine that she is downtrodden in her marriage or anywhere else would be a mistake. She, rather than William, is the more effusive partner. She is also very competitive, especially in sport, and makes no pretence of wanting to win, even against her husband. To suppose that they are anything but equals would be delusional.

Meghan, on the other hand, plays a variety of roles with Harry. On the one hand, she is the ultimate authority on all topics. She is the driving force in their union, but he happily heads in the direction she leads. She is a mixture of the little woman, big mama, leader, faithful follower, siren and nanny. Unlike Catherine, who has equanimity, she vents furiously, casting herself in the role of victim when she faces opposition of any sort, then switching to Boadicea hurtling in her spike-wheeled chariot towards the opposition when that works more effectively. Because Harry is less stable, less intelligent, more emotional and more immature than William, Meghan has him coming and going as she panders to the Alpha male, the little boy, the spoilt brat, the wounded and vulnerable man/child who is still working through childhood issues. Catherine and William's relationship has always been healthy. They are equals in human terms, while some people regard Meghan and Harry's as fundamentally unequal.

After the bombshell announcement of Meghan's lawsuit against the *Mail on Sunday*, the press and the palace became aware of the extent to which she and Harry intended to use their online postings to connect directly with their followers by cutting out the press. One journalist told me that she and most if not all of her colleagues had come to the conclusion that the royal couple was shamelessly hawking their own brand of propaganda. Once the press came to that conclusion, they pored over each and every posting of the Sussexes to try to figure out what their agenda and endgame were. No one was naive enough to take anything they said or did at face value, for the media had come to realise just how canny and wily Meghan and Harry were.

Because Harry is not particularly intellectual and Meghan's *modus operandi* only hinted at her underlying game plan, their postings now became a rich source of inquisition. Their Christmas card was a case in point. While the intended message was that Meghan and Harry had a gloriously happy marriage of like-minded equals, the photograph itself showed that Meghan was first amongst equals. Who the leader is in any relationship is always relevant where any couple is concerned, but when you are dealing with a member of the British Royal Family and his American actress wife who might be inducing him to reject his heritage to keep her happy, who leads and who follows becomes fundamental. Since the British press were vested in the dynamics of the relationship in a way that the foreign press could never be, who was dominant and who submissive became a matter of genuine national interest. The giveaway in the Christmas card was the focal points. All photographs or paintings have only one true focal point. If something has two, it is either a bad painting or a doctored image. In the photo the Sussexes had posted, the natural focal point was Archie. By rights, Harry and Meghan's images should therefore have been equally blurred, for they were equidistant from their son. But in their post Harry's face is expectedly out of focus, while Meghan's is unexpectedly and astonishingly in focus. This was one picture that was worth a thousand words. The message could not have been clearer. Archie and Meghan being the focal points while Harry was not, there were logical conclusions to draw. Both the British press and the internet commentators drew them.

Once that message was picked up, the posting of the Christmas card rebounded, garnering criticism in Britain even though Meghan and Harry had obviously invited only approbation. She was therefore wise to cut herself out of the picture in the next posting, their New Year's message on Sussex Royal, which showed only Harry holding Archie beside the water on Vancouver Island, where they were staying in a $14m house lent to them by a benefactor.

Rather less wise was the accompanying text: Wishing you all a very Happy New Year and thanking you for your continued support!' While this sort of language might have been acceptable in America, in Britain it was not. Royalty does not thank the public for its continued support. Only politicians and traders do. Yet again, the cultural discordance was blighting but also shedding light on the Sussexes' message.

To a discomfitingly large segment of the British populace, many of whom would have liked Harry and Meghan to be enjoying the popularity they had possessed at the beginning of their marriage, it now seemed that he, who used to be able to do no wrong publicly, could no longer do anything right. This was borne out within a matter of days when the couple returned to Britain from their Vancouver Island bolthole, leaving Archie behind with his nanny. In breach of diplomatic protocol, they posted on Instagram that they had visited 'Canada House in London to thank the High Commissioner Janice Charette and staff for the warm hospitality during their recent stay in Canada. The Duke and Duchess have a strong connection to Canada.'

This created a new precedent, and one moreover which would make life impossible for everyone if, every time royalty visits a country, it and the host embassy or high commission has to grind to a halt for a thank you courtesy call. Of course, the true purpose of Harry and Meghan's visit was to ingratiate themselves with the Canadians and, in so doing, whip up public support in that country for their supposed move to Canada, even though their stay there was never intended to be anything more than a stop-gap measure to get Meghan back to her origins in California. However, the press and general public did not yet knew of this or any other planned move; and, since neither the royals nor the diplomats posted to the Court of St James's wanted to be railroaded into having unnecessary courtesy calls, this became yet another instance of Harry and Meghan being out of kilter with what was expected of them as a royal couple. Despite this, their visit did gain them publicity, so to that extent it was a worthwhile exercise.

By this time, the British press and too large a segment of the British public were coming to the conclusion that the couple was playing some obscure game of single, double and triple bluff whose purpose was obscuring by their dazzling public smiles and private contortions what was patently a self-created mystery. When Meghan then posted the 'secret' visit she had made on her own to London's Hubb Community Kitchen prior to dropping in with Harry at Canada House in London's Trafalgar Square, it did not have the effect they desired, namely that she would be praised for being so philanthropic and charitable that she squeezed in visits of encouragement to the needy between courtesy calls on diplomats. This was condemned as a cynical grab for attention.

Because it was obvious to observers that Meghan was sculpting her and Harry's public image into a likeness she wanted their admirers to see, the split reactions being generated through their internet postings forced the conclusion that they were playing exclusively to their supporters in the gallery, while ignoring everyone else in the theatre of life.

It was now apparent that Meghan was a formidable propagandist, on a par with Diana, Princess of Wales, whom Sir David English, head of Associated Press, described as possessing a genius for self-promotion. Because Diana functioned at a time when the internet did not exist, she was handicapped in having to use the press to get her message across. Although Meghan replicated Diana's practice of exploiting her links to sympathetic organs within the media such as *People* magazine, she had direct access to her supporters via the web in a way Diana never had, and was making skilful use of this access to mould her followers' opinion of her and Harry. What was interesting was how she possessed the same cocktail of traits that Diana had: charm and sincerity mixed with contrivance and opportunism, all overlaid with a patina of vulnerability and dextrous assertiveness.

The developing parallels between the two women, as they went about fashioning their public images, were truly remarkable. Both women had the same technique: providing journalists and photographers with the variety and novelty necessary to keep themselves on the front pages of newspapers. Even when they were out of sympathy with both women's viewpoint, these representatives of the media nevertheless guaranteed them attention they would thereafter use to their ultimate advantage as they did the alchemist's trick of turning the base metal of negative publicity into the gold of ever-increasing celebrity.

If variable reinforcement was a tool both Diana and Meghan knew the value of, so too was the lure of letting the public get glimpses of their 'secret' and 'private' worlds. Diana's most outstanding example of this was the Panorama interview with Martin Bashir, but on a daily basis she used to drip-fed 'private' and 'secret' information about herself to friendly journalists such as Richard Kay. It was interesting to see how Meghan was updating that concept, sharing such things as 'secret' visits to charities and in the process shaping her public image into that of a dedicated humanitarian.

In one regard, Meghan's deployment of her media skills was more akin to Queen Elizabeth the Queen Mother's than to Diana, Princess of Wales's. While married, Elizabeth had always taken care to project herself as one half of a golden couple, pushing forward the reticent Duke of York who then became King George VI. In the process, Elizabeth became acknowledged as a wonderful wife and marvellous human being. Diana had never done this. In fact, she had done the opposite, always running Prince Charles down or competing with him to his detriment, but to her daughter-in-law's credit this was one error Meghan was not making. Harry might no longer be the boy who could do no wrong in the eyes of his formerly adoring public, but he remained visibly one half of the Sussex double act, with the core message being that he and Meghan were a great love story, on a par with the greatest lovers of history such as Romeo and Juliet, Abelard and Heloise, Tristan and Isolde, Albert and Victoria, even Bonnie and Clyde. Whenever and wherever they appeared, Harry and Meghan held hands, their overwhelming love and obvious affection for each other evident as they acted out being the embodiment of true love. There should have been no doubt that theirs was a genuine love story, for their every movement and action projected how strongly they felt about each other. Sadly, however, the British press and too large a proportion of the British public seemed unconvinced that they were anything but a conniving actress and her willing dupe. Meghan's public displays of affection were not regarded as marks of sincerity, but methods of control which only Harry could not see through.

Now more than ever it was becoming obvious that Meghan had two hurdles to overcome before either the British press or public would become convinced that she was a genuine humanitarian, let alone a sincere individual. The first hurdle was the unfortunate state of her relationship her father, which perturbed all sorts of people for all sorts of reasons, and the second was her patent lack of respect for the traditions which many Britons held dear. Little did both the press and public know, but they were about to be relegated to insignificance the way her father and British traditions had been. She was preparing to move on from her twin nemeses with a decisiveness which would shock them all.

Few people except Harry and Meghan knew what they were planning as 2020 dawned. Someone close to them said, 'I'm pretty sure neither of them knew exactly how things would pan out. They knew what their objectives were, but they didn't have the nuts and bolts nailed down. He's an innocent abroad and she's a great visionary who feels her way strategically towards her goal without actually being able to read a roadmap. A lot of their tactics are *ad hoc*, spur of the moment stuff. They make things up as they go along. They play their cards close to their chest because half the time they really don't know what they're going to be doing next. What they do know, though, is where they want to be. That's living an A-List billionaire lifestyle in California, feted by the film world as great humanitarians.'

With that in mind, Harry and Meghan had been using social media to put their case in subtle and not so subtle ways for the better part of a year. Their posts had gradually become both mischievous and competitive, begging the question whether the bad old days of Diana had returned. The late Princess of Wales would do anything to grab column inches away from Charles and the other royals, sometimes even the Queen. Such as the time she had started to play the piano as he was about to make a speech, or when she wore a new hairstyle while accompanying the Queen to the State Opening of Parliament, or when she posed in pathetic solitude outside the Taj Mahal.

It certainly seemed that the spirit of Diana had returned in the body of Meghan, and that Harry, who had been too young to appreciate the nuisance his mischief making mother had been, was only too eager to go along with what royalists regarded as the unnecessary and potentially destructive competitiveness which had crept into the Sussexes' PR at the expense of the other royals' activities. In the past year, there had been too many occasions on which he and Meghan had snatched publicity away from the other members of the family, usually by means of carefully calibrated postings. This was just the sort of conduct no one at the palace, in the Establishment or the Royal Family wanted, and while the press were having a field day with it, it was not up to the media to suppress the reporting of valid news by ignoring the obvious antipathies. The way for Harry and Meghan to avoid the criticism that was coming their way was to desist from being newsworthy in a negative way and at counterproductive times.

The first brazen scene-stealing ploy had taken place in April 2019, shortly after the Sussexes had branched out on their own. Catherine Cambridge is a keen photographer who posts pictures of her children for their birthdays. She had posted an adorable one of Louis for his first birthday. Within hours the Sussexes had knocked her out of the news by cranking out wildlife pictures taken by Harry of a lion, a rhinoceros, and an elephant in celebration of Earth Day. These received 787,000 likes compared with Catherine's 1.2m, but royal author Phil Dampier expressed the view of many when he said, 'It starts to look like Harry and Meghan are in competition.'

There was an almost amusing postscript to the picture Meghan and Harry posted. The *Mail on Sunday* published an uncropped version of the elephant, showing that it had been tethered and sedated, while the other two animals had also been drugged into docility. The pictures therefore represented anything but wildlife. Harry complained to the Independent Press Standards Organisation, denying having misled the public, but his complaint was rejected at the end of January 2020.

In June 2019, Meghan successfully belittled Catherine Cambridge's appearance at Wimbledon following her own disastrous appearance there. William's wife is an avid tennis player as well as Patron of the All England Club. In that capacity, she presents the trophies to the winners at Wimbledon. This she did as usual, but Meghan managed to knock her and the champions off the front pages of the papers and acquire 1.3m likes - compared with her sister-in-law's 670,000 - by turning up with Harry for the premiere of the *Lion King* and, after greeting Jay-Z and Beyoncé, who called her 'my princess', successfully garnered sympathy for herself when Pharrell Williams told her how much her 'union' meant to people of colour, and how 'We cheer you guys on.' After thanking him for his words of encouragement, Meghan's response, which was reported upon worldwide along with her attendance at the event, was, 'They don't make it easy.'

What, people wanted to know, intrigued by the apparent anomaly of Meghan's comment, did she mean? Was she struggling? And if so, why? In a few well-chosen words, she had managed to suck the public into a mystery of her own fabrication, in the process making herself and her feelings into the story. Undoubtedly, Meghan was every bit as skilled as her late mother-in-law at winning the limelight away from all competitors.

Despite this, critics wanted to know why Harry, Captain General of the Marines, had missed the memorial concert marking the 30th anniversary of the death of 11 Marines when the IRA had bombed the Royal Marine Depot at Deal. Surely Meghan could have attended the *Lion King* premiere on her own while he attended the memorial concert? This again struck a wrong note with people who genuinely wanted harmony, and moreover wanted to see the Royal Family function as a dignified and unified unit, each one in step with the other, rather than one couple knocking another off its perch.

Controversy, however, had replaced unity, with Harry and Meghan overshadowing the other royals even when it was not in the best interests of the Family or the Nation. Twice in a calendar month they managed to overshadow royal tours, the first being their own in South Africa, the second being the Cambridges' tour of Pakistan in October 2019. This had been an important event, long in the making, with high hopes on both sides for its success. However, it was completely eclipsed by the sensational teaser tapes of the Sussexes' forthcoming interview with Tom Bradby, resulting in a courtier stating, 'This move has certainly overshadowed the Pakistan visit and what has been achieved here during the last few days, as well as a lot of work by an awful lot of dedicated people here on the ground as well as back home for months.'

All journalists press thrill to a competition, and now that they were aware that one genuinely existed between the Sussexes and the other royals in general, and the Cambridges in particular, they focused on it. Even before they discovered that Meghan had instructed her American representatives to make her the most popular woman on earth, with the largest Instagram following, and bigger than Diana, they began noting how Harry and Meghan were using postings to trump his brother and Catherine.

Up to January 2020, the Cambridges had more Instagram followers than the Sussexes. While both couples were small change (11+m followers) compared with the big hitters such as Cristiano Ronaldo (187m), Dwayne 'The Rock' Johnson (159m), Selena Gomez (158m), Kim Kardashian (150m), and Kylie Jenner (148m), Meghan and Harry's postings systematically rained on William and Catherine's parade. Even though Meghan's ambition was ultimately to put Ronaldo in the shade, she nevertheless timed her posts for maximum impact with the seemingly specific purpose of knocking her in-laws out of the running. For instance, on a day that Catherine was fulfilling three official engagements, Meghan managed to steal her thunder yet again by posting a picture of herself, taken two weeks before in London at the Mayhew animal charity, as she beamed beatifically while stroking an infirm dog. The *Daily Express* royal correspondent Richard Palmer felt compelled to tweet, 'Wow what unfortunate timing that once again, just as a senior member of the Royal Family was heralding an important initiative, the Sussex Royal Instagram account kicked into life with some PR pictures at the very same moment.'

Meghan is nothing if not canny. Being a child of Hollywood, she knows what grabs attention. Dogs, kids, and beatific beaming will do it every time, at least for people who like their idols wearing their hearts on their sleeves and showing their admirers what wonderful, caring, feeling, hyper-glamorous but always-down-to-earth individuals they are. There is also the unavoidable fact that Meghan Markle is an infinitely more interesting personality than Catherine Cambridge. People with side are always more unpredictable and entertaining than straightforward women like Catherine. For that reason alone, it is not surprising that she and Harry finally caught up with Catherine and William on Instagram, though their success would remain short lived.

There is also the fact that while Meghan is obsessively competitive, with the stated goal of possessing the largest Instagram following on earth, Catherine did not want to be in a competition with her sister-in-law. Now that Meghan has departed, the Duchess of Cambridge is said to be relieved that the competitive atmosphere has abated. As far as she is concerned, being Duchess of Cambridge who will one day be Princess of Wales then Queen of the United Kingdom is more than enough for her. She does not need to strip Ronaldo of his crown and disliked the air of tension Meghan created as she set about scene-stealing on her quest for ever-greater acknowledgement.

Meghan, however, had a far more American view of her position. Her goals belied her heritage, just as Catherine Cambridge's belied hers. Meghan's target audience was not and had never been the British people but the American worlds of commerce and entertainment. Being a businesswoman, she understood only too well the monetary value a large Instagram following could have. The Kardashians are paid hundreds of thousands of dollars per posting, sometimes even millions, and her goal is to supplant them and derive all the financial benefits they possess.

Meghan understood that she did not have to be popular with every-one, just with those who liked her. She could therefore afford to disdain her critics, for, painful though their disregard of her was, they were not worth winning over because they did not hold the keys to success. Only her supporters held those, and it was to them she and Harry played, making the point time and again that they were the premiere couple in the royal world, not William and Catherine. That, of course, did not mean that she could abide criticism, and that wouldn't work to shut down her critics, but it did mean that she had contempt for those who stood in her way as only someone who is as self-righteous and self-con-fident as Meghan could.

It was therefore not surprising that she and Harry chose the night before Catherine's 38th birthday on the 9th January 2020 to reveal to the world and the Royal Family via Instagram that they would be recon-stituting their roles.

They announced:

'After many months of reflection and internal discussions, we have chosen to make a transition this year in starting to carve out a progressive new role within this institution. We intend to step back as 'senior' members of the Royal Family and work to become financially independent, while continuing to fully support Her Majesty The Queen. It is with your encouragement, particularly over the last few years, that we feel prepared to make this adjustment. We now plan to balance our time between North America and the United Kingdom, continuing to honour our duty to The Queen, the Commonwealth, and our patronages. This geographic balance will enable us to raise our son with an appreciation of the royal tradition into which he was born, while also providing our family with the space to focus on the next chapter, including the launch of our new charitable entity. We look forward to sharing the full details of this exciting next step in due course, as we continue to collaborate with Her Majesty The Queen, The Prince of Wales, The Duke of Cambridge and all relevant parties. Until then, please accept our deepest thanks for your continued support.'

Once more, Meghan and Harry had chosen to use social media to dictate the agenda and shape the narrative. There had indeed been discussions over the past few months concerning their desire to live on both sides of the Atlantic while engaging in commercial activities. These had not gone as well as they would have liked. There was considerable opposition to them 'wanting to eat their cake and have it,' a prince told me. Garter King of Arms Thomas Woodcock, the leading member of the royal household whose brief it is to ensure that the royal image is kept pristine and unsullied by unacceptable commercialism, said, 'I don't think it's satisfactory. One cannot be two things at once. You either are or you aren't.'

Meghan and Harry had asserted in their statement that they intended to be both at the same time. This was despite no member of the Royal Family to date having been allowed to actively participate in commercial activities while at the same time retaining their royal rank with all the attendant privileges, responsibilities and conflicts. The palace did not want any member of the Royal Family to engage in commercial activities for their own benefit, and certainly not while being sponsored financially by the state. 'What they've been proposing is rather like a priest who has taken a vow of poverty going into the usury business, then trying to convince everyone that he's doing it for the good of humanity when it's blindingly obvious he's doing it for his own benefit,' someone from the College of Heralds said. 'The inelegant maxim of getting thieves to guard your treasure springs to mind.'

From the American perspective, what the Sussexes wanted to do seemed not only anodyne, but admirable. They were a grown man and woman, well into their thirties. They wanted to strike out on their own. Good for them. Independence should be encouraged. Best of luck to them.

Of course, America does not have a royal family and therefore such understanding as exists about its functions is superficial. When people like Caitlyn Jenner liken her family or the Kennedys to a royal family, they miss the point entirely. Royalty is not the same as celebrity, nor can politicians be likened to royals. Royals are representatives of their country no matter when or where they are. They are expected to behave at all times and in all circumstances up to a standard few members of the public could achieve and none would aspire to. Unlike celebrities, who differentiate between their private and public lives, no such distinction applies with royalty. You are a prince or a duchess at all times, not just when it suits you to be. If you are engaged in commercial activities, it is supposed to be on behalf of the institution of monarchy, not on behalf of yourself. Such profits as accrue should never be for your own personal enrichment, but for the benefit of the Nation.

What Harry and Meghan were proposing was therefore contrary to everything that had gone before, and was fraught with difficulties. The reality was that their eminence, whence came their desirability commercially, was based upon them being members of the Royal Family. Although each of them had personal attributes that burnished their appeal, the bottom line was that Meghan Markle's commercial value pre-marriage had been fractional compared with what it became afterwards, and for all Harry's jock appeal, no one would ever have found him anywhere as noteworthy or desirable had he been plain Harry Windsor instead of a Prince of the United Kingdom.

The British Crown, as stated earlier, is very sophisticated. It's seen all the angles and knows all the tricks people pull. It knows that commerce can be a dodgy business. Philanthropy is often a cover for the purchase of respectability following acquisition of wealth by dubious means. Now that it was merely a matter of time before Meghan and Harry actively entered the commercial world, the Royal Family had to prepare itself for what would happen if things went wrong. The slightest slip could result in a loss of prestige for the Sussexes and, by extension, the monarchy.

Even more dangerous, however, was the Sussexes' proposal to mix charity and commerce. Modern charitable organisations are run in such a way that the organisers receive handsome financial rewards. It is one thing for professionals to be on salaries that sometimes run well into six and even seven figures, but there is a real danger when royals start receiving sums like that for work which their peers do *gratis*. Should it emerge that Meghan and Harry were deriving financial benefits for their charitable endeavours, what could be regarded as fair recompense with anyone else would be viewed as corruption on their part. The outcome could therefore be toxicity, as Buckingham Palace knew only too well from the fallout when the Socialist Government of Spain went after the Infanta Cristina, second daughter of King Juan Carlos I, and her husband Iñaki Urdangarin, Duke of Palma de Mallorca. These Spanish cousins became enmeshed in a financial scandal involving their non-profit Nóos Institute. For a while it looked as if both the Infanta and her husband would be tried for fraud, but ultimately only he was. Nevertheless, the outcome was disastrous for the Spanish Royal Family. The king abdicated, his son-in-law was convicted and is presently serving a five year ten month sentence at Brieva Prison in Avila, while the Infanta moved to Switzerland with her children and is now *persona non grata* at the Spanish Court.

Because of Meghan's previous business activities, and the surreptitious way in which the couple had gone about laying the foundations for their commercial and charitable endeavours, the worry was that they might end up receiving 'expenses' for their charitable activities which could be interpreted as 'backhanders'. The last thing Buckingham Palace wanted was for any British royal to be caught up in a financial scandal such as had engulfed the Spaniards. They also hoped to ensure that the commercial and charitable activities which the Sussexes embarked upon could never be used, even far down the line, by anti-monarchist politicians, to embarrass the monarch or the Royal Family.

The courtiers are far more sophisticated than either Meghan or Harry, and understand potential pitfalls insofar as they are detrimental to the monarchy in a way that neither of them does. Harry simply does not have the intellectual capacity, and Meghan, for all her canniness, such a newcomer to the big league that she lacked the knowledge, experience, and insight that she could only acquire with time, by making mistakes, or through the wisdom of experienced advisors to the monarchy.

Of course, if their objective was to acquire as much fame and fortune for themselves as they could, with never a thought for the welfare of the monarchy or the interests of the British people, that was another matter. Certainly she and Harry would not be receiving reliable advice from any American organisations, all of which are utterly ignorant and completely inexperienced where British institutions are concerned, and are therefore in no position to estimate risk to Britain or its monarchy, even though they possess undoubted expertise in headline grabbing on both sides of the Atlantic.

These were just some of the considerations which Buckingham Palace hinted at when it stated that Harry and Meghan's desire to step down as senior royals was complex and therefore it would take time for all the issues to be resolved. The couple was not best pleased that what they saw in purely personal terms - their right to earn as much money as they could, and to do it in their own way with reference to no one, including courtiers at the palace - was viewed in less personal terms at the palace.

Intent on getting their point of view across to their supporters and the American public, Harry and Meghan got 'friends' to complain that those who were standing in their way were simply 'naysayers' who were 'spiteful' because they wanted independence and these spiteful opposers didn't want them to have it. To drive the point home that Harry and Meghan were benevolent and loyal to those opposing forces who were so nastily obstructing them, these friends then assured the world that the Duke and Duchess of Sussex would nevertheless do as the palace desired

Although Harry and Meghan wanted the world to know that they were being noble despite being hard-done-by, the view within the palace was that the couple's public relations briefings were jeopardising the future wellbeing of the monarchy. Although no one but the couple wanted them to strike out on their own commercially, the Queen and her senior advisors nevertheless accepted that they might well be able to forge a new career path which, if successful, would lay down a beneficial precedent for their successors. After all, there will always be second sons and minor royals and, if a way could be established whereby royals like them could function commercially without danger to the Crown, that would only be to the advantage of successive generations.

The Sussexes, on the other hand, felt that the palace's concern for the monarchy should be on at least an equal par with their own interests. The message Harry was giving out was that he and Meghan should have absolute control over their options. Why should he, a second son, be hamstrung by putting the monarchy's concerns over his own - which was the aim of the palace - when he was never going to be number one? He and Meghan 'seemed incapable of considering any option but the top job, and since they were never going to be King and Queen of the United Kingdom, they should be freed to become king and queen of something else instead,' a courtier said. They genuinely could not see why their future plans should be curtailed or monitored by the palace. They could not understand why absolute liberty to strike deals as and how and when they pleased might conflict with their continuing duty to the British Crown and the British people. The dilemma of whether Harry and Meghan could ever become entirely free agents, shorn of all responsibility to the Crown and its citizens, and whether they owed a continuing duty of care to both those entities irrespective of whether they were fully functional royals, fully retired, even de-royalised, lay at the heart of the matter. It is still an issue which remains unresolved.

I am informed that William was particularly disappointed by his brother's attitude. He felt that they all have responsibilities which go above and beyond their own personal desires, or even their own happiness. Harry, however, has always had a tendency to think in more personal terms than his elder brother, even when others would deem it more suitable to think in institutional terms. This, in effect, was the result of the way Diana had raised Harry. She had brought him up without limits, to think in personal and emotional terms rather than objectively, to escape the consequences of his actions, to do as he pleased, to regard himself as special, not because he was a prince but because he was the adorable Harry. A bit less personalism and a bit more royalism might have redressed the balance, for the fact is, while some of Harry's specialness is due to nature, an even greater part is due to the position into which he was born. Diana herself had trodden a fine line between self-indulgence and the damage her actions might do to the Crown, but she at least had an awareness that she had to tread carefully even when she was trying to sabotage her ex-husband or discomfit the Royal Family. Always, at the back of her mind, was the knowledge that one day her son would inherit the throne. She therefore couldn't afford to rock the boat too much, and this had a restraining influence upon her. No such compunction existed with Harry.

With fully fledged Second Son Syndrome motivating him, and without the restraining influence of duty before personal satisfaction to curtail his aims or actions, once he and Meghan figured out that their ambitions would be more achievable outside of the royal fold than inside it, they behaved with a reckless disregard that had been absent even with Diana. This made him heedless of consequences in a way she had never been, especially as how he had a wife who did not want to spend her whole life playing second fiddle to the Duchess of Cambridge any more than he enjoyed being in William's shadow. There was also a personal element between the two women which made self-justification easier. Meghan disparages Catherine as 'uptight' and feels uncomfortable around her because their styles are so radically different. Catherine is traditionally stately and Meghan the quintessence of Californian informality, while Harry has adopted Meghan's disdain for traditionalism and now regards William's careful and restrained approach with contempt.

Undeniably, Harry and Meghan had become a potent double act

which went down well in the United States, even if it was not appreciated in the same way in Britain. They also genuinely loved doing things together. They share many of the same goals, values, ambitions and interests. Each of them loves the limelight. They truly enjoy being the superstars that they have become. They thrill to the realisation of their dream as humanitarian luminaries on the world stage, acknowledged and feted for their unique gifts as the only royal superstar couple who can now function as independent agents.

Harry had long chafed at being a second-string player. While there is little doubt that he would have come to terms with his lot had he married a girl like Chelsy Davy or Cressida Bonas and led a traditionally British life, once he was exposed to other possibilities by an outsider like Meghan, his eyes were opened and his love for her blinkered him. Through her, he caught a glimpse of a previously unimaginable way of life which would allow him to indulge himself in a way he had hitherto found unthinkable, and while he would most likely have been happier remaining based in Britain and not cutting his ties the way he has, he understood that the only way his marriage would work was if he supported Meghan in her vision of what their life could be. From her point of view, the only way they could realise their true potential as major players in their own right was to shift the stage from Britain to the United States, and not just anywhere either, but to California, where Meghan's knowledge of the entertainment industry would be an asset which would hopefully bring them rich rewards, not only financial but also in terms of kudos and the international recognition they desire.

Having accepted that the best way forward to achieve their objective was to create their own platform rather than share one with his brother and sister-in-law, both Harry and Meghan were liberated. Undoubtedly, he was having to make difficult choices, many of which he would have preferred not to make and which would not have arisen had he married any other woman. But there was an upside. No longer would they be limited by a system in which they would always be second-tier players. They could step out of the shadows and become the first-raters they regard themselves as being, and which they were acknowledged as in Meghan's native country. It had been extremely frustrating for them,

Meghan especially, to be part of a way of life which would always deny them the central position their vision and ambitions demanded they occupy. Only by striking out on their new path would they have the possibility of creating a platform for themselves upon which they could shine brightly as the central players, rather than sharing the royal platform and with the deck stacked so patently in Catherine and William's favour.

Although a limited number of public figures in Britain, such as the actress Helen Mirren and the writer Hilary Mantel, understood a star's need to shine brightly, this was not shared nationally. The general view was that Harry and Meghan were not only abandoning the British Royal Family and the British people, but they had shown disrespect by issuing their departure statement without giving advance notice to any member of the Royal Family or to the courtiers. This fact was confirmed by Buckingham Palace, which informed the BBC royal correspondent Jonny Dymond that it was 'disappointed' by their decision, that the Royal Family was 'hurt' by the announcement, and that 'no members of the Royal Family were consulted.'

To drive the point home, Buckingham Palace then issued its own statement contradicting the Sussexes': 'Discussions with the Duke and Duchess of Sussex are at an early stage. We understand their desire to take a different approach, but these are complicated issues that will take their time to work through.' This was palace-speak for 'Meghan and Harry have been trying to ram through game-changers on us. We're prepared to give an inch, maybe even two, but they want to take a mile before the race has even begun. Now they've jumped the gun and in doing so have kicked sand in our faces, and have made a grab for all sorts of privileges which we cannot let them have without damaging the monarchy, and even though they've been unreasonable, we're planning to be reasonable and give them as much as we can.'

The Queen, Prince Philip and Prince Charles must have had a real sense of *déjà vu,* for Harry and Meghan's ploy was reminiscent of the way Diana had behaved during the negotiations for her divorce, in particular with regard to her future title. Like Meghan and Harry, she had initiated negotiations privately with the family, and when she thought they weren't going as quickly or as satisfyingly as she wanted, she had tricked Charles into meeting with her, jumped the gun without a definitive agreement, and falsely claimed that she and Charles had agreed on certain issues, when they had not. These included that she was prepared to give up being a royal highness and be known as Diana, Princess of Wales. Because she was the mother of a future king and likely to remarry, there had been the possibility that she would be made Her Royal Highness Princess Diana. This would have allowed her to remarry and still retain a royal title. On the other hand, if she became Diana, Princess of Wales and remarried, for instance if she had married Dodi Fayed, she would have merely been Lady Diana Fayed instead of HRH Princess Diana, Mrs Dodi Fayed. She had outsmarted herself, and I was told that the Queen, furious that Diana had tricked Charles, decided to take her at her word, which is how she came to lose the title of royal highness.

One must never forget the human element. Harry is Charles' son, William's brother, the Queen's grandson. They all love him. They were all fully aware that Harry would have been perfectly happy to remain as a working member of the Royal Family, involved with his charities and maintaining his military links, had he not married a woman who wanted to capitalise upon his royal status and strike out on her own with him. The words 'financial independence' inspired terror at the palace, for all the reasons previously articulated. No one who loved Harry believed that the desire for financial independence lay with him. He had been perfectly happy with his financial situation prior to marriage. Had he married Chelsy Davy or Cressida Bonas he would have remained content with what was on offer for a royal duke, rather than wanting to branch out and lead the life of a rich American entrepreneur. He had more than enough money for his own worldly needs as well as those of a wife who was content with the lifestyle of an ordinary royal duchess. Meghan, however, did not want that lifestyle. She didn't want the boring bits or the hard work. She preferred the glitz and glamour of the entertainment world. In the year and a half that she and Harry had been married, they had been exposed to the A-list celebrity lifestyle of friends such as Elton John and George Clooney in a way neither of them had been before. Meghan's appreciation of all things sybaritic had not changed since the days when she was confessing in *The Tig* how much she relished the perks of great wealth. She wanted that for herself, and Harry, eager as ever to please her, was prepared to go along with her ambitions.

Although none of the royals was happy with Harry and Meghan's plan to have one foot in the royal camp in Britain, and another in the commercial market in the United States (Canada being acknowledged by all as nothing more than a convenient stepping stone), the Queen, the Prince of Wales and William were nevertheless prepared to work towards achieving a *modus vivendi* that would allow Meghan and Harry to leave the royal fold honourably and make their own way in the world with equal honour. They understood by this time that Meghan was a formidable personality who functioned completely differently from them. She was undoubtedly one of the strongest personalities anyone had ever encountered, as her good friend Serena Williams said while singing her praises. Backed up at all times by a husband whose mantra was 'What Meghan wants, Meghan gets,' the Royal Family would have no choice but to cope with the new way of functioning she and Harry were intent on creating. As Princess Margaret's former lady-in-waiting Lady Glenconner put it, 'Meghan didn't stay very long because she didn't realise that to be a royal is jolly hard work and quite boring at times. It's not all fun and glamour. A lot if it is behind the scenes, so it's not supposed to be flashy.' Not only did Meghan want the glamour of a glitzier and more stimulating and exciting lifestyle, but, being a businesswoman, she wanted it to pay as well. This she and Harry intended to achieve by exploiting their royal status for financial gain while basking in the glory of royalty and burnishing the gloss with Hollywood-style celebrity without the boring business of meeting mayors and doing all the other low-key, non-newsworthy activities which are the daily chores of monarchies, but which bored Meghan as rigid as they had bored Diana.

How to reconcile what, on the face of it seemed irreconcilable was the challenge facing the royals. They were only too aware that Meghan, being American, was relished in the United States in a way that only a native royal could be. The positive response there to their stepping back had been overwhelming. Because Americans did not realise how imperative it was for the British Crown and the British people that

Harry and Meghan's departure be effected with as little damage to all concerned as could be achieved, American media coverage addressed none of the national concerns of the British. The American reports were essentially superficial, missing all the more nuanced dimensions with which the British were concerned, indeed often riding roughshod over these considerations.

There was also the misconception that Meghan had been the victim of racism and snobbishness. Snobbishness was simply ridiculous. Sophie Rhys-Jones and Catherine Middleton had also been middle class girls, and they had successfully made the transition to royal, so Meghan's equally middle class background could not be the problem. Nor was racism. In fact, Meghan's race had militated in her favour, so it was a cause of grievance throughout Britain that the fulsome welcome she had been given initially could be converted through ignorance of what had really gone wrong into accusations of racism against any of the many segments of the populace who had welcomed Meghan with open arms and hearts. Her failure to settle happily in Britain lay not with her race, but with her refusal to adjust to a new way of life: one whose lack of financial reward had left her distinctly unimpressed.

It should have been a simple matter for people on both sides of the Atlantic to acknowledge that a mature woman like Meghan, set in her ways and happy with herself, was almost inevitably going to have difficulty adjusting to a new environment with radically different values and expectations from those she was used to. To accuse the British of prejudice because of Meghan's failure to assimilate would be as unfounded as accusing her of being maliciously motivated in her refusal to do so. The fact that she did not, could not, and would not, did not make her malign, any more than Britain's inability to adjust its values, customs, traditions and expectations to her convenience makes us, the British people, racist. Had Meghan been a fully Caucasian blue eyed blonde who behaved exactly as she did, she would have elicited an identical response. It would most likely have been quicker and harsher in tone too, for obvious reasons.

The issue of racism being used unfairly to explain away Meghan's failures caused outrage in Britain. There was a growing consensus that she and Meghan had an obligation, not only to the Royal Family and the monarchy but to the British people themselves, who had welcomed her so warmly, to call time on the red herring. The fact that the couple was allowing accusations of this nature to muzzle justifiable criticism of their actions was interpreted as ruthless cynicism on their part. It did nothing to gain them supporters, and in fact lost them a great deal of respect, for the one thing a nation which prides itself on fair play could not accept was being accused of guilt it did not possess. If Meghan did not know the old British condemnation 'That's not cricket', Harry should have. His silence did nothing to commend him.

How best to deal with a couple who were so intent on getting their own way, irrespective of the cost to his family, the nation, and the institution of the monarchy, now exercised the Royal Family. One of the European royals told me that the Queen, the Prince of Wales and Prince William had, from the very beginning, been 'bending over backwards trying to come to some accommodation' with Meghan and Harry. 'They're still trying. I would imagine they're going to be trying for a very long time, for what the Sussexes want is really incompatible with constitutional monarchy,' hence why a time limit of a year had to be put in place following the Queen's meeting with Harry, Charles and William to see how their commercial activities panned out. Moving forward, 'It's going to be a long and arduous process of trial and error, with most of the flexibility coming from the Royal Family and most of the demands and complaints coming from the Sussexes.'

'Right now, the royals feel they've been betrayed by the Sussexes.' Harry and Meghan's conduct since making that initial announcement of stepping down has had unnecessarily adversarial overtones. I was told that William was furious with both Harry and Meghan for having used her friends to disparage the Queen as a 'naysayer' and for accusing them of acting spitefully when the family has been doing no such thing. The family's declared and sole posture had been, and continues to be, finding a way forward that allows the Sussexes to make as much money as they want without damaging the Crown.

No one enjoys being accused of victimisation when nothing could be further from the truth, but equally, the family understands that there are 'human dynamics at play,' as the European royal explained. 'They understand that when we speak about the Sussexes, we're really saying Meghan with Harry, the compulsively limerenced and therefore useful idiot, tagging along saying yes, yes, yes to everything she proposes - no matter how much it hurts him or the family.'

The royals have found themselves in an impossible situation. They do not deny Meghan's right to pursue her life as she sees fit. They accept that it would be unreasonable of them to expect a woman of nearly forty years old who cannot make the adjustment from one way of life to another to sacrifice her comfort for their wellbeing. 'It's really too sad, but the Royal Family know that this sort of thing happens to millions of families all over the world. They hope people will understand and have compassion for their dilemma - and Harry's. They've embarked upon what is effectively serious damage control.'

This royal explained that the Sussexes' initial announcement of stepping back, was exactly what many in the British press and many at the palace deemed it to be: 'a power grab. It was meant to bounce the Royal Family into accepting what they cannot accept. They (Meghan and Harry) tried to hardball the Family.'

There were strong feelings at the palace that the announcement was also 'an impertinence and shows just how out of touch with reality the Sussexes are. Really, who in their right mind would issue a statement declaring that they are collaborators of the Queen? It confirms how utterly self-important, even delusional, the [couple] is. The Queen is the Sovereign. She is the Head of the Family. She is their SUPERI-OR. Superiors do not collaborate with inferiors. They collaborate with EQUALS. The Queen's only equals are other Heads of State. As an Army officer, Harry knows only too well that his Sovereign is his Commander-in-Chief. All military people respect the chain of command. As a royal, he knows that the grandson of the Sovereign does not have parity with the Sovereign.'

The realisation that Meghan is such a strong character and so self-confident that she regards herself as the equal of any other living individual, irrespective of who they are or what their position is, and that she feels sufficiently empowered by her self-belief that she will take on anyone, including the Queen, and regard herself as fully entitled to negotiate with anyone, including the Queen, as if they are equals, had begun to sink in. While such an attitude is regarded as admirable in many circles in the United States, within the British Establishment, it was viewed as cringeworthy *folie de grandeur*. The royal explained, 'In no way, shape or form would Harry ever consider himself the Queen's equal. I give no rewards for guessing who considers herself on a par with the Queen. I cringe with embarrassment on behalf of that young man. How he could ever have allowed that woman to issue such a statement, using his name, is beyond me.'

It is here that we see how the typical American viewpoint of everyone being equal converges with the viewpoint of the anti-monarchists in the United Kingdom. They too regard everyone as equal, and cannot understand why the position of head of state should be hereditary. They want it open to all, and republicans have even suggested that David Beckham would make a better head of state than Queen Elizabeth II. What they fail to understand is that even when the hereditary element has been removed, equality is only a notional concept, for the head of state in a republican or even a Marxist society, occupies a unique position within that state and is generally acknowledged to be a thing apart from all other citizens. The fact that Meghan had no respect for her own president will have enhanced her belief that the position of head of state is therefore just another position, and that she, being an avowed activist, has a perfect right to challenge it as and when it is in her interest to do so. To people who admire empowerment, there can be no doubt that Meghan has grown into a fully empowered woman who respects no one person or position as much as she respects her right to forge her own path. The fact that she now took on Queen Elizabeth II was awe-inspiring, to say the least. She deserved acknowledgement for having decided to treat the monarch as just another individual with whom she deals, but this attitude caused astonishment in many British circles, not the least of which was the press, who soon saw just how potent and resourceful Meghan could be when she puts on her thinking cap. Hard on the heels of 'stepping back', she and Harry issued a statement declaring that they would be suspending the Rota system. This was like lobbing a live grenade into the media arena.

Alluded to earlier in this work, the Rota system which had been in place for decades was viewed by both the press and the palace as the fairest and most practical way in which these two organs of British national life could co-exist to each other's mutual benefit. By appointing one journalist and/or photographer out of a pool of other journalists representing the seven leading newspaper companies in the country, both the Royal Family and the press were assured of mutually beneficial coverage with the maximum guaranteed for minimal output of manpower, by the sole representative(s) passing on content to all their other colleagues.

The Rota has always worked well because only accredited journalists have access. This assured the royals of having reputable representation and a measure of control that was acceptable to both sides. Journalists who indulged in dubious or unethical conduct would lose their accreditation, while the royals accepted it is the right of the press to criticise fairly, so the system has always had a degree of impartiality which works well for both the Royal Family and the press.

It should be remembered at this juncture that the British royals, like all other public figures in Britain, accept that our media are more robust and critical in their scrutiny than any other national press. Everyone understands it, most public figures accept it and come to terms with it, even though we all struggle through the negatives at one time or another. Public figures who bemoan their lot too loudly lose respect from both their peers and the press, because most public figures in this country appreciate the importance of a free press.

Although Harry and Meghan maintained that they too respected the media's right to call them to account, their every action contradicted these assertions which were viewed by those they were trying to muzzle as both hypocritical and meretricious. Indeed, the couple's own assertions suggested that their interpretation of objective press coverage was a faithful repetition of any instruction they provided, with the journalist plumping out his piece with purely positive or adulatory comments. In essence, they wanted the British press to perform the way the American does when covering celebrities. With the exception of hard news interviews, which are conducted by journalists who are encouraged to write as they see fit, PRs write the script for celebrity coverage and newspapers and magazines in the US either follow it or alter it with the consent of the subject and/or his/her press representatives. This is the system Meghan Markle got used to as a minor celebrity who was insufficiently newsworthy for journalists to take an independent line with. It had been something of a shock for her, when she was confronted by the way the British press functioned, to realise that her views could be challenged, her behaviour scrutinised. It was obvious that the Sussexes' refusal to continue with the Rota system was their determined attempt to impose American style journalism upon the more robust British press. Since they couldn't exclude representatives of the companies they were litigating against, and since Meghan and Harry's policy was to eliminate anyone who displeased them, their alternative was to replace the Rota system with one of their own invention. 'Meghan takes her role of being a force for change seriously,' the journalist Alexis Parr said. 'But the change is always in her favour and, where the press is concerned, to the detriment of its freedom of expression.'

This certainly seemed to be the case. But Meghan and Harry were not prepared to merely replace an impartial system with one partial to them that they could control more easily. They were building towards an even more draconian remedy, for Harry has a rabid and irrational hatred of the press, blaming it as he does for his mother's death, while Meghan had developed a hysterical antipathy towards their criticisms of her, declaring them to be based upon racism, sexism, misogyny, jealousy, envy, and anything else but fair comment. Her self-belief was so solid that she simply could not wrap her head around the fact that some of their criticisms might have merit.

Harry and Meghan now availed themselves of the opportunity to demean their opponents and present themselves as victims. They accused reputable organs of the British press of being hypocritical liars and cheats who were maliciously twisting and turning their actions. They declared that it was 'their wish to reshape and broaden access to their work' and that they would 'invite specialist media to specific events/engagements to give greater access to their cause-driven activities, widening the spectrum of news coverage.' To the British press this was hypocritical cant, for they were restricting access, banning all mainstream reporters, choosing instead only tame journalists who would report their activities in ways that pleased them. Or, as Harry and Meghan put it, 'credible media outlets focused on objective news reporting to cover key moments and events.' Which really meant, North American style coverage, in which we inform you, you faithfully repeat our words, puff us up, or you're out on your ear.

It is hardly surprising that the mainstream press were incensed by this ploy to deny them the access which till then they had had as a right by long-established practice. But Meghan is bright, and she had come up with a way of thwarting her opponents such as no other royal had ever done. To people who want to control their publicity, she had turned herself into something of a heroine overnight.

I am reliably informed that Meghan and Harry feared, with good reason, that the British press could otherwise sabotage their well thought-out strategies for boosting themselves financially as well as reputationally. They were worried that the media might point out the potentially adverse effects their commercial activities could have upon the welfare of the monarchy. This might lessen their prestige in the US, weaken their brand, and scupper business opportunities. They therefore needed to defuse the power of such comments before they were even made. The most effective way would be if they could present themselves as victims of a vicious and unjust media. They also needed to take total control of the narrative. Stories must not emanate from independent and uncontrollable sources, but from themselves solely. Only then could they control the outflow of information while creating a hiatus between the breaking of news and commentary on their initiatives.

This was pure media management. Doubtless Sunshine Sachs was behind it. None of this was new of course, as any student of history knows the shaping of public opinion is as old as the hills. The two acknowledged geniuses in the twentieth century were Hitler's brilliant Minister of Propaganda, Josef Goebbels, and Diana, Princess of Wales. It therefore came as no surprise that her son Harry and his media savvy wife would display an aptitude. What was surprising, however, was the total lack of boundaries. They were not only being innovative, being real 'forces for change' to use Sussex-speak, but were behaving with a vigour and ruthlessness that was truly astonishing, not only to the press and public, but to the palace as well. Undoubtedly, they were being well advised by real experts. Unless the press were very careful, or Meghan and Harry miscalculated terribly and did something which was so offensive that the general public would lose all sympathy with them, their tactics were intended to keep the British press on the back foot. In doing so, they would negate the media's ability to scrutinise, thereby weakening criticism of them because the press would no longer be fashioning the narrative but trailing it.

What Meghan and Harry had set out to do was turn the tables on the press, so that the public would end up thinking that valid press criticism was simply carping, even when the press was really fulfilling its responsibility to the nation by fairly and accurately commenting upon their desire to alter treasured national customs and institutions which the vast majority of the British public did not want changed.

Having come up with such effective exclusionary tactics, Meghan and Harry also made it clear in their announcement what sort of press commentary they would hereafter regard as acceptable. They required 'objective' reporting. They also looked 'forward to continuing their use of social media and believe that their updated media approach will enable them to share more, with you, directly.' This struck the British media as yet more hypocritical cant, and every journalist I spoke to believed that their policy will always be to control access so tightly, and to impart information so guardedly, that the only picture the public will ever see is a heavily curated one.

Nevertheless, Harry and Meghan's promulgations received support in the United States, where there was the perception that they were the victims of the British press rather than vice versa. Those positive reactions showed that there was indeed both a real cultural and a generational divide. Despite Americans treasuring their First Amendment rights, they did not recognise the dangers the Sussexes were posing to free speech in Britain. The British, which in this instance includes the Canadians, did. The young on both sides of the Atlantic took Meghan and Harry's two announcements at face value. They felt that the couple should have a chance to lead their own lives as and how they saw fit. If they wanted to chuck the royal way of life and make money, let them. This sentiment was not shared by the more mature segment of the population, who felt that the royal couple was being greedy, selfish and self-indulgent. Prince Charles's Duchy of Cornwall had stumped up the better part of a million pounds for Meghan's clothing since she had married his son. Their large house on the Queen's Windsor Estate had cost the taxpayer £2.4m to renovate. Neither of them was exactly overworked. In fact, they had a pretty good deal. Why should they be allowed to be royal when it suited them and private citizens when it did not? Why should they be both in and out, as they wanted to be, undertaking the occasional royal engagement when it was in their interest to do so, but otherwise being supported by the tax payer while they went about making fortunes for themselves? When had more and more ceased to be enough?

* * * * *

The splits in society regarding Meghan and Harry's decision to step down as senior royals were what made their decision so interesting. To those of us who had inside information as to what was really going on, it was fascinating to see how even well-placed people like the Canadian Prime Minister could rush in and get things gloriously wrong amidst this societal tangle of approval and disapproval. Harry and Meghan's announcement, which had come like a bolt out of the blue and wrong-footed the Royal Family, contained so much layering that was perceived as being disrespectful or tactical, that only naive, unsophisticated or blinkered people could have read it and thought the cover revealed the contents of the book. Yet Meghan and Harry's good friend Justin Trudeau made the comment that Canada would not only welcome them if they chose to move there, but would share the cost of their security with the British while they were in Canada.

The ensuing hue and cry from politicians and public alike made it clear that the Canadians did not want to pay anything for the privilege of having Meghan and Harry in their midst. Their rebuke of the Prime Minister's generous offer was embarrassing, and some politicians went even further, stating that the Canadian monarchy works well because the royals only visit; they do not reside there.

This never used to be the case. Queen Victoria's daughter Princess Louise and her husband the Marquis of Lorne, later 9th Duke of Argyll, lived in Canada while he was Governor General, and so did Queen Mary's brother the Earl of Athlone and his wife Princess Alice of Albany, granddaughter of Queen Victoria. So too did the former Prince Alastair, 2nd Duke of Connaught, grandson of King Edward VII, who not only lived in Ottawa for three years while aide-de-camp to Lord Athlone, but froze to death when he fell out of an open window at Rideau Hall, the official residence of the Governor General, while drunk during the Second World War. But much had changed since Lord Athlone departed as Governor-General in 1946. The Canadians no longer wanted members of the Royal Family residing in Canada. In an editorial published in *The Globe and Mail* on the 13th January, 2020, this was spelt out clearly and extensively, ending with the following paragraphs:

'..... Canada kept the monarchy, and a head of state we share with various Commonwealth countries. The head of state's representatives here are the governor-general and the provincial lieutenant-governors, who perform essential duties from opening parliaments to deciding who gets a form of government in minority situations. They're as close as Canada comes to having resident royalty, but they're not royalty. Instead, they're merely temporary avatars for a virtual monarch who remains permanently ensconced across the sea.

'Furthermore, since the 1950s, governors-general have always been Canadians. Princes are not shipped over here when no useful duties can be found for them on the other side of the Atlantic.

'The Sussexes are working out their own personal issues, and Canadians wish them the best of luck. Canada welcomes people of all faiths, nationalities and races, but if you're a senior member of our Royal Family, this country cannot become your home.

'The government should make that clear. There can be no Earl Sussex of Rosedale and no Prince Harry of Point Grey. Canada is not a halfway house for anyone looking to get out of Britain while remaining royal.'

This neatly encapsulated the view of many Canadians, while also going straight to the core of the dilemma. While the Canadians felt for

Harry in his quest to move away from royal life, he was not welcome to do it in Canada. Although Meghan and Harry's stepping back was huge news, and the reactions sufficiently mixed to allow each side room for manoeuvre, behind the scenes the family stepped in to contain the fallout to the monarchy and to eliminate the possibility of long term damage, even for the couple themselves. Harry and Meghan, of course, had no intention of residing permanently in Canada, but, being skilful tacticians who understood that their radical decamping from the United Kingdom would be more tolerable if their ultimate destination of California could be concealed beneath the fig leaf of a desire to reside in a Commonwealth country, they were still allowing everyone to suppose that they would end up in Canada. This had constitutional implications, but these were less than the public and press might have realised, because Harry is simply not high enough up the line of succession. At his most important he was merely the spare, and once William had his first child, he ceased being even that. By 2020, he was the fourth spare after the three Cambridge children. Nevertheless, he was still a member of the Royal Family, still beloved, and still someone whose conduct could damage the monarchy and potentially himself. Moreover, what he was allowed to do now would set precedents which could impact upon Princess Charlotte and Prince Louis of Cambridge, so it was important to get things right.

The Queen took matters into her own hands. Within the family, she has always had a secondary role to Prince Philip. However, where her function as Sovereign is concerned, she has consistently jealously guarded her turf, allowing no interference from any member of the family, including the forceful husband she otherwise deferred to, or the domineering mother from whose shadow she emerged only after the Queen Mother's death in 2002 at nearly 102 years old.

For someone who was personally self-effacing, Elizabeth II as queen has always had an astonishing degree of certitude. Her Private Secretary the Hon. (later Sir) Martin (then Lord) Charteris was the first to comment upon this immediately following her accession at the age of twenty five. He noticed how sure-footed she became as soon as she had to fulfill the role of monarch. She had a genuine natural authority and absolute confidence, possibly emanating from the schooling she received in the role of monarch from her father King George VI and her grand-mother Queen Mary.

The Queen put this regal assurance to good use as she conferred with the head of the family, Prince Philip, who by then resided full time at Wood Farm on the Sandringham Estate, having given up public life. Known within the family for his wisdom, practicality, humanity, and unflinchingly royal approach to duty, his viewpoint, according to a European royal was, 'The most important thing was to not let things drag on.' Decisions must be made, and made quickly, so a date was set for a meeting on Monday the 13th January between the Queen, Harry, and the two immediate monarchs-in-waiting, Charles and William. To ensure that decisions would have to be made in a short space of time, the Queen informed everyone that it had to conclude before teatime, which meant that it could not go on beyond 5pm.

I was informed by royal cousins that Prince Philip was appalled at the way in which Meghan and Harry had tried to bring pressure to bear to get their own way. He was happy not to participate in the meeting itself, and, having fortified the Queen with his support, was driven away from the big house by his great friend Penny, wife of his maternal uncle Dickie Mountbatten's grandson Norton Knatchbull, 3rd Earl Mountbatten of Burma just before the meeting was due to start. Harry had arrived from Windsor early, hoping to meet with his grandmother beforehand to influence her, but it did not work. She remained unavailable until the appointed time, waiting until the Prince of Wales and William arrived.

Despite the Queen making it clear that she wanted an agreement before the meeting concluded, there was personal anguish all round. Charles was distraught that his efforts to include Meghan had come to naught and that Harry had thrown them all a curved ball, while William was equally distraught that the brother whom he had loved and protected all his life could be behaving in what he regarded as so foolhardy and destructive a manner. The Queen was disappointed that all the sterling possibilities the union had engendered throughout the Commonwealth might come to nought, and that the warmth, generosity and hospitality the family and public had shown to Meghan had meant so little. Harry himself felt that he was not being supported enough and was upset when it became apparent that he and Meghan would not be able to trip off to North America, cut deals left right and centre, trip back over to Britain for a few photo ops which would keep their earning potential topped up, and generally just do as they pleased. Insofar as their well laid plans to exploit their royal positions were concerned, he was made aware that there would be a trial period of a year's duration. 'A lot can happen in a year,' a European prince said. 'By not coming to a definitive agreement, the family was buying time, allowing the Sussexes to feel the breath on their necks which would hopefully encourage them to strike only acceptable deals. Remember, Meghan is a businesswoman. The great fear is that she loves money so much she'll sacrifice reason for profit and in doing so involve herself and the monarchy in controversy."

Aside from putting the couple on a probationary period, the family made it clear to Harry that he and Meghan would not be calling the shots as to what they could, and could not, do regarding their royal patronages, the way he and Meghan had suggested in their initial posting. He was informed that he would have to give up his links with the Army. This was a big blow to him, for 'he had really envisaged popping back, hunkering down with the men, enjoying the camaraderie which had been one of the high points of his life, then breezing back to America, hopefully on a friend's private plane, to cut more deals while Meghan increased the family fortune, whether to become President of the United States or just an ordinary billionairess was beside the point,' one of his cousins explained. He had not calculated on being forced to stand down from being Captain General of the Royal Marines, a position he had inherited from his grandfather Prince Philip and valued greatly; Honorary Air Commandant, RAF Honington; or Commodore-in-Chief, Small Ships and Diving, Royal Naval Command. The loss of these really hurt, as he would confess a few nights later when he gave a speech at the Chelsea Ivy on behalf of Sentebale, the charity he founded which supports the mental health and wellbeing of children and young people affected by HIV in Lesotho and Botswana. He had also not lost patronage of the Invictus Games foundation, which he had also founded. Nevertheless, the only really meaningful patronages he and Meghan would be allowed to keep would be President and Vice-President of the Queen's Commonwealth Trust, something which was within her personal gift and she could police easily. She also hoped this would leave the channels open for greater cooperation in the future. The Queen genuinely loves the Commonwealth, as everyone close to her knows, so by allowing Harry and Meghan to keep those patronages she was playing to them on many levels.

Last but not least, Harry and Meghan were also made to forgo using their Royal Highness titles. Although they were not stripped of them, by banning them from using those honorifics after they officially stepped down as royals on the 31st March 2020, the Queen, Prince Charles and Prince William were delivering a clear message: You can't be both in and out. It's either/or. This was yet another subtle way of exerting some control over the headstrong couple. If they behaved decorously, no more would be said of further demotions, but the implied threat was obvious: Cross the line and you might end up losing your royal rank altogether.

Although it is unlikely that Meghan and quite possibly Harry will have known that there was a precedent for royals being prevented from using their royal titles, in 1917 Her Highness Princess Maud, Countess of Southesk was ordered by her uncle, King George V, to cease using the style and title of princess, with which her grandfather King Edward VII had endowed her in 1905. Thereafter, she was known by her married name, Lady Southesk. Although she remained a highness and princess, and enjoyed precedence immediately after those members of her family who were royal highnesses, and although her coronation robes were those of a royal princess and not a countess, she was referred to even in the Court Circular by her aristocratic dignities alone. Had she persisted in using her royal titles, King George V would have stripped her of them.

Because Harry and Meghan are now in a similarly anomalous position, and no one yet knew whether Meghan would turn out to be as much of a maverick commercially and politically as some feared she could be, both doors were being kept open. If she and Harry respected the boundaries behind which royals must function commercially and politically, they would be allowed to keep their royal status. If they deviated from the high standards required, they could be deprived of it.

This was not an empty threat, and constitutionalists who argue that Parliament would have to vote to strip Harry of his royal status are wrong. Although peerages cannot be withdrawn except by an Act of Parliament, King George V with one stroke of the pen in Letters Patent dated 20th November 1917 deprived a whole host of his royal relations of their royal status. These included King Edward VII's grandson Prince Alistair of Connaught who became Lord Macduff; Queen Mary's brothers Princes Adolphus and Alexander of Teck who became the Marquis of Cambridge and Earl of Athlone respectively, while their heirs Princes George and Rupert were demoted to Earl of Eltham and Viscount Trematon with all the other children mere courtesy lords and ladies; and the Battenberg princes Henry and Louis, whose marriages to Queen Victoria's daughter Beatrice and granddaughter Victoria did not prevent them from becoming the Marquises of Carisbrooke and Milford Haven, while all their little princes and princesses became mere lords and ladies. The Queen might not be able to strip Harry of his dukedom without proceeding through Parliament, but she could certainly strip him of his royal status with the ease that her grandfather had shorn those just mentioned.

A friend of Harry and Meghan's told me that neither of them understood the weakness of their position at the time they made these moves. Once they became alert to the dangers, Meghan showed her mettle by trying to brazen things out. She declared that people would consider them royal whether or not they remained highnesses. To an extent, she was right. In America, people have a different concept of what it means to be a member of the Royal Family. As long as you are related to them, you're regarded as being royal. Even in Britain people do not appreciate how narrowly defined the Royal Family is. Princess Margaret's son and daughter are often called royal, as are Princess Anne's children. In reality, none of them is royal. The Royal Family is in essence limited to the monarch, his or her children, and all grandchildren in the male line. Latitude is extended to the children of the children of the heirs into the third generation, hence why the Cambridge children are royal, but no legitimate child of Harry's is a member of the Royal Family until such time as his father ascends to the throne. But Meghan and Harry are members of the Royal Family, and even though they have been demoted by having usage of their Royal Highness titles denied to them, they will continue to be royal, albeit semi-detached, unless their royal status is removed from them.

Remote as that possibility seems, it is not beyond comprehension. If they should become caught up in a scandal like the Infanta Cristina and her husband, they might well find themselves stripped of their royal status the way Cristina and Iñaki Urdangarin were stripped of their ducal titles. The British monarchy has proven itself to be amazingly resourceful and inventive when it is in its interest to lay down new precedents. So it is not beyond the realms of possibility that Harry could find himself ceasing to be a royal highness. It's doubtful that people would then still consider them royal, but even if they did, the level of kudos would be infinitely inferior to that of a royal dukedom.

All this, of course, may seem far-fetched, but then so was the extra-legal ruling which prevented the Duchess of Windsor from being styled Her Royal Highness, or the invention by which Prince Edward's children, who by right are lawfully His Royal Highness Prince James of Wessex and Her Royal Highness Princess Louise of Wessex, became known as Viscount Severn and Lady Louise Windsor.

The royal world is subtle. It issues shots across the bow before it sends in the fire ships. The most contentious of all the Sussexes' plans as they sought to paddle their canoe beyond the safe harbour of British royal life into the rough seas of Americana was their registration of trademarks for their Sussex Royal brand. The incredibly wide net they cast when they registered over a hundred items ranging from the purely commercial to the purely charitable, with unhealthy mixes of both in a discomfiting number of the items, set alarm bells ringing at the palace. Meghan and Harry were warned by the Garter King of Arms, Thomas Woodcock, who told the Times, 'I don't think it's satisfactory,' when questioned about their declared intention to continue using the word royal in their brand. Of course, they had gone to a great deal of trouble and expense to trademark the items they intended to exploit commercially, and Meghan would not have been a capable businesswoman if she hadn't tried to hang onto the brand she had already spent so much time, trouble and money creating. It was inevitable, nevertheless, that they would be prevented from marketing themselves as royal, for the word is a restricted one, and, by making the announcement that he did, Garter was in effect shutting them down, which of course subsequently happened.

That this anomaly arose at all shows how genuinely naive Meghan and Harry were, or how brazen, depending on your perspective. They could easily have trademarked something else - their names, their initials, anything beneath the ducal coronet such as the obscure Archewell which they have subsequently come up with - and not fallen foul of the law. But in presuming that they could simply exploit Sussex Royal they showed, at the very least, how ignorant they both were of even the most basic elements of English society, or then how confident they were that they would prevail over both precedence and the law.

Although Garter's actions were on behalf of the Queen, and it is she who ultimately prevented Meghan and Harry from using the word royal in their branding, Her Majesty nevertheless had been intent on doing her utmost to paper over as many cracks as she could, despite always putting the good of the Crown before all personal considerations, as she has done time and again during her long reign.

In the past, there had been occasions when Elizabeth II's personal choices were stark, such as when she accepted the advice of Sir Winston Churchill to retain the surname of Windsor for the dynasty in preference to Mountbatten, and in so doing created an issue between herself and Prince Philip which took the remainder of the decade to resolve. Or when she remained resolutely neutral during Princess Margaret's marriage crisis over Group Captain Peter Townsend, which caused problems between her and her sister. Harry should have appreciated that his grandmother was no pushover, but possibly neither he nor Meghan understood the limitations to which they were subjected where exploiting their royal identity was concerned.

Despite being no cinch when the family trespasses on hallowed royal turf, the Queen nevertheless has been an extremely indulgent mother and grandmother. It is likely that this is what allowed Harry to believe that his and Meghan's extraordinary demands would succeed. She has been the antithesis of the controlling parent and grandparent. Her critics would say that she has been too understanding. Had she been less so, she would have had less to understand.

Of all the royals present at that meeting in January 2020 when she, Charles, William and Harry were deciding how best to proceed, the Queen was the most inclined to take a lenient view, aiming for the couple to achieve as many of their objectives as would be realistically possible without damaging the monarchy - even if that meant recalibrating customs.

Her attitude was reflected in the statement she issued at the end of the meeting:

"Today my family had very constructive discussions on the future of my grandson and his family.

"My family and I are entirely supportive of Harry and Meghan's desire to create a new life as a young family. Although we would have preferred them to remain full-time working members of the Royal Family, we respect and understand their wish to live a more independent life as a family while remaining a valued part of my family.

"Harry and Meghan have made clear that they do not want to be reliant on public funds in their new lives.

"It has therefore been agreed that there will be a period of transition in which the Sussexes will spend time in Canada and the UK.

"These are complex matters for my family to resolve, and there is some more work to be done, but I have asked for final decisions to be reached in the coming days."

Understandably, the press examined the statement from all angles, including a few that have never existed. In reality, Meghan and Harry were sailing into uncharted waters. There was talk of them 'abdicating', and they were linked to the Duke and Duchess of Windsor.

There were indeed parallels between Harry and Meghan Sussex and David and Wallis Windsor. Both Meghan and Wallis were American and both were divorcees. Harry and his great-great-great uncle did indeed throw over their royal positions for the love of a woman. Both of them were compulsively and obsessively in love with the women who became their wives. Both were co-dependent upon their love objects, as indeed were David's brother and Harry's great-grandfather King George VI upon Elizabeth Bowes Lyon, later Queen Elizabeth, then the Queen Mother. This extreme co-dependency was a feature of several of the Hanoverian royals over the centuries, including their common ancestor King George III and his son the 1st Duke of Sussex, who was Queen Victoria's Uncle Augustus. He had two unsuitable, indeed invalid, wives, the first being Lady Augusta Murray, the mother of his two children, and the second, Lady Cecilia Buggin. Ever the romantic, Queen Victoria took pity on her uncle and his invalid second wife once she became queen, and since it was not possible to revoke the Royal Marriages Act of 1772 and make Aunt Cecilia Duchess of Sussex, she instead made her the Duchess of Inverness in her own right. This was truly astonishing, and showed to what extent Victoria was both a romantic and flexible, an attitude some courtiers believe Queen Elizabeth II inherited from her great-great-grandmother.

There the similarities between the Sussexes and the Windsors end. Meghan wanted to marry Harry from the word go, and ensured that she did by being the living embodiment of everything he had ever wanted in a woman. Wallis never wanted to marry David and did all she could to discourage him from marrying her. Meghan is from of a *petit bourgeois* background while Wallis was from an upper class Southern family. Wallis valued the royal way of life to such an extent that she never wanted to marry the King but to remain his mistress so she could remain a part of the royal system. Meghan's disregard for the royal system was evident not only in her conduct while she was living in England, but in the manner of her departure. Meghan is essentially a lone wolf with social skills, while Wallis was genuinely a people person. In her own way, Wallis was a romantic, although one with a wide and frankly acknowledged streak of pragmatism. Her uncle Sol Warfield was one of the richest men in America and she was his sole heiress until she threatened to divorce her first husband, a wife-beating alcoholic named Win Spencer. Uncle Sol warned her that he would cut her out of his will and leave his money to a home for fallen women if she became the first Warfield to divorce.

She divorced, he left his $2.5m estate as threatened. Although Wallis loved beauty and had style, her actions show that when push came to shove, she chose the heart over the bank. Her behaviour, once David abdicated, also showed that she was indeed the 'good and honest woman' Chips Channon labelled her in his famous diaries. Notwithstanding her genuine horror of finding herself living out her worst nightmare as the Duchess of Windsor, she put a brave face on it, was a loyal and devoted spouse to the man she never wanted to marry, created a truly regal lifestyle for them in France and the United States, maintained a dignified silence publicly about the reality of her life, and used to laughingly remark privately how taxing it was to be one half of one of history's greatest romances.

Many of the comparisons between Harry and the Duke of Windsor are fanciful, born of ignorance or miscomprehension. While it is true that both men were prone to depression and had mental health issues, the Duke of Windsor was the archetypal royal. There was never any doubt that you were in the presence of a former king when you were around him. By the time I met him he might have been a doddering old bore, but he was always regal, immaculately turned out, and lived according to royal etiquette. There was nothing bovverish or oikish about him, which is certainly not true of Harry. The former king would no more have played strip poker in Vegas than have sex in the middle of the Mall. He used to sit on the edge of a room and people would be brought over to him, one by one, to talk with him until he indicated that he had had enough and was ready for someone else. There is nothing regal about Harry. This, of course, has been one of his charms. There certainly has never been anything stylish about him. He always looks as if he's just crept out of bed or is about to head into it.

I knew the Duke and Duchess of Windsor slightly when I was a young girl in New York and they were coming to the end of their lives. She was a game old bird while he was rather pathetic, with an air of sadness, indeed defeat, about him. Nevertheless, he was very dignified. I knew a very great deal about them through family connections. My great family friend John Pringle, founder of the iconic Round Hill Hotel, where Harry and Meghan stayed when Tom Inskip had his wedding reception there, had been the Duke's ADC during the war and was full of stories about the Windsors. My stepmother-in-law, Margaret Duchess of Argyll, was a longstanding friend of theirs. My sister-in-law Lady Jean Campbell, whose grandfather Lord Beaverbrook had been one of the Duke's strongest supporters when he was king and wanted to marry Wallis, gained a wealth of information about them from her grandfather. Had Edward VIII followed the Beaver's advice, he would have remained on his throne and Wallis would have become either Duchess of Lancaster or Queen of England. However, he was so terrified of losing her that he preferred to give up his throne rather than be separated, then ironically had to endure a separation of six months to validate her divorce.

The single greatest difference between the Sussexes and the Windsors was that Wallis never wanted to marry David while Meghan wanted to marry Harry from the outset. Wallis never wanted to be anything but *maîtresse-en-titre* while Meghan wanted to become a royal princess and duchess. Wallis loved her husband and wanted to remain Mrs Ernest Simpson while being the King's mistress. Rather than losing a fortune to marry a man for love, the way Wallis did, Meghan has ensured the acquisition of wealth through a series of dextrous manoeuvres, some commercial, others personal, but all with her businesswoman's eye firmly fixed on the baseline. Wallis' idea of hell was the life she ended up with, saddled in perennial exile with a man-child (whom she and Ernest used to call Peter Pan), condemned for a lifetime to have him worship at her altar. Meghan, on the other hand, has encouraged Harry to embark upon a life of semi-exile and seems very comfortable with the pedestal he has put her upon.

Contrary to popular belief, Wallis did everything in her power to keep Edward VIII on the throne, but he was so 'insanely in love with her', as his cousin Prince Christopher of Greece put it, that he recklessly threw away his crown rather than run the risk of being separated from her. Knowing the sacrifices he had made out of love for her, Wallis spent the rest of David's life responding to a love she really didn't feel, though, with the passage of time, she did develop a deep affection for him. Wallis also had sufficient humility to appreciate that her way was not the only or necessarily the best way. She was no egomaniac. She recognised that the royal world was a richer, more ancient, layered and textured one than she was used to in America. She did not believe that she had much to teach an older and more established society than hers. She appreciated that they had much to teach her, and set about learning. Margaret Argyll used to recount how Wallis went from being a relatively unsophisticated newcomer in the early 1930s to one of the world's most sophisticated women by the end of the decade. She became the world's leading hostess, her dinner parties a byword for taste, style, and elegance. No one entertained like the Duchess of Windsor.

For all their differences, Meghan and Wallis have one or two defining features in common. Wallis was and Meghan is an obvious, upfront woman on the make. Wallis did and Meghan does exult in luxury. Materialism and an awareness of quality have mattered to them more than they matter to most women. Wallis was honourable enough to pay the price for her position. She understood that her prince had given up a lot for her. If Meghan truly believes her comment that her 'love for Harry has made possible' his stepping back from the royal way of life, she has not only failed to appreciate the tremendous sacrifices he has made for her, but she hasn't even listened to what he has said. Harry stated in front of hundreds of people at the Chelsea Ivy how 'saddened' he was to give up his links with the military and indeed his country, family and friends. Can she truly believe that she has liberated him from bonds which were not shackles but valuable moorings to a past life which, for all its imperfections, was a glorious one? Can she genuinely accept that there was no sacrifice in substituting a splendid position laden with possibilities for doing good, with one full of uncertainty?

Meghan's flattened affect where the sacrifices of others are concerned is one of the many concerns the royals have for Harry's future with her. They understand his predicament even though they do not like or approve of it. They appreciate that they are powerless to intervene, that this is one river which must flow into the ocean, and any attempts to divert it might result in an unfortunate outcome. For that reason, William has tried to mend fences insofar as it is possible for him to do so, though I am told that there is now so much water under the bridge that it is unlikely that the brothers will ever again be close the way they used to be. Charles, I understand, is utterly perplexed as to what he can do to help, having moved mountains for Meghan, only to have them come crashing down on him. It was he who managed to get for Meghan, a divorcee like him, what he could not achieve for himself; namely a church wedding conducted by the Archbishop of Canterbury at St. George's Chapel.

A royal told me that the Queen has been more relaxed than anyone else, 'possibly because she realises that if things work out for Harry and Meghan, they will have broken new ground where other junior royals can follow, and if things don't (work out), it won't be the end of the world. The monarchy has survived far greater threats.'

Already, it is evident that the British public have accepted that the Duke and Duchess of Sussex are detached. They have bidden them farewell, sometimes with regret, sometimes with relief, sometimes with impatience, but with no perceptible difference to anyone's life. As such, they're now in a different category from the rest of the family. 'In my view,' the royal said, 'they've already been downgraded in the [British] public's eyes from royals to celebrities.'

If this is the case, Harry and Meghan's position is not as enviable as optimistic PRs might think it is. There has been talk that they will be able to earn $100m per annum, maybe even more, that they are a billion dollar brand, that they could become a second Barack and Michelle Obama or even, God forbid, a variation of Tony Blair. This is to ignore some basic facts while misinterpreting how status works at the highest levels of society. Harry has never been the President of the United States, nor has he been a Prime Minister like Blair, who might have deceived Parliament into entering a war which made him popular in the United States and the Middle East, but earned him the hatred of millions of Britons once they saw through his lies. If Tony Blair's trajectory is anything to go by, Harry and Meghan had better strike while the iron is hot. Tony Blair's heyday lasted for only a few years. His money-making glory days were wrapped up with his reputed prestige, and once that evaporated he became a busted flush, reviled in so many quarters of society and parts of the world that his utterances are treated with contempt, his presence an embarrassment to such an extent that I know of many people who have declined to meet him (yours truly included), and even more who refuse to be in the same room as him (yours truly again), much less the same photograph. Nor was Tony Blair's politics the only thing that destroyed his reputation (although they did not help). It was the perception of him as a narcissistic, hypocritical, messianic, virtue-signalling money-grubber that buried his reputation. Hectoring people with one hand while coining it in with the other is not the ideal way to gain or retain respect. Once enough of the public lose respect for a public figure, their earning potential begins to wane. This is something Meghan and Harry would do well to note, for none of us who wish them well wants them to go the way of Blair, whose story really is a cautionary tale.

Even so, Tony Blair did lead a country, and did do so for an extensive period of time. He won three general elections and might well have gone down in history as a great Prime Minister had he not deceived Parliament and the British people into the war with Iraq which no one in Britain but he wanted. Even then, he might well have become an eminent retired statesman had he not shown himself to be the acquisitive hypocrite he is now regarded as being. Nevertheless, Blair was, if only for a short while, respected. In that interval, he was able to capitalise upon his reputation, his former position, and his undoubted experience, to make a fortune.

Harry, on the other hand, has never led a country. He has never been elected to any position. He has no experience as a leader. He was only ever a minor ranking army officer who happened to be the second son of the heir to the British throne. Yes, he had star quality. Yes, he was a revered figure until his marriage. Yes, he had a great position, but he was never going to be number one, much less President of the most powerful nation on earth or Prime Minister of Great Britain. Moreover, he walked away from his position to seek his fortune in the great bazaar of commerce. In doing so, he lost the most prestigious part of his position, his transcendence above the fray. As Garter put it, you either are or you aren't.

It remains to be seen, now that Harry and Meghan have stepped back from their royal roles, whether their frank commercial take on life will enhance or demean their earning capacity. Certainly, they were forthright in their announcements and their pitches, as was demonstrated by that famous clip of Harry nobbling Disney CEO Bob Iger at the *Lion King* premiere. Harry not only abandoned well-bred reticence, but he replaced it with a hustling technique that even Trevor Engelson would find enviable. 'You do know she does voiceovers?' Harry unexpectedly asked an astonished Iger, who spluttered, 'Ah, I didn't know that,' before Hustling Harry zeroed in for the kill saying, 'You seem surprised. She's really interested.' A clearly embarrassed Iger then rolled over, saying, 'We'd love to try. That's a great idea,' while his wife, the journalist Willow Bay, looked on with a face like thunder. Harry and Meghan had clearly planned their ambush, because they then turned their attention to the director Jon Favreau, with Harry declaring, 'Next time anyone needs extra voiceover work, we can make ourselves available,' while Meghan stated, 'That's really why we're here - it's the pitch.'

It worked too. Disney signed a deal with Meghan to do voiceover work in return for a donation to the charity, Elephants Without Borders. Whether she received expenses, possibly running into the hundreds of thousands, has not been announced, but she did the work prior to departing for Canada in November 2019. When the programme aired in April 2020 the reviews were mixed, with an unfortunate proportion accusing her of being over-eager to please or being just on the right side of annoying, though a minority found charm in her performance.

Success or failure, when the Royal Family found out that Meghan and Harry had not only used an official engagement to pitch for work, but had successfully concluded negotiations behind their backs, they were furious, accusing the couple of entering into contracts 'with firms like Disney' without following procedure. Meghan was unrepentant. She told friends that her 'work with Disney is far from over. The voice-over is just the beginning and there's (sic) more collaborations to come. Meghan has no regrets and the sky's the limit.'

This foray back into the entertainment industry was testing the water in more ways than one. They and their advisors needed to feel their way towards success, which meant maximising the Sussex brand and its earning potential while boosting the couple's prestige. Make no mistake about it, this was one brand where there was a holy alliance between money and reputation. One was intended to feed the other, and there was a whole team in the background working away at making the Sussex brand successful in every way possible. Meghan and Harry's American advisors fully intended them to be on a par with the Obamas in terms of earning capacity. But comparisons with the former Presidential couple seemed optimistic. Just as how Harry does not compare with Barack Obama in practical terms, in personal terms, how does a former cable television network ensemble actress and blogger, with political aspirations but no political experience and only a handful of personal appearances to her credit, compare with a successful lawyer, university administrator and two term First Lady like Michelle Obama? The Obamas were at the forefront of the world's stage for eight years. They were admired for their accomplishments and their successes. There were many millions of Democrats who voted for him and still admire them. During their eight years in office they did not denigrate treasured national customs and institutions. They did not complain about how hard done-by they were, did not take on the press in an attempt to neutralise or control them, nor did they jump ship to earn themselves more money than they were already making in their appointed roles.

For all the optimism of their financial team, the Sussexes were not the equals of the Obamas in terms of status and accomplishment, nor did they have the wealth of experience or the scale and scope of vision of the presidential pair. What they did have was huge ambition and self-belief, and these, together with their royal status, should play well in the United States even as they have lost respect in Britain.

* * * * *

To fully appreciate the danger the Sussexes now find themselves in, one needs to understand that at all levels of society there are gradations. This is as true of a local hospital in Missouri as it is of a bank in San Antonio, the social world that David Patrick Columbia covers in the New York Social Diary, or a palace in Europe. Status is like wine. It doesn't always travel well, though sometimes what is second or third rate in one place becomes first rate in another.

Meghan discovered that fact to her advantage when she moved to

Canada and found herself embraced by a category of person who would have shunned her in her native habitat. The lesson was reiterated in Britain, once it became apparent that she and Harry were headed for the altar. The press presented her as a bigger star than she had ever been, and Andrew Morton, who had boosted Harry's mother's reputation in a panegyric, did the same thing for Meghan in his pre-marital best-seller *Meghan: An American Princess*. Whether all this exaggeration clouded her judgement, and she forgot the lessons of her roots, or she simply wasn't sophisticated enough to understand the dynamics of the situation she found herself in, or she was indifferent to any externals save her own ultimate desires, Meghan misunderstood the power of the monarchy and the relative fragility of the royals within the system. As Anne Glenconner put it, Meghan thought that marrying into the Royal Family assured her of 'instant popularity' and an exciting and easy life spent travelling in 'a golden coach', when in fact the royal way of life is hard and often boring to boot.

Had Meghan been born into an established family, she would have appreciated that the whole is infinitely greater than its parts. Great families and great institutions value the individual, but they also know that each individual is dispensable. No matter how important, powerful, rich, talented, beautiful, intelligent or anything else you are, you are on this earth for only a limited period. Durability becomes a matter of each individual making his contribution in the knowledge that he will be replaced and hopefully his family or institution will continue to flourish, with him having added something to it rather than subtracting from it. The greatest mark of success is that you leave things better off than you found them. It is this balance between your own importance and your relative unimportance, your replaceability and your unique irreplaceability, which gives the holders of great positions the sense of proportion necessary to fulfill their destinies. The King is dead; long live the (new) King.

These were nuances which Meghan might well have understood, but since she gave no indication of having done so, the only conclusion onlookers could come to was that the whole thing was way above her head. One of the greatest insults you can level against an individual in the British Establishment is that he is out for himself, rather than out for the greater good. One of the greatest insults you can hurl at someone is to say that he is exploitative. There is an awareness of the necessity for each person or cause to leave room for others. Greed is not good, nor is being mercenary. Striking too hard a bargain is not seen as a virtue, the way it can be in certain segments of American society, but as a vice. You add to your cause, and if you benefit personally, so much the better, but you never put yourself before your cause, nor do you squeeze such a good deal for yourself that you are sucking into your province what by right would have gone to others had you left enough space for them to benefit as well. Balance, justice, fair play and decorum also play invaluable parts in this way of life. 'There is a time and place for everything,' is one of the cornerstones upon which the edifice of all well brought-up traditionalists was constructed. For instance, when you are attending a premiere of a movie and the proceeds of the event are going to a charity with which you are involved, you do not hustle the CEO and the director for a job for your wife as soon as you meet them. You at least have the good grace to wait until the after-party, though Harry and Meghan were able to get away with this flagrant breach of etiquette because the people at Disney believed that they, being royal, were begging for charity and not themselves, and that they, being royals, were above the cut and thrust of commerce. This illusion has now been well and truly dispelled by their admission that they wish to achieve financial independence. The danger is that now that they are commodities who will have a price for their services, their presence will be less prestigious than it would have been when they stood to make no personal gain from any of their transactions.

In the world whence Meghan originated, and to which she has returned with Harry, many people consider it admirable to be as aggressive as Harry and Meghan were with the Disney CEO. Hustling has its purpose, and to hustlers that is more important than the place in which it is exercised. However, not everyone regards such directness as desirable. I spoke to several well-placed people in Hollywood (producer, director, heir to the heritage of one of the Hollywood Greats etc.) who thought Harry's conduct let the side down. Such conflicting attitudes again highlight the clash of one world's values against another's. But it was noteworthy that the condemnation was exceeded by the admiration, which demonstrates why Meghan and Harry will always have followers, especially in her homeland.

While Harry remained a senior member of the Royal Family, he undoubtedly had a great position. This was enhanced by the perception that he had something which money could not buy. Added to this was his reputation for being a down-to-earth, affable guy. He also had the physical attributes to shine within the role. Position plus personal assets always have a potentiative effect, the position exaggerating the personal qualities and vice versa. HIs mother was a case in point. Diana would never have been known as a great beauty had she not become the Princess of Wales. Nor would a Princess of Wales, who lacked her style, charm, personability and graciousness, have become the worldwide star which she was.

The danger for the Dianas and Harrys of this world arises when they receive consistent feedback about their personal qualities exceeding the value of their elevated positions. Once they begin to believe the hype, they are on rocky ground. The temptation to overestimate your personal worth while denigrating the worldly advantages which exaggerate it can become irresistible, unless you take the attitude that Prince Philip stated he and the Queen took when, in the early days of their marriage, especially after her accession to the throne, they were revered as the most desirable, glamorous, appealing couple on earth. They decided that they would go about their business as if none of that acclaim existed. Taking the praise with a pinch of salt, they felt, was the only way to avoid having their heads turned. The ways their lives turned out proves the wisdom of their choice.

For Harry and Meghan, the danger of their initial popularity was not only having their heads turned, but also misjudging their appeal and how it could be made to work for them. Any miscalculation could do long term damage to their 'brand', and could result in them setting out on a path thinking they could become more commercially successful than was possible. The fact that Harry had no experience of the American way of life, crucially to include commerce, while Meghan had no real knowledge of how their royal position could be converted to maximum financial advantage, meant that they were, to an extent, the blind leading the blind, and therefore liable to make mistakes, not the least of which might be in what their true earning capacity could be. Yet there are indications that Meghan is indeed the brilliant tactician, strategist and businesswoman that Nelthorpe-Cowne assessed her as being. She has organised the best business brains for Harry and herself, and has positioned them so that they will become Hollywood's regnant royal couple. In America, where people are often taken at face value, and where one's estimate of one's worth is frequently used as a benchmark of one's true value, Meghan's positioning of Harry and herself as regal, hyper-glamorous, stylish, down-to-earth, caring, woke, left-wing, yoga- and nature- and family-loving conscionables who care deeply about the world, their fellow humans, the environment, animals, children, and family life, has been supremely clever.

There is no doubt that Harry and Meghan made a bold move when they left Britain for California via Canada. It takes courage to strike out onto such an unscripted path. I am told that Harry's ambitions were simple enough. He wanted a happy wife and a happy family life with her. I am also informed that Meghan's ambitions were also simple, albeit different. They were a cocktail of elements which owe more to the dreams created by Hollywood - and which have influenced just about everyone in the world - than to the values of an older and more tradi-tional way of life. She is Hollywood given flesh. The values she espouses, no matter how heartfelt, are basically new, cutting-edge ones. She often talks about change, but she has no cohesive overview, nor does she ever bog herself down in what the consequences of change would be. Change always brings about new problems, but these are never mentioned, much less defined; nor are the potential solutions addressed. Noble though Meghan's motives might be, she is actually a novice in the world of realpolitik. Rhetoric does not solve society's problems, though superb rhetoricians throughout the ages have been able to employ this gift to gain support for themselves from the public.

The palace understood that it was never going to be enough for a royal to simply deliver moving speeches. From their point of view, every word spoken by a royal must be carefully considered so that public expectations were not played upon, whether through ignorance, cynicism, ambitiousness, or even naiveté, as public expectation raised too high would result in unwanted disillusionment.

Meghan's values, being the values of a new and to a large extent untried world order, inevitably came into conflict with the tried and tested values of an older, tried and workable order. She seemed not to understand to what extent she had set herself up to be in conflict with not only the British way of life, but with the more traditional elements within America as well. Yet any examination of the difference between Haves and Have-Nots will show to what extent Meghan's values were those of a Have-not clashing with those who already have.

In any society, whether it be a constitutional monarchy, a free republic, a totalitarian regime, even a Communist state, the emphasis of Haves has always been on preservation and survival, while those on the make have traditionally valued change and acquisition. One was not necessarily better than the other. Each had its merits, depending on the circumstances of an individual. One might even say each was desirable, for those who were materially lacking and aspired to a richer life could not do so without changing their circumstances. They needed to aspire, while, for those already in possession of assets, the emphasis switched from more and more to keeping what one had, not only for oneself, but for future generations. Obviously, the traits, skills and mind-set were different for each group, but of one thing you could be certain. Once those who had aspired had achieved, their focus invariably expanded to include the goals of preservation and survival that were the characteristics of the Haves.

It will be interesting to see at which point in her development Meghan switches from acquisitiveness to preservation. To date, Meghan has moved from a No Money world to a New Money then an Old Money one when she married Harry. She and Harry have set about joining the Real Money world, in the stated hope of making enough for them to end up with having Real Money. Old Money, New Money, No Money and Real Money all have distinguishing features, and each has impacted upon the couple's lives.

Old Money has the grand houses, castles, and palaces that are stuffed full of chattels which would seriously deplete the bank accounts of New Money and even make a dent with Real Money, should they be able to buy the items which are seldom if ever for sale. Old Money might not have readily realisable assets, but what they have is an accumulation of riches, now mostly in everything but cash, which New Money can only replicate, in a contemporary setting, by consuming its funds in a latter-day version of the real thing. Old Money also has some things that New Money and Real Money cannot buy. It has history, tradition, and breeding. These can be very discomfiting to a newcomer like Meghan, for the one thing that someone like her would find difficult is relating to people who, because of their heritage, are so unconsciously themselves that they wear their every advantage lightly and take no one, including themselves, too seriously. This conflicts with neophytes who are far more conscious of themselves and invariably take themselves far more seriously.

The philosophical differences between Old Money and New Money are at the root of many a misunderstanding. Several of Harry's friends have confirmed that Meghan never fitted in with his old crowd. Not only did she not fit in, but she pointedly made no attempt to do so. From the very outset, her attitude was, 'This is me. I am inflexible. I bend to no one.' It is ironic that she would have had this attitude, bearing in mind that she had gone out of her way to scale the heights of Canadian society, and had done so successfully by doing her utmost to fit in. But there are differences between the upper reaches of Canadian and British society. Canadians of all classes are more similar to their American counterparts than to the British. They are also more simplistic than the British. Here, use of language, pronunciation, phraseology, body language, overt and unstated demeanour are radically different. If you are an American or Canadian who is authentically yourself, you will fit in without any difficulty into all strata of society in Britain. On the other hand, if you are a personality whose development has been as self-conscious as Meghan's, the only class in Britain into which you will fit comfortably is the *arriviste*. This is because all other segments of the British population are renowned for their adherence to the mores of the worlds in which they function, with only the *arriviste* adopting new modes of behaviour and the attitudes to go along with their newfound status.

Had Harry been an entrepreneur who had started out in a council house in Dagenham prior to making a fortune and acquiring the trappings of wealth while remaining proud of his working class roots, or had he done a Cecil Parkinson and replaced his ordinary origins with a 'classy' persona, Meghan would have been perfectly at home in Britain, and would have found both scope for and comfort in her new way of life. She would then have lacked the option of returning to her birthplace as a great star, and would doubtless have settled in a way she never did as a royal. Meghan's revulsion against Harry's friends was not surprising once you realised what her origins and interests were. Although she was really of the No Money category, she had had enough worldly success to have acquired New Money tastes and attitudes, all fuelled with a generous amount of self-awareness. Meghan was intelligent enough to realise that Old Money, whether in the US or the UK, generally finds many of New Money's practices vulgar and crass, and therefore unpleasant to be around.

New Money, on the other hand, finds what it regards as the prissiness and restraint of Old Money constraining, tiresome, and boring. It is also seriously disconcerted by the sudden way Old Money often lapses into unrestrained political incorrectness, riding roughshod over New Money's treasured politically correct attitudes. Inevitably the values of these two worlds collide, and there is no doubt that they did with someone as dogmatically woke and politically correct as Meghan. Of special objection to her was their relish for the traditional country lifestyle, with its emphasis on blood sports; but worst of all, their supreme distaste for personal publicity. Also odious to a luxury-loving fashionista like Meghan was their tolerance of personal discomfort, born of their lifestyle's activities such as hunting, fishing, shooting, and stalking, not to mention the tendency for their houses to be seriously under-heated. This, of course, was because Old Money homes are usually so large (a small house might be thirty rooms, a large one two or three hundred) that only the rooms the family uses on a regular basis will be heated constantly. Even when you stay in beautifully appointed castles like Naworth, you walk from one warm room to another via something on the more Arctic side. Old Money understands that comfort is always relative, that each individual must sacrifice some of what he would prefer in an ideal world if he is to retain the endowments good fortune has provided him with in this one. New Money does not accept like trade-offs like this, the New Age concept of Having It All being something it lives by, or at the very least, aspires to. Old Money would never waste its time on trying to have it all; it knows from generations of acquisitiveness that you can't. It even goes as far as disapproving of such a mandate, dismissing it as greed. Over the centuries, it has learnt that possession might be nine tenths of the law but retention requires self-sacrifice.

New Money is therefore both more demanding and less hardy than Old. What Old Money accepts unflinchingly, New Money regards as a personal assault on its right to be comfortable at all times. Meghan's conduct, with its insistence on her personal comfort being considered before anything else, showed that she was an archetypal evocation of the New Money school of learned softness. It also explained why she saw nothing untoward with frank acquisitiveness and pronounced materialism. New Money is materialistic in a way that no other class in society is. It uses not only itself, but others, to get what it wants. It is ruthless in a way Old Money seldom is. It thinks money is more important than it actually is, that cash can buy what it cannot, and that money is a magic stick rather than a means of exchange. It too often thinks people have a lower value than they do, and that anyone and anything can be used by them without damaging consequence. Usually, it learns the error of its ways in the second and succeeding generations, by which time it has been absorbed into the Old Money set, replicating its values.

Although Meghan is the exception that proves the rule, Old Money people are generally very comfortable to be with as long as you understand what their values are. They have codes of conduct which stretch back to the beginnings of civilisation. They have invisible boundaries which regulate their conduct and wellbeing from the cradle to the grave. New Money and Real Money are far more exciting. Their very lack of knowledge of these invisible boundaries makes for a freedom that is refreshing until you realise that you're at sea with someone who doesn't know how to paddle the boat. Prince Charles's former butler Grant Harrold once said in my presence that he much prefers working for Old

Money rather than New, because people with Old Money treat their staff better than people with New. There are reasons why expressions such as 'rough diamond' or 'not polished' used to be used. New Money people simply do not have the awareness that comes with a heritage stretching back generations. But now that so many of the Old Money people have lost prominence and so many of the New Money people have joined the feast, there has been a relaxation of the rules, which has loosened up behaviour and allowed cross pollination between different social groupings. It is this influx that has allowed even No Money people to take seats in the banqueting hall. Hence why Meghan not only gained access but was welcomed with open arms.

To all intents and purposes, prior to her marriage to Harry, Meghan would have been categorised as a No Money person. While she had made reasonable money following her success in *Suits*, she did not have enough to even buy and furnish a decent sized house such as she and Trevor used to rent, and maintain a reasonable lifestyle, which is the acid test between New Money and No Money. She really was Cinderella at the ball. This provides a partial explanation for why she regards financial independence as being so important. It must be remembered that Meghan's success came late in life. She's only enjoyed it for the last few years. Before that, she was dependent upon men for a roof over her head and the wherewithal to have a half-way decent existence. This dependence on men also explains why she became such an advocate of feminism once she made enough money to stand on her own two feet. Her appreciation of wealth and her left-wing sympathies can also be explained by her antecedents. With her father and mother, she led a *petit bourgeois* existence while being schooled with children from sometimes infinitely richer backgrounds than hers. With Trevor Engelson, she enjoyed a significant upgrade, but it was still only a *bourgeois* existence. Even in Canada, her house was in a resolutely middle class area. Although she got glimpses of a grander way of life, it was only when she married Harry that she actually transited from middle to upper class.

Changing both class and country at the same time is not an easy or straightforward proposition. Inevitably, there has to be a period of adjustment if you are going to make the transition successfully. What worked well in one environment might not in another. In America, where class and classiness have distinctly different connotations from Britain, Meghan's demeanour came across as 'classy'. This was why she had been given the role of Rachel Zane in *Suits* and why she had acquired the followers she did with *The Tig*, where she was able to present herself as an arbiter of style, taste, and discernment, and be accepted as such by her two million followers. In Britain, however, where 'classiness' is something else entirely, Meghan's heightened appreciation of all things material or superior affected the way people reacted to her. They recoiled from her overt materialism and a demeanour which she might have thought was classy but which they regarded as pretentious. The lashings of charm which she deployed to convince people that she was a nice, regular person were also counterproductive; often her manner struck recipients as superficial over-eagerness to please. This got people's backs up the way it did the critics of *Elephants Without Borders*, whose dismissal of her performance had one common thread: insincerity.

For all the doubts about her motives, Meghan is proudly and openly *arriviste*. Initially, this lack of heritage was viewed by the British as a plus, the way it had been with Catherine Middleton and Sophie Rhys Jones. Britons like ordinary people making the grade to greatness as long as they don't get all lah-di-dah and forget their roots. The worst possible message Meghan could have delivered to the British working class was that she was ashamed of those roots, yet this has been the precise message her cold-shouldering of her family conveyed. The fact that Meghan was foreign should also have helped Britons to warm to her, for most Britons take the view that Americans are so different that normal British rules cannot be applied to them. This gives the average American who moves to the United Kingdom a great advantage. Irrespective of the modesty of their antecedents, they are usually welcomed with open arms in a way no Briton with a similar social background would be. All they need to do is show that they respect British ways; they do not even need to ape them, though if they do, that is appreciated. A recent case in point is the television presenter Julie Montagu. A girl from a modest background in Sugar Grove, Illinois, she married the Earl of Sandwich's heir Viscount Hinchingbrooke, and has gone from strength to strength with her natural, unaffected charm and down-to-earth manner. She has never tried to come across as 'classy', which is where Meghan went wrong right from the outset. Unbeknownst to Meghan, what had been her great selling point in the United States and Canada, would become a millstone around her neck in Britain. Had she been less self-consciously 'classy' as she set about asserting how discerning, indeed expert, she was in the finer things of life, she would have escaped the pejorative label of 'common' which Nicky Haslam so pointedly dismissed her with. Had she been like Julie Hinchingbrooke, or frankly North American middle class in her manner like Autumn Phillips, who married the Queen's grandson Peter Phillips and made a very successful transition from being ordinary Canadian girl to distaff connection of the Royal Family, her lack of background would not have been a stumbling block. Autumn is valued as a fully paid-up member of the royal world, and will remain so even though she and Peter have parted. What worked for Autumn and Julie but prevented good adjustment on Meghan's part was her reluctance to unbend and relax into the royal and aristocratic world by ceasing to be 'classy', by being just sweet and charming the way she had been in New York with Serena Williams or in Canada with the Mulroneys and the Trudeaus, instead of believing that once she became a royal highness, it elevated her beyond its natural level.

Meghan's Uncle Mike Markle, who is fond of her and has tried to find an explanation as to why she not only withdrew from both branches of her family but is also so consciously 'classy', believes she has a chip on her shoulder, plainly born of the 'greyness' her identity caused her in her youth. Whether that is so or not, Meghan is certainly a complex individual with much sensitivity who, by her own account, had to swallow many a slight as she worked her way up the ladder. This might have resulted in her creating an outer skin which protects her feelings as it projects to the world the view of herself she would like people to see. Nevertheless, by projecting such a 'classy' exterior and allying it to a consciously woke, left-wing, politically-correct activistic stance which made clear that she disapproved of much of what Harry's friends and their world stood for, she alienated people who wanted to like her but sensed that she did not regard them as worthy of engagement with her. This made many people feel uncomfortable in her presence, causing them to withdraw, though she did hit it off with Charlie van Straubenzee's wife Daisy Jenks, bonding over their shared love of shoes.

Of course, there is another interpretation which is worth considering as to why Meghan failed so utterly to make friends in Britain. She might well have decided from the word go, or from early on, that she wanted no part of Harry's world. Although she was too canny to say so, the indications are that from well before the marriage, it was obvious to everyone - and would therefore have also been clear to someone as bright as Meghan - that she was unsuited to the role of royal duchess and that she was not fitting in comfortably to Harry's personal world. Maybe it would never have been a good fit, if only because she and it were so alien to each other, but she certainly made enough of an effort between meeting him and marrying him to move from girlfriend to fiancée then to wife, strengthening the relationship with each passing day until they were an indestructible unit.

Because of the concerns as to how she would fit into his world, none of his friends or relations wanted him to marry her. Several of them, such as his brother William, his good friend Tom Inskip, his grandfather Prince Philip and his grandmother the Queen, tried to counsel caution. In each case, Harry resented the concern, which he took to be unwarranted intrusion and reacted against emotionally.

It is a testament to the strength of their attraction that within weeks of meeting Meghan, Harry was completely in her thrall, and has remained so. Patently, she wanted him too. She is extremely loving towards him, supremely tactile, and even people who dislike her and doubt her sincerity will acknowledge that she covers him with love. Those who admire the couple are convinced that they are ideally suited, while those who do not hope that she wants him for himself and not just for the springboard to greatness. Which is what many people in Britain of all colours, creeds and classes fear is her real motive.

CHAPTER 11

What makes Meghan and Harry's story so interesting is how split perceptions are regarding them. Harry is more easily explained. The couple's admirers think that he has found himself his ideal mate, that they are well suited and that they balance each other out perfectly. This view is shared even by astrologers. WASP America's Astrologer Suprema, Mary Michele Rutherfurd, states that their charts are astonishingly compatible, down to such things as Meghan mothering Harry and Harry liking being mothered. Off this premise, which is ratified by the evident affection the couple has for each other, they will go on to have a long and happy marriage.

On the other hand, their detractors claim that Harry is Meghan's useful idiot, a 'pussy-whipped' dolt who deserves the nickname 'Blow Jobs Harry' as he has fallen under the spell of a brighter but ultimately ruthless spouse who is using him and will discard him when she is through milking the situation for all she can get out of it. Theirs is a harsh assessment, but they maintain that Meghan is a lone wolf who disguises her motives with charm as she develops what Nikki Priddy called 'strategic' relationships for her own advancement and self-aggrandisement. They cynically believe that whenever she is ready to move on, she does it with such alacrity that it must raise doubts as to whether her connection with them was ever as deep nor as heartfelt as they thought it was. Until then, though, she is so wonderful that she seems too good to be true.

Her detractors claim that no one who is sincere makes such a show of being extravagantly loving and self-abnegating the way she does. Some of them even disparage her acting ability, stating that she consistently behaves in such an extreme, over-the-top, hyper-emotionalistic, actressy way, even as she is covering Harry with love, that she comes across more as a parasite clinging to a tree than someone who is sincere emotionally. They say that she substitutes effusiveness for profundity, and that her main talent is not even her acting ability but her energetic ruthlessness. Rather than praise her for the consistency which is one of her more pronounced characteristics, they regard it as proof that her whole life is an act. Off that hypothesis, it doesn't matter whether she is behind a camera, in front of it, or even in front of an audience of one; as long as there is someone to play to, she does so from a script (which might be written for her when she is in front of the camera, but at all other times she writes herself), projecting an image that is self-serving for the duration the act works in her favour. They believe that she uses people to achieve her goals, and that her interest in others lasts only as long as their presence provides her with the opportunities and rewards she requires from them. They do not accept that her independence of spirit is a quality; they regard it as evidence of something altogether more ominous.

Despite their scepticism, her critics cannot avoid conceding that Meghan develops intense relationships, some of which last for years, and that the people with whom she is involved invariably sing her praises for the duration of the relationship. Although she does have a pattern of ghosting people when relationships sour, her supporters feel that this is not because she is the ruthless opportunist her detractors regard her as being, but because she is a sweet, sensitive soul who prefers terminating relationships with a minimum of fuss and unpleasantness rather than sullying herself with the unpleasantness of explanations and recrimina- tions. Irrespective of your take on the merits of her exit strategy, there can be no dispute that she has the ability to convince those with whom she is involved that she is a warm, sincere, self-denying individual who thinks only of others and never of herself, though she also expects men to make and keep her happy.

So many people to whom I have spoken have used the same words to describe Meghan that a pattern emerges. She is bright. She is opinion- ated and passionate in expressing her beliefs. She can be vivacious and charming. She is devoted, radiating warmth, interest, and care. She is energetic. She has a truly sweet manner and strikes people who like her as vulnerable. She is high-octane and functions at a fever pitch emotion- ally. She is both sensational and sensationalistic. She can be huge fun. She can be enthusiastic to the point of freneticism, but people who like that about her believe that she is delightful and sincere, though others who prefer people functioning in a lower key hear the clanking sound of an empty vessel making a lot of noise. She is very exacting and demanding. She is so upfront about what she wants that her admirers regard this as a commendable virtue indicating honesty and integrity, though her critics view it as a deplorable vice suggestive of insensitivity and bumptiousness. She is so open about being ambitious, so proud of the relish she has for the things of this world, that she comes across as honest to those who sympathise with her worldliness, while at the same time turning off others. Like her or loathe her, she is charismatic. She draws you in, and those who relate to her find her wholly convincing, while those who do not accuse her of having the feigned sincerity of a practised actress or true phoney. The two most frequently used phrases to describe her are 'strong' and 'hard as nails', but people who do not take to her also consistently say 'there is something about her that is slightly off'. When I tried to nail down why they felt like that, they often could not articulate anything specific, though they all ended up saying that she somehow doesn't ring true. As one of Harry's friends said, 'He thinks she's so good that she's true. I think she's too good to be true.'

In private, Meghan complained bitterly about her critics. As Harry has confirmed in his postings, they both found it extremely painful to her to be doubted the way she often was. I am told they really struggled to understand how so many people could fail to recognise how self-evidently well-meaning and wonderful Meghan is. This created a feeling of being unfairly martyred, and they blamed not only the 'nasty' people who thought like that, but anyone who provided them with a platform. This fed their hatred of the press, which one royal told me 'borders on paranoia'.

Reconciling the opposing perceptions of Meghan is well-nigh impossible. To those who know and love her, she is almost the 'angel' her mother calls her. Rather more controversial is the opinion of a psychologist to whom I spoke. While her admirers consider her an extremely sensitive person whose every thought and feeling are governed by a sweet-nature and a good heart, he concluded that descriptions of her correlate with sociopathic as well as narcissistic tendencies. Meghan has pronounced charm, charisma and social skills, all of which narcissists and sociopaths possess in greater measure than the average person. But what tipped the scales for him as the decisive factor was her propensity for wanting sympathy. People with sociopathic tendencies evidently possess a greater need for sympathy than the general population. As one in every twenty five individuals falls within this spectrum, and few of them typify the popular view of murderous crazies while many are high flyers in high functioning roles, sociopaths, or people with sociopathic tendencies, proliferate far more than the public realises. In his opinion, Meghan's interview with Tom Bradby was a dead giveaway not only of her hunger for sympathy but also of another sociopathic trait, namely lack of insight into how inappropriate her requirement of having her needs fulfilled, even in disproportionate circumstances, can be.

Possibly it was not Meghan's fault that the tape was cut the way it was. Maybe ITV was responsible for how self-obsessed and self-pitying she seemed as she complained about her great pain, in not receiving the emotional support and attention she required while adjusting to her new life of even greater privilege and opportunity than her old life, which had not been exactly underprivileged either. But her complaints seemed weirdly disproportionate to this psychologist, made as they were while she and Bradby were surrounded by South African women with genuinely significant daily struggles for life, liberty, health, food and safety. These women and these issues were meant to be the true focus of the programme. Yet, so complete was Meghan's self-belief, so pronounced her need to obtain the support of viewers by gaining their sympathy for the hardships she was enduring in her difficult life, that she did not stop to question whether a royal duchess, happily married to a man who adores her, who has a beautiful, healthy son and a life of extreme privilege, should be maintaining in the face of so much genuine deprivation that her own suffering was so great that it could even warrant a mention alongside poverty, rape, mutilation, murder, starvation, and the many other issues that had been addressed by the programme as the South African women's lives unfurled in their full horror.

Harry acquitted himself with equal emotional fervour during the interview. While his admirers may have been filled with sympathy when he confessed how every time he sees a flash bulb he is catapulted back to his mother's death, those who take a more measured view of the responsibilities and privileges of a prince had cause to question whether he too had started to wallow in rather too much hyper-emotionalistic self-pity when a healthy dose of gratitude for his advantages might have been a more appropriate response to the many privileges that went along with his position. It is interesting that no one to date has questioned whether Harry has narcissistic and sociopathic tendencies commensurate with those questioned about Meghan, when, in every respect save intelligence, he has mirrored her, as his conduct throughout the Bradby ITV programme demonstrated. He too came across as someone who wants sympathy intermingled with admiration, all of which is offset by a notable lack of insight as to how blessed he truly is. Every criticism levelled at Meghan could be fairly directed at Harry. The only member of that triumvirate who justifiably escaped criticism was Tom Bradby. A journalist, who asks a question that pushes the boundaries of an interview into terrain it has no business occupying, cannot be fairly criticised, nor can his producers and editors when they come to compile the programme, if a couple as experienced in PR as Harry and Meghan decide to compare their own anguish with the Golgotha of others.

There are moments in life when people open their mouths and in a few choice words reveal more than they intend to. This happened to Oscar Wilde during his second trial for sodomy, when the prosecution barrister Sir Edward (later Lord) Carson asked him if he had ever kissed a certain servant boy. Wilde, who had been maintaining that he was not homosexual, truthfully and revealingly replied, 'Oh dear, no. He was a particularly plain boy - unfortunately ugly - I pitied him for it.' Just as how the jurors were able to conclude that no heterosexual man would have answered that question with reference to the looks of the boy, and thereby found Wilde guilty of the offence for which he was being tried, so too did many viewers of the ITV interview leap to an elementary conclusion when Meghan said that she often tells Harry that the purpose of life is not to survive, but to thrive. To her admirers, she was being her frank, honest self, articulating one of the guiding principles of her life. Her admission was not merely a sign that she has the healthy appetite of someone who appreciates a fully laden table, but that she is honest and up-front about her desire to have the best and the most of everything.

In doing so the way she did, she also confirmed that she does not regard it as shameful to want more. This is something that does not perturb her admirers, who see nothing wrong with someone wanting to have it all if they can get it all.

Her detractors, however, took another view. To them, only an unconscionable egotist, and a rapacious one at that, could state on television, in the middle of a South African wilderness surrounded by some of the poorest people whose everyday life is an uncertain struggle for survival, that the purpose of life is not survival but thriving. What appeared to be insensitivity had the possibility of another interpretation, and a more harmless one at that. The psychologist hypothesised that Meghan, who has a very American attitude to poverty, was simply being frank. She accepts it more frankly and shamelessly than Europeans do. To many of the Britons watching her on television, however, she came across not as an enlightened woman who loves the poor, but as an entitled, insensitive First Worlder. What her admirers saw as healthy and frank self-empowerment, her detractors saw as a spoilt brat who has never learnt where the boundaries should lie, who has been raised to have boundless ambition, who displays boundless greed and boundless entitlement, and is so shameless about self-aggrandisement as to flagrantly, almost boastfully, denounce the ability of some of the poorest people on earth, whose struggle is elemental, to know what the true purpose of life is, which by her pronouncement was to thrive rather than just survive.

There might also have been more to Meghan's tremulous confession of the hardships she had faced than meets the eye. She had studied Diana Wales closely. Her stated ambition is not only to emulate her, but to outstrip her. Just as how Diana used the books that I and Andrew Morton wrote, the press through friendly journalists such as Richard Kay, and her television interview with Martin Bashir, to manoeuvre herself from one point to another, so too might Meghan have been laying the ground for her departure from the confines of the royal way of life by establishing grounds for the public sympathising with her misery, and therefore giving her their blessings to return to her homeland.

Undoubtedly, Meghan disliked the royal way of life. She disliked its constraints, its sacrifices, its drudgery, its discipline, its lack of financial reward. She had never seen any reason to get out of bed and give herself away for nothing, which is what the royal way wanted her to do. No Mayors of Surbiton for her, thank you very much, when she could be paid hundreds of thousands of dollars, maybe even a million or more, to make appearances for the same length of time on the other side of the Atlantic. If she wanted to give her time or self away to charitable causes, she would do it, but on her terms, for her ultimate enrichment, whether that be spiritual, emotional, or financial, and not to embellish the cause of the British monarchy.

Since then, she and Harry have shown that they fully intend to put their money where their mouths are. They have not only expanded their financial horizons, but have also set up a financial structure which allows them to acquire a marital pot that is indisputably their own. This means that, in the event of a divorce, each of them will have access to the joint fortune they will make. Until that new development, Meghan had no access to any of Harry's money because the British legal system fully protected his fortune. It says much about Harry's love for and belief in Meghan that he would do something like that. In Britain, people with inherited wealth, being alert to the dangers of divorce settlements, have their money so tightly tied up that adventuresses cannot gain access to it. This has become especially necessary since recent changes to English divorce law have made London the divorce capital of the world. There have been cases in which childless wives, whose marriages were only a few years old, were granted 50% of their husband's entire wealth. Old Money has been so threatened by inheritance and income tax for the last seventy-five years that its possessors already had strictures in place which lessened the danger of greedy spouses getting sizeable divorce settlements, but even so people have still had to implement new safeguards to protect their palaces, castles, properties and chattels against nest-feathering divorces.

While it would be unworthy of us to think that Meghan wanted anything but love from a prospective spouse, despite Lizzie Cundy's confession that she had asked her to introduce her to a rich and famous Englishman, once she ended up with Harry she found herself in a whole new ballpark. Up to then, her men had been No Money men bordering on New Money. Now, however, she was married into one of the oldest and most tightly sewn up Old Money families. This meant that she would walk with little or no money in the event of a divorce, for Harry's assets were ring-fenced. Being unable to make money while they remained proper members of the Royal Family, with all the financial constraints inherent in those positions, the reality was that should their marriage end in divorce Meghan would leave with only what she had brought into it. Moreover, the Hague Convention, to which the United States is a signatory, meant that she would be trapped living in Britain in the event of a divorce, for any children of the marriage would be obliged to remain in the UK as long as she and Harry were living there at the time of a separation. As Harry is a devoted father, Meghan will have known that there was no way he would agree to her taking his child or children back to the US should they separate. She, however, is extremely maternal as well as foresighted, so she had a second good reason to move her base of operations.

From here on in, not only will Harry be the one trapped in a foreign country should the marriage end and he wants to be where his children are growing up, but any money they make will go into the marital pot. Meghan will walk with a whole lot more money than she would other-wise have done had she remained a proper royal. Because Harry has been so willing to step out of the protection of Britain into the exposure of America, he must trust Meghan implicitly; or he is truly as desperate as one of his cousins believes him to be.

Their move to the United States has seriously undermined Harry's position in other ways too. Meghan, it must be remembered, is an American citizen. Harry cannot become an American without losing his title and royal rank, both of which he would have to renounce to become naturalised. At the very most, he can only become an American resident. That is a process that takes time for most people and, judging by the abusive way he and Meghan have spoken about Donald Trump, it is very unlikely that the President will be cutting any corners on their behalf. This means that Meghan is the only partner with earning capacity at the moment. Even if Harry accompanies her to events, he will not be able to be financially recompensed until his status is regularised. Meghan will therefore be the only earner in the family for the foreseeable future. In the event of a divorce, that puts her in an even stronger position financially.

Meghan is a planner. She is proudly strategic, thorough, and considered. She seeks and takes the best advice. Long before her and Harry's departure from Britain, she had her business manager Andrew Meyer reincorporate in Delaware Frim Fram Inc., the California-based company which ran *The Tig* and was shut down in 2017 before her marriage to Harry. The merit of Delaware is that Meyer could be listed as the company secretary without its owner's identity being revealed, but the mere fact that Meghan opted to revive a company rather than start an entirely new one shows that on some level she intended to leave traces rather than assure herself of the privacy a new name would have done. This her admirers will say is reflective of the fact that she is such a loyal person that she even retains connections to her old companies, while her detractors will conclude that she leaves clues lying around so that the press will make the connection and write about her, in the process helping her to fulfill her ambition to become the most famous woman in the world.

Whatever her motive, Meghan and Harry set about fine-tuning their other priority as soon as they arrived in the United States. Controlling the British press while also managing their publicity in America so that the public would see only the facade they wished to present became their prime target. This did not require quite as much skill or finesse as the uninitiated might imagine. Meghan had *People* magazine in her pocket and Sunshine Sachs behind them. The American press, as previously stated, is basically a lot more amenable to printing what celebrities want than its British counterpart. As long as Meghan and Harry could drip feed *People*, *Page Six* and a few other vital portals the stories they wanted written, that was their American coverage taken care of. They had also done a Diana, cooperating with two amenable journalists, Omid Scobie and Carolyn Durand, who would be publishing a book in the summer of 2020 which detailed their version of events. They had no doubt that this would become a worldwide bestseller, increasing their fame and adding to their fortune by opening up all sorts of new opportunities for them.

The British press was another story entirely. Harry's irrational and longstanding hatred and Meghan's determination that reports about her must reflect only what she regarded as fair representation were backed up by Sunshine Sachs's aggressive tactics. They were all still feeling their way towards victory, namely the muzzling of any dissent while rewarding tame journalists with information. But they were building up to another attack, which would come soon enough.

In the meantime Instagram proved useful, as the couple proclaimed their desire for privacy on the one hand while on the other hand embarking upon a series of posts that increased their profile. Harry, still in England working out the details of their departure from the Royal Family while his wife had returned to Canada at the first opportunity, then launched a second excoriating attack on the British press, stating that Meghan's privacy had been violated by a paparazzo photographing her with a long distance lens as she walked their dogs Guy and Oz, with Archie strapped to her front and two protection officers, one Canadian, the other British, bringing up the rear. Once more admirers and detractors of the couple were at loggerheads, the former sympathising with poor Meghan, who couldn't even take a walk with her two protection officers, baby, and dogs without being interfered with by what Ken Sunshine so eloquently called the stalkerazzi, the latter deciding that Meghan, who was photographed smiling broadly for the benefit of the camera, must have colluded with the photographer as no one walks around like that unless they know they're being photographed.

To the British press, this was reminiscent of Diana, who was always accusing them of violating her privacy while covertly setting up photo ops with them. It left them unmoved but irritated at what they regarded as the couple's hypocrisy and uncalled-for victim-signalling. The Royal Family are public figures, supported by the state, i.e. the British taxpayer, and when they are out in public they are fair game to be photographed, especially when it appears as if the photos were staged.

Americans, with their different approach to the press and no royal family of their own to provide them with a common point of reference, might find it difficult to appreciate to what extent Harry and Meghan's complaints damaged the couple's interests. The royal couple had successfully avoided any press attention they had not themselves orchestrated for some considerable length of time. It was therefore felt that they were rather underhandedly trying to kill two birds with one stone. On the one hand, they were keeping themselves in the news, while they casting themselves as victims - yet again, their detractors said. The fact that Meghan and Harry had been coming and going for two months without the paparazzi having violated their privacy, suggested to cynics that it wasn't only the press who were being set up, but the public as well.

No sooner did Harry return to Canada that he and Meghan gave an insight into how adept they were at avoiding the press when it suited them. They snuck out of their bolthole on Vancouver Island undetected, were driven to the airport, boarded the JP Morgan Gulfstream company jet, flew to Palm Beach and landed that same evening, all in absolute anonymity. This suggested that the press might not have them under constant observation the way they were suggesting it did.

No matter what, Meghan and Harry remained assiduous in protecting their privacy. Now that they were private individuals rather than working royals, they no longer bothered about the contradiction inherent in eco-warriors like them, who had warned the world how 'every action counts' and people should not do anything to increase their 'carbon footprint' as 'the planet's in danger and it's up to each of us', significantly expanding their footprint by using private jets. But Harry had an answer for his critics. He had to protect his family by that mode of travel. It was not a luxury. It was a necessity. Their circumstances were so special that commercial travel was simply impossible.

Still undetected by the press who were clearly not adept at discovering their every move, Meghan and Harry spent their first night in Palm Beach with Serena Williams in her villa. The following day they journeyed to Miami, where they joined 425 guests who included the discredited former Prime Minister Tony Blair, half Greek half Irish (Guinness) shipping heir Stavros Niarchos III and his new wife, the ex-Mrs Roman Abramovich Dasha Zhukova, Alex Rodriguez and Jennifer Lopez, Magic Johnson, British architect Lord Foster of Thames Bank, and Patriots owner Robert Kraft, at the JP Morgan Alternative Investment Summit. This was held in a sprawling tent erected in the grounds of the five star 1 Hotel on Miami's South Beach. To reaffirm the importance of those who were present, security was tighter than usual, with a six foot wall erected to prevent tourists who would be walking along the beach's famous boardwalk from peering in.

This was the Duke and Duchess of Sussex's first post-abdication engagement and they could not have chosen better in financial terms. Irrespective of whether they were actually earning money for the talk they were about to give, Meghan and Harry now had access to JP Morgan's coffers. There was no question of them resisting the lure of that lucre hereafter, nor of spurning the offers of the other major financial institutions who were being lined up by their representatives to avail themselves of the soon-to-be post-royals' services. This was what they had swapped the constraints of Britain for, and there was no doubt, from the way they behaved, that they were absolutely thrilled to be there.

Meghan's friend Gayle King introduced her in the warm, exciting and friendly manner that a true professional has. Meghan then played on the audience's heartstrings by revealing how very much she loves Harry, who is, of course, a wonderful man worthy of the love of a good woman, and how her love had saved him from the horrors of a royal life without financial independence. Having set the stage amongst this clutch of multimillionaires and billionaires, all of whom would be sure to appreciate the importance of money but equally understand the significance of royalty, which usually isn't for sale or hire, hence the high premium placed upon its worth, she then introduced Harry. He gave an impassioned, highly emotional speech about the mental challenges he has had to face as a result of his mother's death. Meghan is known to write her own speeches as well as Harry's, and the end product was moving and held nothing back. Harry's suffering was laid bare for all to see and empathise with. He hit home with how badly his mother's death had affected him, resulting in his entering therapy aged 28. He talked a lot about his and Meghan's decision to step down as senior royals, laying the blame at the feet of the trauma he had suffered and how he doesn't want the same to happen to his family. In so doing, he introduced a non sequitur, for there are no parallels between Harry and Meghan's situations and Diana's or indeed Harry's childhood circumstances, nor has there ever been any prospect that what happened to him as a result of her death happening to Archie. He then shared how painful separating from the Royal Family had been for him, but confessed that he had no regrets about the decision he had made, for this was the only way to preserve his family unit. In so doing, he implied that his marriage might not have survived without his sacrifice of giving up his country and royal life for what would essentially be a California life. He maintained that he and Meghan remain optimistic about the future, optimistic about being able to be financially independent, while working on the projects that mean a lot to them, and how they will be supporting the charities they believe in. To one canny observer, 'it was a neatly packaged bundle, somewhat illogical but very emotional, all adding up to: Gimme the money in exchange for my class.'

Mark Borkowski was but one of the many commentators to question whether such conduct wouldn't ultimately 'cheapen' and 'tarnish' the brand. 'This shows how difficult it's going to be. They've got to make a lot of money and they are going to slip up along the way. The worry is; How many of these types of gigs are there going to be? How often can Harry play the card about his mental health?'

Piers Morgan, who lost his father when he was a little boy, condemned Harry for 'profiting' from his mother's death by sharing intimate details of how he had coped with it in a commercial setting, stating, 'there's a big difference between talking about it to raise public awareness of grief-related mental health issues, and doing it privately for a big fat fee to a bunch of super-rich bankers, business tycoons, politicians and celebrities. By commercially exploiting his mother's death to make vast pots of money like this, Harry is surely behaving in exactly the same way he professes to despise from the media?' A disproportionately large percentage of social media agreed, accusing Harry of cashing in on his mother's memory. A Twitter user summarised the consensus: 'I'm literally disgusted that Harry is now dragging up Diana's death to earn money. I really didn't think he would stoop that low. This is disgusting on a whole different level. Shameful. Their titles must be stripped completely.'

Not everyone shared these sentiments. Forbes Magazine, knowing that financial considerations usually come before high-flown beliefs, had the opinion that 'it was a very smart move to get in with some of the world's richest people. The conference is all about building wealth for future generations, and making the world better for future generations, a topic close to Harry's heart.' There was no doubt that Meghan, who has a longstanding reputation for being a networker *par excellence,* understood that the way for them to make money was to link up with the richest companies and the richest people on earth. There was speculation that the Sussexes received $1m for the speech he made. What was less speculative is the way that world works. From here on in, they will have forged a relationship with JP Morgan, who will trot them out as ambassadors, or guests, or whatever is the most convenient or appropriate label to give them, as and when required. All for fees ranging from $250,000 to $1m+, depending on the occasion and their degree of input.

While commentators in Britain have decried their selling out, and believe that the Sussexes will inevitably becoming an increasingly busted flush, the more seasoned and sophisticated ones in America will understand that there is always a clientele ready and willing to pay good money for personalities, even those on the decline as long as they once possessed sufficient eminence to be categorised as A-listers. Tony Blair's presence alone confirms that JP Morgan is none too fussy about associating itself with eminences who have peaked, including politicians who have been accused of fostering war crimes, albeit war crimes on the right side of the fence. While the former Prime Minister clears rooms in Britain, he still has drawing power in the US, and Meghan's statements confirm that she fully expects Harry and herself to emulate Blair not only in earning power but to surpass him as a star attraction in her native land. Her assessment, that British royals will be more valuable and prestigious than a former Prime Minister, might well turn out to be right, for Meghan and Sunshine Sachs understand how America and American attractions work, and, if they have anything to do with it, the Duke and Duchess of Sussex will turn into the main attractions of the A-List world.

CHAPTER 12

The Sussexes, whose royalty is their main attribute, are still royal, if only just, and therefore they will continue to have a value, especially in the United States, where their reputations remain unsullied in a way they no longer are in Britain. It is difficult to envisage them losing popularity in the United States to the extent they have in Britain, or to such an extent that they become a valueless commodity. They will therefore more than likely always have people who want to read about them. With that will come commercial activity to fill their coffers and enhance such popularity as they possess amongst their followers. Nevertheless, they face the danger of ever diminishing returns with the passage of time. The dilemma for public figures like Tony Blair and Sussexes is simple. The more you sell yourself, the less desirable you become. But that does not mean they still won't have a high monetary value. It's just that busted flushes are less valuable than they would have been, had their reputations remained pristinely above commercial activity.

To their supporters, Meghan and Harry's pursuit of wealth is not an ignoble activity but a noble quest for financial independence. But to their critics, the couple has been justifying what is essentially greed as a quest for financial independence when they already possess it. Harry is worth some $40m, while their income from the British state, exclusive of expenses amounting to at least another $2m, was well in excess of $3m per annum. Meghan herself was worth at least $4m. According to that reasoning, they have been trying to excuse extreme acquisitiveness as a quest for financial independence, when in fact the former is greed and the latter is a sleight of hand.

Criticism aside, the reality is Meghan and Harry simply do not have the amount of money they require to fund the lifestyle she, as opposed to he wants, or to secure her future irrespective of what it is. Because they cannot say this, they pass off what to the average Briton looks like inexcusable rapacity as something that is intelligible and desirable to the average American: financial independence.

Both Harry and Meghan have well-trodden track records with charity, and while the Doubting Thomases point out that her forays were always to her ultimate benefit, his were not. There is no doubt that Harry has a streak of care born of exposure through his royal links, to include his mother's charity work and his father's even greater charitable accomplishments. Royalty always supports charity, so it was inevitable that this would continue to play a part in their lives. Prior to Meghan's entry into his life, the idea of actually mixing such activities with personal benefit would have been beyond contemplation.

In Spring 2020, they took the first steps to set up the entity which they intend to utilise as they go about doing their charitable and humanitarian activities, by hiring as their chief of staff and executive director Catherine St. Laurent. She was the director of Pivotal Ventures, Melinda Gates' foundation for women and families. They later announced that they had named this entity Archewell, following the Queen's refusal to allow them to use Sussex Royal, when the prestigious right-wing broadsheet *The Telegraph* in Britain asked them about it. They explained on one of their direct posts to supporters, 'Like you, our focus is on supporting efforts to tackle the global COVID-19 pandemic but faced with this information coming to light, we felt compelled to share the story of how this came to be. We connected to this concept for the charitable organisation we hoped to build one day, and it became the inspiration for our son's name. To do something of meaning, to do something that matters. Archewell is a name that combines an ancient word for strength and action, and another that evokes the deep resources we must draw upon. We look forward to launching Archewell when the time is right.'

This was not the first time they had taken the time and trouble to explain that their charitable enterprise would be neither a charity nor a foundation but an entity which will assist others as and when they feel the need. Their flexible and unstructured approach will assure them of maximum scope for manoeuvre as they go about finding causes to support while also providing them with financial freedom. Although Harry and Meghan have maintained that a fundamental part of their goal will always be their humanitarian work, the reality is that financial reward has been an equally powerful consideration. Had altruism been their sole or even their main motivation, they would have been able to exercise far greater influence and do far more sterling work from within the Royal Family. As independent operatives, they will always be in a different category and will, as such, be able to coin in rewards that could never have been theirs had they remained working royals.

Had they remained in the royal fold, Meghan and Harry would have had to rub along in what they now regard as relative penury: an approximate income from the royal coffers of $3m or $4m per annum, another $1m or $2m per annum in expenses, an equal sum for her clothes, aside from top-ups from Prince Charles's Duchy of Cornwall into another seven or so figures, not to mention the free housing they would have been given. If you compare all that labour with being flown by private jet from wherever you're basing yourself, turning up at an agreed venue and speaking for forty five minutes about yourself or some cause dear to your heart, and earning a quarter of your annual British income in less than an hour, it's obvious what will win if you desire financial independence, as they have said they do.

Hopefully Meghan and Harry will be able to create a charitable entity which is convincing enough for them to achieve some of the good they would otherwise have been able to do as royals. Nevertheless, they will find themselves saddled with problems that would not have existed had they remained within the royal fold. By linking charity and humanitarianism with themselves now that they are avowed financial agents, they will inevitably find themselves being suspected of profiting for their own monetary reward. Where formerly their presence would have been perceived as being a pure benefit, they will hereafter have to guard against questions being asked as to how the financial rewards are divided between their entity and the couple themselves. Of course, they have excellent financial advisors as well as superb PR representatives who are well practised in presenting one thing as another and vociferously lambasting any who question their claims. Nevertheless, the danger they hereafter face is one aspect of their operation demeaning the other.

As a result, they will inevitably have to cope with the overt and covert ill effects that suspicion brings in its wake. That is not to say that they will not be able to accomplish some good in their charitable endeavours, but it is to say that they will accomplish less than they would otherwise have been able to do, unless they are very careful and resourceful. Their aim is to end up covered in glory, acknowledged as the world's most benevolent couple, and they might well achieve their objective. But they will need to be very careful as they go about doing so, for the one thing the press on both sides of the Atlantic likes more than the privileged flourishing is the privileged tripping themselves up.

In America especially, there are a thousand and one ways in which charity, philanthropy and humanitarianism benefit the individuals raising funds. These include such standard subtleties as generous expenses, tax breaks, and quid pro quo deals. These are the creative processes which Buckingham Palace has always avoided and would have wished Meghan and Harry to avoid. They are also what will bring the Sussexes the financial independence they want, and with those benefits will come a host of dangers unless they are careful.

Although it might have appeared to the uninformed outside that JP Morgan had been the only financial institution with which Meghan and Harry have been dealing, since 2019, they have also been forging links with Goldman Sachs, ostensibly on behalf of charity but again with the couple benefiting financially once the fig leaf of humanitarianism is cast aside and both sides get down to the real business of exploiting each other financially. For woke activists whose concern for the environment is so great that Harry sometimes struggles to get out of bed, his and Meghan's choice of Goldman Sachs as their second institutional benefactor might seem surprising. This is a company which was criticised during the Credit Crunch for unethical conduct as it bet against financial products it was also recommending to clients, in the process making itself billions while costing its clients a commensurate amount. This resulted in them agreeing to pay $5.1 billion to settle accusations of wrongdoing in their RMBS business with the US Justice Department and state agencies including the New York Attorney General's Office. A decade later, they were still being fined for malfeasance, this time £34.3m by the British Financial Conduct Authority for misreporting more than 200 transactions over a ten year period. Had Harry and Meghan still been functioning under the aegis of the Royal Family, there is no doubt that they would have been prevented from entering into ongoing relationships with institutions whose performance has attracted such penalties. But now that they are free agents, they are able to make what deals they wish, though the hope remains that they will not end up tainted the way the former Duke and Duchess of Palma de Mallorca were.

To ensure that they retained the liberty to wheel and deal as they saw fit, Meghan and Harry closed down their royal office in England. This meant that the limited policing to which they were subject disappeared. They gathered their Buckingham Palace staff together and gave all fifteen members of them notice at the same time. 'This came as a bolt out of the blue,' one of them told a friend of mine. 'No one saw it coming.' All of them had displayed commendable loyalty and tremendous dedication, sometimes in the face of great provocation, as they were the ones who were the frontline operatives dealing not only with a critical press but also an upset couple who could not handle the frustrations placed in their way. As a result, neither Meghan nor Harry had been easy to work for, nor had their staff found the tasks with which they were faced cut and dried. Despite this, they were, to a man and woman, committed, and expected, when they were hired, that they would remain *en poste* for a considerable length of time.

Royal positions used to be for life, and while they have become merely long lasting, they are not expected to be transient appointments. Yet that is what all the Sussex jobs turned out to be. Some, like Sarah Latham, were controversial, though she has behaved so impeccably that she has been snapped up by the Queen to advise on special projects, reporting directly to Her Majesty's Private Secretary Edward Young. However most, like Fiona McIlwham, their Private Secretary who was on secondment from the Foreign and Commonwealth Office, were not. David Watkins, poached from the fashion house *Burberry* to act as their social media expert, found himself out of a job when he had been promised job security, as was Marnie Gaffney, assistant communications secretary who had helped to organise their tours of Australia and Africa. All had performed excellently, had given constructive advice, had often tried to fulfill their tasks under extremely trying conditions, not the least of which was the counterfoil office across the Atlantic Ocean pushing a different agenda and causing many of the problems with which they then had to deal. This of course is what sealed their fates, for Meghan and Harry did not want to hear that associating with companies like JP Morgan or Goldman Sachs on an ongoing basis was tantamount to despoiling their royal status, nor were they prepared to run the risk of having their Buckingham Palace office scupper deals by tipping off the powers-that-be about activities that would be deemed dubious in Britain but would be regarded as admirably sharp in America. Like all people who operate at the highest level, Harry and Meghan wanted to achieve the maximum that the traffic would bear, and did not wish to be limited with what the palace regarded as the niceties of what is suitable and unsuitable for royalty. As someone from the palace told me, 'Meghan's attitude is: All dollar bills are green, and once they're safely in the bank, it doesn't matter whence they came. All that matters is that they're there. Harry backs her up totally, in this as in everything else.'

Ultimately, Harry and Meghan have only one thing to offer that no one else does: his royalty. Neither of them has a talent beyond putting themselves forward as performers on the world stage. Being good public speakers is one thing, another is what do they have to say? As long as they were functioning under the royal umbrella, they were protected against the perception of opportunism, but now that they are openly in the marketplace, they no longer enjoy the kudos that non-commercial royals possess. They are in reality royals for sale or hire, a tricky position to be in while having to retain the prestige customarily associated with the non-commercialism of royalty.

Other royals, over the decades, have tried to convert their prestige into dollar bills. Ultimately, all failed. Whether it was King Michael of Romania, whose grandmother Queen Marie had been so popular that she was given a ticker tape parade down Wall Street, or King Peter of Yugoslavia, or the descendants of Russian, German and Austrian, Italian, Greek, Danish and Spanish monarchs, none of them found it possible in the long run to alchemise the glitter of royalty into serious money. They either married it, or they learnt to do without it, for, after the initial flurry, during which they were offered coinage appropriate to their rank, interest waned. Of course, Meghan has an advantage none of them had. She is an American, and moreover one who is experienced in working the entertainment industry to her advantage. On the other hand, she has so far been more Hope Cooke, former Queen of Sikkim, than Grace Kelly, late Princess of Monaco. The appeal of royalty, as the Canadians noted so clearly when it appeared that Harry and Meghan hoped to join them permanently, is that it is foreign, non-resident, and inaccessible.

Despite this, Harry and Meghan have a game plan and they have adhered to it. It is well thought out and maximises their chances of success, though this is far from assured, at least at the level and to the extent to which they aspire. The tariff for their services has been set so high that only billionaires and their ilk can afford them. The only billionaire couple to step forward incontrovertibly has been Bill and Melinda Gates. With their international profile as humanitarians involved in global health, and with similarly woke credentials, the Gateses had everything they could possibly want in terms of prestige except for a royal couple in their stable. Now they have the Duke and Duchess of Sussex, and it will be interesting to see how this relationship evolves. To what extent will the four of them embark upon cooperative arrangements or joint ventures? They have enough in common to forge a strong, ongoing relationship, and behind the scenes they have been developing it.

There have even been rumours that Bill Gates might run for president in 2024 or even 2028. If that is so, it will only be a matter of time before some journalist sympathetic to the Sussexes suggests Meghan as a running mate.

Life at the top is not so cluttered that couples with a lot in common can fail to welcome each other. As mentioned earlier, the human element should never be discounted. Bill and Melinda Gates have so few other couples who share their level of prestige, allied to their political and humanitarian sympathies, that it should be no surprise that they have relished associating with a couple whose identities reflect theirs in significant ways. As that couple has brought to the relationship something they lack, they have reciprocated commensurately.

However, the couples are clearly unequal in important ways. Meghan and Harry are paupers relative to the Gateses. This has proven to be a win-win situation for all concerned, similar to the relatively poor King Juan Carlos of Spain and the tremendously rich King Abdullah of Saudi Arabia. When the seriously rich regard themselves as being on a par with others who are significantly poorer than themselves, what is a large sum to one party might be a *bagatelle* to the other. It is whispered in certain circles that the Microsoft magnate has assisted the Sussexes, albeit in a minor way compared with how Abdullah rescued Juan Carlos.

Of course, there are important differences between the circumstances of Juan Carlos, who was a reigning king with all the constraints imposed by his position, and the flexibility that Harry and Meghan have created for themselves as they set about making their fortune. Nevertheless, it is instructive to learn that in 2008 the Saudi monarch ordered his Foreign Policy Advisor and sometime Minister of Foreign Affairs, Adel al-Jubeir, to pay $100m into an account held by the Panamanian company Lucum, owned beneficially by the Spanish sovereign, at the Swiss Private Bank Mirabaud. This was an outright gift, as the form regarding the origin of funds confirmed, and shows how generous a rich man can be to what he called his poorer 'brother'.

Of course, Harry and Meghan's financial ambitions far exceed a capital sum as paltry as $100m. Their 'people' have been predicting that they can earn two, three, and five times that amount in a year. It remains to be seen if the couple will be billionaires in five years, as they and their advisors hope. In the meantime, it is not suggested that Bill and Melinda Gates have so far been tempted to endow Harry and Meghan with such a generous gift, but the word in certain circles is that they have eased the path of the couple by helping them while they have been settling into their new life in California.

Certainly, some benefactor has been assisting them. Even with Prince Charles's private contributions, Harry and Meghan's expenditure as they settled into California life far outweighed their means. Even their security was a problem. They no longer enjoyed the status of 'internationally protected people' and therefore did not qualify for state funding for their security. Indeed, their security bills had been one of the problems which had convinced the Canadians that they would prefer not to have them resident in their country. Harry and Meghan decamped from Canada to California a day or two before the Canadians withdrew their protection. The Americans also refused to assume that burden, which was hardly surprising considering Meghan's withering comments about Trump being divisive, misogynistic and a host of even worse remarks delivered both publicly and privately, while Harry was recorded opining to Russian pranksters, who he thought were Greta Thunberg and her father, that the American president had 'blood on his hands' because his climate change policies do not accord with theirs.

I am reliably informed that there is no way Prince Charles would be coughing up £4m per annum for protection even if he had it to spare - which he does not.

Living the billionaire lifestyle requires serious income. If you're Meghan and Harry, you'd be at least twenty times too poor to cover even the basics. While house hunting for the California mansion that would consume at least half your capital, there'd be the house to rent, costing thousands per diem in excess of your overall income. Then there's be the staff to pay and everything else that would set you back a sum you don't have in income.

Short of a few good deals bringing in a minimum of $30 or 40m per annum, it becomes impossible to maintain this lifestyle without outside assistance. Only with a benefactor who has been as generous to King Juan Carlos as King Abdullah was, can Harry and Meghan maintain their lifestyle and avoid the ignominy of hawking their wares in so inappropriate a manner that their prestige plummets along with their earning capacity.

Meghan and Harry have cast a wide net. Not only have their applications for Archewell suggested that they will be aggressively marketing product, but that their range will be so comprehensive that they might well end up the billionaires they wish to be, just off selling chachkas which might have no real relevance but will be desirable to buyers who want a bit of their 'classy' and humanitarian dream. Not that Meghan is limiting herself to such activities. Although she is rapidly approaching forty, and therefore has a very short shelf-life left as a leading lady, she has nevertheless expressed interest in reviving her career as an actress in the hope that she can achieve her twin ambitions of winning an Oscar while making a vast fortune at the same time. A story was planted by her 'people' that she had received many offers, none of which she would be considering as they were too 'cheesy' for someone of her stature. Nevertheless, she remained open to offers from serious A-List directors who could showcase her acting talents in the exemplary light someone as prestigious as the Duchess of Sussex would require. It was mischievously observed that no A-List directors stepped forward, so time will tell whether her ambition to be taken seriously as an actress while earning big bucks in a major production will materialise.

A far more certain route to great fame and fortune rests in the safety of mutually advantageous relationships with billionaire sponsors and major companies whose budgets allow for the luxury of vanity projects passing themselves off as humanitarian activities. Such sophisticated methods will assist Harry and Meghan to successfully make the transition from royal non-earners to majestic earners.

By Easter 2020, the word in royal circles was that this was the route Meghan and Harry intended to go down as they operated at the highest level in order to retain as much of their royal prestige as they could, while maximising their financial potential. Confirmation came when Catherine St-Laurent wrote to her colleagues stating, 'After nearly nine years alongside Melinda and the Gates Foundation and the Pivotal Ventures teams, I am moving on to begin a new chapter and wanted to make sure to share my contact info so we can stay in touch. Beginning next week I will be acting as Chief of Staff and Executive Director of the new non-profit enterprise for Meghan M and Harry. They are embarking on a new chapter themselves and I am thrilled to be able to play a supporting role in realizing their vision and enabling them to achieve impact on issues that matter most to them.'

People who thought that the royal couple would have no story to tell beyond his pain at his mother's death were clearly underestimating Meghan's resourcefulness. Harry doesn't have to offer great depth or intellect. As the son of one future king and the brother of another, he will always have kudos. Meghan has also demonstrated over the years what superb judgement she has in attaching herself to institutions and people who take her from one level to another. Even if the good ship Meghan sails through some squalls, it is unlikely that she will ever lose this aptitude. If she and Harry end up developing the philanthropic entity they envisage to the full extent of their ambitions, she will have made the right career move in disentangling herself from the royal fold, for she will have set them up as the supranational king and queen of humanitarianism and, as such, will have the respect of much of the world. They will therefore have no need of the approval of people in Britain. Whether that degree of success will ever fill the void created within Harry by abandoning his country and all he held dear within it, is something else.

Even if Meghan and Harry should divorce in the future, as long as they manage to successfully pull off their hat trick of becoming billionaires or even just multi-millionaires while being acknowledged as the world's premiere humanitarian couple, she will by then be covered in so much philanthropic glory that her eminence will be pretty much inviolate. In that eventuality, it would be very surprising if she did not continue to associate herself with a charitable entity of her creation, thereby perpetuating her distinguished position and securing her position on the world stage for the remainder of her life. Quite possibly, like Jackie, on the deck of some billionaire's superyacht.

If anyone should fall by the wayside, it will be Harry.

Had Meghan not encouraged Harry to make the move they made, they would not now be on the cusp of possible magnificence such as he would never have been able to envisage before she opened up his eyes to the possibilities before them. From here on in, barring some great slip-up, the doors that will open to them contain not only great wealth but also renown and recognition beyond anything he could ever have imagined when he was merely the second son of the Prince of Wales. Thanks to Meghan's vision, determination, and resourcefulness, their options now have the potential to grow exponentially. It is very unlikely that Meghan is going anywhere but to the bank via the portals of glory, irrespective of whether Harry is by her side or not.

It is ironic that a couple who are so demonstrably in love can have generated so much speculation as to how long their union will last. Yet from the very beginning of their marriage, bets have been laid as to whether it will last two years, or three, or five. Cynics say that Harry is in for the long haul but that Meghan will have factored into the equation the possibility of being a divorced Duchess of Sussex. That she will have been canny enough to see that it would far more difficult for the ex-wife of a royal duke to set up a prestigious charity, and extract from it the benefits, that will now accrue to them as a result of having opened it up while they were married. 'He, poor darling, is the faithful puppy following its master,' one of his cousins told me. 'He doesn't see that the more they feather their nest abroad, the more incentive she has to leave him one day, walking off with the lion's share of the proceeds. We all despair for him.'

Poor darling or not, the undoubtedly faithful Harry has been backing his wife up to the hilt. Both of them know that they will sink or swim together, and they have been vigilant in protecting their 'brand'. This was nowhere more apparent than in the lengthy statement they posted to 'update' their followers when they realised that their royal status had been dangerously called into question in the early days of their 'stepping back'. Trying to shore up their prestige as a result of losing the right to use the style of royal highness, they stated that they 'will retain their "HRH" prefix, thereby formally remaining known as His Royal Highness The Duke of Sussex and Her Royal Highness The Duchess of Sussex. The Duke and Duchess of Sussex will no longer actively use their HRH titles as they will no longer be working members of the family as of Spring 2020.' They asserted that '(w)hile there is not any jurisdiction by The Monarchy or Cabinet Office over the use of the word 'Royal' overseas, The Duke and Duchess of Sussex do not intend to use 'Sussex Royal' or any iteration of the word 'Royal in any territory (either within the UK or otherwise) when the transition occurs Spring 2020.' They reminded their admirers that they 'do not plan to start a "foundation", but rather intend to develop a new way to effect change and complement the efforts made by so many excellent foundations globally.' They complained that 'the trademark applications that had been filed as protective measures and that reflected the same standard trademarking requests as done for The

Royal Foundation of The Duke and Duchess of Cambridge, have been removed,' and that '(w)hile there is precedent for other titled members of the Royal Family to seek employment outside of the institution, for The Duke and Duchess of Sussex, a 12-month review has been put in place.'

To those in the know, Meghan and Harry had swung into action to protect their 'brand'. There was no doubt who had drafted the statement. 'Iteration' is a word that is seldom used, except by Meghan, who has an affinity with it going back to the days of her two blogs. Friends of hers were also quoted in *People* magazine disparaging those who disagreed with her plans as 'naysayers' and 'spiteful' because the palace were insisting on a twelve month trial period. This, her 'friends' alleged, was because they were punishing her and Harry for wanting their freedom.

To people in the know, the Sussexes' statement was not only disrespectful but riddled with inaccuracies. It was misleading on virtually every point it made, and there was a strong suspicion that it had been created to boost Meghan and Harry in America without a care to the unfairness of the claims or the potential damage it could do to the monarchy in Britain. Firstly, Harry and Meghan's assertion regarding their royal highness titles was unequivocally wrong. While technically remaining royal highnesses, they had been banned from using that title. It was not an elective on their part. They no longer had the right to use what they referred to as their 'HRH prefix' either formally or informally. Patently, the distinction between the meaning of the words technical and formal had been lost on whoever composed the statement, but the reality was that while they formally retained the titles they had technically ceased to have the right to use them.

As for their assertion that the Monarchy and Cabinet Office did not have international jurisdiction over the use of the word royal insofar as it applies to the British Crown and all businesses registered in or linked to the United Kingdom, this was not only factually inaccurate but was perceived in Britain as being an impertinent and unwarranted challenge to the right of the Crown to maintain its purity. The idea that members of the British Royal Family could be challenging the legal means whereby the British Royal Family ensures that no one abuses their royal status by restricting everyone's right to the use of the word royal, was viewed as beyond belief. There is a raft of legitimate and legally binding legislation such as the Companies Act of 2006 which specifically gives the Secretary of State for Business jurisdiction over royal names for 'any type of business'. This backs up the Paris Convention for the Protection of Industrial Property of 1883, which protects all royal trademarks. The USA and Canada were but two of the many nations which signed the convention, in 1887 and 1923 respectively, so any attempt by the Sussexes to claim that they had the right to use the word royal without the permission of the Crown would fall foul of trademark laws internationally.

Canada, being a country whose Head of State is the Queen, is also subject separately to rules governing the use of the word royal, and all requests to use the designation royal have to be addressed to the Governor-General's Office at 1 Sussex Drive, Ottawa. This made further nonsense of Harry and Meghan's claims that they had the right to use their Sussex Royal brand internationally. Their further assertion that they would nevertheless indulge the British Crown in its petty refusal to allow them to market themselves under their Sussex Royal brand might have seemed like magnanimity in the United States, but in Britain it was seen as the pretentious and irresponsible score settling of a spoilt and over-indulged couple who didn't care how much damage they caused to the institution which had given them their prestige as long as they were able to present themselves in a flattering light to their target audience.

By this time, the British press had come to the conclusion that Harry and Meghan were arch hypocrites who thought that the rules applied to everyone but themselves. They had been getting flack throughout much of the previous year for not living by the rules they preached, but which they nevertheless advocated everyone else abide by. They did not help themselves by advocating their right to breach national and international trademark laws while demanding that the press respect other laws which they and their agents, rather than the press, had broken, in particular Meghan's friends leaking the contents of the letter she had written to her father to *People* magazine, then suing the *Mail on Sunday* when it was her friends who had breached her privacy, causing her father to defend himself against her 'friend's' allegations. While this was not an anomaly which perturbed the American press, it did the British, whose sense of justice rankled.

What caused further offence in Britain was Harry and Meghan linking the Cambridges' trademarking of their brand with the Sussexes'. By bringing in the Cambridges, the statement revealed how adept the Sussex public relations machine was at muddying the waters in their favour and to the detriment of others. Once more, the trans-Atlantic difference could not have been more pronounced. In the US, people did not even notice the importance of the point being made, largely, of course, because the British Royal Family is not their own institution but merely a source of glamour, admiration, interest, or indifference, depending on the perspective of the reader. In Britain, however, the swipe was noticeable, notwithstanding there being no justifiable parallels between the situations of the Sussexes and the Cambridges. There has never been any concern at the palace about the Cambridges indulging in commercial activity that might result in negative consequences for the monarchy, nor has that couple ever baulked at revealing their commercial intentions to the powers-that-be. The same was not true of the Sussexes. The Duke and Duchess of Sussex's commercial plans had been a bone of huge contention at Buckingham Palace for the past year. They wanted the licence to do as they pleased, without reference to the palace. No oversight, consultation, and certainly no recrimination such as occurred when the palace discovered that they had struck a deal with Disney and she had taped the voiceover from Elephants Without Borders in autumn 2019.

At the time of writing, the harbingers are that Meghan and Harry have set themselves up to be cooperating royalty to American liberal billion-aires, with each party promoting the other's philanthropic ventures and garnering the rewards of their humanitarian enterprises. How seriously Meghan and Harry as a double act will be taken in the years to come depends on many variables. These include the following they amass, the mutually advantageous links they forge with financial institutions and people like Bill and Melinda Gates and Oprah Winfrey, even whether there is or isn't much news that day, causing their latest posting to achieve greater or lesser attention. I do not foresee them retiring from public view any time soon, because Meghan and Harry both understand that fame is a commodity with a price tag, and the coinage isn't only money but also glory and the ability to use their profiles to further their causes.

As regards fame and fortune in America, Meghan is right. America is not the United Kingdom. Its values are in some ways entirely different from ours, and what works there does not work here, and vice versa. My good fortune is to have been partly educated in the United States and to have lived in New York until my mid-twenties. I have friends and family there, and visit often. I can therefore see both sides of the coin. The British press might wish to delude itself into believing that Meghan and Harry will wither on the vine and die without their attentions, but nothing could be further from the truth. Even as a busted royal flush, Meghan and Harry, or Meghan on her own, will continue to have appeal. Maybe not as much as they would have had, had they retained their rank, or, should they be divorced, had she remained his wife, though that might change depending on which billionaire she marries afterwards.

There will always be institutions who want what are billed as first tier speakers or celebrities, even though they are no longer of the first rank except in PR circles. In the commercial world, there are also companies which will pay good money for celebrities like the Sussexes to assist them in marketing their wares, upping their profile, or enhancing their prestige. That too will remain a potential source of revenue. Meghan and Harry's aptitude for publicity, together with her stated desire to be the most famous woman in the world, will doubtless continue to coalesce with her ambition to end up having the world's largest Instagram following. One will feed the other, while she uses her entrepreneurial skills to exploit both for her maximum financial and reputational benefit. I for one will be very surprised if we don't see a lot more of the Meghan show, with or without Harry, in the future. She is an operator of the highest order, and I fully expect her to do all she can to operate at the highest level, for as long as she can, and for all the rewards she can obtain for Harry and herself. All of this will be done while she and Harry espouse humanitarian causes in rhetoric that will appeal to those of their political bias. Critics will be dismissed as racists, anti-feminists, and everything else that can be thrown at them by her team as well as by her and Harry's supporters. The one thing that these people will never acknowledge is the possibility that others might simply not like Meghan because they aren't convinced by her.

As for Harry, I doubt that he will persist in sharing his suffering with the world except as and when it engenders the response they both require. He will doubtless come up with other strings to his bow as he sings for his supper and plays a tune that his and Meghan's admirers want to hear. You can only share your grief so often before it becomes a bore. Moreover, Harry's grief accounts for only a part of his mental health issues, as one royal told me. 'Harry blames his mother's death for things that have nothing to do with it. He's not overly bright and the fact is, Diana messed him up from the word go by spoiling him rotten. She refused to acknowledge his place in the scheme of things, just as she refused to acknowledge her own. Many of his underlying problems have been due to this lack of boundaries. He's never going to be healthy until he faces the facts. Personally, I don't think he has the brainpower (to do so).' There is, of course, another way of looking at Diana's legacy. By encouraging Harry to believe that he, as a human being, was special, she released him from the bondage of his position and enabled him to function outside of the royal world. It took Meghan's influence to show him how he could establish his own platform outside of the royal box, but he has been empowered by his mother as well as by his wife, and will make his mark in the world in a way he could never have done without their input.

The turn Harry has taken under Meghan's influence is instructive. Prior to meeting her and becoming so empowered under her ministrations that he now feels that they are such potent forces that they can change the world, he used to have a degree of self-doubt born of the awareness that he was not a genius. Thanks to her confidence in herself and her encouragement that he shouldn't let himself be 'limited' by all the 'crap he was brought up to believe in', he seems to have shed these inhibitions and now accepts her premise that they are both a lot brighter than the jeremiads who preach caution and the value of boundaries. They believe that the only thing they have to fear is fear itself, and since each of them is fearless in his and her own way, together they make a fearsome combination.

The boundlessness that Harry and Meghan share must be very exciting. It must also make for some amazing prospects for them to consider. Meghan's boundlessness, unlike Harry's, was inculcated from an early age. She was brought up to believe, especially by her father, that she is a force to be reckoned with and that she has an entitlement born, not of rank or privilege or even talent or achievement, but of her right to 'have a voice' by virtue of being herself. Patently, she knows her strengths, most of which are allied to determination rather than education or even information. Undeniably, her strengths are considerable. Critics such as Gina Nelthorpe-Cowne suggest that she might have so overused them that they are morphing into weaknesses. Meghan has given free rein to her desire to rule, to control, to call the shots, to achieve without the consent of others when they stand in her way or do not agree with her, as she has demonstrated time and again since she married Harry and decided to take on the royal establishment and beat them at their own game. She is firmly convinced that her way is the best way, that she is entitled to what she wants for no other reason than that she has a right to it as a result of being the individual she is, and that those who stand in her way should not be allowed to prevail. This suggests a woman who is fully empowered, who is a formidable ally as well as opponent, who should not be underestimated. Her critics say that she teeters on the brink of megalomania, that she has encouraged Harry to become more potent than is healthy for him, that he lacks her control or intellectual prowess and will therefore be more at risk than she ever will be. Potent though their strengths may be, they have aimed too high to be in a healthy place.

Meghan and Harry, however, espouse values and support positions which are popular with large swathes of people, and, as long as they continue to do so, and as long as she remains as measured and considered as she is, and as long as she persists in being the driving force in the relationship, the likelihood is that they will play the fame game successfully. Of course, this could change if she should enter politics, for there are huge differences between the fame and the political games, chief of which is that the former is mostly about front-of-house presentation, while the latter is frequently about what goes on behind-the-scenes.

Meghan's story is instructive in how powerful supreme self-confidence can be. It might get you a place at the top table, but if it then creates such odium that you clear the room, as has happened in Britain, you're hardly in a beneficial position. Meghan's limitless self-confidence has so far resulted in relative wealth, approbation, and the recognition that she used to confess on her blogs that she hungered for. The royal setting was too small and restrictive for her. While her detractors might conclude that she is like Norma Desmond in *Sunset Boulevard*, the reality is, she saw that the setting of being a royal highness, a royal duchess, and a senior member of the most important royal family on earth, were simply too small for her ambitions and needs. As Harry himself has said, 'She's not changed. She's the same woman I met and married.' She saw the opportunity to create a new platform, one which would allow her the use of her voice, one that she could shape to her own requirements that would bring her the wealth, power, recognition, approbation and approval she yearned for. By achieving all of this, she will have shown everyone, both admirers and critics, that she is indeed an extraordinary, possibly even a unique, individual, and love her or loathe her, no one will ever be able to dismiss her again the way people used to when she was a lowly supplicant in Hollywood trying to make it.

The reality is that Meghan's needs and ambitions were simply incompatible with being a member of the Royal Family. But she was canny, and while she might have handled her exit in such a way that she has earned the contumely of the British people, she has nevertheless accomplished it in such a manner that she has set herself and Harry up successfully where matters to her: America. The way she did it says much about her. She understood the need for a good excuse. Like Diana Wales, who understood that she would lose supporters and her privileges if she admitted that she wanted her freedom, so blamed Charles for the collapse of her marriage when in fact she was more to blame than he was, Meghan had to come up with a better reason for leaving a situation most people would give an arm and a leg for. Rather than admitting, 'I want the admiration of people, not criticism, and I also want to make hundreds of millions of dollars, billions if I can, and the palace is preventing me from doing it,' she started saying that the royal way of life was 'crushing my soul' as well as 'Harry's' and that she needed to get them out 'for our mental health.' In a few short sentences, Meghan had turned her desire to swap the limited and restraining royal platform for one which would give her the freedom of movement she required as well as the ability to control it, into a matter of life and death, with her and Harry at risk of a lifetime of mental illness.

Not everyone in Britain was blind to how astute Meghan was at spinning things in their favour. One courtier who admires what he calls her 'unblinking *sang froid*' said, 'You wouldn't've been able to blast her out of here with an atomic bomb if she'd been given free rein to make all the money she wants to.' What Meghan wanted was the freedom to exploit herself and Harry to the maximum commercial advantage, while remaining a working member of the Royal Family. Even so, she would still have sought to create an American platform, not only because there she wanted to gain the approbation she needed but because she would be able to control the narrative more successfully with a tame American press rather than an uncontrollable British one.

At the palace there was genuine shock that Meghan would 'stoop to using mental health as the cover for what is essentially greed and self-indulgence,' as one courtier said. 'Only spoilt brats think that their mental health is affected if they don't get everything they want in life. Mature people cope with frustration and frustration is something that everyone has to cope with. You only have good mental health if you can cope with it positively. If you can't, it means you're a spoilt brat who needs to grow up.' While her blogs indicate that she always had a propensity for believing that the frustration of not achieving her ambitions would affect her mental health, the palace misunderstood her attitude and believed that she was only exploiting it cynically, having become involved with Harry and discovering that he, William and Catherine already had such an interest in the topic that they had created the Heads Together movement in 2016.

In the mental health sector, there is a general awareness that you can remain mentally healthy even as life deals you a bad hand and you have to tailor your ambitions to reality, but there are times when life so overwhelms you that you need help. Mental health is not the same as facile happiness. It is coping well with what is happening even when things are not so good, or maybe when they're so good that they disrupt your equilibrium. William and Harry were well known in Court circles to have had their own mental health issues resulting not only from Diana's death, but from the emotional turbulence of their early life. They were the typical children of divorce, and this gave them an insight into how misery affects mental health. Catherine, on the other hand, was from a happy family, but her brother James Middleton had suffered from depression, demonstrating that a happy family background does not guarantee good mental health.

By alighting upon mental health, Meghan and Harry were placing themselves in an unarguable position whereby their desire to 'stand on their own two feet' and achieve 'financial independence' could be explained away as a 'mental health' issue. This had a powerful appeal to the younger generation, as well as to the Americans who were their ultimate target group. It also showed the palace what clever operators they were in spinning their ambitions into something with which their target audience could sympathise.

According to one of Harry's friends, 'Meghan thrives only when she's able to do as she pleases. He used to thrive mostly when placed in a secure structure with clear boundaries and clarified expectations, like the Army.' According to his friend, 'Harry did not necessarily have to be doing only what he liked to be in a good space.' He was happy to share his part of any load with colleagues, even when the tasks were not pleasant. As long as they were necessary, and made sense in the relevant context, he was 'up for it'. Meghan is not similarly self-sacrificing. What she likes, she likes; what she doesn't, she wants no part of. She no longer sees any merit in changing herself to accommodate any system; the system must change itself to accommodate her. Say what you will about her, it takes gumption, courage, and ability to marry a royal prince, become a royal duchess, decide the lifestyle doesn't suit you, and manage to do what no other royal wife has ever done before, namely convince him that there is a viable and even more attractive alternative which will give you everything you want. That is demonstrably self-actualisation in its frankest form, a paean to the efficacy of empowerment and determination. Although Harry has gone along with it all, the fact is, it's Meghan's creation, and she deserves the credit.

Well, they've left. Meghan and Harry have got their way. They've freed themselves of a system that they regarded as limiting their possibilities and have replaced it with one of their own making. She instructed her friends to announce to the world via *People* magazine that she was happy that they'd left Britain, that they were excited about their prospects for the future. They're now in California, laying the foundations for the lifestyle they wanted - Californian, A-List, luminous in a contemporary way. Despite their stated desire for privacy, they have moved to a place where the paparazzi will have access to them in a way it never would have had in Britain or Canada. The truth is, both Harry and Meghan want ever-increasing fame; they simply want it on their terms. They want the Hollywood version, not the British, royal one. They do not want to do what the other royals do, which is get out of their beds at six thirty in the morning to get dressed so that they are ready for an 8am helicopter ride to the Midlands of England, where they will meet a group of workers, cut a ribbon or two, meet groups of school children before unveiling a plaque prior to having lunch with the Mayor and local worthies, after which they will continue with a series of unglamorous meetings and interactions for the remainder of the afternoon, before returning home for a quick change and an equally dull but worthy evening engagement. They have freed themselves to have what they have announced is an ordinary life, though ordinary is strictly relative, for it is the ordinariness of the hyper-privileged. They say they like going for long walks, doing yoga together, playing a lot with Archie, and cooking. They like a lot of downtime so that they can focus on themselves and Archie, whom they want to bring up to be an 'ordinary' person. This is plainly a simpler life, with fewer demands and more focus on themselves than would have been possible had they remained as working royals. But it's doubtless only a part of the picture, for Meghan is a powerhouse who intends to make a great fortune and has not given up on her other great ambitions, including outstripping Diana, being the most famous woman in the world, with the largest Instagram following, and maybe down the line even becoming President of the United States of America. Much time is therefore spent in what her detractors might view as plotting and scheming, though her admirers will understand that it is the creative and resourceful strategizing of a truly extraordinary individual.

For all the sacrifices he's made, Harry appears to be supremely attached to Meghan. He has willingly if not happily given up his own world for the one she envisioned they could create together. By April 2020, however, it was apparent that he was struggling to cope. Primatologist and anthropologist Dr Jane Goodall, a friend of the couple, was the first to break ranks and confirm that Harry was finding it 'challenging' to adjust to his new life. Another of his friends said that he complained that 'I didn't sign up for any of this' when he got married and was questioning 'what he's got himself into.' Alarm bells began to ring back in Britain when he began to question the advisability of having left the Army. As he 'floundered', the ever-watchful and concerned 'palace crew' swung into action. By May, I was being rung up by an impeccable source and informed that the palace had started making plans for his eventual return. Alone.

Patently, Meghan's forceful personality had not been enough to provide him with the structure and security he used to get from the Army, nor were her plans for their glorious future together proving to be such a satisfactory substitute. Quite how he will cope, in the long run, with a wife who regards external constraints as provocations to be conquered or avoided, remains to be seen. Could Meghan be making the same mistake Diana had made? A wife who rules the roost too fully and demands too consistently that her husband give up everything that he holds dear, to keep her happy, might push even the most obliging of husbands into concluding that the sacrifices aren't worth keeping the marriage intact. There had come the point when Prince Charles realised that he'd compromise himself out of existence unless he beat a tactical retreat. That had sounded the death knell of the Wales marriage. Would Meghan's demands break the back of her marriage too?

By her own admission, she never wants to deal with 'any negativity'. This means that the word no is something she finds unacceptable. There is no certainty how that will play out if and when Harry deviates from her script so entirely that he ceases to sing from the same hymn sheet, or even just raises her hackles by silently opposing her. In any marriage, there has to come a time when a couple, even one as well matched as Harry and Meghan, diverge. Whether Harry's losses become so great that they will break the back of the marriage is now a question that would have been unthinkable even in January 2020. Although Harry is still in love with Meghan, the vacuity and unpredictability of their make-it-up-as-you-go-along way of life has already shown that he and Meghan have fundamentally incompatible approaches. One factor that might influence him to endure such an uncertain and unstable way of life is the reality of what will happen with Archie if he and Meghan should separate. Meghan has already stacked the decks in her favour by moving the family to California. Unless he manages to get himself, Archie and Meghan back to the United Kingdom prior to a separation, she hereafter has the right to keep Archie with her in California. This will condemn father and son to a trans-Atlantic relationship.

Meghan has a formidable ally in her mother. Doria has evidently expressed the view that the best thing her daughter could have done was leave Britain to forge a new way in the United States. She claimed to be worried about Meghan's mental health because she was so unhappy in Britain. 'She doesn't understand that you can be mentally healthy and cope with not getting your own way all the time,' a courtier told me. 'She doesn't realise there's a huge difference between the demands of a spoilt, entitled, overgrown brat, and the healthy expectations of a reasonable person.' Doria, with her social worker's training and her experience of dealing with the deprived and inadequates who enter the social system, does not have the experience of dealing with people whose lives are so big that privilege is counterbalanced with abnegation, with lives that make demands upon you, that require you to grow into them and cope with discomfort as a concomitant. Growth is sometimes painful but ultimately enriching for you and everyone else around you. 'They are small-minded people whose lives have been very restricted by their modest circumstances. Mrs Ragland is a pleasant and dignified woman but she has very little experience of the world at large, much less of the royal world. As for her daughter, she is the most spoilt, demanding so-and-so I have ever had the displeasure to encounter,' a courtier said.

This is not a view shared by Meghan's admirers. They do not regard the way she has influenced Harry to detach from his friends, family and royal heritage as anything but liberating him from a way of life that was preventing him from focusing on what really matters. To them, he is a beneficiary of her largesse, but to a significant number of Britons, he has lost the plot, and though he has been ever-increasingly dismissed as a spoilt brat, his obvious desperation to do anything and everything to keep his wife sweet engenders both pity and condemnation.

Once more, the human element kicks in. The family has come to understand, in a way they did not in the early days of the marriage, and certainly not before it, how fragile in terms of mental health both Harry and Meghan are. They are cauldrons of bubbling, overheated emotions which not only threaten to erupt, but frequently do. Their misery prior to moving to the US was palpable. It took loved ones aback to see how truly desolate they were, despite having so much going for them and despite being so in love with each other. While Harry's emotional instability had been containable before his marriage, under Meghan's encouragement he had learnt to 'get in touch with' and indulge his emotions, giving full rein to them the way she has done ever since they got married and she gained a companion in arms who encouraged rather than restrained her. As they have sparked each other off to greater and greater heights of ambition, determination, and passion, it has not been joy but wretchedness that has been the overriding emotion. This discordance caused both worry and perplexity. The attitude was succinctly expressed by Mike Tindall, husband of Princess Anne's daughter Zara Phillips and therefore Harry's cousin by marriage, who summarised the view of the whole family by saying, 'The only thing I want them to be is happy. They have got to find their way, and as long as they're happy and Archie is happy, then that is all you can ask for them. I am sure they will do that.'

Avoiding misery when a couple has so many advantages and privileges might seem like a pretty niggardly aim, but if that is the difference between a deeply miserable couple and one with some surcease from anguish, it starts to explain why the Royal Family has taken the view that Harry and Meghan's path to independence needs to be encouraged.

All couples spark each other off in different ways. Harry and Meghan's interaction has been a fascinating combination of how a pair, wholly absorbed in each other and believing that restraint is a failing to be avoided as opposed to a virtue to be deployed as and when necessary, can access all that is positive and negative in both their personalities, and, having done so, set in motion a train of consequences which have turned them from one of the most popular couples on earth into one of the most reviled in his homeland, all within the space of eighteen months. Each of them has deep reservoirs of passion, self-indulgence, entitlement and aggression, which have brought them to this pass. While no one fears for Meghan's survival, many of Harry's loved ones are terrified as to what will happen to him should the limb that he has climbed out onto, with Meghan's active cooperation, snap off. 'The prospect is too dreadful to contemplate,' a princess told me. 'There are some words that one does not even want to think of, much less utter.' This fear that Harry could entirely lose the plot, maybe even harm himself, is what is behind the latitude which has been granted them.

The most cursory of examinations show that Harry and Meghan are indeed individuals who have admitted to suffering deep emotional pain, and who are also considerably more emotional than the average person. Although both have laid the blame for their misery at obvious doorsteps - his at his mother's death, hers at her racial identity - their critics have some justification in maintaining that such suffering as they have admitted to is also tied up with more fundamental aspects of their identities such as their excessive emotionalism and tendency to over-personalise. Harry was always slated to be much more emotionally unstable than William, not because of his mother's death but because of the way his mother spoilt him, while Meghan's anguish appears to owe more to having been over-indulged by her father from a young age, resulting in her having difficulty even as a child with coping with the frustration that comes from not getting her own way. As one of the friends she left behind when she became a success on *Suits* put it, 'I don't for a nano second accept that Meg ever experienced any racial prejudice. I may be doing her a grave injustice, but I am sure as I draw breath that it's all false memories. No one can remember one instance of her experiencing any of the suffering she now lays claim to. The only pain Meg ever suffered was to have to wait for her ambitions to be achieved. That must have been pretty painful for someone who'd always got everything she ever wanted while growing up.'

Of course, if Meghan is prone to self-dramatisation, which her demeanour suggests she is, her suffering would still be heart-felt, so to that extent she is still deserving of compassion. Recent studies have shown that there is little psychological difference between the effect of real and false memories, so someone who lies to himself and others about having suffered as a result of an incident he invented, ends up being almost as badly scarred emotionally as someone who actually suffered the experience. This is a lesson Meghan should have learnt, for she was effusive on her blog about how effective self-hypnosis was when she was telling herself that she was a booker. If she failed to understand that blaming her racial identity for her own failures would inevitably bring her misery rather than the comfort she sought, that does not make her present suffering any the less real. All it means is that she is ultimately responsible for the pain she has entrapped herself into experiencing, at least on one level. However, she is no more responsible for having been over-indulged than Harry is. A parent who spoils a child does it no service. Diana and Tom Sr deserve the blame, and while the former never lived to see her handiwork, the latter has. Had he brought his daughter up to have a slightly lower opinion of herself and to accept that boundless ambition is not necessarily the road to happiness, she might well have accomplished less, but she would have also have been spared a lot of pain. Yes, she might have ended up the waitress her sister Samantha has said she would've been without their father's input, but a happy and satisfied waitress might have been a better fate than the miserable duchess she became.

Like many people whose parents' destructively indulged them, Meghan and Harry are prone to blame everyone and everything but themselves and their own character defects for their inability to experience the fulfilment in life that they yearn for and believe they are entitled to. It should not have come as a surprise to anyone that they would end up blaming the British press for their inability to enjoy the plenitude with which they have been blessed. The fact is, the press have given them a hard time, and they would not have been human had they liked it, but she and Harry have nevertheless conveniently conflated the issues and in attributing blame unjustly, have confused the public as to where responsibility really lies. A handy enemy is always a useful tool to chide rather than accepting responsibility for one's own failings. This is especially useful when one is breaking new ground and trying to win popularity contests with the Hollywood elite, the way Meghan and Harry were. While Meghan and Harry's supporters have bought their explanation that it is the British press that has caused their problems, the better informed and more knowledgeable observers on the other side of the fence understand that they are ultimately responsible for their own happiness. The idea that one cannot lead a constructive and fulfilled life even while being subjected to adverse publicity is nonsense. I am the living proof. Nor am I unique.

Irrespective of one's point of view, there can be no doubt that the most damaging course of action Harry and Meghan embarked upon once they arrived in California was declaring war on the majority of the British press. The day before the Queen's 94th birthday on the 21st April 2020, at the height of the coronavirus pandemic, when most of the world was in lockdown and everywhere people were dying or suffering serious hardship, they got their 'people' to issue a declaration to the editors of the *Sun*, the *Daily Mail*, the *Daily Express* and the *Daily Mirror*. In pure Sunshine Sachs lingo, they were informed:

'As The Duke and Duchess of Sussex now settle into the next chapter of their lives and no longer receive any publicly funded support, we are writing to set a new media relations policy specifically as it pertains to your organisation.

'Like you, The Duke and Duchess of Sussex believe that a free press is a cornerstone to any democracy - particularly in moments of crisis. At its best, this free press shines light on dark places, telling stories that would otherwise go untold, standing up for what's right, challenging power, and holding those who abuse the system to account.

'It has been said that journalism's first obligation is to the truth. The Duke and Duchess of Sussex agree wholeheartedly.

'It is gravely concerning that an influential slice of the media, over many years, has sought to insulate themselves from taking accountability for what they say or print - even when they know it to be distorted, false or invasive beyond reason. When power is enjoyed without responsibility, the trust we all place in this much-needed industry is degraded.

'There is a real human cost to this way of doing business and it affects every corner of society. The Duke and Duchess of Sussex have watched people they know - as well as complete strangers - have their lives completely pulled apart for no good reason, other than the fact that salacious gossip boosts advertising revenue.

'With that said, please note that The Duke and Duchess of Sussex will not be engaging with your outlet. There will be no corroboration and zero engagement. This is also a policy being instated for their communications team, in order to protect that team from the side of the industry that readers never see.

'This policy is not about avoiding criticism. It's not about shutting down public conversation or censoring accurate reporting. Media have every right to report on and indeed have an opinion on The Duke and Duchess of Sussex, good or bad. But it can't be based on a lie.

'They also want to be very clear: this is not in any way a blanket policy for all media.

'The Duke and Duchess of Sussex are looking forward to working with journalists and media organisations all over the world, engaging with grassroots media, regional and local media, and young, up-and-coming journalists, to spotlight issues and causes that so desperately need acknowledging. And they look forward to doing whatever they can to help further opportunities for more diverse and underrepresented voices, who are needed now more than ever.

'What they won't do is offer themselves up as currency for an economy of clickbait and distortion. We are encouraged that this new approach will be heard and respected.'

Not surprisingly, this letter overshadowed Elizabeth II's birthday, proving once again that no occasion was so significant or insignificant that Harry and Meghan's activities would not swamp it. No sophisticate reading it would ever have doubted that it was crafted by slick, clever American media manipulators. Aside from the language, which was pure Americana, the tone was New York knuckledusters dipped in Malibu saltwater. It was a *tour de force* of cant and hypocrisy, whose main purpose was to shut out those organs of the press who had not been sufficiently adulatory while deliberately confusing the issues and thereby deceiving the unwitting public into accepting that Meghan and Harry's suffering equated with the 'real human cost.....this way of doing business..... affects' its genuine victims.

As one of those people whose 'lives [have been] completely pulled apart for no good reason, other than the fact that salacious gossip boosts advertising revenue' over the last forty six years - and who has sued all four companies successfully and is in fact suing one as I write this - I am better qualified than most to say that Harry and Meghan's actions were unjustified, unjustifiable, and dangerous to the wellbeing of the British people and the freedom of the British press. I was bemused that they and their advisors could have had the temerity to so cynically attach their cause to the real sufferings of others, myself included, as if a broken fingernail equates to the loss of an arm.

What Meghan and Harry were trying to do wasn't only unconstitutional. It was a direct challenge to the protocols by which two of this country's greatest institutions, namely the monarchy and the press, conduct themselves. They were trying to justify creating a new and dangerous policy which could weaken the whole edifice upon which our freedom of expression was based. Their claims to victimhood were spurious. Yes, they had been criticised, but by and large those criticisms have been based in fact. They were not based upon lies. Just who did they think they were, seeking to overturn and thereby endanger established protocols which were finely calibrated to protect everyone in this country, not only those who were written about, or those who did the writing, but those who worked in the newspaper industry? Because they **felt** they had been wronged? They were being reckless and uncaring of the consequences their actions potentially had to the nation as a whole. In their sensitivity and, dare I say it, misguided sense of how entitled they were to protect their own feelings, they had equated those feelings with the greater injury they exposed everyone else to as they weakened the press. Could they truly be so blind as to where reality lay that they genuinely believed their wounded feelings justified endangering a whole industry, when there were already safeguards built into the system whereby those who were damaged could gain protection or justice?

What made Harry and Meghan's actions so fearsome was that they seemed to be mindless of the consequences to anyone's interests but their own.

Ian Murray, the Executive Director of the Society of Editors, which aims to protect media freedom, responded by explaining, 'Although the Duke and Duchess say they support a free press and all it stands for there is no escaping their actions here amount to censorship. By appearing to dictate which media they will work with and which they will ignore they, no doubt unintentionally, give succour to the rich and powerful everywhere to use their example as an excuse to attack the media when it suits them.'

While Mr Murray might have thought their ploy unintentional, I had no doubt, having researched how aggressively, indeed abusively, Sunshine Sachs approaches any segment of the media which does not fall down at the feet of its glorious clients and lick the soles of their dirty shoes as if they were gods to be worshipped, that Harry, Meghan and their media advisors had set out, very intentionally, to give succour to the rich and powerful everywhere to bash the media. As Martin Niemoller, the anti-Nazi pastor pointed out to the German people in the 1930s prior to being imprisoned at Sachsenhausen and Dachau Concentration Camps, 'First they came for the Communists, but I did not speak out, because I was not a Communist......Then they came for me, and there was no one left to speak for me.'

Meghan and Harry's unique attempt to reshape the way the British press works had taken no account of the fact that the British press is an integral part of British national life, and scrutiny is an acceptable part of the package. As Prince Philip has put it, 'It's the role of the press to be intrusive. It's a fact of life and one we accept.' As members of the Royal Family, albeit semi-detached ones residing abroad, both Harry and Meghan have a duty to respect and abide by the protocols and customs of the country over which his grandmother reigns and of which his father and brother will one day be king. There are already elaborate protocols, safeguards and laws in place, some quite recent, but others going back decades, sometimes centuries, protecting the rights of those who write in the press, and those about whom the press write. All British newspapers are obliged to refer to an individual about whom they are writing for his or her comments. This right cuts both ways, protecting not only the subject of an article but also the publication publishing the piece.

Because the American media were being fed stories that Meghan had been victimised because of her race and class, there was considerably more sympathy for her and for Harry on that side of the Atlantic than there would ever have been, had they known that the facts were being misconstrued to protect the Sussex brand.

I for one found it depressing that clever operators could so subvert the narrative and misrepresent the reality to the detriment of a whole nation. But the world had changed out of all recognition because of the coronavirus pandemic. Things that had seemed significant pre-lockdown simply became irrelevant post. Inevitably, Harry and Meghan were affected along with everyone else. While the other members of the Royal Family endeared themselves to the British public with sensible, down-to-earth and relevant demeanour, Harry and Meghan were finding it difficult to strike the right note from their temporary accommodation in California.

As the pandemic raged and people started dying in their thousands, as hospitals filled up and the Prime Minister Boris Johnson was struck down and nearly died, surviving only after being taken into intensive care at St. Thomas' Hospital in London, and chaos reigned worldwide as to what was the best course of action for fighting and avoiding the virus, Harry and Meghan's postings did nothing to enhance their reputations. They advised people, who had been told weeks before that they should wash their hands, to do that, then grandly informed the world that they would be providing updates as to the best and most accurate information. Since the consensus was that not even the experts knew what they were dealing with, Harry and Meghan found themselves being mocked for laying claim to a level of expertise they could not possibly possess. Then their website was closed down and they had to rely on friendly journalists and postings from their supporters. By this time, they were coming across as irrelevant and out-of-step, and those of us who wished them well hoped they'd go to ground until the crisis was over.

Fortunately, they did go quiet, but it was for only a few days before they surfaced, offering their support and encouragement to a variety of people. Their professionally paced and heavily curated contributions were obviously conceived with their advisors to keep their profiles up with drip-feeding. Each of them contacted someone who was then proud to share the experience with a wider public. Since it was unlikely that any of these people would have been violating the couple's privacy, the conclusion had to be that Harry, Meghan and Sunshine Sachs were providing encouragement behind the scenes. This was borne out when the executive director of Project Angel Food, a charity Doria Ragland likes, informed Instagram, 'In honour of the Easter holiday, the duke and duchess spent Sunday morning volunteering with Project Angel Food. And on Wednesday they quietly continued delivering meals to relieve our overworked drivers. It was their way to thank volunteers, chefs and staff who have been working tirelessly since the Covid-19 crisis began. We're completely honoured.' This was much more the sort of tone Harry and Meghan wanted than what they had been getting from the British media, and sure enough, the American press not only covered the story with the positivity that is such a feature of their press, but even managed to obtain photographs of Meghan in her face mask and Harry in his bandana delivering the meals. *People* magazine, whose coverage of them is akin to what it was with his mother when she was alive, not only faithfully reported upon those activities, but also managed to obtain the couple's uncomplaining approval when it ran a story, with photographs, about them taking their dogs for a walk. Plainly, Harry and Meghan were, Kardashian-style, keeping themselves in the news by curating their profiles as and when it suited them. But this did not help their cause in Britain, for people questioned why Harry and Meghan would consider it acceptable for American publications to photograph them walking their dogs but complain, as they did, when the British press did the same and provided equally inoffensive coverage.

Looking behind what was happening to Harry and Meghan's motives and aims, they seem to have believed that they had embarked upon a win/win scenario in their battle with the tabloids. If they beat the four newspaper companies into submission, they would have achieved their goal of micromanaging their publicity, but if they failed, they would have made themselves even more famous and warrior-like than they were already were. On the theory that there is no such thing as bad publicity, they would therefore have won even if they should lose.

Although both their actions support that hypothesis, Meghan appears to be the driving force behind the ploy. The lawsuit she brought against the *Mail on Sunday* for breach of privacy, data and copyright demonstrated her determination to face down her adversaries even though she has cast her father in the role as one of them. If the matter goes to trial, it promises to be a humdinger. It will be the number one show in town: town being the whole of the world. If the name of the game is keeping her profile high, Meghan succeeds no matter the outcome.

As things stand, the evidence Meghan has submitted is a double-edged sword. It confirms her father's claims that she never once responded to his numerous attempts to contact her following her wedding; that she cut him out of her life with a decisiveness which would have resonated with Harry, not only because he displays the identical characteristic of dropping people when they displease him irrespective of how long or close the relationship was, but because it was also a feature of his late mother's *modus operandi*. And he seems to have adopted it questioningly.

Possibly Meghan has given up caring what anyone thinks of her except for Harry and her supporters. She knows they will accept whatever she says uncritically, so she does not need to concern herself with any response beyond theirs. Or maybe her position really has gone to her head the way Tom Quinn recounts in *Kensington Palace: An Intimate Memoir From Queen Mary to Meghan Markle*. Maybe she really was on the power trip the staff who served and observed her insisted she was on. Could there be any justice in their having nicknamed her Me-Gain the Duchess of

Difficult who was Di Two and Di Lite and expected everyone to bow down before her and accept as gospel whatever she said? Her conduct in the lawsuit against her father certainly gave merit to that interpretation. She made the most unlikely and anomalous claims. Because her case would have no merit if she admitted that she had set her five friends up to leak the contents of the letter to *People* - you cannot legally claim that your privacy has been violated when it has been done at your behest - she swore that they had done it behind her back, without her knowledge, consent or approval. This, if true, was astonishing, but if untrue, was perjurious. Either way, it was an incredible claim to make. Meghan had clearly not recriminated against any of the five who had betrayed her confidence. Rather than sue them for preaching her privacy, which is where the real breach occurred, she had sued the newspaper which had given her father, the real victim of the breach, a forum to defend himself. Incredulity piled upon incredulity when the scope of the lawsuit was addressed. It had been blown up out of all proportion from a simple tort into an approximation of a public enquiry in which the *Mail on Sunday* would be tried for every wrongdoing Meghan wished to throw at them, irrespective of relevance to the matter at hand. A prince with knowledge of the law observed, 'It's very unlikely that her lawyers recommended this course of action. She seems to think because she worked in a fictional law firm on *Suits* that she is a legal expert.' Of course, lawyers have a duty to advise, but a client is the one who instructs them, and since lawyers get paid whether a client wins or loses, it is up to the client to exercise good judgement and make sound choices. Meghan clearly did anything but this, and following an application from the Mail on Sunday to throw out the lion's share of her claim, Mr Justice Warby duly did so. It was but the first of the many rounds in what promises to be an exercise in loss.

Who really wins and who really loses, except financially, is open to question in this game of double and triple bluff. The *Sunday Times* journalist Camilla Long wrote in April 2020, 'Who wins is irrelevant - in many ways she has already lost. There will be a day's headlines if she prevails after two, three or even four weeks of lashing stories about her destructive ambition and unedifying obsession with her image. Meanwhile she is reducing the pair of them to supermarket magazine fodder, telling Harry he's getting better when in fact he's getting worse.

She will brush the whole trial aside as yet another injustice, no matter what happens.'

Long is 'no fan of the royal family, and in many ways I'd hoped she would expose them as the pale, stale charisma vacuums they are, but at least they have the humility to know when to stop.' But Meghan is 'someone who thinks that she can win at anything; be the centre of all attention; have the moral upper hand in any dispute. Her ego blinds her; it even blinds the people working for her.'

But does it? What the British and Americans fail to understand is how different each of them is from the other. Beyond a common language, there is little else the two nationalities share. In Britain, reputations once destroyed are seldom reparable, but that is not so across the ocean. Much of what turns the British off about Meghan's character is viewed far more sympathetically in her native land. What passes as chic and classy in the US is regarded as precious and pretentious in the UK. What is regarded as arrogance here is admired as confidence there. The same is true of pushiness, aggressiveness, and what in the vernacular is abbreviated as BS. Because Meghan is an American and royal, her coverage there will always have elements of native pride unless she so overreaches that even they get fed up with her.

Meghan is also the beneficiary of the misconception that she has been a victim of racism and snobbery. She and Harry have been happy to allow these canards to stand, possibly because they have convinced themselves that they are true, though there is every reason to suppose that they know them to be the fig-leaves which they have conveniently clutched at as they conceal their naked deficiency in ways they find inconvenient or intolerable to reveal. Possibly they really do lack insight, and really do believe that their flaws do not exist, that their critics are vicious and prejudiced when in fact they simply see that the Emperor's new clothes are not the glorious raiments he thinks they are. Either way, it should make little or no difference to the outcome of the fame game as long as Meghan and Harry continue to play it the way they've been doing it.

American-style fame is a much easier commodity to float and maintain than British. For instance, when Meghan and Harry informed the world that they and Archie had facetimed with the Queen to wish her a happy birthday, the Americans accepted the confidence at face value, the tone of the stories being, 'How sweet. Happy families'. In Britain, however, they were accused of hypocrisy yet again, for the Queen had asked that all communications within the family be kept private. Meghan and Harry, despite their avowal of wanting to keep their private lives private, had violated not only their privacy, but hers as well. But the Americans don't even know about such nuances, their press lacking the interest in scrutiny the way the British do.

To date, Meghan's management with Sunshine Sachs of her and Harry's public profile has appeared to be working the way they wanted it to. Doubtless they were all mindful of the tremendous success the Kardashians have achieved on the back of attention-grabbing tactics of dubious taste such as sex-tapes, vaginal displays, and the daily sharing of the most anodyne, mind-numbing detail of their self-centred lives, which, despite its innate vacuity, vulgarity, gross materialism and dullness, nevertheless fires the approval of their many fans. If such offences to good taste can become the successes they have, there is no reason why Meghan Markle and Harry can't up the ante, trade upon their 'classiness' and titles, and become the royal version. All Meghan needs to do is sustain the regard her fellow Americans have for her, with the devoted Harry following in her wake as long as they remain a double act.

At present, they seem to be benefiting in the United States not only from their superficial appeal as royals but also from the fallacy that Meghan was victimised by the British. This mixed bag has enhanced her profile on a variety of levels. On the one hand, there was admiration for her undoubted style and beauty, while on the other hand her admirers sympathised with the fact that she had been womanfully fighting and slaying the dragons of racism, snobbishness, misogyny, jealousy, lack of appreciation and the multitude of other challenges she and Harry have hinted at whenever they have shared their journey with their supporters.

Many of these hints will be given flesh around the time this book is published, because Meghan and Harry have done a Diana. They have provided cooperation to Omid Scobie and Carolyn Durand for a panegyric, due to be published this summer. If Andrew Morton's and my experience are anything to go by, they will be bending the facts to burnish their subjects' images and settle scores with a skill not seen since Josef Goebbels unleashed his talents for propaganda on an unsuspecting German populace. Already, there are indications from Meghan's evidence in her lawsuit against the *Mail on Sunday* that she and Harry will be laying a considerable burden of blame on the doorstep of a malign British press. This will include her fractured relationship with her father, which she has been blaming on the press rather than her failure to engage with him. Doubtless, Harry and Meghan's struggle will not be represented as that of an ambitious and over-confident woman who has linked up with a troubled and well-meaning but none-too-bright prince, but as brave humanitarian warriors who are fighting the good fight and being unfairly labelled greedy, hypocritical, spoilt and self-indulgent by a jealous and malicious contingent who wish to bring them down and prevent them from doing all the good they can as they change the world for the better.

This is a scenario which will work better in America than it will in Britain. One of the many benefits of fame in the United States is that Americans are much more willing to admire without nit-picking the way the British do. They are willing to take at face value that which the British never would. They don't want their heroes to have feet of clay, which is why fame in the US is so much easier and headier than it is in the UK.

Another, very important but little acknowledged distinction is the differing roles the tabloids play in each country. In the US, they are more or less disregarded as fantastical organs of nonsense. This is because they often are. In the UK, however, they are serious publications whose content is justifiably taken much more seriously. This is where Sunshine Sachs and the Sussexes have been so clever. Americans think they're fighting the good fight against maligners and will therefore disregard anything the British tabloids say. This will only change when Americans wake up and realise that tabloid doesn't mean what they think it means. They're dismissing the British at their peril.

Despite the differences between the two cultures, and despite Harry and Meghan's complaints about how much they've been suffering from the ill-effects of fame, there is no doubt that they enjoy theirs. If they did not, they would not be so assiduously courting publicity. No event that can be exploited, no matter how mundane, ever goes to waste in the dustbin of silence. Harry used to be more restrained in terms of 'sharing' than he now is, but both he and Meghan have always had an eye to the main chance where publicity was concerned. The difference between them is that Harry used to mine that rich seam for the benefit of charities like Sentebale and countries like Lesotho, with never a thought for personal gain, while nowadays everything they do is influenced by how it will impact upon their brand, not only reputationally but financially.

Without a doubt, Harry and Meghan are an extremely tight couple. They have common aims and motivations which influence everything they do. All couples spark each other off in different ways, and Harry and Meghan's interaction has been a fascinating combination of how a couple, wholly absorbed in each other and believing that restraint is a failing to be avoided as opposed to a virtue to be deployed as and when necessary, can access all that is positive and negative in both their personalities. Having done so, they then set in motion a train of consequences which have turned them from one of the most popular couples on earth into one of the most reviled in his homeland, all within the space of eighteen months.

Each of them has deep reservoirs of passion, self-indulgence, entitlement and aggression, which have brought them to this pass. While no one fears for Meghan's survival, many of Harry's loved ones are terrified as to what will happen to him should the limb that he has climbed on, with Meghan's active cooperation, snap off. 'The prospect is too dreadful to contemplate,' a princess told me. 'There are some words that one does not even want to think of, much less utter.' The fear, that Harry could entirely lose the plot, maybe even damage himself irretrievably, but no matter what be utterly destroyed as a personality, is what is behind the latitude which has been granted the couple.

Both Harry and Meghan have been frank about being people who have experienced deep emotional pain. Although both have laid the blame at obvious doorsteps - his at his mother's death, hers at her racial identity - their critics have some justification in maintaining that such suffering as they have endured is no excuse at this stage of their lives. Despite having lost his mother at nearly thirteen, Harry has had more advantages than most. Many other youngsters who have lost a parent do not ask for a free pass on the grounds of such a loss, so why, the reasoning goes, should a prince of the most eminent royal family in the world be accorded one? And Meghan's anguish was born of the pain of someone used to instant gratification being forced to develop patience and exercise it the way less spoilt people have had to do since early childhood.

Of course, if Meghan is prone to self-dramatisation, her suffering would still be heart-felt. Recent studies have shown that there is little psychological difference between the effect of real and false memories, so someone who lies to himself and others about having suffered as a result of an incident he invented, ends up being almost as badly off emotionally as someone who actually lived through the experience. This is a lesson Meghan should have learnt, for she was effusive on her blog about how effective self-hypnosis was when she was telling herself that she was a booker. If she failed to understand that blaming her race for failures which had nothing to do with it would somehow spare her the consequences of a suffering she had never experienced, she has lived to experience pain which is really of her own creation. As there is the suspicion that Meghan used the pain of a prejudice she had never experienced to gain the admiration of people she sought to impress, in the process turning herself from spoilt woman of colour into a brave battler for human rights, such suffering as she now feels leaves her detractors cold, for they regard it as the just deserts of a self-promoting fantasist. Self-created or not, her pain is nevertheless genuine, as is Harry's, which, even his critics concede, was anything but self-generated.

This shared bond of pain seems to have permitted Harry and Meghan to become caught up in mythological struggles, he against a murderous press who were never responsible for the death he seeks to lay at their doorstep, she against a racist and hostile world which is meant to have spurned her when her race was the one thing which never played a factor in the process. They are both trapped in a cauldron of pain, but they are laying blame fruitlessly when the solution to their problems lies in entirely different and more positive directions.

Pain or no pain, Meghan and Harry are a double act who protect themselves using any resource at their disposal. To date, their associates have thrown her father, his brother, his sister-in-law, even his 'naysaying' grandmother under the bus. Whether they are responsible for these veiled attacks, or they only benefit from them but do not actually set others up to launch them on their behalf, the fact that they do not dissociate themselves from the stories, while creaming in the benefits, leaves a mystery as to their level of knowledge and involvement. Responsible or not, they nevertheless hide behind a rich arsenal of aggressive supporters who do not flinch from attacking on their behalf, and the aim of each attack is always to preserve them while burying everyone else under a fusillade. This was also a game Diana played, and, as this is the absolute opposite of how the royals function, Harry and Meghan need to take responsibility and discourage their friends and associates from playing such a nasty, destructive game.

Quite how destructive it can be was driven home to me in the most forceful way when I received an uninvited tip-off which I was asked to accept, whether justly or unjustly is another matter entirely, had emanated from Harry himself. Presumably there was the hope or expectation that my sympathies would be engaged, and, since I was already known to be an impartial commentator who was rooting for them but questioned the advisability of some of Meghan's conduct, I had to conclude that they or someone close to them was trying to shape the narrative on their behalf.

It has been no secret in royal and aristocratic circles that I was writing this book. The cooperation that I have received, as can be seen from the content of this work, was so comprehensive that I was catapulted back nearly three decades, to when I was writing my Diana biographies. As January 2020 was coming to an end, history repeated itself in a wholly unwelcome but enlightening way. After Britain's Channel 5 aired its interview with Thomas Markle, in which he made it clear that he loved his daughter and was distraught at the loss of their relationship, and was perplexed as to the reason why she refused to get in touch with him,

I received a telephone call from an extremely eminent, well-connect-ed aristocrat who has a direct connection to Harry through one of his closest friends. Did I want to know the real reason why Meghan had had to sever ties with her father? Of course I did.

A song and dance then ensued with the informant asserting that the truth was so awful that she could not possibly bring herself to utter the words. I had to point out that a writer cannot consider, much less use, an allegation that is not spelt out clearly. I was then informed that Harry himself believed the information to be true, as if that would somehow mitigate for something that was so mysteriously awful that it could not be put into words. Yet I was supposed to write it.

I was then invited to guess what was the worst thing that a daughter could have against her father. Not being a simpleton or three years old, I immediately cottoned onto where this was going, but still refused to be drawn, pointing out that a responsible author does not guess but relies upon information that is freely imparted. After the most tremendous palaver, the informant then managed to spit out the odious word 'inter-ference'. I asked what the word meant in that context, and was left in no doubt as to what it did mean.

I am terribly sorry, but anyone with scruples or a heart, invited to accuse a man whose daughter was full of praise for his parenting skills only weeks before she met her prince, would have to be low indeed to give credence to such a debased piece of information. I felt duty-bound to point out to the informant that Harry could not possibly believe any such thing. If he did, it meant that he accepted that Meghan was a brazen liar who had fabricated a truly loving father to impress the readers of her blog as well as everyone else with how worthy she was of the love of such a wonderful man. Either that, or she was lying now, or someone had mischievously made up the whole thing to gain my sympathy.

That certainly cast me right back to the bad old days of the 1990s, when bizarre stories were invented which had so many permutations that their objective was frequently obscure, though their source was as transparent as the freshly cleaned glass at Kensington Palace.

Of course, one must acknowledge the possibility that Harry might not, despite appearances to the contrary, have known anything about the telephone call. Notwithstanding the fact that he was in Britain at the time, this could well have been a coincidence. His friend, knowing that I am neither a supporter nor a detractor, could have been trying to influence the narrative in such a way that I would be tempted to look more favourably upon Meghan's treatment of her father. One must always keep an open mind until all the evidence is in, but when the wind is blowing strongly in a certain direction, the weather vane naturally registers that fact.

It looks increasingly unlikely that Meghan and Harry will be returning to live in Britain any time soon, if ever again. All the indications are that they will remain in the United States. Whether they will make the big bucks they are aiming for is another matter. They might well do so, though there is also every possibility that they might make less than they hoped. Either way, Meghan has destroyed her acceptability within the British Establishment in a way no one else has done since Diana Wales slit her own throat while spewing out her bile to Martin Bashir in the hope that she would deprive Charles of his right to the throne. From then until her death, most doors, including within her own family, were shut to her. Even before that, she had become so marginalised that she was playing serious catch-up with people she had fallen out with, including me.

Harry falls into another category. While there is no doubt that Harry has damaged his reputation by decamping, should he need to return to live in Britain, he will be reincorporated with dignity and even compassion. But reputation in Britain is like a beautifully wrought glass vase. Once it's broken, even if it's repaired and looks okay, it doesn't ever hold water the way it used to. Its fundamental function being altered, it has less value. Harry's glory days are over as a public figure in Britain, not only because he abandoned his post, but because too many people have voiced the opinion that he is 'weak', 'pussywhipped', and 'pathetic'.

The speculation continues as to whether Meghan and Harry's marriage will last. As stated earlier, from the very outset, people at the palace were taking bets as to whether they would give it two or five years.

Even Germaine Greer waded in, hoping that Meghan's professions of love were sincere. I too hope they are, for there is no doubt in my mind that Harry genuinely loves her and will be heartbroken if she turns out to be a mirage instead of the oasis he believes her to be.

I know as a fact that Harry's family is hoping the marriage lasts but will not be taking any bets on it. Privately, they have reeled from the way Meghan has influenced Harry into withdrawing from his birthright. Royalty is like a secular religion. You do not become an apostate without earning the disapproval of all true believers. Nor could even the most open minded family have a high opinion of anyone who caused a beloved family member's departure, and the fact is that their opinions reflect their loss.

Even the Queen, who is the most anodyne of all of them, has expressed her displeasure in no uncertain terms. She has many friends, and she has been forthright in expressing her viewpoint. I have been told by two separate and utterly reliable sources that she feels that Meghan's demeanour has been only a cut above a floozy's and her conduct has been no better than a strumpet's. That does not mean that she regards Meghan as either a floozy or a strumpet, but simply as someone whose sense of obligation, responsibility, and self-aggrandisement is reminiscent of a category of woman who is out for herself in a way that other women would not be. These remarks by no means compare with Queen Elizabeth the Queen Mother's description of the Duchess of Windsor as the lowest of the low, but they do show how disappointed and hurt even the Queen has been by Harry and Meghan's stepping back.

Despite this, the Queen's policy is to keep the door open for them to return to the royal fold if they want to, and if they do not (as seems likely, at least where Harry is concerned for the duration of the marriage), to maintain enough of a publicly approving profile for them to be included in the occasional event. Her ideal scenario is for Harry and Meghan to make infrequent appearances when they come back to the UK, or for them to represent her in some Commonwealth capacity from time to time, thereby delivering the message to the world that all is well and Harry, Meghan and Archie, who remain 'beloved members of the family'. This show of harmony is the ultimate aim, for no one seriously expects Meghan and Harry to resume their place in the chorus line of royal theatrics. Intermittent displays of acceptance as they float across the stage will also endow them with just enough respectability for them to become what they truly want to be: commercial operatives at the highest level. But the royals and their advisors are aware that the true beneficiaries of this policy will be Harry and Meghan. Any patina of acceptability will benefit them far more than it does the Royal Family, whose prestige will remain undented no matter what happens to theirs.

There is little doubt that the family regrets Harry and Meghan's departure, and minds awfully the manner of and motive for the departure. Financial independence when you're worth tens of millions does not strike people who take their duties seriously as a good enough reason to chuck away a life of service and privilege for one of hustling for real money and Kardashian-style fame. Yet the family understands that there is nothing they can do to influence a couple hell bent on doing things their own way.

Hopefully, Meghan and Harry will prove their critics wrong. Hopefully they will do sterling humanitarian work, earn money nobly, and ultimately she might even realise her ambition of becoming President of the United States of America. Hopefully they will resolve their dilemma where privacy is concerned. Hopefully, they will make a genuine success of their lives, not only by demonstrating how adept they are at acquiring fame and fortune, but in fulfilling the high hopes of the hundreds of millions, maybe even billions, of people of colour who looked up to Meghan as a beacon of hope when she first became Duchess of Sussex.

Meghan and Harry have struck out onto a new path. I for one hope they make a success of it. If I were a betting woman, I would not be giving any odds, because Heraclitus put it better than I ever could: Character is destiny. The harbingers are so mixed that the only thing I will predict with any certainty is that Meghan and Harry will be ensuring that today, tomorrow, next week, next month, and next year, their actions will keep them at the forefront of everyone's attention.